HINDSIGHTS

HINDSIGHTS

An Autobiography

John Heath-Stubbs

Hodder & Stoughton
LONDON SYDNEY AUCKLAND

British Library Cataloguing in Publication Data

Heath-Stubbs, John
  Hindsights
  I. Title
  821.912

  ISBN 0-340-59132-3

Published by Hodder and Stoughton,
a division of Hodder and Stoughton Ltd,
Mill Road, Dunton Green, Sevenoaks, Kent TN13 2YA.
Editorial Office: 47 Bedford Square, London WC1B 3DP.

Photoset by Rowland Phototypesetting Ltd,
Bury St Edmunds, Suffolk

Printed in Great Britain by St Edmundsbury Press Ltd,
Bury St Edmunds, Suffolk

Contents

Illustration Acknowledgments

The frontispiece is by John Cherrington. The illustrations, which appear between pages 186 and 187, are unless otherwise stated the property of the author. Other credits: Howard Coster – 2; Bembridge School – 3; Aero Pictorial Ltd – 4; Barbara Rawson – 5; Renée-Jane Scott – 7; Polyphoto/Michael Meyer – 8; OUP – 9; Leeds University – 10 and 11; Courtauld Institute Galleries, London – 13; Carnegie Art Gallery, Pittsburgh – 14; Hulton Deutsche Collection Ltd – 15 and 18; Chris Barker – 16, 21 and 23; Samir Fahr – 17; Alistair Elliott – 19; Christopher Dean – 20; John Cherrington – 22.

John Heath-Stubbs,

Drawing by John Cherrington

1

Origins

It must have been some time in 1917 that four sisters were walking near my grandfather's house, Butler's Marston, near Leamington Spa in Warwickshire. The ladies in question were my aunts Mary, Beatrice, Lily and Florence – the last of whom was to die tragically young at the age of sixteen, as she had inherited a family tendency to consumption. With them was a woman friend who was supposed to possess some kind of psychic gift. Suddenly she said: "If I believed in ghosts I would say I saw one just now." They asked her what she meant, and she replied that she had seen a man dressed in odd, old-fashioned costume, riding over the ploughed fields. Later they heard from an old lady in the village that there was a legend that in 1642 the then owner of Butler's Marston had ridden out to fight on the royalist side at the Battle of Edgehill, on his wedding night. He never returned. The story was that if the ghost were seen there would shortly be a wedding from the house. Not long after this, my mother, who was a friend of the family, came on a visit, and a little later my father was invalided out of the army with what was diagnosed, wrongly as it turned out, as "shell-shock". They fell in love and were married from the house.

There were other ghosts associated with Butler's Marston. One of these was a house spirit, the kind that haunts many old houses in Britain and other parts of Europe, and is particularly important in Russian folklore. These spirits will do the housework after dark, but must be rewarded with a bowl of cream or porridge. The one thing you must never offer them is clothes. They are naked and, although they put the clothes on with great delight, they will never be seen again. I suspect that this is because they were originally thought of as the spirits of the unborn, and the putting on of clothes symbolises birth as human beings. Another ghost was sadder. There was a ball-room which was supposed to have been built by an owner of the house for his daughter, but at the inaugural ball she saw the man to whom she was betrothed dancing too frequently with another woman, and in consequence she hanged herself from one of the beams. Her ghost ever after haunted the ballroom.

My grandfather's family, the Stubbses, traced their ancestry to the time of Charles I, when the first recorded member of the family, Francis Stubbs, married a woman called Elianor. He wrote on his marriage settlement: "Francis Stubbs, yeoman", whereas his son, John Stubbs, was to describe himself as a gentleman. This was fairly typical of that period: the yeomanry were rising by buying lands which the Tudor nobility had, in all probability, acquired as a result of the dissolution of the monasteries and had then cumbered with debt. The yeomanry were sending their sons to be educated as lawyers in the Inns of Court, and law became the traditional profession of the Stubbs family. Some of them, at any rate, were members of Lincoln's Inn. This opens the possibility that one of my ancestors may have been that John Stubbs (member of Lincoln's Inn) who wrote a pamphlet opposing Queen Elizabeth's intended marriage to the Duke of Anjou entitled: *A Discoverie of a gaping gulf whereinto England is like to be swallowed by another French marriage* . . . Among other things, he pointed out that the Queen was probably too old to have children. This, one may be sure, particularly offended her. He was sentenced to have his pamphlet burned by the public hangman and his right hand cut off. It is recorded that he raised his hat with the other one, shouting: "God Save the Queen!" This is sometimes cited in history books to indicate the essential loyalty of the opposition during Elizabeth's reign.

The Stubbs family seems to have originated at Walsall in Staffordshire, and the name is still common in the North-West Midlands area. George Stubbs, the painter, came from Cheshire, a neighbouring county. Although there is no record that he was related to my family, it would be surprising if, traced far enough back, a connection was not found. There is a tradition that the Stubbses played a part in Charles II's escape after the Battle of Worcester, and that one of my ancestors was offered a knighthood after the Restoration but refused it on the grounds that it would entail too much expense to come up to London. Yet I have read the King's own account of his escape, *His Majesty Preserved*, and there is no mention of any Stubbses or their close kinsmen, the Heaths. In fact, most of those who helped Charles during his escape were Roman Catholics, and my own family were, for the most part, firmly Anglican. But there may be some truth behind the legend. There appears to have been a scheme at the Restoration to found a new order of knighthood, the Knights of the Oak (in memory of Charles II's hiding in the Boscobel oak), to reward those who had been loyal to the throne during the Commonwealth period. The scheme collapsed because it did not get enough support – those who had lost their estates during the Commonwealth were not compensated adequately and may well have disliked the expense that a knighthood would have entailed.

The Stubbs family crest shows a "demi-eagle displayed or" (half an eagle with its wings spread, in gold), holding in its beak an oak branch "fructed proper" (of its own natural colour) with acorns. One of the best-known Stubbses is the famous Bishop of Oxford. His family was from Norfolk, but their crest also was a demi-eagle displayed, although, in this case, holding a laurel branch. This suggests there may have been a connection. The laurel, a more obvious emblem symbolising victory, may have been changed by the Staffordshire Stubbses to an oak branch in memory of the Boscobel oak.

A distant relative was Sir Henry Newbolt, whom I never met. His mother was a Stubbs. Newbolt, who as a poet was a kind of naval Kipling, was the official naval historian for the First World War, although I do not know quite why, since he was never in the navy. He had a romantic interest in genealogy and compiled the Stubbs family tree. There were connections between our family and two Welsh families, the Rollings family of Merionethshire and the Thomas family of Monmouthshire. Like most Welsh families, they could claim remote ancestors among the Welsh princes of the early Middle Ages. Wales being a poor country, estates were only inherited by the eldest son, and the younger sons usually reverted to the status of peasants. The same is true of the Cornish and, to some extent, the Irish and the Scots. The Thomases claimed descent from Sir Rhys ap Thomas. Although he was merely a knight, he had been stripped of all sorts of princely and royal titles by the English. He played a devious role during the Wars of the Roses, his main motivation being the preservation of Welsh independence. He supported the Earl of Richmond, the future Henry VII, and is mentioned in *Richard III*. There is a story that he had vowed that no King of England should enter Wales except over his body. Consequently, when Henry VII came to the throne and proposed to enter Wales, Sir Rhys had to lie under a bridge over the river Wye in order to fulfil his vow. Thomas is, of course, a very common name in Wales, but limiting it to the Monmouthshire Thomases opens the possibility that I might be distantly connected with Dylan Thomas and Edward Thomas, both of whose families originated from Monmouthshire, as did, on the maternal side, the family of Barbara Pym. I like the idea, anyway.

There was also a vague rumour in the family that Sir Henry Newbolt had traced a connection with "Fair Rosamund", Rosamund de Clifford. This legendary lady was the mistress of Henry II, who is said to have kept her in a labyrinth in Woodstock Park in Oxfordshire. She had two sons by Henry: one became Bishop of Salisbury, and the other was known as William Longsword. My aunt Beatrice, who told me this story, believed that we might be descended from the latter. It is true that the Stubbses were always remarkably tall. Sir

Henry Newbolt, in his autobiography *My World as in My Time*, recalls the tradition that if any member of the family died the Stubbses could provide four men to carry the coffin who were taller than anyone else in the county. But I think that the idea of the Stubbses being descended from the de Cliffords is a confusion, as the Stubbses only emerged from the yeomanry in the early seventeenth century. Possibly Newbolt found a connection between one of the two Welsh families with whom the Stubbses were related by marriage and the Welsh Cliffords, of whom the Cliffords of Woodstock were a branch.

Although the Stubbs family tradition seems to have been always firmly Anglican, my great-great-grandfather became a Unitarian. He was also an extreme Tory and resigned from all his public offices with the passing of the Reform Bill of 1867, which he held to signal the total annihilation of England. There is an account of him in Sir Henry Newbolt's autobiography, as he was Newbolt's guardian.

The Stubbses had close ties with the Heaths, another legal family from the same part of the country, and there were many marriages between them. Eventually the Heaths died out, and in my grandfather's time the last Miss Heath left money to my family, on condition that we adopted the name Heath-Stubbs. My grandfather, my uncle George and my father's sisters changed their names by deed poll, but my father had been christened Francis Heath Stubbs and there seemed little point in paying five pounds for a hyphen; so, quite legally, he simply added one.

My paternal grandmother's family, the Emmets, originated in the area of Halifax, Yorkshire. One branch emigrated to Ireland, eventually producing the Irish patriot, Robert Emmet, while another branch emigrated to New England, where Emmet is still a well-known name. Whereas the Stubbses were mainly lawyers, many of the Emmets were clergy. It was an evangelical family with considerable intellectual talent. Among its surviving members is my second cousin once removed, Dorothy Emmet, the philosopher, who now lives in Cambridge. She was a pupil of Whitehead, and a professor of philosophy at Manchester University. During the 1960s she edited, with a group of friends of like interest (the Epiphany Philosophers, who met regularly in an old mill in East Anglia), a periodical called *Theoria to Theory*. This journal dealt with topics where theology, science and philosophy possibly meet.

My mother's name was Marr. Her father was a Scottish businessman who moved south. I do not know very much about the Marr family, but the name originated in Aberdeenshire, and the Marrs are a sept of the Gordons. An extremely talented pianist, my mother had earned her living as a concert performer from the age of sixteen. She was accepted as a pupil by the great teacher, Tobias Matthay, among whose other students were Myra Hess, Harriet Cohen, Irene Scharrer and York Bowen, all contemporaries of my mother. Like many women of her generation, my mother gave up her professional career on her marriage and was only to resume it some fourteen years later.

My father was the youngest surviving member of his family. His elder brother, my uncle George, I know very little about. Educated at Rugby School, he seems to have been the only member of the family to have had a public school education. My father was educated at some kind of private academy he referred to as "Old Black's". (He once told me of the initiation which new boys had to go through. They were obliged to tell three stories, sing three songs, climb from one end of the dormitory to the other on the ceiling beam, or drink a glass of soapy water.) My uncle George never married, and died in 1925 in the South of France, where he had a yacht. He inherited the bulk of the family fortune, and at his death it was left, by his will, to the RAF Benevolent Fund. It seems that he was not altogether pleased by my father's marriage to my mother. In this he may have been influenced by his sister, my aunt Lily. My father's marriage meant that she and her sisters had to sell Butler's Marston, which they shared with my father, and they therefore had to give up fox-hunting, to which my aunt Lily was passionately devoted. I do vaguely remember once seeing my uncle George when he came on a visit to us, and it was said that he showed signs of relenting. There was even a rumour that he had made a new will in favour of my father, but that this was destroyed.

My father qualified as a solicitor but never practised. He had just enough money at that time to live on without working. I think he sometimes felt guilty about this. During the First World War he enlisted, despite his extremely bad eyesight, resulting from a congenital condition of glaucoma which I was to inherit. It was said that as the war progressed the army was taking in so many recruits that when they were put through their eye tests there would often be more than one man in the room. My father, who had a good memory, was able to get by heart the letters, which were up on display, as the man in front of him in the queue read them out. He did not see any action in the trenches, but was, in fact, an ambulance driver. Nevertheless he was invalided out, and it was on this invalid leave that he met my mother in his father's house in Warwickshire. My father proposed to my mother when they were cub-hunting. Cub-hunting is performed to cull the young foxes and train the young hounds. Hunting, to me, has always been a wholly barbarous occupation and I remember only once, as a small boy, attending a meet and seeing the fox fleeing, as it seemed to me, on the horizon.

My grandfather also owned estates in Monmouthshire and

5

Merionethshire. The mountainous country of Merioneth is not suitable for fox-hunting, but there was a story in the family that a nouveau-riche gentleman who had acquired a country house in the neighbourhood wished to hunt. In those days foxes could actually be ordered from a firm in London. This is testified by Surtees. Keepers used to trap foxes, which they ought to have preserved for hunting, in order to send them to a dealer who then sold them to those who required to hunt them. Unfortunately, the fox which this gentleman acquired was not a fox but an Indian jackal. The hounds, as they caught up with what was supposed to be their prey, did not smell the characteristic scent of a fox, which is offensive to all dogs, but that of a jackal. A dog and a jackal are almost the same species, and instead of hunting it they fraternised with it.

My parents' wartime wedding was by special licence from the Archbishop of Canterbury. I was born on 9 July 1918 in a private nursing home in Streatham, in room number nine. My mother, consequently, used to describe number nine as her eventful, but not lucky, number. The effects of the war were harsh at this time and it is possible that poor nourishment of my mother during her pregnancy, and perhaps of myself in my early months, may have been a cause of glaucoma, in that a want of fat is said to be a factor. I remember my mother telling me how she, like most people, had given up taking sugar in her tea during the war. After I was born, the nurses brought her a cup of tea and, as a special treat, sweetened it. My mother, no longer used to this, found it nauseating.

Normally at baptism a boy is provided with two godfathers and one godmother. I was born when the war was at its height and, unusually, my father was one of my godfathers, the other being his close friend, George Tyrrell. My godmother was my aunt Mary. Tyrrell was a remarkable man. He had been a friend of my father's from their earliest days and had been with him in the army during the war. He had a scientific and philosophical training, but devoted the greater part of his life to research into extrasensory perception. His work in this field was far more rigorous than the better-known work done by Joseph Banks Rhine.

George Tyrrell discovered that the governess he employed for his two children had apparently some kind of psychic power. For example, if any object in the house was missing she would immediately say where it was to be found. He therefore embarked on a long series of experiments with her. For this purpose he constructed an ingenious device, which I remember seeing. Tyrrell operated a typewriter keyboard, the keys of which lit up one of a series of electric light bulbs inside boxes on the other side of a screen, behind which Nancy, the governess, sat. There was a series of rotating devices

6

between the keyboard and the bulbs, so that Tyrrell himself did not know which key would light which bulb. Nancy had to open the box which, she intuited, contained the lighted bulb. In case anyone might say that she was abnormally sensitive to heat radiation through the box, there was a suspending mechanism whereby the bulb did not actually light until the lid of the box was raised. Furthermore, as soon as the box was opened the result was automatically recorded, so there was no possibility of her cheating in any way. These experiments, which must have been very tedious, went on for years, and Tyrrell maintained that the number of right answers Nancy gave was statistically much higher than might have been expected. It also sometimes appeared that when she was wrong she was actually anticipating the box in which the next bulb was to be lit. He eventually incorporated his results in a book entitled *The Personality of Man*, published by Penguin Books in the 1950s.

George Tyrrell never received as much recognition as he deserved, and one has to say that in some ways he was an unhappy man. I feel that through these rigorous experiments he was desperately trying to prove some kind of spiritual basis to the universe, something which is better authenticated by the imagination and the intuition than by the intellect. Tyrrell had very little imaginative or aesthetic sense. The pictures he had in his house were appalling and he positively disliked music of any kind. He once sent a professor of English literature a piece of verse which a medium had been given in a trance, and which Tyrrell thought was a remarkable and inspired poem. He was very disappointed when the professor told him it was nothing of the kind, but a bad imitation of Longfellow's *Hiawatha*. These experiments fed back badly into his personal relationships. His wife, Tina, always struck me as an embittered woman. I think she was jealous of the amount of time he spent every day closeted with Nancy, although I am certain there was nothing improper in their relationship or that Tina suspected there was, as Nancy remained living with the family after Tyrrell's death.

George Tyrrell's work received a great deal of hostility, notably from the scientific community. Scientists in general have nearly always been bitterly opposed to any theory of extrasensory perception, since such theories cut across the entire scheme of empirical, deductive knowledge on which scientific thinking has been based since Newton and Locke. But Tyrrell was equally disappointed that his work was not well received by the Church either. In his later years he came to the conclusion that the personality of man is not an entirely closed individual unit, that we are, as it were, like islands – projections above the sea of the unconscious with a common continental base. I suppose such a theory might be particularly suspect to Christians of an

7

evangelical turn of thought for whom individual conversion and individual salvation are all-important, but it does not seem to me altogether at variance from the Christian doctrine that we are all members one to another. Tyrrell was eventually to die of cancer of the throat, an affliction which was particularly tragic in his case, for he was unable to dictate to a secretary his final conclusions about human personality.

My father and Tyrrell, in their younger days, were interested in recording their dreams, to find out if any were precognitive or telepathic. My father told me about a dream he had had at the time of his engagement to my mother. He dreamt he was a member of Sinn Fein and had been arrested by soldiers of the British army. They searched him and found a letter to him from his sweetheart which they read aloud and jeered at. In my father's dream this was a letter from his real fiancée, my mother. He felt so indignant at their behaviour that he woke up in a rage. It is curious that my father should have had such a dream. He had no particular interest in Ireland and the family tradition had been Unionist. The episode is one which might well have actually occurred in Ireland at the time he had the dream.

My godmother, my father's elder sister, Mary, was the intellectual one of the family. I eventually inherited her library which contained a large number of books on philosophy, theology – especially mystical theology – and poetry. She contributed articles to the *Hibbert Journal* and also published a collection of short stories, *The Golden Rose*, as well as writing the official history, *Friendship's Highway*, of the Girls' Friendly Society, of which she was a leading member. This admirable society existed to help working girls who were leaving home for the first time. Members of the society would arrange to meet a girl at the station of the city she was moving to, find her lodgings, provide her with social facilities and see that she did not get into bad company. When I once mentioned this society to a friend who came from a mining family in Durham, he could not speak too highly of it.

My aunt Mary and her brothers and sisters reacted against the strong evangelical education they had received from their Emmet mother, and embraced a High Church, or Anglo-Catholic, position. In my aunt Mary's later years when, I think, she was in her seventies, she was suddenly possessed with a desire to hear the liturgy recited in the Holy City of Byzantium. She set off with a woman friend to journey all the way across Europe, and on the way she managed to obtain a private audience with the Exarch, the head of the Bulgarian Church. He blessed her and she kissed his ring, but I do not know what their conversation was about or, indeed, what common language they used.

At the time of my birth my father and mother were living in a house in Hampstead, but my earliest memories are of Shoreham, near Sevenoaks in Kent, where they had a house called Cherrydale. I can remember riding in a pram which was being pushed by one of the local girls who was acting as my nanny. We were proceeding along a tarmac road that ran between an avenue of tall trees. Some leaves seemed to have fallen on to the canopy of my pram, and my nurse gave me them to look at and hold. As I seemed to enjoy this, she then deliberately put sticks, leaves and pine cones on to the canopy, saying that these had also fallen from the trees. Next she placed a handful of change on to the canopy, but did not give this to me, as she said she had to take it home to my mother. It was obviously change from some money my mother had given her for an errand in the village. At this point I immediately rumbled her and have had a strong sceptical tendency ever since.

I played with the village children and I recall one slightly un-pleasant incident. One of the girls showed me her baby brother in his pram, and remarked to one of her companions that whenever her mother cut her finger she put the blood on a lump of sugar and gave it to the baby to suck. I do not know how widespread this practice was amongst the English peasantry at that time.

The life of the village was to some extent dominated by the artist Harold Copping. Shoreham had a tradition of being an artists' village. Samuel Palmer had lived there about a hundred years before. Copping was then a fashionable popular painter who was best known for an illustrated Bible, and also did wash drawings for the short stories in the *Strand* magazine. He rather disrupted the economy of the village by paying all the young men and women who were at all personable to be his models. My parents had my portrait painted by him at the age of three. I remember sitting for Copping and disconcerting him by a tendency, when compelled to be still, to go off into a kind of dreamy trance. He made his young daughter, a girl of about fourteen or so, distract my attention by holding up books and pictures for me to look at. I inherited this painting at my mother's death, but somehow I could not bear to have such a sugary version of myself as a three-year-old looking down at me from the walls of my flat, and let it be sold. I am told it eventually came on to the open market and got quite a good price, so perhaps I ought to have kept it.

Another distinguished inhabitant of Shoreham was Lord Dunsany. This Irish writer was very well known at the time, especially for his plays, many of which had a fantastic theme. In a one-act play called *A Night at an Inn*, three sailors have stolen the "red eye of the great green god". Like the protagonists of Wilkie Collins's *The Moonstone*, they are pursued by the priests of the god, who wish to reclaim the

9

jewel. The sailors entrap and murder the priests, but the idol turns up in person to reclaim his eye, and destroys them. This play, which was put on at a staff concert at Bembridge School which I later attended, gave me nightmares for years. Dunsany's plays are not, perhaps, much remembered today, but his fantasy story, *The King of Elfland's Daughter*, was reprinted in the 1960s. The vogue for Tolkien had made this kind of thing popular with the young.

I recall being taken to a garden tea party at Dunsany's house at the age of about three. I dimly remember a man with a beard. This was a period when most men of middle age were beardless because they had served in the army in the First World War, so the beard remained in my memory. I also recall a large dog whose image remains in my imagination as an Irish wolfhound, though I am not sure that it really was. According to my mother, Dunsany was, frankly, something of a bore. His single topic of conversation was a well-known proprietary brand of salt which he maintained no one should ever use because it contained powdered glass.

It was when I was still three years old that something was discovered to be seriously wrong with my eyesight. I was taken to an oculist in London called Bishop Harman. Bishop was his Christian name, though he was, I believe, a minister in the Unitarian Church. At any rate he was a very pious man. There is a story, which my father told me, that a lady, recovering from an anaesthetic which had been administered in the course of an operation on her eyes, on regaining consciousness overheard Harman saying to the surgeon: "The Almighty has blessed me with sixteen children." This alarmed her, as she was in a slightly confused and disorientated state and, for all she knew, might have been in a maternity home. I was given the usual eye test of reading illuminated letters on a screen. Harman wondered whether, at the age of three, I would be able to identify them, but my parents told him, proudly, that I already knew all my letters. He diagnosed glaucoma (a condition of the eyes which usually comes on in later life), prescribed glasses, and advised that I should be discouraged from reading or using my eyes for close work, and that I should take up a healthy outdoor life. The glasses were tinted green in order to abate the glare of the sun. The trouble was that, precisely because I was short-sighted, I was quite inept at outdoor occupations, and later on at school I loathed football, cricket and other games. But I was drawn intensely to the world of the imagination and to books. Although I was never encouraged to read – though in my early years books were read to me – I began reading widely in early childhood.

2
New Milton

My parents did not remain very long at Shoreham. They moved to various addresses in the south of England, and also lived for some while in France. At that time, it was cheaper for middle-class people with a small income to live abroad. I remember spending my fourth birthday in Brittany in a village called Saint-Jean-du-Doigt, which took its name from the fact that its church possessed, or had possessed, a relic of the finger of St John the Baptist. There was a tradition in the Middle Ages that after the beheading of St John the Baptist Herod ordered the body to be burned, but the finger with which he had pointed out Christ, saying, "Behold the Lamb of God", would not burn. A number of churches are said to possess this relic. Saint-Jean was still a primitive place and midsummer bonfires were lit on St John's Eve. This is the eve of Midsummer's Day, according to most reckonings, and was, from pre-Christian times, an important folk festival in Western Europe – especially in the Celtic areas. But most celebrations had died out by the early 1920s. It was said that the Church allowed this rather pagan celebration because it fulfilled a useful function in helping to keep the gorse down.

Somehow or other I became dimly aware of the Celtic tradition in Brittany, and I remember my father reciting to me:

> When great King Arthur ruled this land
> he was a goodly King.
> He stole three pecks of barley meal
> to make a bag pudding.
> A bag pudding the King did make
> and stuffed it full with plums
> and in it put great lumps of fat
> as big as my two thumbs.
> The King and Queen did eat thereof
> and serving men beside
> and what they could not eat that night
> the Queen next morning fried.

This was always a favourite rhyme with me, especially as heavy suet puddings were a great feature of our family cuisine, as was the custom of frying the leftover pieces for breakfast. So I was familiar with the rhyme, which gives, perhaps, a better historical account of King Arthur than Tennyson does. But my father now added, "You know, this was one part of the world where King Arthur fought his battles," because there was a tradition that Arthur landed in Brittany, before he tried to take on the Roman Empire, and killed a giant at Mont-Saint-Michel, and also the monstrous cat, Pelag. This saying of my father's caught my imagination and has remained with me ever since. It prompted me when at the age of fifty I was to write my longest and most ambitious poem, *Artorius*, an attempt to restate the Arthurian theme. My father also acquired a collection of Breton fairy-tales in French, and translated some of them for me. They included the story of the fairy Melusine, who was supposed to have been the ancestor of the Lusignan family. A mortal married her, but she made a strict condition that she must be allowed to remain in her own chamber on Saturday afternoons when, in my father's phrase, "she was on no account to be disturbed". Eventually her husband peeped through the keyhole and saw her in the form of a serpent. Finding out that she was discovered, she vanished with a banshee cry, which was always heard when any of the family was about to die. This is a widespread story. (I think it may have to do with women's totemic snake rites, and is found as far afield as Japan.)

There was an American family in the hotel where we were staying, and I remember being left in their charge when my father and mother went out on their own for a time. One day I was playing with a little toy pig, which was always known simply as "the pig with the turned-up nose", and I also had some wooden bricks. The American lady said: "Why don't you make a pen for the little pig?" I had never heard the word "pen". I knew that a pig lived in a sty, but I realised that because she was American she was using a slightly different English from mine. Perhaps this shows an early sensitivity to language.

Before we returned to England we spent a short time in Paris. I remember a great, brightly lit city, and riding in a miniature train in the Bois de Boulogne. Unfortunately I contracted bronchitis, but was cured of this by being cupped. This method of treatment had, I think, died out in English medicine, but had been retained by the French. I must have been one of the last English people to be cupped. It was pretty drastic, though familiar to our eighteenth- and nineteenth-century ancestors. The idea is to draw out the bad humours by placing cups, from which the air has been expelled by heating, upon the chest of the patient. My mother told me that I suffered acute pain. Curiously enough, I can remember the operation very well, including the matches being lit to heat the cups, and the French doctor trying to placate me for my sufferings by offering a piece of chocolate – which I refused – but the memory of the pain itself has entirely vanished from my consciousness.

After returning from Paris we occupied various addresses, first of all, I think, in London. I have distinct memories of furnished rooms, with service, in Courtfield Gardens near Gloucester Road. I recall my uncle Philip, my mother's brother (who, after the death of my grandmother, quarrelled with my mother over the inheritance), standing with me at a window and pointing out a priest in a long soutane who was coming along the road. This must have been one of the Anglican clergy from the nearby church of St Stephen's, Gloucester Road. My uncle was consumed with an intense Protestant hatred of this sight, and was urging me to join him in jeering at this figure. I also remember, in Courtfield Gardens, the muffin-man coming round, ringing his bell on darkening winter afternoons, and a little later the lamplighter with his long pole.

Most of our various addresses were in the country. In fact, the doctors had advised that I should live in the country, as I found life in the town too stimulating to my mind. Eventually we came to New Milton, Hampshire. This conurbation is divided into three subsidiary villages: Old Milton, the original village with the parish church and two village inns; New Milton, to the north, built when the railway station was opened and containing most of the shops and a water tower (constructed in a sensational redbrick Gothic style and looking like an enormous chess castle); and Barton on Sea, which was being developed as a seaside resort. Barton had the reputation of being "bracing". At this period resorts were very strictly classified as either "bracing" or "relaxing", but I have never been able quite to make out what the criteria were. It was well known that the east coast was bracing and the south coast, especially the south-west, was relaxing. Barton on Sea and, by extension, the two Miltons were definitely bracing. We rented a cottage in Barton Lane on a road which led from Barton on Sea to Old Milton village. The whole area was being intensely developed. Barton on Sea had come into existence with the sale of the Barton estate, just after the First World War, when there was enormous scope for speculative new building, usually of the bungalow type, for middle-class people, mostly retired.

My health began spectacularly to improve, and my mother determined that there should be an end to the wandering life to which my father seemed prone. We planned to settle there and direct the building of a house which should be our permanent home. When this decision was made our clothes, books, china, and so on, which had been in store in London, were brought down to the Barton Lane cottage. One lunchtime I was finishing up my meal (rhubarb and custard). I was a slow and finicky eater, and my mother had left me to it and was doing the washing-up in the kitchen. I suddenly heard a tremendous crackling sound. I thought at first that this was a sudden burst of rain pattering on the roof tiles, but in a corner of the room, at the level of the cornice, flames suddenly burst through. I called out to my mother: "The house is on fire." She rushed in and pulled me out of the house. My father was not there, as he had gone out for a walk. The upshot was that the entire house went up in flames. Apparently the builders, in constructing a flue for a geyser which heated the water in the bathroom, had not given it a proper access to the outer air. There was, above the ceiling of the first storey, an empty space which was used by the owners of the house for storing a lot of old clothes, books, children's toys and other highly inflammable articles. The flue, which should have found a vent in the air, terminated here, and occasionally emitted sparks which had ignited a beam of wood that had smouldered for a long time before bursting into flames.

My mother took me to our next-door neighbours, who told me to lie down, and shut me up in a room on the other side of the house where, to my disappointment, I was unable to watch the conflagration. Our next-door neighbours were, in fact, the Goudge family. The father was a canon of Christ Church, Oxford, and the daughter was, a few years later, to become well known as the novelist Elizabeth Goudge. We were all to read with delight her first novel, *Island Magic*, which together with its successor, *Green Dolphin Country* (which was filmed), dealt with life in Jersey at the beginning of this century. Her mother had been born there, and she relied on her mother's memories of this place. I was very touched, some years ago, when a friend showed me an anthology of poetry edited by Elizabeth Goudge, which he had picked up in a second-hand bookshop. She had included a generous helping of my own verse, although we had not met since I was a boy.

In due course the fire-engine arrived. It was simply an old Ford car, carrying a tank of water with a hose attached to it. The hose played upon the burning house, which had a course of asbestos tiles that were meant to render it fireproof, but the tiles simply became red hot and, as the water was played upon them, exploded. The whole house was completely destroyed, apart from the central chimney, which stood for many years. We had lost almost everything we possessed, except for the clothes we stood up in. We moved to The George, one of the two village inns in Old Milton, until other arrangements were made.

My father suffered an acute paralytic stroke at this point, from

14

which he subsequently seemed to recover. He had had such a stroke when serving in the army during the war, and this had been the reason for his discharge. The authorities had put it down to "shell-shock", a vague term employed at that time for a variety of conditions resulting from trench warfare. Similarly, the stroke which followed the fire was attributed to shock. It was not until a third such stroke occurred, while he was staying in Devonshire with his friend George Tyrrell, that serious medical attention was paid, for on this occasion there was no external cause which could be held to blame. In fact, he was found to be suffering from multiple sclerosis, a disease which afflicted him for the rest of his life. He died in 1938.

We moved from The George to an annexe flat in a large rambling house at Barton on Sea owned by a family called Gunter, who became our close friends. Mr Gunter was a retired clergyman, though he continued to do a lot of voluntary work for the Society for the Propagation of the Gospel. The Gunters were a rather bohemian family. The younger children, the son, Paddy, and the daughter, Doreen, became my playmates. We spent a lot of time on a nearby rubbish tip, full of interesting objects. The house was not kept in very good repair. A particularly nasty incident happened to me at this time. I had always been subject to extreme night terrors, and I cried out on account of such an attack while staying in the Gunters' flat. My mother and father came and found me trembling from head to foot. They thought it was a nightmare, but it turned out that there was, in fact, a rat in my bed. While we were staying at the Gunters' flat, the building of our house, which we called Seaward Cottage, at Barton on Sea, was under way. We moved into it in the early 1920s, and it remained our home until the Second World War.

I first began to attend school at the age of five, when we were still living at the cottage in Barton Lane which was shortly to be burnt down. It was a large private girls' school, the lower form of which took little boys as well. I think I was only there for one term, and I do not remember much about this except for a French lesson from a Frenchwoman. I had already been taught some French when we were living in Brittany. I also remember trying, rather ineffectually, to copy letters in a copy-book. The following term I attended another private school in the village, kept by a Miss Barnes. Her pupils consisted of not more than two or three boys and one or two girls, as far as I recall, but she was a good teacher. Miss Barnes taught us history out of a book called *Our Island Story*, which told all the familiar stories of English history that everyone ought to know, and began, very properly, with our mythological history – the giant Albion (a son of Neptune) and Brutus the Trojan. Geography was taught out of a similar book in which some children are visited by a genie who transports them to various parts of the globe on a magic carpet. After a while an aviator takes over – his function being simply to transport the children to different parts of the British Isles.

It was at Miss Barnes's school, also, that I first became aware of poetry, as opposed to the nursery rhymes which, from an early age, I had read in a book illustrated by Lovat Fraser. Miss Barnes read us "The Lady of Shalott" and, inevitably, "Daffodils". I do not know why it has become traditional that this poem of Wordsworth's, which is really a sophisticated poem, seems to have been adopted as the English child's introduction to poetry. Miss Barnes also read us the first canto of *Hiawatha*. A few years later I was to read the whole of *Hiawatha* in a rather good annotated edition which gave a detailed account of the folklore of the native Americans, on which Longfellow drew. The trouble about Longfellow's poetry is that it all seems to be in glorious Technicolor. The metre of *Hiawatha*, unrhymed trochaic verse, is far too easy in English – it is scarcely a metre at all. You can improvise it till the cows come home. Longfellow derived it from the *Kalevala*. This national epic of Finland was stitched together from oral lays and ballads extant among the Finnish peasantry. Most of this poetry had its roots in pre-Christian mythology. It was intelligent of Longfellow to adopt this metre for *Hiawatha* because the civilisation depicted in the *Kalevala* is a shamanistic one – in which the heroes are wizards rather than warriors – which was in many ways similar to the civilisation of the native Americans of Michigan.

A few years ago I heard a passage from *Hiawatha* read on a BBC schools programme and it brought back memories of a poem I had not looked at for over fifty years. It was the passage which deals with Hiawatha's initiation. He retires to a wigwam in the centre of the forest and fasts for a long period. Then a golden-haired young man arrives, dressed in a green robe, and challenges Hiawatha to wrestle with him on three successive days. On the third, Hiawatha overcomes the young man, and he dies. He tells Hiawatha to bury him, and he will rise again as a gift for Hiawatha's people. He does rise again because he is the maize plant. However inferior the verse may be, the imagery of this is powerful, and I realised that its deep anthropological symbolism had had a strong impression on my unconscious at the early age at which I had read it, and had prepared me for James George Frazer's *The Golden Bough*, T. S. Eliot's *The Waste Land*, and a lot more.

It was in Miss Barnes's school that I first made acquaintance with the still novel invention of the radio. Lessons were suspended while we observed the two minutes' silence which marked Armistice Day. Miss Barnes was listening to the Cenotaph ceremony through headphones, and retailing to us what was going on. She then passed the headphones round for us to listen ourselves. What we heard was a snatch of a hymn from Westminster Abbey, presumably "O God, our help in ages past". It was, I suppose, within a year or two that almost every household owned a radio.

I am not sure how many terms I spent at Miss Barnes's school, but it cannot have been more than one or two. I proceeded to a more sophisticated establishment called Speedwell, in New Milton. It was called Speedwell after the wild flower that had grown abundantly on the ground where it was built. Each of the boys wore a little bright blue blazer, and a bright blue cap, to recall the colour of that flower. It was a day school kept by two brothers, Mr Warren and Mr Roland Kershaw, and their elder sister, Miss Kershaw. Their elderly mother also lived with them and cooked the school lunches. The number of boys was not more than a dozen or so, but it did function as a regular preparatory school. The lowest form was taught by Miss Kershaw, who read us Bible stories, parts of *Uncle Tom's Cabin* and also a book called *Tommy Smith's Animals*. In this, a boy called Tommy Smith, who is extremely callous towards wildlife, is suddenly faced with the animals talking to him and putting their own point of view, which I am glad to say reformed his character. The upper form was much more rigorous. Mr Warren taught us mathematics and French, Mr Roland, Latin, Greek, English, history and scripture. Mr Roland was the more attractive character of the two, being a less strict discipli-narian, and with more humour, than Mr Warren. Not only did I prefer him but I did better in the subjects he taught. It was in his classes that I was given the only Greek lessons that, to my lasting regret, I have ever had. He taught us the alphabet, the declensions of nouns, part of the conjugation of verbs, and then, rather prematurely, perhaps, plunged us into the early chapters of Xenophon's *Anabasis*, translating it for us as we went along. His scripture lessons consisted in reading remorselessly through all the historical books of the Old Testament. I do not think we ever reached the prophets or the New Testament.

Mr Roland was also a keen amateur naturalist. One afternoon he suddenly opened the box which he called his museum. It was full of wonders: a Chinese toy, which was a carving of a tiger, a piece of smoked glass, the skeleton of a sparrow, snail shells and the skin of a snake. He also told us of observations he had made on the mating of snails and how he had seen a specimen of one of the rarest of English reptiles, the coronella (or smooth snake), lying by the road near Beaulieu in the New Forest.

Life in the country was already awaking in me an interest in natural history. My father took me for daily walks, and identified the songs of the birds that we heard. Seaward Avenue, where our house, Seaward Cottage, was built, had only just been changed from open fields into a housing area. Consequently it had birds and insects that you would not normally expect to find so close to human habitation. The alarming "Devil's Coachhorse", or rogue beetle, was common in the garden. This insect, which has the habit of turning up the end of its abdomen in a threatening manner and opening its large and formidable jaws, is perfectly harmless, indeed a friend of the gardener, as it eats slugs and other destructive creatures, but it is often (never by me) mistaken for a scorpion or something of that kind. Stonechats nested in the bramble bushes which fringed the edge of the road, and I remember, at the age of eight or so, standing beside a bush and seeing, only a few inches away, the male stonechat, with his brilliant red breast and black head, guarding his nest and sounding his characteristic call note, which is exactly like the sound of stones being chinked together. Also, at one point in the early autumn, there was a weird sound in the air above us: it was the call of curlews, migrating to the coast.

My father had inherited his knowledge of birds from his own father, who had studied the standard book of that generation, Yarell's *British Birds*. Many years later, reading a book by James Fisher on sea birds, which had been sent to me for review, I found that a Mr Stubbs had recorded seeing the body of a Wandering Albatross, hanging up, in order to attract customers, over a poulterer's stall in Leadenhall Market. I think this Mr Stubbs must have been my grandfather. The bird had been newly killed, as blood was dripping from its beak. There is no certain record of this bird ever occurring in Britain, although this specimen may at least have been shot in British waters. The Wandering Albatross, with its eleven-foot wingspan, is the most spectacular of the species. The smaller Black-Browed Albatross, which is not much larger than a large seagull, has been recorded in England on one or two occasions. It must have been one of the smaller albatrosses that the Ancient Mariner shot – you could not possibly have a bird with an eleven-foot wingspan hung round your neck. Coleridge did, in fact, witness the shooting of an albatross, on his voyage to Malta, although this was after he had written *The Ancient Mariner*; but I dare say it was the Wandering Albatross that Baudelaire saw, on his voyage to the East, impeded by its enormous wings when captured and compelled to walk on the deck of a ship. For Baudelaire, it is a fitting symbol for the poet – lord of the air and the sky, but inept and clumsy on mundane earth.

Barton on Sea and, later on, New Milton itself were to be my home until, at the age of twenty-four, I came up to London to work, remaining there permanently for most of the rest of my life. New Milton in its extended sense was a strange community. There was very little left of its original rural character, though the nearby villages of Ashley and Bashley, which were in the same parish, and the nearest New Forest town of Brockenhurst were still traditionally agricultural. Most of the inhabitants of New Milton seemed to be members of the middle classes, living in little one- or two-storey houses which, like my parents, they had often designed themselves, surrounded by gardens, on which they lavished great care, with an obligatory tennis court. I heard a rather shocking story of a man who had lived in Japan for many years and had brought a Japanese gardener back with him to design the garden of the house he had built for his retirement. The poor Japanese gardener had to incorporate a flat, square, tennis court into his carefully designed landscape of little hills and rivers, at which the Japanese excel, and almost resigned the commission – it was an affront to his aesthetic sense.

Most of these people were retired members of the armed services or the colonial administration, or former businessmen who often had worked abroad in the British Empire. Our closest neighbours at Seaward Cottage were a family called Parker-Rees. Their younger daughter, Daphne, and her brother, Alistair, were my constant friends and playmates. Mr Parker-Rees had had some kind of business in Hong Kong, and had brought back with him a Chinese nurse, or amah, to look after his children. This poor woman, elderly, and hardly speaking a word of English, must have lived an extraordinarily lonely life with nothing to devote herself to but the children in her care who treated her with not a great deal of respect. I myself was slightly frightened of her, for the stereotype of the Chinese in the popular literature of the period was that they were at best quaint, at worst incredibly sinister and cruel. Dr Fu Manchu was the figure who sprang to mind.

The society of New Milton was in many ways very like that described by E. F. Benson in his novels, though the community he was writing about was Rye in Sussex. Apart from the eternal bridge parties and tennis parties, there was a variety of amateur artistic projects. This was an advantage, I think, of the pre-television age. There was a local dramatic society, and an operatic society which usually put on the old musical comedy hits of the first part of this century, such as *The Arcadians* and *San Toy*, though they were ambitious enough, at one point, to put on *Faust*. Later, when my mother resumed her musical career, she founded a local orchestra which collaborated with the operatic society to provide the music for *Faust*. There were also various chamber music groups, amateur fiddlers, cellists, a clarinettist, a flute player and a choral society. I remember that this last went so far as to perform, not the whole of *Hiawatha*, but *Hiawatha's Wedding Feast*. *Hiawatha*, a dramatic cantata by Coleridge Taylor, was extremely popular among English choral societies in the pre-war period. A performance of it was given annually by massed choral societies at the Albert Hall, in which all the participants dressed in Red Indian costume, and an underground stream, which runs under the Albert Hall, was brought to the surface and made to work as part of the décor.

In the 1920s, during the era of silent films, there was only one cinema in New Milton. Later a new cinema was built which showed the talkies. I remember gazing at the stills outside the cinema and wondering what the stories they illustrated could be, because unlike most children of my generation I was not taken to the cinema at an early age. There were two reasons for this: in the first place, a large part of the middle classes, including my parents, did not regard the cinema as anything but cheap entertainment for the servants; and, secondly, my parents believed that the old flickering screen would be detrimental to my already weak eyesight. I was taken once or twice, under supervision, to films which were thought suitable, for example, a film with the child star Jackie Coogan, and later on to some boring films about wild animals which my parents thought would please me. Naturally we sat in the more expensive seats at the back, where the glare of the screen would be less damaging to my eyes, but because of my poor eyesight this meant that I could not read the captions, and to this day I have not a clue what the Jackie Coogan film was about.

There was not, as far as I remember, a literary or debating society in New Milton. Contemporary art and music seemed only to have been known as the subject of jokes in *Punch*, while contemporary literature, apart from the popular novels provided by Boots library and W. H. Smith, scarcely existed. A former rector had been a Mr Kelsall, who must have been one of the last of the Victorian scholar-naturalists. An old lady in the village had known him, and she told me how she had taken him round her garden and invited him to inspect her scillas. "Scillas!" said Kelsall contemptuously. "Say 'squills', woman." Kelsall had been a friend of the Reverend C. A. Johns, whose two popular natural history books, *Flowers of the Field* and *British Birds in their Haunts*, were still in print in my youth, though they were not really good natural history, especially the book on birds. The same lady told me that Johns, who had a parish near Winchester, had a notice in his garden designed to keep out intruders: "Beware mandrakes and creeping jenny". Kelsall left his library to the town and it was housed in a local institute. I think I was the only person who ever read in it. It contained a copy of the old 1888 *Encyclopaedia Britannica* and some valuable books on natural history, such as Jerdon's *British Vertebrates*, as well as some books on the Old Testament, interpreted in the light of the knowledge of mythology which was coming into fashion in Kelsall's youth.

Barton on Sea aimed to be a seaside resort. It had, however, a rather unattractive shingly beach, a cliff which was always falling down, and quantities of the local blue slipper clay which formed dangerous shifting bogs. This blue clay, known as the Barton Beds, was rich in fossils of the Eocene period. The subsidence of the cliffs continually occupied the local council, who tried building breakwaters and dams to prevent the erosion. This was not the right solution; a better one was to drain the clay beds. The latter policy was advocated by a member of the council, an Irishman whose proper name was Captain The O'Donovan. This surname indicated that he was the hereditary head of the O'Donovan clan. He insisted that the other councillors should address him in full form, which annoyed them extremely. Eventually they wrote to the College of Heralds, who replied, saying quite firmly that Captain The O'Donovan was entitled to be addressed in this way and they should do so. In spite of Barton's disadvantages for bathing, there were numerous beach huts built on the undercliff. Adders were not uncommon in the grass there, and coltsfoot grew abundantly. During the war, a friend and neighbour of ours collected coltsfoot leaves by the sackful in order to make his own herbal tobacco.

At the eastern end of Barton was a common, so called, though I think it was no longer actually common land, and part of it had been turned into a golf-course. This common, although subject to frequent fires, also formed a fascinating part of my boyhood. A stream debouched into the sea at this point. It ran through a valley which was known as Becton Bunny. The word "bunny", which appears to be connected with the word burn (a stream), is the traditional name in this part of the country for such a valley, which in other parts would be called a syke or a drain. There was a similar bunny to the east of New Milton in the nearby village of Highcliffe. This had acquired the pretentious name of Chewton Glen, but the older people still called it Chewton Bunny. Although to some extent polluted, Becton Bunny still harboured some interesting wildlife. I saw swifts hawking for flies above it, and further along on the sandy cliff was a colony of sandmartins. Also, while walking by the stream, I saw the extraordinary sight of a number of the cast skins of the sub-imago stage of the mayfly, sitting for all the world as if they were living creatures on the branches of a willow tree.

My brother George was born in Seaward Cottage on 1 December 1925. I had not been prepared for his birth. I do remember, some time before it, my father scolding me for some misdemeanour. I was always being scolded, and from time to time beaten. Although I do not know why, I always seemed to be in the wrong. I was not a vicious child, I am sure, but I was dreamy, impractical, clumsy, forgetful and unpunctual, and this must have been extremely irritating. My father said to me that, if I did not behave better to my mother, God might take her away. I realise now that he was afraid that the worry I caused her might be prejudicial to the birth of my brother. This was, I think, a terrible thing to say to a child. I had my own bedroom at Seaward Cottage, and woke up one morning to find I had been moved to a spare room. My grandmother, my mother's mother, who lived with us, came in to wake me and tell me that a lady had arrived late the previous night, and that she had wanted my room. She was, of course, the midwife. I was then taken down to see my mother, whom I knew to have been ill for some time, and suddenly introduced to my small brother. By all modern ideas of child psychology this whole procedure seems to have been totally misjudged, and it did, I think, lead to my feeling jealous and resentful. Consequently George and I were not on good terms through most of our boyhood, though I believe he admired and looked up to me.

When the Second World War broke out my mother decided to send my brother to Rhodesia (as it was then called) to live with her brother, my uncle Fred, a Commissioner for Native Affairs, and his wife. George finished his education there and served in the South African army in the Italian Campaign. After the war he settled permanently in Rhodesia as a farmer, but decided to leave his farm in the charge of a partner for a while, and go round the world in search of a wife, taking in America and the Far East. But when he arrived in New Milton he took to frequenting one of the pubs and fell in love with the landlord's daughter and married her. I encountered, in George, a young man whom I genuinely liked and respected. We remained on friendly terms until his death in 1983.

Servants, in the 1920s at any rate, were plentiful and easy to find. We had one servant living in, a house parlourmaid called Dolly, and another, Dora, who acted as cook, and had some three miles to travel on her bicycle every morning. Servants got up at extraordinarily early hours, before six o'clock, to light the fires, and so on. Dora had come to my mother when very young and my mother had largely trained her. She had had a place as a kitchen maid in a big country mansion in the neighbouring village of Hinton Admiral. The family who owned this house still kept up a traditional, squirearchical way of life. When the railway line was brought through their lands they secured the right to stop any train that was passing through the little station that adjoined their estate, if they wanted to use it to go up to London. In church, when there was a communion service, no one would dare go up to the altar until the squire's family had done so. Dora was a remarkable girl. Never, I think, in her whole life did she leave her native county, and she had a great sense of tradition; for instance, she would say to my mother: "It is Michaelmas next Monday so I have ordered a goose." One of her great specialities was a dish called Hampshire apple cake which you eat hot as a pudding rather than as a cake. I have tried to make it myself but never with entire success. I wish I had managed to get the recipe from her. When my mother had company for tea in the drawing-room, I was sent to have mine in the kitchen with the servants. I enjoyed this, and spent my time reading the cookery books which were kept in the kitchen. There was, of course, *Mrs Beeton* and other books of that kind, and also Mrs Marshall's cookery book which was very upmarket. My mother had once had a cook who had been trained at Mrs Marshall's school and who insisted on our having a copy of her teacher's magnum opus, though it really gave recipes which were quite outside the range of a middle-class family.

Besides these two maids, we had a sewing-woman who came in fairly regularly to help us and, in later years, a charlady for the rough work. There was also a gardener called Matcham. My mother in addition engaged a series of au pair governesses from Scandinavian countries and in one case, I think, from Switzerland. My mother was suspicious of engaging au pair girls from Catholic countries. I remember one of the Danish girls teaching me the Danish version of "Baa, baa, black sheep" – "Baa, baa, hvid lamme". It struck me at the time that the Danish poetic imagination appeared to be inferior to the English, as it concerned itself with such an obvious phenomenon as a white lamb instead of the much more interesting anomaly of a black sheep.

We thought of all our servants as friends and members of the family, and my mother worked closely with Dora in the kitchen. There was a great spate of marmalade-making in May, when the big bitter Seville oranges came into the shops, and in the late summer jam-making and fruit-bottling, using not only fruit from the garden – strawberries, raspberries, gooseberries, blackcurrants, greengages, plums and apples – but also the wild harvest of blackberries and elderberries. We did not make wine with the elderberries, however, but stewed them with apples. The only alcoholic drink that my mother did make was sloe gin. You prick the sloes and steep them in gin. I have seen sloe gin on the market these days that is bright red. Sloes are black. I cannot think what they put in it. One of my students at Oxford simply could not understand when I explained that "sloe eyed" was an epithet of eighteenth-century popular poetry for dark eyes.

Dora would never allow us to have blackberries after 1 November: "The devil spits on them." In some parts of the country, it appears, it is said more bluntly that he pisses on them. They are certainly not good eating in the later part of the season, and this, I suspect, is because there are four hundred-odd different "infra-species" of blackberry (the group is a botanist's nightmare) and the ones that become ripe at this time are inferior. But it also may be that the blackberry, because of its colour, is regarded as the food of the dead, and the dead are widely believed to be released temporarily from purgatory, or the underworld, during November. They wander about the lanes and feed upon the blackberries. We always had blackberry and apple pudding and blackberry and apple pie in September and October. My father used to say that whenever he heard the prayer which asks God to bring forth in due season "the kindly fruits of the earth" he always thought of blackberries and apples. He also had a strong sense of tradition. After we had been to church on Good Friday he would always plant his spring seeds, so they would rise, presumably, with the risen Christ, or at least be influenced by the waxing Easter moon.

Our milk, groceries and meat were delivered daily by an errand boy on a bicycle, who would then take the orders for the following day. In the twenties, neither we nor any of our neighbours – with the exception of those, like doctors, who needed them for professional purposes – had telephones. Fish was delivered every Friday from the fishmonger, but sometimes a fisherman would come round peddling, from door to door, fish he had caught in Christchurch harbour. These included some unusual kinds, for example the gar-fish. Its appearance is against it. It has a long snaky body with spiny fins, and a head like that of a miniature crocodile with a beak-shaped mouth and formidable teeth; moreover, its bones are bright green. Nevertheless, it is excellent eating. For special occasions we could always buy game, presumably shot on neighbouring estates. The Christchurch Avon is also a salmon stream.

At the heart of the community was Old Milton, where was the parish church to which my father took me every Sunday. My mother, although a devout Christian, did not usually go to church because she saw it as her duty to assist Dora in cooking a hot Sunday lunch for us. There had been a church, in fact a chapel of ease, belonging to Christchurch Priory as early as the reign of King John. The present church was mostly a Victorian restoration, but there was an Elizabethan tower. The greater part of the community (apart from substantial Methodist and Baptist minorities, and the small Roman Catholic congregation) still went regularly to this church and often, if one was not there early, one had to go up into the gallery. This had originally been a musicians' gallery before the period when, under the influence of the Oxford Movement, organs were introduced into country parish churches. The old custom of having a group of musicians playing to accompany the psalms and hymns is described by Hardy, and I think the discontinuation of this custom was something of a loss. The rector,

Mr Hutchinson, though doubtless a well-meaning man, had an unfortunate personality and did not altogether get on well with his congregation. He was rather High Church and most of his congregation were not. The conflict between them seemed to hinge on his attempt to introduce the English Hymnal to replace *Hymns Ancient and Modern*. Once, when he was away on holiday and a guest preacher advocated prayers for the departed, several of the congregation strode out.

About a mile to the north of the village the New Forest began. The forest is not by any means all woodland: a great deal of it is open moorland and peat bog. At least at that time a lot of it was planted with quick-growing conifers which were sold as pit props. Nothing much will grow under conifers. The older deciduous woodland, especially the oak trees which once provided timbers for the English navy, is far more environmentally friendly. There is, or was, remarkably little wildlife in the forest, apart from the half-wild ponies and the deer. The ponies, which in those days were often sold as pit ponies, were very tame, and in winter, sometimes along with the deer, would come into New Milton itself, entering people's gardens and doing a certain amount of damage. One had to be careful when driving along the forest roads because they had no fear of man or, it seemed, of motor cars.

Some of the peculiarities of the New Forest fauna, which I found described in my natural history books, seemed to have already vanished. In fact the New Forest has always struck me as a forbidding place. One would go on excursions to see the Rufus Stone, the monument erected in the nineteenth century to mark the spot where William Rufus was mysteriously killed by an arrow. Margaret Murray in *The God of the Witches* maintains that William's death was really a ritual sacrifice and that he was a secret adherent of the old pagan religions, of which she saw witchcraft as a survival. William was certainly unpopular with the Church, but I do not think this necessarily means that he was a pagan. Unfortunately, Margaret Murray went on to maintain not only that Thomas à Becket's murder was in the same category but in a later book, *The Divine King in England*, that practically every king or royal consort or favourite who died in any violent or mysterious way down to Stuart times was a ritual sacrifice. As they obviously all cannot have been, it logically follows that probably none of them was. I find it hard to believe that when Charles II said, "I'm sorry to be an unconscionable long time dying," he was apologising for not expiring in the right ritual month. I have even heard it said that Margaret Murray maintained that the death of Lord Wavell's son in Africa was really a sacrifice planned to coincide with the coronation of the present Queen.

There were rumours that popular belief in witchcraft still lingered

25

on in the New Forest. The modern witchcraft cult was founded there, just before the Second World War, by Gerald Gardiner, a disciple of Aleister Crowley. Whether Gardiner and his followers drew on any real ancient tradition is, I think, doubtful. Francis King – not to be confused with the novelist of the same name – says in his book, *Ritual Magic*, that during the Second World War the witches courageously did their best for the country by performing their ritual naked dance, in the depths of the forest, without applying the customary bear's grease, so that one of their number would inevitably die of exposure and thus be accepted by the gods whom they worshipped as a sacrifice on behalf of the war effort. Whether this is true I do not know. But it is a fact that a Rosicrucian theatre was founded near Christchurch at about this time. I never went to this theatre, which I regret, though I would not like to have met the Rosicrucians and possibly been commandeered into their cult at an impressionable age. Among the plays advertised was one called *Henry VII*, which I imagine was a work posthumously delivered by Shakespeare, through a medium, to complete a gap in his series of historical plays.

There were other, more modern associations with the New Forest. Somewhere in the forest was a house in which an old lady lived in retirement. Everybody had heard of her, but nobody seemed to have met her. She was Alice Liddell.

3

Bembridge

After a year or so I was sent away to a boarding-school called Dorset House, in Littlehampton, Sussex, where my friend Alistair Parker-Rees was already a pupil. Dorset House was a small preparatory school, taking not more than about thirty children. It was kept by a Mr Monroe and his wife, a large and kindly lady. Mr Monroe was also kindly in his way, though a ferocious exponent of corporal punishment. He had a graduated series of instruments of punishment. At the lowest end of the hierarchy was a little cane called "Tickler" or "The Children's Friend", which he would bring into class and strike out at any boy who made a very bad mistake in his Latin, which was what Mr Monroe mainly taught. For more serious misdemeanours he would use a Woolworth's cricket bat. Mr Monroe would sometimes over-indulge in port and come into the classroom quite tipsy, assigning marks not because the boy had answered the question correctly but because Mr Monroe felt well disposed towards him. The two Monroes had the endearing habit of going round the dormitories and saying goodnight individually to each boy, but the boys would get wise when Mr Monroe was a bit drunk and put chairs in his way so that he fell over.

Besides the Monroes – Mrs Monroe did not in fact do any teaching, though she did sometimes read books to the junior boys – there were two assistant masters, both of whom were neurotic and alleged to be suffering from "shell-shock" acquired during the war. Mr Sims, who had been a sergeant-major and put us through military-style physical training exercises for an hour every morning, also taught French. He was something of a sadist, I think, and we did not like him. Mr Furley was the master who assisted Mr Monroe in teaching classics. Prematurely grey, he had aquiline features which, to my eye, resembled the portrait of Julius Caesar, taken from the/so-called Naples bust, which adorned our school text of the *Gallic Wars*. I developed a private fantasy about him, which I used to illustrate with drawings, that he was indeed Julius Caesar, and had even existed from the beginning of time. I remember drawing a picture of him pursuing dinosaurs over a primeval landscape. He was a kind man with some odd habits. It was said that if he did not like the pudding that was served at lunch he would withdraw, saying he had to meet a man to play golf, taking some of the pudding with him. If it was a bread pudding, he would make it into pellets which he flicked at the boys as they emerged from the dining-hall. He used sometimes to take us for walks round the town. We would go down to the seafront where there were old shops selling maritime junk of various kinds, and a sweetshop where he used to buy us humbugs. I gather that what are called humbugs now are little sweets, not very different from what we would have called bull's-eyes, but the humbugs Mr Furley bought in Littlehampton were another matter. About three inches by two inches, they were delicious, tasting either of peppermint or cloves.

Besides these two masters, there was an assistant mistress, Miss Dormer, who taught mathematics. I was not good at this subject and do not think that she helped me in becoming more adept at it by her method of personal supervision of my work. She made me sit at the table where she presided and do my sums in front of her. Every time I made a mistake she rapped me sharply over the knuckles with an ebony ruler. She had her own room, and hanging on the mantelpiece was a large photographic reproduction of the statue of the Mannequin Pis in Brussels. This is a fountain in the form of a little boy peeing, and the photograph caused a certain scandal among Miss Dormer's pupils.

The teaching at Dorset House was, I suppose, fairly old-fashioned even for its day. We spent a great deal of time on Latin, doing drill in learning the principal parts of the verbs and reciting them every morning, and reading from a book called *Fabulae Faciles* which retold some of the well-known myths from Ovid. I was already well acquainted with these through the medium of Hawthorne's *Tanglewood Tales* and Charles Kingsley's *The Heroes*. There was, I remember, a particularly dodgy passage in the account of the career of Perseus, the episode which recalls his rescue of Andromeda from the sea monster: "tunc propter omnibus ad rupem alligata est" – "and then in the sight of all she was tied to the rock." It was, of course, inevitable that sooner or later someone would translate it: "and then in the sight of all she was given up to the alligator."

Our readings in English literature seemed to consist mostly of Macaulay's essays on Warren Hastings and Clive, which, since our study of history never got past the Tudors, we found difficult to understand. For poetry we had Macaulay's *Lays of Ancient Rome*. Later, when I got to university, I despised these poems, but now I admire them. Already, in Macaulay's time, scholars were beginning to opine that Livy must have drawn on traditional oral sources for the stories in his *History of the Roman Republic*. Macaulay was trying to reconstruct these sources in imitation of an English ballad, or romance style.

In the junior form, which was taken by a Mrs Brown, we studied a collection of English poetry known as *Gems* – I think its full name must have been *Gems of English Poetry* – which contained poems by Longfellow, Mrs Hemans and others. It even included *Lycidas*, though none of us was up to tackling this poem at that age. A poem that I particularly liked, and decided was my favourite, was Thomas Campbell's "The Soldier's Dream", which seemed to me to express the deep sense of homesickness I felt at this boarding-school.

Mr and Mrs Monroe both followed the admirable Victorian practice of reading aloud to us on Sunday evenings. In the junior form Mrs Monroe read us Kingsley's *The Water Babies* and collections of fairy-tales. I remember "The Yellow Dwarf", by Madame d'Aulnoy, and some of the stories collected by Andrew Lang. Our doctor and family friend, Dr Francis Henderson Begg, who many years later, after the war, was to become my stepfather, gave me a present of John Masefield's *The Midnight Folk*. This is far and away Masefield's best work. For the most part he is derivative, both as a poet and as a novelist, but *The Midnight Folk* is a wonderful creation of the fantasy world of a lonely Victorian child. It is much better than its sequel, *The Box of Delights*, which is nowadays better known, as it was adapted for television. Mr Monroe read to the older boys, who remained in the school up to the age of twelve or thirteen, from the romances of Rider Haggard and the tales of Arthur Conan Doyle – both the Sherlock Holmes and the Brigadier Gerard stories. There was a reasonably good school library from which one could borrow books. At a very early age I had had *David Copperfield* read to me, at least in part, by my grandmother, and I had read and reread it myself. At Dorset House I followed this up with *Oliver Twist* and *Great Expectations*, but did not finish the latter. I suppose *Great Expectations* was too difficult for me, though I now think it is a much more interesting and subtly written book than the other two.

On Sundays we were all taken to church, wearing little straw boaters. At one time Eton collars had been *de rigueur*, but Mrs Monroe had abolished them as barbarous and cruel inventions, though I recall sometimes having to wear the uncomfortable things at parties during the holidays. After church we had two duties to perform, then the rest of the day was free. One of these duties was to write a letter home, the other to learn the collect for the day. This again, I think, is a Victorian custom, as it is one of the duties which Kay, the hero of Masefield's *The Midnight Folk*, had to perform. In many ways it is an excellent custom, for Cranmer's Prayer Book collects are wonderful examples of English prose, but unfortunately, in spite of having to learn them all by heart, I could not recite a single one of them now.

Every night before we went to bed we were supposed to read a chapter from the Bible. At the beginning of term a printed reading list produced by some evangelical organisation was given to us, but nobody ever supervised these readings or enquired whether one was reading the recommended passages. This left me free to explore the Bible on my own. It was the poetry of the Bible which most captured my imagination – especially that of the Song of Songs and the apocalyptic books, Revelations, Daniel and Ezekiel – but the scientist in me also delighted in the lists of clean and unclean beasts in Leviticus, and the description of the Leviathan and the Behemoth, which are probably the crocodile and the hippopotamus, in the Book of Job.

In many ways Dorset House was a fairly brutal school. The rooms were bare and uncomfortable, and the food was bad, except on Sunday mornings when we were given sausages. The boys themselves devised a rigid hierarchy. For purposes of administrative convenience, each boy was given a number which reflected, I think, his general academic and other success. The boys created out of this a desperately oppressive system, whereby any boy had absolute power over any other boy with a number higher than his own, and had the complete support of the rest in this. He could "turf" him, that is, make him go away, he could hit him, with the other boy having no right of retaliation, and he could "turf" any rubbish or unwanted material by putting it into the desk of the other boy, who could dispose of it or, more likely, "turf" it on to a boy lower than he in the hierarchy.

Boys are essentially primitives and like to belong to totemic clans. Some of these clans were institutionalised; for example, there were the "Crusaders", whose badges were borne on the lapel. The Crusaders were some kind of evangelical Christian organisation whose members were pledged to virtuous actions. Besides this there were the "Gugnuncs" and the "Mustard Club". The patron of the "Gugnuncs" was Wilfred, and the badge showed his ears. Wilfred was part of a trio – Pip, Squeak and Wilfred – who appeared regularly in a children's comic strip in the *Daily Mirror*, then not so much a populist paper but designed for the bright young things of the twenties. Pip was a dog, Squeak was a penguin and Wilfred was a mentally retarded rabbit. Unlike his two companions, he did not have the gift of articulate speech, but had a limited vocabulary of "gug", which indicated approbation, "nunc", which I think indicated enthusiasm, "ick ick" for fear, "pah" for disgust and "boo" for anger. The members of the Gugnuncs, who paid a small subscription to the *Daily Mirror*, and pledged themselves to be kind to animals, to defend the British Empire, and things of that sort, would greet each other by a series of secret passwords made up from Wilfred's vocabulary. Other characters in this strip, which had a very strong conservative political line, included a Russian Bolshevik called Wtzkowski who appeared, like an anarchist of the turn of the century, in a long cloak, long beard and large hat. He carried bombs around by the sackful or, sometimes, by the sledgeload. His accomplice was a communist dog, Popski. There was a mysterious character called Aunty. She was Squeak's aunt and was a slightly senile penguin, who also, I think, was not gifted with the power of speech. The Gugnuncs had an immense number of adherents right down to the thirties. When the Nazi youth of Germany were assembling in Nuremberg, shouting "Heil Hitler", hundreds of English children were assembling in the Albert Hall, calling out: "ick, ick, pah, boo".

The Mustard Club was a publicity stunt which owed its inception to the genius of Dorothy L. Sayers, who was then working in an advertising agency. This suggested the setting for her detective story, *Murder Must Advertise*. The Mustard Club was created to advertise Colman's mustard, but as Colman's had practically a monopoly of mustard its name never had to be mentioned. Dorothy L. Sayers invented an imaginary fashionable West End club, the committee of which consisted of the Baron de Beef, Lady Hearty, Miss Di Gesta, Signor Spaghetti, Lord Bacon and Master Mustard. Reports would appear almost daily in the popular newspapers, dealing with the adventures of this group of characters, who reflected the fashionable smart set of the twenties. Children do not really like mustard, but most of us delighted in the adventures of these characters. Many of us belonged to the Mustard Club, and wore a little mustard-pot badge. Another totemic club was the private invention of myself and two of my friends. We secretly identified ourselves with a badger, a fox and a ferret, and had an imaginary life in which we played the parts of these animals, keeping an archive of paintings and drawings in a tin box.

We slept in large, chilly and uncomfortable dormitories. After lights-out, boys used to tell stories, or even read aloud, for we all read with a cheap electric torch under the bedclothes. In these circumstances, I absorbed most of *Dracula* from another boy's retelling of it. There was a boy, Gary, who had the pre-pubescent boy's intensely scatological and sexually obscene imagination developed to a high degree. He would entertain us at night with a long saga about a character called Charles Augustus whose adventures I forbear to relate here. When I was about thirty I was walking along the Bayswater Road one evening when, suddenly, a man a year or so older than I stopped me and said: "Aren't you John Heath-Stubbs?" I replied that I was. He then introduced himself as Gary, and I said, "Oh, I remember you very well. You taught me the facts of life." He assumed a horrified expression and quickly departed. I think he

31

thought I was accusing him of initiating me sexually, but he had only done so verbally.

Every summer we boys used to go on a holiday excursion in a little steam or motor launch up the river Arun as far as Arundel Castle. On the way we passed through a heronry, and it was a delight to see those great grey birds perching on the trees. We were all supplied with a lunch consisting of a Cornish pasty and a bottle of fizzy lemonade or ginger beer, in a glass bottle closed with a glass marble. It was very ingenious. When the bottle was full, the glass marble was forced down the neck so that it got completely wedged because of the pressure of the carbon dioxide inside the beverage. The way to open the bottle was to push the marble further down into the liquid. Sometimes it was necessary to use an umbrella or a walking-stick.

When I was twelve my parents decided to send me to a public school, and their choice was Bembridge, in the Isle of Wight. Bembridge was a recently founded public school, the creation of its Warden, J. Howard Whitehouse. Whitehouse came of a wealthy Lancashire family of industrialists whose background was Quaker. He was not himself a practising Quaker but advocated a vague, liberal, non-denominational Christianity. An enthusiastic disciple of Ruskin, whom he had once met, Whitehouse had entered Liberal politics in the early years of this century and had held a junior post in Lloyd George's administration. The school was intended to reflect the ideas of Ruskin, Morris and the Arts and Crafts movement of the time. My parents chose it for me, I suppose, mainly because of the injunctions of the oculist that I should not read too much and should be encouraged to do things with my hands; and also because, although there was compulsory cricket and football, sport – for which I was obviously unfitted – did not have quite the same fetish value as it had in traditional public schools. Bembridge was more liberal than most of these, and it did not include the barbarous institution of fagging. But in other respects it was fairly traditional; for instance, there was frequent corporal punishment which Whitehouse usually administered himself – and I believe he took some pleasure in doing so.

Although my parents' motives for choosing this school can be understood, it did not suit me at all, and I look back upon it with bitterness. One of the few friends I made there with whom I am still in touch, Judge Peter McNair (now retired), wrote to me a few years ago: "Isn't it strange that you, I and Robin Day all went to the worst school in England?" The academic teaching was of a low standard. Whitehouse, who did not believe in the educational value of the classics, allowed just enough Latin to be taught for us to scrape into

32

Oxford or Cambridge, though hardly any of the boys ever did this. No Greek at all was taught. I had already had a good though old-fashioned grounding in Latin, and added nothing to it during my years at Bembridge. I deeply regretted not being able to go on with Greek. I used to huddle away in the library with a copy of Dr Smith's Greek Grammar, desperately trying to teach myself, but this was not really practicable.

Since the classics were skimped there should have been good teaching of English literature, but there was not. English was taught by the form master in each class. Not one of these had a degree in English. Whitehouse's own strong liberal and pacifist politics were forced upon us without our being in any way encouraged to debate or question them. This set up a deep tension in my own personality, which I have never entirely resolved, between the liberal ideas of the school, which were associated with a regime and teachers I in many ways disliked, and the philosophy of my father's family whose values were not so much conservative as deeply rooted in an old Tory tradition of loyalty to Church and Throne.

Bembridge was divided into a junior and a senior school. The junior house, of which one was a member until the age of twelve or thirteen, was run by a staff of two, a Mr Hughes and a Miss Kingsnorth. Mr Hughes was the art master for the entire school, though he taught general subjects in the junior house. The memory I have of him is of a slightly perverted and somewhat sadistic man. As an art teacher he favoured a style which, I suppose, could be classified as art deco. We were encouraged to illustrate whimsical poems about the goings-on of fairies and elves, or to draw scenes involving wooden Noah's ark animals. Their rectangular structures offered an exercise in another of his passions, the teaching of perspective. For example, he would draw on the blackboard a picture of a square box, placed on a round table in front of a mirror, with one of its corners towards the mirror. If you know anything about perspective you will appreciate that that subject is extremely difficult to draw accurately. Another exercise was to draw a spiral staircase. The staircase in question led down from the portico of a palazzo in Venice, and a lady dressed in rococo costume was descending it in order to enter a gondola which was waiting for her. A spiral staircase is almost impossible to draw in correct perspective, but in any case we were never expected to do much but copy what Mr Hughes had drawn on the blackboard. Later on, when I was in the senior school, his place was taken by a much better art master, a Mr Basil Rock, who encouraged free expression and creativeness in his pupils.

Mr Hughes had a certain talent for acting. On Sunday evenings he would come into the dormitory and read to us from the works of

33

Clifford B. Poultney. These books consist of extremely amusing and witty monologues by a Clapham housewife, Mrs 'Arris. She has a well-off sister, Hemma, who is married to Mr Hearl, "a large butcher in Putney and very affluent". Mr Hearl frequently goes on excursions, for example to the country (a savage, alien area somewhere out of London), or else on business trips to Paris. At the annual staff concert, Mr Hughes used to dress up in drag to do his impersonation of Mrs 'Arris. He did not learn the text off by heart but pretended to be making pastry with a cookery book beside the basin. In other scenes of this revue he dressed more flamboyantly, in a long evening gown and ostrich-feather plumes, to join in the chorus. Mr Hughes's Sunday evening readings enthralled us, but listening to them did not give us a chance to prepare for the dreaded first lesson of Monday morning. This was a scripture lesson in which we had to repeat a psalm by heart to Mr Hughes, who sat grimly behind his desk with his Bible open in front of him. Boys with good eyesight could usually manage to read the psalm upside-down, but those who could not, if they stumbled, were told peremptorily to go away, write out the psalm six times and learn it by the evening. If they failed to do that they were beaten severely.

Miss Kingsnorth had a more kindly personality and was, I think, a good teacher of English literature, among other things. The junior school library had a reasonable collection of books, including a complete illustrated set of Scott's Waverley novels. Miss Kingsnorth would recount the plots of these novels to us in her classes, and in this way went through *The Talisman, Ivanhoe, Guy Mannering, The Antiquary* and *Rob Roy*. Her method of telling these stories was sufficiently accomplished actually to encourage me and some others to read these books. I also read one which she had not recounted to us. This was a lesser-known novel, *The Betrothed*, set in the Welsh marches during the time of the Crusades, but I was attracted to it because of the stories of our Welsh ancestry that my father had told me. The library also had annotated editions of *Hiawatha* and of Kingsley's *The Heroes*. Both of these texts opened up my mind to the possibilities of studying mythology and folklore in a comparative spirit, an interest that has remained with me.

Some masters in the senior school instructed us in subjects not covered by Mr Hughes and Miss Kingsnorth. One of these was a short, stocky, dark-haired Welshman, a Mr Rhys Lloyd, who, although he was the mathematics master, acted as science master for the junior school. This he did rather well. He had a distinguished brain and later entered Liberal politics. He was eventually raised to the House of Lords under the title of Lord Lloyd of Kilgareth. In the senior school he was one of the members of staff who treated me with some kindness and encouraged my writing. At one point he actually gave us an exercise in verse writing. He read us Byron's poem "The Destruction of Sennacherib", and then told us to read the passage in the Book of Judges which deals with Gideon's destruction of the Midianites, and to write a poem on that subject in the style and metre of Byron's poem. I enjoyed doing this, and knew perfectly well that I had done better than any of the others. Mr Lloyd knew that I knew that, and in order not to over-encourage me simply wrote on the script: "Not pure anapaests." I probably deserved this. I have never been very good at triple metres, though later on I heard it stated that Byron's poem is not in anapaests but in amphibrachs. Mr Rhys Lloyd had, however, one disadvantage for a teacher – an extraordinarily violent temper. If a boy annoyed him by ill-attention or fooling around he would turn bright scarlet, walk slowly up to the boy's desk and then cuff him over the ears with all his force. It could easily have caused serious injury, and nowadays would have got him into court.

The boys were a mixed bunch. There was no entrance exam and many of them would never have made it into a normal public school. A few of them, indeed, were little more than high-grade morons. These lived a terrible life, associating only with their own kind, and were the butt of the other boys and the masters. I believe that modern education theory maintains that children with mental handicaps should not be educated at special schools but alongside normal children, who, out of their natural tendency to goodness, would help and assist them. My own experience teaches me that this is profoundly not true. Human beings are, at bottom, primate mammals actuated by the selfish gene. They have a deep animal instinct to keep out of the genetic pool any members of the species who are inadequate, just as chickens will peck injured members of their species. Education can enable us to lift ourselves out of this, but it is an essential human condition. I witnessed the persecution of these unfortunate boys, and with my own bad eyesight and rather awkward manner was subject to a good deal of it myself. On the whole, life at school was one of perpetual war against the other boys and the members of the staff. If I meet anybody who tells me they were happy at an English boarding-school, I know I am talking to a sneak or a bully.

I have spoken of the Ruskinian ideals of the school and the emphasis on arts and crafts, which was one of the reasons for my being sent there. Unfortunately, my bad eyesight, combined with a rather poor muscular co-ordination, made me absolutely hopeless at the crafts part of this curriculum – which I disliked intensely – though I did succeed in the painting and drawing classes when I had a good teacher in Mr Basil Rock. We also had lessons in woodwork and printing from a Mr Muirhead. I had no aptitude for carpentry and was eventually given the task of picking up the wood that other boys had dropped. In printing, similarly, I was relegated to picking up the type that had fallen. In carpentry we made various fancy goods which were sold by the school to raise a fund for building a chapel, one of Whitehouse's ambitions which he eventually succeeded in accomplishing. In the printing classes we produced the school magazine, in which all the contributions were either written by Whitehouse or specifically commissioned by him from the older boys. Although the school theoretically believed in self-expression, it was from top to bottom a monolithic and dictatorial regime. We also set up various works of Whitehouse himself. Every year he would write a Nativity play for the boys to perform. This was printed and sold, of course, for the chapel fund. It would have been much more sensible if he had encouraged the boys themselves to create these Nativity plays, but nothing of the sort ever happened.

When finally erected, the chapel was a great barn of a place in which cold and uninspiring non-denominational religious services were conducted. It had one piece of decoration, a small panel of stained glass by a contemporary artist. The subject was apparently Elijah and the ravens. It showed the prophet dressed in a purple robe, and on a bough above him were perched two large yellow birds, about three times his size. It was perhaps more conducive to a contemplative frame of mind than the principal picture which hung in the main assembly hall of the school which was used for regular morning and evening prayers before the chapel was erected. This was a painting by Henry Scott Tuke (1858–1929). He worked in Falmouth and, according to Timothy Darch Smith in his book *Love in Earnest*, liked to paint boy models, whom he took from among the local fisherfolk, and is said to have suffered from blackmail threats from their parents. This picture showed three boys of about eighteen or so bathing from a rowing-boat in a harbour. Two of them are lying back in the boat, the other is standing and is about to plunge into the sea. He has unwrapped a towel from about his waist and is just about to discard it. This picture verged on high-grade pornography and I found its continual presence during religious services intensely distracting.

There was no chaplain at the school. Whitehouse, with his Nonconformist background, disliked the Established Church. His subwarden, Mr Dawes, who I think had been a colleague of his for a long time, was an idealist and an Anglican evangelical, and seemed a little lost in the venue in which he found himself. Whitehouse, who was a monster of egotism, delighted in preaching long sermons in a slow rhetorical manner suited to the bad acoustics of the House of Commons. We discovered a method of getting through these sermons while showing apparent attention. It is a game I recommend, for it has often come in useful to me in later life. This is how to play it. You wait until the speaker has pronounced a word beginning with "A", then you have to attend until he has pronounced a word beginning with "B", and so on through the alphabet. You might have quite a hold-up for letters such as "Q", and I think you can be excused if you do not discover an "X" or a "Z" towards the end of his peroration.

My literary talent was encouraged by Rhys Lloyd and others, particularly by my friend and contemporary, Peter McNair, who came from a cultivated background. His mother was a painter and had studied with Walter Sickert. She and Peter had the utmost contempt for the drawings and paintings which the boys produced under Mr Hughes's supervision and which were annually exhibited. Music was scarcely encouraged at all. In fact, I think Whitehouse had a real dislike of it. My mother, being a professional musician, insisted on my taking up the cello. I did not really want to play the cello at all, but she hardly gave me any choice in the matter. My brother George had to take up the violin, the idea being that we should all eventually play chamber music together. The cello is a particularly cruel instrument to wish on an adolescent boy – it is large and difficult to transport and makes one conspicuous. My original teacher from Bournemouth, a kindly man called Samuel Clifford (by origin a Dutch Jew), was a bad teacher and I made little progress. Under him I learnt a series of trivial salon pieces by such composers as Popper and Squire. At Bembridge I was allowed to practise the cello for an hour while cutting another subject, and I elected to cut the printing and woodwork classes which were doing me absolutely no good at all. In addition to arts and crafts, Mr Muirhead also taught us something called nature study. My own interest in natural history had developed and I had read widely on the subject. After a bit I elected to cut his classes too because I was too embarrassed in knowing far more about the subject than he did. He appreciated my contributions to his class and called me his "pet scientist".

It was probably quite difficult for Whitehouse to keep the school going during the depression period of the 1930s, but we suffered considerably. The premises were cold and uncomfortable, and the food inadequate. Pocket-money for tuck was not allowed. We had to hand in all our pocket-money at the beginning of term and could withdraw it only with special permission. Some of it was converted into a series of fourpenny coupons and we were allowed to spend one coupon a week on sweets or fruit. Most of the boys secretly hoarded pocket-money and bought, in the neighbouring village of Bembridge, stocks of food to consume in the dormitories. These were not luxuries, but simply items such as bread, cold meat and cheese. Eventually the school authorities got wise to this and were apparently under the mistaken impression that school stores had been pilfered. One Saturday afternoon, when all the boys were out of school, the authorities went round all the lockers and confiscated any food they found. This led to actual protests and riots, with boys refusing to speak during meals. Whitehouse was away at the time but was summoned back to deal with this dangerous situation. He employed all his skills of parliamentary rhetoric to cow us into submission. He told us, in an odd phrase, that we were like "little children in the depths of Russia", and having delivered his oration demanded that every boy who was prepared to apologise for his disgraceful conduct should rise to his feet. There was a slight pause and then somebody rose, and after that, of course, everybody rose. Each boy then had to write a personal letter of apology to Whitehouse. Two boys were, in fact, the organisers of the rebellion. They were both to some extent influenced by the political ideologies of the 1930s. One had communist sympathies and the other was a fascist. The latter, having a rather flamboyant personality, had kept a diary of the whole episode. Eventually the school authorities, by searching his private property, found this diary, and used it as evidence against him. Both boys were summarily expelled.

I can find little good to say about this school or its teaching, but it did have a reasonably well-stocked, though ill-planned, library in which I spent much time educating myself. The basis of the collection was evidently the family library of Whitehouse himself. It contained a complete set of the 1888 *Encyclopaedia Britannica*, standard reference books such as Brewer's *Dictionary of Phrase and Fable* and Lemprière's *Classical Dictionary* (a highly sensational work to put into the hands of the young). Since Whitehouse was, of course, an avid collector of the works of Ruskin, he would go to auctions where any early editions of Ruskin were on sale and acquired various other curious books at the same time.

The *Encyclopaedia Britannica*, I think, was the main source of my education. The 1888 edition contained lengthy scientific and literary papers in which the authors often put forth their latest and sometimes controversial theories. The papers on biology, which I read with avidity, were by such writers as Ray Lancaster and Thomas Huxley. I also read Andrew Lang's article on mythology, a very important essay in which he disposed of the then current theories of Max Müller, and pointed out the importance of studying not just the classical texts in Greek and Sanskrit, as Müller had done, but the beliefs of primitive peoples in all parts of the world. Müller believed that primitive people made metaphorical statements about physical phenomena, and that these were converted into myths. For instance, they might express the idea that the sun follows the dawn by saying: "The shining one pursues the burning one." The "shining one" is the literal translation of the Greek Phoebus, and the "burning one" of Daphne. The laurel bush is also called Daphne because it burns readily, therefore the myth of Apollo's pursuit of Daphne and her transformation into a laurel bush is created. There may be one or two instances in which this kind of thing has actually occurred, but this approach Lang, Frazer and others successfully discredited. A later edition of Müller's work on mythology, published at the end of the nineteenth century in a series of classics, included, as an appendix, an anonymous essay (I suspect that Lang may have had a hand in it) entitled "The Oxford Solar Myth". It pointed out that Müller was said to have come from the east (from Germany). The sun, which rises in the east, may be called a miller because it grinds up the clouds, and reaches its highest eminence at a place in the centre of England called Oxford – and so on and so forth. It follows, therefore, that Max Müller had no real historical existence.

As well as these reference books, I, of course, read poetry and fiction. We were taught a good deal of poetry at school, but in an unsystematic way, most of what we were taught being that of the so-called Georgians and their contemporaries. The Georgian School started in 1910 with the accession of George V. The trial of Oscar Wilde, fifteen years earlier, had brought poetry into disrepute among many readers, and most of Wilde's contemporaries, such as Johnson and Dowson, led dissipated lives and came to early deaths. The Edwardian age (1901–10) is, on the whole, a bleak period for English verse. Kipling was almost the only poet widely read. In 1910 Edward Marsh and Rupert Brooke came to the conclusion that much good poetry was being written but not getting published. They therefore sponsored a series of annual anthologies of "Georgian Poetry", which continued, latterly under Sir John Squire's editorship, well into the 1930s. Typically, the Georgian poets avoided the affectations of diction which later Victorian poetry, including that of the 1890s, had developed, and sought a return to a sort of Wordsworthian plainness.

The Georgians wrote largely about the English countryside. This was the age of the weekend cottage, when the invention of first the bicycle and then the motor car made access to the countryside easy. "Georgian" latterly became a byword for escapism, and many reputations made at this time were swept away by the triumph of the modernist school, initiated by T. S. Eliot and Ezra Pound, and continued by W. H. Auden and other poets of the 1930s. These last were the poets most characteristic of the period when I was at Bembridge.

I had never heard of any of them. In fact, I read parodies of Eliot in *Punch* before I had ever heard of Eliot, for example:

> The lifted face of Mrs Lumpleigh-Smith
> grins at the threshold of the unknown;
> she has a few short hours to dally with
> ere putrefaction claims her for its own.

While I was still in the junior house at Bembridge, I had begun to write verse myself in, naturally, more or less a Georgian style. I think my first poem was written quite spontaneously at the age of about twelve. It was not the kind of humorous jingle which all boys indulge in, but a perfectly serious descriptive poem called "Winter", in regular rhyme and metre. I was encouraged in this by Peter McNair and some of the teachers. I discovered that I possessed a magical power which the rest of the boys, whom I mostly regarded as my enemies, did not, and from that time forth I have never really looked back. Some of my early poems – a hymn to the Moon Goddess; a poem on London; and one to the night (by this time I had discovered Keats) – appeared in the school magazine, and the one about London was reprinted in an anthology of schoolboys' verse, published by Blackwell, along with early work by Alex Comfort, Maurice James Craig, Nicholas Moore and others. After I had left Bembridge, the school published these poems in a little pamphlet, which inevitably they sold in aid of the chapel fund. I was not even sent a copy, and the school was, of course, in breach of copyright, since they had not obtained either my permission or that of my parents. It was not until many years later, in the seventies, that a master at the school, Roger Sawyer, who made my acquaintance and became a good friend, gave me a copy of this pamphlet, which contains one bad misprint.

Our teachers taught us nothing about what was really living in contemporary poetry, and the same was true of fiction. The only serious modern writers I learnt about, largely through finding them in the library, were Shaw, Wells, Galsworthy, Bennett and Chesterton. Wells's books influenced me greatly, above all his science fiction from *The Time Machine* onwards. I read *The Outline of History* and *The Science of Life* (the latter work appearing in fortnightly parts at this time). Wells completely indoctrinated me with his liberal neo-Darwinism, and this was reinforced by the writings of Thomas Huxley and Ray Lancaster whom I had read in the *Encyclopaedia Britannica*. I also read Shaw's *Back to Methuselah*, with its so-called neo-Lamarckian philosophy.

I did not make progress in the realistic novel. Galsworthy I found tedious, and still do, and I was not ready for Bennett, who wrote about worlds – that of the industrial Midland urban bourgeoisie, and of rich people in London – which were quite foreign to my own background. I had developed a taste for detective novels which led me to Chesterton's "Father Brown" stories, and then to his other fictional fantasies, *The Man who was Thursday* and *The Ball and the Cross*. Here I found a world with values quite different from those of Wells and Shaw which were eventually to deliver me from total slavery to Darwinian ideas. I also enjoyed Chesterton's poetry, though it is what George Orwell calls "good bad verse".

Apart from Robin Day, the broadcaster, there were, at different times, various alumni of Bembridge who were to become well known, though none of them was my actual contemporary. One of these, as I learnt from reading his memoirs, was Mervyn Stockwood, who became Bishop of Woolwich, but he was only there for one term. Francis King, the writer on magical subjects, was also at this school. But the star old boy was Dingle Foot, who had been there before I came, and who entered Parliament with a promising political career before him, ending up as Solicitor-General in Harold Wilson's government. Isaac Foot, the father of Dingle Foot, Hugh Foot and Michael Foot, was a friend of Whitehouse and would sometimes appear at school speech days. It will be noted, however, that he did not send his two younger sons to the school. Whitehouse and he shared the tradition of Nonconformist radicalism (the Foots were Methodists), though it was much more hard and passionate in Isaac Foot's case.

Dingle Foot occasionally visited the school, but I was not to meet him personally until many years later. This was in Chalfont St Giles in 1974 during celebrations of the bicentenary of Milton's death. I was asked to take part in a public symposium on Milton, along with Dingle Foot, Joan Bakewell and a fourth participant, whose name, I fear, escapes me. Miss Bakewell did not seem a Milton scholar but was charming and intelligent. Dingle Foot was drunk. I mentioned to him that we had been in the same school, to which he replied that as long as a school had compulsory Latin and corporal punishment it was all right. In the course of the symposium it became obvious that he had not done his homework. As a historian, he regarded himself, following in his father's tradition, as an expert on the Commonwealth period. But this did not prevent him from confusing Satan and Beelzebub throughout, and in a defence of Oliver Cromwell's regime against the charge of its being hostile to culture he said that women first appeared on the stage under the Commonwealth. I pointed out that this was obviously absurd as the theatres were closed. In fact, a French company, including actresses, had appeared on the stage in the reign of Charles I, but had been hissed off. Actresses began regularly to appear on the stage some time after the Restoration. Dingle Foot replied, bluntly, that I was wrong and he knew what he was talking about. Foot must, in fact, have been giving a confused interpretation of the role played in the history of the theatre by William Davenant. Under the Commonwealth, Davenant, who changed sides rather notoriously during the civil war, attempted to circumvent the ban on the theatres by introducing to England the opera, which had already developed in Italy and then in France. His opera, *The Siege of Rhodes*, which is lost, was performed during the Commonwealth period, and did include women singers, but not actresses.

Although I have, on the whole, unhappy memories of Bembridge School, I retain a good deal of affection for the Isle of Wight itself. It retains some of the Victorian character it acquired when it was made fashionable by Queen Victoria's residence at Osborne House, and the Cowes Regatta. The Isle of Wight has its own dialect, quite distinct from that of Hampshire, for it was settled not by the West Saxons but by the Jutes. We are told that the founders of this settlement were two chieftains called Stuf and Witgar. Stuf may possibly be the earliest form of the name Stubbs.

Bembridge School was built on the sea coast and had its own semi-private beach from which the boys bathed in the nude. As tourism became more frequent on the island, the police put a stop to this. To the west of this beach was a high chalk cliff called Culver Cliff. Culver means dove, and it must once have been the haunt of the wild rock dove, though there was none there in my time. At the cliff's foot was a tidal reef on which I used to spend hours studying the sea-shore life. I remember on one occasion, at the season of the neap tides, going further west to a little indentation in the cliff where there was a space which was always just above high-water mark. In this was a colony of most curious creatures which I was not, then, able to identify. They had long legs and pincers and measured about an inch. One of them had something red on its back which was, in fact, a parasitic blood-sucking mite. These creatures must have lived on scraps of organic material, which they found above the tidemark, or on very small organisms, like mites and sandhoppers, which fed on the seaweed. They began to advance towards me slowly. I can only suppose that they smelt the sweat from my body, and thought that there might be a source of food there. They had very good eyesight. Whenever I moved, they rapidly jumped back. I suddenly became slightly afraid of them. They seemed somewhat sinister, though they were, in fact, perfectly harmless. It was not until many years later that my researches told me what they were. They were False

42

Scorpions. These creatures resemble scorpions, though they belong to a different order of arachnids, which includes one species which is commonly found at the base of high cliffs. I had already met another member of the group, the little Book Scorpion, under mossy stones. It is also found among old books, where I suppose it feeds on book lice, and has the odd habit of hitching lifts by hanging on to the legs of flies.

Culver Cliff was a breeding ground for a vast number of gulls and other sea birds. In the rock pools one could find various kinds of fish as well as sea anemones, the little beadlet (which is common), but also the large and much more spectacular oplet. There were also, of course, shrimps and crabs, and numerous kinds of seaweed and molluscs. Another terrain for my studies in natural history was Brading Marshes, a mile or so from Bembridge. This was a breeding ground for wild swans, ducks and wading birds such as water-rails, coots, moorhens, redshank and lapwings. They are, at present, under threat from drainage.

For summer excursions we used to go to Ventnor, some miles away, and walk back across the chalk downs to Bembridge. Here was the site of a well, known as St Boniface's Well, which had long been closed up. In fact, its sacred waters are used as the water supply of Ventnor. I hope that it does the inhabitants some good. In a guide-book I read that if you climbed to St Boniface's Well without looking back or pausing – and quite a steep climb it was – any wish or prayer you made would be granted. I introduced this custom among my companions, and every year we would climb to the site of the well, which was marked by a concrete slab.

4

Worcester College for the Blind

My parents wished me to be confirmed, but Whitehouse put every
obstacle in the way of this. He seemed to see no point in the Church
of England sacraments. None of the other boys, with the exception of
two or three who were sons of clergymen, was confirmed. Whitehouse
dragged his feet so much over this that I was not confirmed until the
age of fifteen. On Saturday afternoons I had to walk to Bembridge
village, three or so miles away, where I was prepared by the kindly,
but elderly, rector of the parish whose instruction was not of a very
high order. When the day came for the actual ceremony I was taken
on a bus by one of the matrons to the other side of the island, where
I was confirmed by the suffragan Bishop of Portsmouth in a local
village church, and then brought back again. No indication whatever
was made that this was a day of any particular significance for me
or for anyone else. At the same time my religious faith was under
strong pressure from my reading in biology and in the works of H. G.
Wells. But the book that was perhaps most crucial was *The Story of
an African Farm* by the South African writer Olive Schreiner, which
Peter McNair had lent me. In particular, the fable of the man who
seeks for the great white bird of truth and finally dies on the mountain
with one feather of its wings clutched in his hand made a powerful effect on me, as did Olive Schreiner's general indictment of the
cruelty and injustice of the world. I was beginning to become aware
of this cruelty. Like everybody else, I was conscious of the constant
threat of war and the rise of Nazism in Germany. There was also the
economic depression of the north of England, Mussolini's invasion
of Abyssinia, the Spanish Civil War and the show trials in Soviet
Russia.

  Though I do not think these external events impinged on me
strongly, on a personal level I was seeing my father becoming more
and more incapacitated by the continuing onslaught of multiple
sclerosis, a disease which attacks with more and more frequency,
then gives a remission, followed by a severer stroke. This disease was
not well understood at the time, and there has not been much progress
since. All sorts of strange treatments were tried, for example my father
had to drink, in alternate months, a bottle of colloidal gold and a

bottle of colloidal arsenic – a remedy which sounds reminiscent of mediaeval alchemy. At the same time the economic depression of the 1930s had struck at my own family's security. My father had had sufficient private means to live comfortably, but modestly, with his family in New Milton, and pay for the education of myself and my brother. My brother was sent to the King's School, Bruton, and later on took a choral scholarship to Lancing College. (His voice broke almost immediately afterwards.) But after 1932 my mother was forced to become the breadwinner.

She took up, once more, her musical career, no longer as a concert pianist, though she did give recitals from time to time in Bournemouth and New Milton, and also gave chamber music concerts, especially with the violinist Albert Salmons. But the main force of her enterprise was to found a Tobias Matthay School with branches in Bournemouth and New Milton. The fact that she had been a pupil of Matthay gave her the right to found such a school, with Matthay's own particular method of teaching the piano as the core of the curriculum. Matthay's method was based on the relaxation of the hand and forearm on the keyboard, rather than the percussive action of the fingers. This was, I think, particularly effective in the interpretation of Chopin and Schumann – but less so for Bach, and certainly for Liszt, with his virtuoso approach to the piano. The rival to the Matthay method was that of Leschetizky who had been a pupil of Liszt. Sometimes I wonder whether these two rival approaches to the keyboard have roots going back to the difference between the playing of the clavichord and that of the harpsichord, respectively. As well as teaching the piano, my mother's school employed teachers for violin, cello and singing, and a lady who offered to teach Dalcroze eurhythmics (though there were never enough people willing to form a class). My mother worked extremely hard, more than twelve hours a day, both as a teacher and in the organisation of the school, in spite of continual tiredness and pain brought on by arthritis. She gave up the school when she married Dr Begg at the end of the Second World War, but continued to do private teaching up to her death in 1972.

My lessons with Samuel Clifford continued, though I made very little progress with the cello, as my heart was not really in it. I might have enjoyed playing the classical guitar, but this was not an instrument taken very seriously in those days, and there was probably no teacher anywhere within range. Later on I was taught by Miss Hanson, a much more accomplished teacher who introduced me to compositions by Bach, for example, and the Italian baroque violinist composers of the eighteenth century. I took the Associated Board examinations up to the advanced standard, which included playing unaccompanied Bach. At the Bournemouth Festival I was awarded a bronze medal for playing the cello sonata by John Eccles, the late seventeenth-century English composer (the silver medal was withheld). It had never really been my choice to learn music, but my mother had such a strong personality that it was difficult to resist her. Finally I took the decision to make a clean break when I went up to Oxford in 1939 and have never really wished to go back to it. Nevertheless I am now grateful for this early musical training. It has helped my appreciation in listening to music, and I also learnt from her teaching methods and, when I came to write verse, the importance of structure. I found the study of harmony and the rudiments of composition more interesting. My harmony teacher was a local church organist called Mr Russe, an elderly man, kindly but rather uninspiring. The lessons mostly seemed to consist of filling in the inner parts of hymn tunes and Anglican chants. Once Mr Russe asked me: "What do you think of Johann Sebastian Bach?" I said something vague about my appreciation of his music, but this was not enough for my teacher. His old eyes shone as he said: "I think he was the greatest man who ever lived."

I had begun reading the great rationalist classics of the past. These were available in the 1930s in an excellent series of cheaply produced books called "The Thinker's Library", published by Watts and Co. at 1s. 3d. a volume, and sold at station bookstalls. The series was sponsored by the Rationalist Press, a branch of the Secular Society. From these little books I went on to Gibbon's *Decline and Fall of the Roman Empire* and Frazer's *The Golden Bough*. I had read all through the three-volume edition by the time I was sixteen. The Thinker's Library reprinted the poet James Thomson (BV). His *City of Dreadful Night* is one of the most remarkable poems of the Victorian age. It is a statement of utter despair. Thomson was a melancholic and an alcoholic, and his poem curiously anticipates T. S. Eliot's *The Waste Land*, a fact which has been noticed by several critics. Many years later when I met Eliot, I asked what he thought of Thomson's poem. His reply was a characteristically ambiguous one. He said that it had been his favourite poem at the age of sixteen. But I am not quite sure whether this meant it had influenced him profoundly or, alternatively, that he regarded it as an adolescent taste.

In New Milton my mother also founded amateur chamber music groups and an orchestra. The orchestra was conducted by a Miss Ciceley Card, and apart from myself there was only one other cellist, a Mr Lubbock (a member of the distinguished Liberal intellectual family). When he found that his son Mark (who was to become the conductor of the BBC Light Orchestra) possessed musical talent, Mr Lubbock sent him to Germany to study the violin and, in order that Mark should not waste his time or fall into bad habits while living away from home, went with him, studying the cello himself. I really have some sympathy with Mark Lubbock.

There was also plenty of musical entertainment to be had at Bournemouth, which was twelve miles away and was our nearest large town and our main shopping centre. Bournemouth boasted three theatres: the Bournemouth Pavilion (supported by the town council), to which theatrical, operatic and ballet companies from London used regularly to come, and where the municipal orchestra performed under the conductorship of Sir Dan Godfrey; the Theatre Royal (an old-fashioned repertory theatre); and the Little Theatre, which was semi-amateur and put on what were, by the standards of the time, more advanced and intellectual plays. My first visit to the Bournemouth Pavilion was at the age of about seven or eight, to hear Elgar conduct his cello concerto, the soloist being Beatrice Harrison. I was much too young to appreciate the music, but I am glad to have seen Elgar, an impressive old man with white hair. Later on, in the thirties, I was to hear a solo recital by Kreisler, and one by Horowitz. The latter took place in 1936, just after the death of King George V. The concert interval was prolonged in order that King Edward VIII's accession speech, broadcast by the BBC, could be relayed to the audience in the concert hall. Consequently the second part of his recital was delayed, to the evident annoyance of Horowitz. This was probably exacerbated by the understandable hatred of many Russian Jews, who had suffered under the Tsars, for European royalty. At any rate, before resuming his recital, the pianist spat at the audience.

I also saw Pavlova dance at the Pavilion, when I was about twelve. She was becoming elderly at this time, and perhaps past her prime. I was in no position to judge the quality of her dancing. In fact, I found ballet dancing slightly shocking, with its short tutus and erotic imagery. My parents, however, commented adversely on her famous dance of "The Dying Swan", to Saint-Saëns's music. They said it was like a swan dying in a fit. Later, on the day that Pavlova died, her company played Saint-Saëns's music before an empty stage. So great was the power of association that some people thought that they saw her white ghost upon the boards. The Pavilion also received annual visits from the newly formed Sadler's Wells Opera, and one was also able to witness there the beginnings of English ballet under Anton Dolin and Alicia Markova. I particularly remember Dolin's dancing the role of Satan in Vaughan Williams's *Job*, which the composer described as a "masque for dancing". The sets were based on Blake's illustrations for the Book of Job. Particularly impressive was the moment when Satan was cast down from heaven. Dolin did a tremendous roll down a long flight of steps, which must have been rather painful and, I should think, dangerous.

47

The first opera that I saw was *Lohengrin*, which I enjoyed, and this was followed by *Madame Butterfly*, which I disliked, and still do – intensely. Puccini seems to me to have no tunes (well, not anything you could play on a barrel organ!). Furthermore, I disliked the cruelty of the story and its obviously phoney pictures of Japanese life. But the Sadler's Wells production of Mussorgsky's *Boris Godunov*, based on Mussorgsky's manuscript version, not on Rimsky-Korsakov's arrangement, was tremendously impressive. For me, *Boris Godunov* is one of the greatest of all operas. You cannot say one of the greatest half-dozen, because half a dozen of the greatest operas were written by Mozart, and another half-dozen by Wagner. *Boris* tells you everything you need to know about Russia.

Another company which made annual visits was the D'Oyly Carte with their Gilbert and Sullivan operettas. I remember seeing *The Mikado* and *Patience*, as well as amateur school productions of *The Gondoliers* and *Iolanthe*. It was really the Gilbert and Sullivan operas that were for me the way into classical music. At Bembridge I had a friend called William Taylor Allen. He had a talent for science and mathematics and was destined by his parents for the profession of civil engineer. Although he had no musical training and could not play any instrument, nevertheless he taught himself the principles of harmony and composition from popular reference books such as the *Children's Encyclopaedia*. Every Christmas his family had a big gathering when they would put on amateur productions of Gilbert and Sullivan and other musical plays. Somehow or other Allen and I got the idea of providing our own operettas for these occasions. We embarked on a series of works in the style of Gilbert and Sullivan, for which Allen wrote the music and I the libretti. None of them ever got a stage production, but I think one of them, *The Nymphs of Normandy*, did achieve production in the family puppet theatre. *The Nymphs of Normandy* combined my interest in Gilbert's work with that of the early history of zoology. I had read that during the time of the French Revolution Lamarck had been a tutor to an aristocratic family in Normandy. The plot of this opera, which partly derived from *Iolanthe*, hinged on the love of a dryad for the son and heir of the family, and I think she eventually rescued them from the Jacobins. At the same time, Lamarck and Cuvier were introduced as having opposed views on the subject of evolution. Allen and I also began, but I think did not complete, a more ambitious serious opera of the Wagnerian character, whose subject was the rape of Proserpine.

I spent one of my summer holidays as the guest of Allen and his parents in their house at Acton. The high spot of this stay was to be a visit to Sadler's Wells to see *The Magic Flute*. I had by this time read Dent's *Life of Mozart*, and was fascinated by the Masonic symbolism of

The Magic Flute. The libretto used to be dismissed as trash, but I agree with Ernest Newman who said that it was arguably the best opera libretto ever written. It does not make much dramatic sense, but it provides Mozart with a series of powerful, archetypal situations. We spent days studying the score of *The Magic Flute* and learning the principal tunes, but when we went to Sadler's Wells we were met at the door with an announcement that the soprano singing the role of the Queen of the Night was ill and so they were putting on *Madame Butterfly* instead.

The 1930s was a period of a great upsurge of enthusiasm in England for Mozart's music, which was largely stimulated by the foundation of the opera house at Glyndebourne. However, the price one had to pay for a visit to Glyndebourne put it quite outside the range of either my family or my friends. A Mr Watson, a retired colonial civil servant, lived in New Milton and played the viola in the orchestra. He had been bitten by the Mozart bug and gave several enthusiastic lectures on that composer's music. Today, a year or two after the celebrations which marked the bicentenary of Mozart's death, we tend to forget that for a long time the supremacy of Beethoven was taken for granted almost everywhere, and that, although Mozart was always admired by musicians and composers – Tchaikovsky, for instance – audiences at large often regarded him as rather old-fashioned.

I did eventually get to see *The Magic Flute*, when the Sadler's Wells Company brought it to Bournemouth. But for me the real revelation of Mozart came when at the age of about nineteen I listened to the famous production of *Don Giovanni* broadcast from Glyndebourne. It opened up for me a whole world of eroticism. At the same age, I heard for the first time, in a broadcast, Bach's Mass in B minor. This also had a profound effect on me, though of a different kind. It seemed to me to be impossible that such great music could merely be prompted by an illusion – if God were an illusion.

I left Bembridge when I was fifteen. The teaching I was getting there was not good enough, and my development was being retarded. In terms of class removes, I was always one year behind the others. This was principally due to my weakness in mathematics. This was, I honestly believe, the result of bad teaching in my early years, for mathematicians have told me that I have not got such a bad mathematical brain. At school I was far more interested in, and better at, a more abstract kind of mathematics, such as geometry and algebra, than in the routine business of doing sums. My parents asked the school if I could have extra tuition in this subject, but none was forthcoming. I was therefore removed, and finished my education with private tutors.

Some years later, His Majesty's Inspectors gave such a bad report of the school that it was struck off the Public School Register. There were also allegations of sexual abuse of the boys by Whitehouse. During the fifties, when I was in Leeds, I met Leonard Clark, a minor poet and an inspector of schools. When I asked him about Bembridge, he said: "Oh yes, I could tell you all sorts of tales – but, of course, I must not." A year or two after I left the school, Whitehouse was injured by a cricket ball that struck him in the eye. This accident affected his brain. He was retired from the post of Warden but remained resident at the school, and used to wander round it, vaguely thinking he was still in charge. Bembridge later regained its status as a public school, and I hope that it is better run and provides better teaching than in my day.

Before leaving school in those days, one took the School Certificate Examination, and possibly proceeded to the Higher Certificate, or alternatively the London Matriculation Examination. I prepared for the latter. My tutors were two ladies, Miss Ludwig, and her friend, Miss Edwards. At this time they were living at Christchurch, though formerly they had kept a small school in New Milton. They gave me excellent teaching. A graduate of Edinburgh University, Miss Ludwig was a sister of the first wife of Herbert Read. She fired me with an enthusiasm for the poetry of Wordsworth, among others, and introduced me to the novels of Thomas Hardy and Jane Austen. Hardy, of course, as a Dorset novelist, was something of a local divinity, though I have never much cared for his novels or his poems. I have some sympathy with Chesterton's description of him as the "village atheist brooding over the village idiot". It is not that he was an atheist that I find offensive, but that he was a "village" atheist. He really seems to have thought that nobody else had had the kind of doubts that bedevilled him. Jane Austen was, of course, a Hampshire writer and it is surprising how close her world, of the late eighteenth and early nineteenth centuries, still was to our world of the 1920s and 1930s. If there is a Hampshire literary tradition, middle-class Hampshire is represented by Jane Austen, and working-class Hampshire by William Cobbett. It has always struck me that Jane Austen is the earliest English writer for whom one does not have to make adjustments and say: "Well, this is not something that could actually have happened, or have been said, but is convention." One has to do this even in Shakespeare and Fielding, but there is nothing that happens in Jane Austen's novels that one cannot suppose to have been possible.

Miss Ludwig also brought me on in Latin. I had always enjoyed Latin, seeing its logical structure and the way it behaved, but now, at last, I began to touch the fringes of Latin literature. I prepared with Miss Ludwig, for my London Matriculation Examination, the sixth book of Virgil's *Aeneid*, perhaps the profoundest of all the books of that poem, from which paths lead on to Dante. At last, I had found in Latin not just a linguistic exercise but great poetry. I also read, with enormous enjoyment for their dramatic power, the Catilinian orations of Cicero. Miss Ludwig died some years ago, and I am sorry never to have had the opportunity of meeting her again and thanking her for what she did for me. She became very deaf in her old age and suffered from other bodily weaknesses. A nephew of hers told me that on his last visit to her he had asked her: "Is there anything you would like?" "Yes," she replied, "a new body."

I passed my London Matriculation Examination at fifteen, and the obvious next step was to prepare for a university. What I really wanted to study was biology, and my father opined that I had better do this at a modern university, such as London. My father's family had not had a tradition of university education and he was a little suspicious of Oxford and Cambridge, fearing that one might get into bad company there. At this period also the Oxford University Union passed its notorious motion "That this House is not prepared to fight for King and Country". This may actually have been an aid and comfort to Hitler, persuading him that if he were to attack Britain he would meet with no strong resistance. My father, and some of his friends, also disapproved of Oxford's having admitted women, and for that reason rather tended to favour Cambridge. There were, of course, women studying at Cambridge, but they were not full members of the university. In order to read for a science degree at London University, one had to have achieved a good pass in mathematics, and I had only passed the mathematics paper with difficulty. My future, therefore, seemed problematical.

I continued my studies with another private tutor, a Miss Hunkin, who also lived at Bournemouth. Miss Ludwig and Miss Edwards had moved from the neighbourhood. Miss Hunkin did not like Wordsworth, but nevertheless widened my horizons in poetry. She had, during the 1920s, frequented Harold Monro's Poetry Bookshop in Bloomsbury, which had been a meeting place for both the Georgians and modernists, and where the practice of poets reading their work to an audience really began. We know that both Pope and Tennyson were remarkable interpreters of their own work, but they seem only to have read to private gatherings of friends. It was generally assumed at the beginning of this century that poetry could only be interpreted by actors, and the bad tradition of over-rhetorical reading thus grew up. Miss Hunkin was knowledgeable in modern poetry, and urged me to buy Monro's own anthology, *The Century's Poetry*. This is a remarkable work, published not long before Monro's death in 1932. He had a foot in both the Georgian and modernist camps, and his anthology contains some of the best work of both these schools. There are early examples of Eliot, Pound, the Sitwells, Roy Campbell, and the Imagist poets, F. S. Flint and HD, as well as one poem each by Stephen Spender and Cecil Day Lewis. Unfortunately the book did not include any work by Auden. Miss Hunkin also introduced me to the poetry of John Donne (who was, of course, a kind of totem for the modernists) with a warning not to leave the book lying about where some elderly relative might find it. I was not quite as enthusiastic about Donne as she expected me to be, and he still leaves me a little cold. Miss Hunkin possessed a copy of Eliot's *The Waste Land*, but would not lend it to me because it was a first edition. She had known Munro personally. He had died in an alcoholics' home, and she explained to me that this was, in fact, the subject of what is perhaps his best poem, "Bitter Sanctuary".

When I was eighteen I went for my annual check-up at the oculist's. The oculist was a Mr Basil Graves of Bournemouth. It was suddenly discovered that my eyesight was deteriorating rapidly. My right eye could just distinguish light from dark, while the range of vision in my left eye was much restricted. I was therefore told that my eyes must be operated upon immediately, and that I ought to be sent to a special school for the blind. My operation took place at a private nursing home in Bournemouth, named, rather smugly, "The Home of Good Hope". It coincided with the abdication crisis, accounts of which I listened to on the radio. I had different reports, morning and evening, from the nurses, since the day nurse and the night nurse had diametrically opposed views on King Edward.

Another topic of conversation in this nursing home, which Graves had sent me to because it specialised in eye cases, concerned the two leeches belonging to the establishment. The nurses took an affectionate interest in these creatures, which were called Cuthbert and Alfonsine, though leeches are, in fact, hermaphrodite. I believe that leeches are still used in eye operations. They are very efficient in removing a pocket of blood which may collect behind an eye after an operation, and are provided with a natural anti-coagulant. It was some years later that I heard on the radio that leech farming is still a possible enterprise, though one has to beware of ducks and other birds eating one's stock. About once a month, the leeches are fed with newly drawn blood from a horse, which is lowered into their pond in a skin. My aunt Mary, some years before my operation, had had a leech applied to her, I forget for what purpose. It remained with her after it had done its work, and, being a humane lady, she was not quite sure what to do with it. Eventually she released it in the Round Pond in Kensington Gardens, where I am afraid it would probably immediately have been eaten by a duck or a swan. The reader will recall Wordsworth's "Resolution and Independence", one of the greatest of his poems, and one which speaks most sharply to our twentieth-century consciousness. In that poem, the leech gatherer says of his quarry: "Once I could meet with them on every hand / But they have dwindled long by slow decay." I have often wondered whether this is not an indication that the pools of Cumberland and Westmorland were already being polluted by smoke from the mills of Lancashire. But it has to be said that in Dorothy Wordsworth's account of the same encounter the leech gatherer attributes the scarcity of his quarry to over-exploitation.

The operation saved the sight of my left eye, and I had no difficulty in using it for reading until 1961. My right eye was more or less useless, and had to be removed in 1956. Glaucoma usually attacks people in their later years, and it was quite unusual to perform the operation, which consists of making a hole in the eye to relieve pressure from the fluid within, on a person as young as I then was. I believe that Graves published a paper on this particular operation in a medical journal.

However, the operation meant that at the age of eighteen, when I should have hoped to go to university, I was sent to Worcester College for the Blind, which was situated in the village of Whittington, just outside the City of Worcester. It was assumed that I should need to learn Braille in order to get through a university course. I did learn Braille, but I never, in fact, found it necessary to use it. My sight for reading print remained quite unimpaired for a long time afterwards. So it came about that in 1937, when I might have expected to enter upon the freedom and responsibilities of young manhood, I found myself trapped again in a school. Worcester College for the Blind was founded as a public school for – to use the phraseology of its prospectus, which had a curiously Victorian ring – "the blind sons of gentlemen". In fact, however, many of the boys there came from working-class backgrounds, and were supported by grants of various kinds. The atmosphere was a strange one. Most of the boys had been deeply traumatised, some of them from being blind or partially blind from birth or a very early age, others from having become so from an accident in later years. Only about half of them were totally blind. Many had eyesight much the same as mine or a little less efficient, and were able to read print. On the whole there was a more friendly atmosphere than I had found at previous schools. The boys helped each other in their infirmity, and those with better sight would guide the others on walks in the country or into the city, and would read to them. I remember reading books to boys less fortunate than myself. These were books I obtained from Salmon and Gluckstein's, a firm of chemists who had branches in most provincial towns and ran a lending library at the back of the shop, presumably in imitation of their rival, Boots. One could borrow a book for tuppence a time. I soon discovered that the section labelled, quaintly, "Books for the sophisticated", contained almost the only works worth reading. I borrowed from this section Robert Graves's two Claudius volumes, and a work by an author I was later to meet, and who was to have a decisive influence on me. This was Charles Williams's *Descent into Hell*, which I hardly understood at my first reading of it.

As I have said, many of the boys at Worcester College came from working-class backgrounds, and I think I can say without sentimental romanticism that I found a warmer comradeship than I had found with the middle-class boys with whom I had previously mixed at my earlier schools. I particularly remember the friendship of one boy from a mining village near Durham, and of another from industrial South Wales. But not everything was sweetness and light. The traumatisation of most of the boys manifested itself in two ways, often simultaneously in the same individual. There was a deep cynicism and at the same time a vulnerability, which easily led to their being entangled in the more emotional religions. A year or so back one of the masters at the school had been a member of the Plymouth Brethren, and he had influenced many of the boys into embracing his own strongly fundamentalist views. The school itself, and its headmaster, Mr Brown, were Anglican. I was told of an incident when the Plymouth Brother master had arranged for a number of the boys to be taken by bus to some evangelical meeting. Mr Brown, learning of this, had appeared just before the bus was about to start and ordered all Anglican boys out of it immediately.

The headmaster read morning and evening prayers every weekday, as had been the custom at my earlier schools, but on Sundays we were expected to go to church and to make our own ways there, possibly walking in couples. The choice of church was left open to the boys themselves. Some came from Nonconformist backgrounds, and there were two or three Roman Catholics. Others went to St Swithun's, an extreme Anglo-Catholic church whose rector was a well-known Anglo-Catholic clergyman, Father W. B. Monahan. Such boys absorbed Father Monahan's views, and this formed a kind of counterpoint to the fundamentalism which was found among some of the other boys. I myself had by this time adopted an extremely negative and sceptical point of view, and tended to resist the opinions of either party. On Sundays I usually made my way to the cathedral. It is a magnificent building on its site by the Severn, and the music was splendid. The then organist was Sir Ivor Atkins, a not unworthy successor to Elgar. One of the canons, a charming old man whom I met, was Canon Hutchinson, an authority on George Herbert.

Mr Brown, the headmaster when I arrived, was an elderly man

who was shortly to retire. I think his grip was slipping a bit as there were curious disciplinary anomalies in the school. All those over six-teen were permitted, even encouraged, to smoke. Medical authorities at this time regarded tobacco as a useful sedative for the tensions which often afflict those with defective sight. There was also a good deal of drinking, and if any of us went to the local pub the habitués were only too glad to stand us pints of beer. Also there were events, including rowing and chess, in which we challenged other schools. Some of the boys were formidable exponents of chess and, for fun, could play the game without using a board or men, having such a strong power of visualisation. I never joined the rowing crew but usually managed to accompany them. A prodigious amount of beer was consumed on these occasions as well.

This was more or less my first experience of alcohol. Although my family was not in principle against it, little was consumed in our household. My father would have liked to have wine with his dinner, but in the 1930s the duty on it was heavy and he could not afford it, except when he had a guest or at Christmas. Beer, I think, he had no taste for, and he told me once that he had never entered a public house in his life. This should not surprise one as much as it might nowadays. On the whole, public houses were the preserve of the working classes. The middle classes consumed wine or spirits in their own homes. It was for this reason that public houses had so-called snugs, or private bars, where middle-class people could, if they wished, drink unobserved by the rest of the customers. This began to change at the beginning of the century when a romantic cult of the English public house was created, first by Chesterton and Belloc, and later on, in the 1920s, by writers like A. P. Herbert and Sir John Squire. My first encounter with alcohol, in the form of copious pints of beer, had a liberating effect on me. My experience at previous schools, which, as I have indicated, was on the whole unhappy and unfriendly, had made it difficult for me to relate to other people. I found that beer helped me to do so, and, although I never became either an alcoholic or a compulsive solitary drinker, beer and pubs became necessary crutches for many years to come.

The boys at Worcester College were being prepared for rather a limited range of professions. Those who were not particularly aca-demically gifted were expected to become masseurs, for which they had to acquire a small amount of medical knowledge. The more gifted were being trained to be lawyers or clergymen. In the case of the latter, under Mr Brown's regime there seems to have been no more idea that they should have a vocation than had been the case with the clergy in the eighteenth century. One of the studies was occupied by a set of boys who adopted a fairly raffish style of life, drinking

55

heavily, and playing poker and other games for small sums. There are special playing cards for the blind where the denomination is marked in a corner in Braille. The leader of this set was a boy who was destined for the Church. When Mr Brown retired, and a new headmaster, Mr Bradnock, a sincere evangelical Christian, took over, he attempted to alter this tradition. The potential clergyman preceded me to Oxford. When I last saw him, he confided to me with alarm that he had got a girl pregnant at an indiscreet sherry party. What happened to him in the end I do not know.

Before I entered Worcester College for the Blind, it was discovered that Queen's College, Oxford, offered the Barker Exhibition for a student who was either blind or in danger of losing his sight, and who wished to read English language and literature. It seemed clear that I should try for this, though what my career should eventually be seemed obscure. I was accepted for Queen's College. I remember the Provost, Dr Hodgkin, an authority on the Anglo-Saxons and their civilisation, being kind enough to come down to Worcester specially to interview me, though I could probably have made the journey to Oxford on my own. Among other things, he asked me what I was reading at present. I replied that I was reading Ben Jonson. "No," he said, "what are you reading for pleasure and entertainment?" Well, in fact, I was reading Ben Jonson for pleasure, but I mentioned that I was reading Aldous Huxley's *Antic Hay*. That seemed to satisfy him, and he remarked that many of the young men seemed to be interested in Aldous Huxley. But I was actually reading Huxley because I felt it my duty to catch up with modern literature. My reading pattern has always tended to be along these lines.

In my third year at Worcester College, as a senior boy of promise, I was often invited by Mr Bradnock to meet distinguished visitors for dinner in the headmaster's house. One of these was a peace worker for the Quakers who in the year of Munich affirmed, with absolute certainty, that two things had saved us from war during that crisis: one was the united prayers of all Christian people, and the other was that the ordinary Germans had lain down on the railway lines in one of the Berlin stations, thus preventing troop trains from moving forward. This was obviously a total fiction and a piece of wishful thinking. It was all too typical of the pacifists at that time. Another distinguished visitor was Lord Baldwin of Bewdley, the former Prime Minister. I remember sitting next to him at lunch, though I could not think of anything whatsoever to say to him. He did not really encourage conversation. He seemed to exude gloom much as a snail exudes slime, and no wonder, for the country was slowly moving towards the Second World War as a result, to some extent, of his own policies. Most of the conversation was monopolised by Lady

Baldwin who, in contrast, was extremely lively. She was wearing a long dress in brilliant colours, which was not at all the fashion of the period. When Baldwin was due to address the boys, he and his wife did their little act. She pressed his hand before he went to the front of the platform. This was obviously a routine which they always followed on such occasions.

There were three assistant masters, two of whom were blind, one totally and one partially. The former, Mr Sumner, taught English literature and economics, and the latter, Mr Bonham, mathematics. Besides these, there was a resident classics master, a physical training instructor who came in daily, and a very elderly and pathetic old Frenchman called Monsieur Callet who taught his native language. He was unmercifully and cruelly ragged by the boys. They could indeed be cruel, and did not spare the blind and partially sighted masters either. Monsieur Callet had little defence, except to pick on the two Roman Catholic boys in his class whom he could threaten to report to Father Gibb, who was their parish priest as well as his own.

I took over the editing of the college magazine, and contributed a series of parodies in the form of variations on "Little Miss Muffet". One parodied Housman:

> When I was two and twenty
> I saw my love one day,
> Upon a tuffet seated
> And eating curds and whey.
>
> A spider hung above her:
> A distant church bell rang –
> Today the spider hangs there,
> Tomorrow I shall hang.

The senior boys at Worcester College ran a jazz band with a few old instruments which had been handed down from one generation of boys to another. These included a double bass with no back to it, which I learnt to strum. We used to play at college dances and other occasions, for example at the annual parish dance in the church in Whittington. This was a curious affair. The young men and women of the village lined up on opposite sides of the hall. The young men were, for the most part, much too shy to ask the girls to dance who, in consequence, ended up dancing with each other. There was an upright piano, and when refreshments came round it appeared to be a tradition among the boys to take a portion of the meat pie offered and then to deposit it inside the piano.

5

Queen's College, Oxford

So it came about that at the beginning of the Michaelmas term of 1939 I went up to Queen's College, Oxford, to read English language and literature. I had never previously visited Oxford, and was immediately struck by the architectural beauty of the college which was to be mine for the next four years.

Being new to Oxford, I was too shy to ask anybody for information. I had been shown to my room on the ground floor on the right of the back quad, but had not found out where the hall was or what time dinner would be. I went to bed hungry, having eaten nothing other than a banana which had been left over from the lunch I had taken to eat on the journey. In consequence of missing the hall dinner, I did not hear the instructions which the Dean had given to the freshmen on how they were expected to behave. A small booklet, called "Guide for the Conduct of Junior Members of the University", was then given out, but of course I did not receive a copy. I knew that we were subject to a number of disciplinary measures, but I did not know what they were. I was particularly interested in the rules about frequenting public houses. In fact they were forbidden to undergraduates, though in practice everybody did frequent them. The secret was to keep away from the centre of the town between the hours of about eight and nine, after which the proctors, having finished their after-dinner port, proceeded with their servants, known as bulldogs, to parade the town and to challenge any undergraduate who was found in a public house. Anyone so discovered was fined the next day at the proctors' court, and if caught more than once or twice might well be sent down. I, myself, was caught on only one occasion and this was really because I had been to a party in somebody's rooms, the beer had run out, and I had gone out with another young man to collect fresh supplies from a nearby public house at the wrong hour. There was no objection to undergraduates drinking. The ban on drinking in public houses was simply an extension of the convention that gentlemen did not frequent public houses. One could get wine and beer from the college buttery, though in wartime this was often in short supply, or one could drink in the bar of the Union. The Union at Oxford, of course, is the debating society, but it is also the social club which anyone can join.

In order to find out what these restrictions were, I had to wait until I was formally matriculated a week or so after entering the college. At the matriculation ceremony one is handed a certificate with one's first name in a Latin form – the authorities, however, balked at trying to translate the great variety of girls' names into Latin – and along with it a large volume of the statutes in Latin. I looked into these and saw that one was not only forbidden to frequent public houses, but also "oficinas ubi herba Nicotiana sive tobacco ordinarie venditur". In consequence of this, for some time afterwards I was sneaking into tobacconists hoping to be unobserved. The statute, of course, had long been obsolete. Basically, the statutes in force at Oxford are those instituted by William Laud when he was Vice-Chancellor and were intended for boys of what we would consider secondary school age.

I soon embarked upon my studies. In my first year I had to take an examination, known as Pass Moderations, in four subjects of my choice. One of these had to be an ancient language – Greek, Latin or Hebrew (I believe that classical Asiatic languages – Arabic, classical Chinese or Sanskrit – were accepted from students of Asiatic nationalities). The subjects I chose were Latin, English, Anglo-Saxon and French. The Latin paper involved studying Tacitus's *Agricola* and *Germania*, and a selection of Pliny's Letters. The French paper consisted of Corneille's *Le Cid*, Molière's *Tartuffe* and de Tocqueville's *L'Ancien Régime et la Révolution*. These texts had been selected by the examiners as being of use to students going on to study other subjects in the Arts Faculty. For instance, the *Germania* of Tacitus is invaluable for anyone wishing to study English literature – a course which, at Oxford, includes Old English (Anglo-Saxon) – for Tacitus gives a detailed account of ancient Germanic society as it was in his time (which was centuries before the Anglo-Saxon invasion of England). It is necessary to know something about that if one is to understand poems like *Beowulf*. The Pliny text is of no particular value to students of English but the selection that we studied contained the letter which Pliny wrote, as governor of Bithynia, to the Emperor Trajan, asking him what he was to do about the Christians. Pliny had discovered a cell of this abominable sect even among his own household slaves and, arresting two women who acted as deaconesses, forced them to reveal, under torture, what their worship consisted of. It did not include eating babies or sexual orgies, which he had rather expected. This letter is, of course, important for historians of the early Church. Trajan's answer was eminently sensible. He told Pliny that if any Christians were caught they were to be punished severely, but he was not to hunt them out. This would only encourage the growth of informers and there had been far too much of that sort of thing under Trajan's predecessor Domitian.

The English literature paper consisted of several dramatic texts – Shakespeare's *The Merchant of Venice*, Ben Jonson's *The Silent Woman*, Congreve's *The Way of the World* and Dryden's *All for Love*, as well as Dryden's essay on dramatic poetry. These I began studying with my academic tutor, with whom I should remain for the next three years, Herbert Brett-Smith. The Anglo-Saxon texts for Pass Mods I studied with his daughter Hilary. These were the lives of St Oswald and St Edmund and parts of the *Anglo-Saxon Chronicle*, mostly dealing with the career of King Alfred. I attended lectures on the dramatic texts by Nevill Coghill who was later to become a friend.

My Latin studies were presided over by Craddock Ratcliffe, a clergyman and a Fellow of Queen's. Ratcliffe was primarily a liturgiologist, and had been largely responsible for the service used at the coronation of King George VI which we, the nation, had lately witnessed. Ratcliffe struck us undergraduates as rather formidable, though he was actually a kindly man. I went to classes in his rooms with two other students, one of whom had a Nonconformist background and was rather prim. Ratcliffe would usually offer us cigarettes, and occasionally a glass of sherry. This student ostentatiously refused the cigarettes. One day Ratcliffe said to him: "Do you drink?" He replied very firmly that he did not. "Then", said Ratcliffe, "I suspect you of the worst vices."

I passed all four papers of the Moderations examination in my first term and then proceeded to work for Finals. This consisted of two tutorials a week, one with my English literature tutor, Mr Brett-Smith of Corpus Christi, and the other with my English language tutor (for Anglo-Saxon in my first year, and Middle English in my second), Mr John Bryson of Balliol. Brett-Smith was an old, white-haired man. I think if it had not been for the war he would have retired. He had been a favourite pupil of the Edwardian scholar Sir Walter Raleigh and had published a small volume of verse when he himself was an undergraduate. Brett-Smith had a real love for English literature, especially books marked by a broad humanity and a convivial sense. He was good on Chaucer and Fielding, and a special favourite of his – in fact the latest author that I read, since the English literature course ended with the year 1837 – was Thomas Love Peacock, whose works he helped to edit. Brett-Smith once told me that he could pick a team of four clerics whose names began with the letter "S" which he would back for their wit against a similar team whose names began with any other letter of the alphabet. The list was John Skelton, Jonathan Swift, Laurence Sterne and Sydney Smith. Brett-Smith did not, however, stretch me. I would write him an essay every week and read it to him. He would not really criticise it but just give me a subject for a new essay and a reading list. I felt that I was not getting as much value out of him as I should. Knowing that Fielding was a favourite of his, when he asked me to write an essay on that author I wrote a violent attack on him, hoping that this would rouse Brett-Smith. He was quite unperturbed, however, and said, mildly, that he must read Fielding again.

The Anglo-Saxon and Middle English classes with John Bryson were a tougher option. Like many undergraduates, I resented having to learn Anglo-Saxon, but I was to change my mind about this. During those war years, the heroic, stoical attitude found in Anglo-Saxon poetry was of immense value. Several of the works of the Edwardian scholar W. P. Carr were part of our reading list. He described the Norse myth of Ragnarok, in which the gods are finally destroyed by the hostile powers: the evil and treacherous Loki, the giants of frost and fire, and Hel the goddess of the underworld with her army of ghosts and monsters, such as Fenris the wolf. Commenting on this, Carr said: "The gods know defeat, but the gods also know that defeat is no refutation." The end of the story of Ragnarok (we did not have to read the Old Norse of the Eddas, but I read it in translation) is immensely poignant. After the world and Valhalla have been destroyed by fire, Balder, the god who had died, returns from the underworld with his companions and they find in the grass the golden toys which the gods had played with before the beginning of the world. In 1936 J. R. R. Tolkien published his famous British Academy lecture entitled "Beowulf: the Monsters and the Critics". In this he showed that *Beowulf* should by no means be treated as simply a philological document, but as a great and tragic epic poem. The demand which surfaces every few years or so for the abolition of compulsory Anglo-Saxon at Oxford, and which at present looks as if it may very well succeed, I regard as disgraceful. I am almost tempted to say that English literature since *Beowulf* is a history of steady decline.

The assumption that English literature ended with the 1830s owed its inception to C. S. Lewis, and had been introduced in 1931. Lewis felt that a work did not have classic status unless it had lasted a hundred years. There is something to be said for this point of view, but this deadline remained in force for at least another couple of decades. Nowadays, people reading for the Oxford English School can, theoretically, write an essay on something that was published yesterday. As students of English literature, we obviously lost a lot in not studying the great Victorians. In fact, I graduated without reading at Oxford a word of Dickens, George Eliot or Carlyle. There was an optional Victorian paper, but this, I think, was intended for students who had already graduated at other universities – in America or the commonwealth, for instance – where the examiners had been sufficiently misguided as to include the Victorian writers in the syllabus. The examiners tended to have fun, I suspect, when setting the questions for this paper. I remember such questions as: "'The most corrupt and corrupting author of the period.' Justify this claim in relation to Swinburne, Carlyle . . . etc." and "'The poetry of Robert Bridges is an acquired taste.' Is it worth acquiring?" This examination system also meant that we learnt about twentieth-century literature from each other, not from our teachers. Brett-Smith always insisted that the only poems of T. S. Eliot he could understand were *The Practical Cats*. Nevill Coghill, however, who had been Auden's tutor, was very aware of the poets of that generation. I remember Coghill's quoting a poem of Charles Madge in the course of one of his lectures. It was to illustrate the principle of allegory or symbolism. Madge is now, I think, largely forgotten but during the 1930s he had a high reputation and was regarded as "the white hope of modern poetry".

This was wartime Oxford, and many of the younger male dons were in the army. We had some impressive women teachers like Helen Gardner (later Dame Helen), who wrote a commentary on Eliot's *Four Quartets*. Of the male lecturers in English, the most prominent were Coghill, Professor David Nichol Smith and C. S. Lewis. There was also Lord David Cecil, but he tended to lecture on Victorian subjects which most of us did not have to study. Nichol Smith, who later became my supervisor for postgraduate work, was an expert on the eighteenth century, and edited the then current *Oxford Book of Eighteenth-Century Verse*. I had developed an enthusiasm for the Augustans as a reaction against Bembridge's emphasis on romanticism and Pre-Raphaelite art. In the library at Bembridge I had found a copy of Pope's Homer. I was not ready to appreciate Pope's verse at that time (I would have preferred to have read Homer in the Butcher and Lang translation, had it been available), but I was delighted by Flaxman's illustrations which had a coolness and precision so unlike that of the Pre-Raphaelites. I attended Nichol Smith's lectures on Swift, Pope and Johnson. He was a sound scholar but a rather dry and uninspiring teacher.

Certainly the most exciting lecturer in English was C. S. Lewis. I remember attending his course entitled "A Prolegomena to Mediaeval Literature", the material for which was later incorporated into his book, *The Discarded Image*. These lectures were a revelation to me. They were largely an exposition of the mediaeval world picture, and one learnt that there was another way of looking at the cosmos beside that of modern scientific humanism. Lewis to a large extent rejected the modern world and had turned back nostalgically to a mediaeval one. I never met him personally, though as a postgraduate student I attended his seminars on textual criticism. Lewis was unsympathetic to most of contemporary literature. He rather grudgingly accepted T. S. Eliot as a fellow Christian. The only modernist writer whom he seemed genuinely to admire was Kafka. I think this was because Kafka is, in some ways, an allegorical writer, and allegory was the dominant form of the later Middle Ages. Lewis's critical-historical book *The Allegory of Love* is probably his best work. In some of his fictional works, notably *Pilgrim's Regress* and *The Great Divorce*, he himself essayed the form of allegory. The best of Lewis's fictional works, in my opinion, is *Till We Have Faces*, written after the death of his wife, but he is probably best known now for his children's books. I cannot wholeheartedly admire them, in particular the first of them, *The Lion, the Witch and the Wardrobe*, which owes so much of its imagery and story to George MacDonald (an author whom Lewis certainly admired) as to be very close to plagiarism. It was, in fact, Roger Lancelyn Green, a contemporary of mine who later became librarian of Merton, and an expert on Lewis Carroll and other children's writers, who persuaded Lewis that it was worth publishing. Lewis's friend, Tolkien, who was attracted to the early Middle Ages (the world of the Anglo-Saxons, the Norsemen and the Celts), disliked allegory. In his lectures Lewis had a pithy way of stating things memorably. For instance, he would expound the meaning of the word "realist" in its mediaeval sense, where it is in contrast to "nominalist". The realists believed that general ideas alone had a real existence, whereas the nominalists held that reality only resided in particulars and that general ideas were mere names. Lewis then contrasted this meaning of the word realist with that commonly used in modern philosophy, which is almost its exact opposite. He summed up by saying that in popular modern speech a "realist" is a bad man on your own side, and an "idealist" is a good man on the other side.

Nevill Coghill was an excellent lecturer. I attended a course he gave on *Piers Plowman*, but I suppose his greatest importance was as a dramatic producer both within and outside the university. During my years at Oxford I saw his productions of *Timon of Athens*, *Twelfth Night* and *Measure for Measure*. All these were outdoor productions in college gardens in the summer.

One don whose lectures I never attended was Edmund Blunden of Merton. Blunden was the first published poet whom I ever met. My friend, Sidney Keyes, greatly admired Blunden's work but it has come to be underrated. This is because Blunden is judged by his later work, rather than by his early poetry which provides a mirror of the English countryside. He suffered deeply in the trenches during the First World War, and my first impression on meeting him was the terrible expression of pain in his eyes. Blunden liked to give his tutorials in the Bear public house opposite Merton, rather than in his rooms in college. I recall a particular evening with him in a pub in Abingdon. In his later years, Blunden had become interested in minor eighteenth- and nineteenth-century poets whom I was myself in the process of discovering at this time. One poet whom we discussed was Henry Kirke White (1785–1806), a slightly older contemporary of Keats who died, at a similarly early age, of consumption. Kirke White was, for some time after his death, much better known and more admired than Keats. He was a boy from a humble, poverty-stricken, background in Nottingham who managed to get a scholarship to Cambridge, where he more or less worked himself to death. His poetry is pietistic and weakened by a morbid self-pity, for the poor boy knew that he was dying. There has been a tendency for English anthologists to end their collections with a martyr poet. Once this was Chatterton, then it was Kirke White, then it was Keats, then much later on it was Rupert Brooke, and after the Second World War it was Dylan Thomas. Blunden told me that he thought there was a lot of unpublished material by Kirke White in the hands of a collateral descendant of his, a Colonel Kirke White, who resided in Norfolk and whom Blunden had corresponded with. He pointed out that the first of the volumes of Kirke White's poetry, which Robert Southey edited, contained all the popular pietistic poetry, and that there were some better poems in the second volume. Blunden was of the opinion that Southey knew his audience and had first of all published what he thought would please the readers of the time, and then others, which were less easy to appreciate, which he valued more. If so, the unpublished material of Kirke White might be well worth examining. As far as I know nobody ever has, and I drop this as a hint to future scholars.

Another poet who was lecturing at the university at this time was Charles Williams. An editor for the Oxford University Press, he had come to Oxford, along with the rest of the staff, when the London offices of the OUP were moved there because of the war. Williams had given adult education classes at the City Literary Institute in London, and when he came to Oxford immediately became adopted by Lewis and Tolkien as part of their Inkling circle. Lewis secured an honorary MA for Williams which enabled the latter to give lectures in the university. Williams himself had won a scholarship to King's College, London, in his youth, but the poverty of his family, brought about by his father's blindness, had prevented him from finishing the course. I attended Williams's lectures. Later on, I was to meet him and had at least one interesting conversation with him – but of this, more later.

University life at Oxford was in many respects overshadowed by the war. In contrast with the First World War, when the universities were almost empty, Oxford, like other universities, was full during the Second World War. Men and women came up and did short courses, maybe for one or two years, before they were drafted into the armed forces or other war work, and then could come back after the war to complete their degrees. Because of my eyesight I was totally exempt from military service. In order to get as much time in as possible before being drafted into the army, many clever boys came up at an unusually early age, some as young as sixteen or seventeen.

Among many undergraduates there was a conscious attempt to ignore the war and, almost as an affectation, to hark back to the old Oxford life, even the life of the 1920s. Evelyn Waugh's novels were cult books with us, and the poetry of John Betjeman was just beginning to be discovered. His later popularity would have seemed inconceivable at that time. Some of us also admired Ronald Firbank, although he was a Cambridge man and does not deal with university life in any of his novels. I do not think the undergraduates of my generation can be condemned as escapist. They knew perfectly well that they would have to enter the war very soon and have a high probability of not surviving it. But some members of the press were extremely hostile. Beverley Nichols, on a visit to the Oxford Union, condemned the undergraduates for these affectations. He was hissed. Next day appeared a headline in the paper for which he contributed: "My old university hissed me, and I was proud." Nichols, who as far as I know never did any war service, had written during the 1930s a book entitled *Cry Havoc* in which he embraced an uncompromisingly pacifist position. This was followed by another book in which he just as firmly declared his allegiance to the Buchmanites (the so-called "Oxford Group").

All physically fit undergraduates were required to do a certain amount of military training in the OTC, but some of my contemporaries were exempt because they were conscientious objectors, who, when they were eventually called up, would have to go to a tribunal and hope to be drafted into some kind of non-combatant service. A number of these changed their minds when Germany invaded the Soviet Union and that country entered the war on the side of the Allies. In many cases, the pacifism of my contemporaries was more of a protest against fighting for what they regarded as a corrupt capitalist system; they were prepared to fight for Soviet socialism.

Most of the undergraduates I knew belonged to the Labour Club. Round about 1941 there was a big split in this body, which had hitherto been dominated by those with Marxist sympathies. An independent Democratic Socialist Club was now founded. I did not myself belong to any political party. My experience at Bembridge, when a moderately left-wing ideology was more or less forced on us, and where we were compelled to attend meetings passing resolutions of a pacifist nature, had tended to make me a Conservative for life. But I never went so far as to join any Conservative clubs.

When I arrived at Queen's I was unfamiliar with the ways of Oxford, and to some degree a psychologically damaged person, finding it difficult to make contact with any of my contemporaries. It was not until my second year that I began to make friends. Among my contemporaries at Queen's were Edmund Dell and his friend, George Lehmann (a connection, I think, of that well-known theatrical and literary family). Lehmann, who was reading French, seemed to be brilliant, and was one of those who had matriculated at the age of sixteen. Both he and Edmund Dell were committed communists and I was quite terrified of them. Dell had a darkly handsome countenance but never seemed to smile. Someone is said to have once asked: "Why is Edmund always scowling?" The answer was "He's going to go on scowling until the revolution comes." His later career was to take a rather different turn. He was a junior minister in Harold Wilson's Labour government, and is now, I understand, a successful merchant banker. George Lehmann, who became a lecturer in French at Reading University, and published a worthy but not wildly exciting book about the small literary magazines of the French symbolist period, later joined the University of Buckingham, the only university in England not financed by public funds, and scarcely a left-wing institution.

But there was one of my contemporaries it was impossible to ignore. This was Drummond Allison, who was very boyish in his appearance and manner, and an unstoppable and witty talker. There was something about his character which made him talk almost non-stop. He was entirely without inhibitions or shyness in tackling other people. I was later to meet his parents. He was the child of their old age, and the youngest of three brothers, one of whom was killed in the air force during the war. His father was a worthy Nonconformist businessman, his mother of Viennese descent. Her father had been a jeweller. I do not know whether he was Jewish. Drummond did not either, but rather hoped he was. This was not because he had any romantic ideas about Jewishness, but because he always wanted to identify with any persecuted or disadvantaged minority. Drummond combined English puritanism with something of a Viennese charm.

He had a good knowledge of contemporary literature, of which I was almost totally ignorant. He modelled himself, in his prose stories, upon Ernest Hemingway and, in his verse, largely upon Auden. In his schooldays, like many adolescents of that period, he had been intoxicated by the poetry of Swinburne, but as he matured, a highly individual tone entered his work and he produced poetry which still finds devoted readers. Apart from Auden and Hemingway, he had a great enthusiasm for, and knowledge of, Malory's *Morte d'Arthur*. Many of Drummond's poems are on Arthurian subjects, but adapted to make them comments on the contemporary world. T. H. White, the author of *The Once and Future King*, was a friend of the Allison family. As a boy at Bishop's Stortford School, Drummond had been strongly influenced by the left-wing ideas of the times. Many of his poems exhibit an anguished conflict between his Marxism and his Christian conscience. While the puritanism of his Christianity made him feel that socialism was the only just system, he was at the same time repelled by the inhumanity of Marxism, and its rigid use of class as the only criterion of value. This conflict produced some remarkable poems. A general disillusionment with Marxism had begun at the beginning of the war with the Russo–German pact and the occupation and partition of Poland by Germany and Russia. Many of the intellectuals of the 1930s had adopted Freud's mechanistic view of the human psyche and attempted to synthesise it with Marxism, but in the 1940s the influence of Jung was beginning to replace that of Freud.

Drummond would tackle anybody he thought might be writing poetry and persuade them to show it him. It was he who, in my second year, introduced me to Sidney Keyes in the cloisters of the college. Sidney had a striking, almost un-English appearance. He was not very tall but broad-shouldered. He had fine eyes, thick, dark hair and an olive complexion. The Keyes family had originally been millers from Essex, and Sidney's mother was the daughter of a Manchester clergyman. I know nothing about the antecedents of her family, but there might have been a streak of exotic blood. Later on, when he became friendly with Milein Cosmann, who is Jewish, they were often mistaken for brother and sister.

Drummond Allison, Sidney Keyes and I were to become very close friends and to form a focus of poetry at Queen's College. Anybody whom Drummond discovered to be writing verse would be invited to Sidney's tea parties where we read our poems to each other and profited from the criticism the group might offer. Sidney had a very different character from Drummond's, nor did he share Drummond's enthusiasm for writers like Auden. In fact, almost the first remark he ever made to me was: "Auden is not a poet." He also quoted with some approval, though admittedly humorously, a remark attributed to Sir Maurice Bowra, the Warden of Wadham College, that Auden was "the Martin Tupper of our time". Martin Tupper was a highly popular Victorian versifier whose bestselling work was entitled *Proverbial Philosophy*. Certainly Maurice Bowra's remark was quite unfair to Auden, who hardly retails moral platitudes, and was not, on the whole, an exponent of free verse, as Tupper was. But this general reaction against the influence of Auden marked quite a number of the poets of my generation, at Oxford and elsewhere. Drummond, however, always championed Auden, and said in a letter to me: "Everybody's being so beastly to him that I have definitely taken him under my protection." My own knowledge of contemporary poetry was so slight that I had not encountered Auden before I went up to Oxford, and he was so unfashionable in our circle that I did not read him seriously until many years later. During the 1950s I found the later, American-based and Christian, Auden more to my taste than the early left-wing Auden. It was not until after his death, when Faber published a volume entitled *The English Auden*, which brought together, in their original form, all the poems he had written before he emigrated to America at the beginning of the war, that I at last understood why Auden had been a figure of such importance to his generation. My considered opinion of Auden is that he is a remarkable poet, but of the second rank. He is not an explorer like Wordsworth, say, or Eliot, but one of those poets (others include Pope, Tennyson and Kipling) who retails in an eminently memorable form what a lot of intelligent people were thinking in his generation. Pope does this so brilliantly that he almost breaks into the first rank, and there is a dark side of Tennyson which evinces a far more original and sensitive poet than is exhibited in his Laureate persona.

I was not to meet Auden personally till towards the end of his life, on one of his visits to England. He had been advertised to give a reading in a Bloomsbury bookshop in aid of some important charitable cause. So many people turned up to hear him that the event had to be hastily transferred to the nearby church of St George's, Bloomsbury, but a reception at the bookshop followed the reading. I noticed Auden in a corner talking to my friend and Oxford contemporary, the Reverend Gerard Irvine, who had always been a great admirer of his. Auden was explaining to Gerard, in precise theological terms, the difference between sinful and natural pride – a distinction which I think Gerard would have been perfectly capable of defining himself. Stephen Spender very kindly took me over to meet Auden, who received me affably. He evidently knew my name, though I do not think that he knew very much about my work. Later on I met him at the Poetry Society where he was giving a reading. I remember his refusing to take an easy chair which was offered to him. He spoke of Edwardian virtues and how his mother would punish him if he ever lolled about in an easy chair. On this occasion, he invited me to look him up at his cottage in the grounds of Christ Church when I was in Oxford. I was at that time regularly teaching at Oxford one or two days a week. I have since regretted that I never took up this invitation. It involved rather complicated manoeuvres in order to find Auden's telephone number. I had first of all to contact Spender, and in order to find Spender's number I had to look it up under the name of his wife, the pianist Natasha Litvin. There would also have been for me, who had by this time lost my eyesight completely, some difficulty in finding my way to Auden's cottage through the grounds of Christ Church. But perhaps it might not have been a fruitful meeting. One gathers from Auden's biographers that at this stage he was not interested in exchanging ideas with others, but merely in laying down, rather dogmatically, his own conclusions.

Sidney Keyes had a strong belief in the philosophical or metaphysical mission of the poet. The poets he most admired were Wordsworth, W. B. Yeats and, above all, Rainer Maria Rilke. Those of us who did not know German read Rilke in the translation by J. B. Leishman and Stephen Spender which had appeared about this time. In spite of Sidney's quasi-philosophical approach to poetry, he had no close acquaintance with philosophy as such. When I mentioned Nietzsche to him, he said that he assumed that he was "a negligible thinker". Keyes had adopted the popular view that Nietzsche was simply the mentor of Hitler and the philosopher of fascism. There is a lot more to Nietzsche than that, especially the early Nietzsche of *The Birth of Tragedy*. I had read quite a lot of *Thus Spake Zarathustra* when a boy, though in an immensely turgid official translation sponsored (and also expurgated and distorted) by his ghastly sister, Frau Forster Nietzsche, and her despicable friend, the racialist philosopher Houston Stewart Chamberlain.

Sidney Keyes and Drummond Allison both read in the history school, though Drummond subsequently transferred to reading English literature with Brett-Smith. History plays a considerable part in the poems of both of them. Sidney was a fluent and prolific writer of verse. He showed me most of his poems as soon as they were written and asked for my criticism. I remember on one occasion his reading me a poem on "Queen Nefertiti". I indicated that I thought the final stanza was a bit over the top (that was not the actual phrase I used), whereupon he picked up a pair of scissors, snipped off the final stanza and let it fall into the waste-paper basket. Sidney and I, with Drummond and the rest of our circle, used to enjoy playing verse games in which each member of the party writes a line and, as in the game of consequences, hands it to the next player, who writes another line.

We also wrote sonnets to bouts-rimés in which each member of the party has to write a sonnet with the same set of rhymes. Such games can be of considerable value to aspiring poets. One may note that Keats and his circle used to write sonnets on set themes, and Rossetti and his sister used to play bouts-rimés. I have often recommended it to young poets in my later years.

Sidney Keyes could be facile. He would sometimes use learned allusions in his poems which were not taken from his own reading but were something I or somebody else had told him. He was sometimes almost unethically careless in his journalistic articles for *Cherwell*. For example, the two dancers, Sally Gilmour and Walter Gore, came to Oxford and performed an interesting experiment in combining ballet with poetry. The poem which they interpreted was Browning's "The Confessional". It was first read from behind the scenes and then represented in ballet and mime. This poem is set in Italy – the Italy of Browning's own time with its numerous subversive secret societies determined to establish a united and independent Italy. The plot is as follows: a girl is speaking from a madhouse cell and tells how she confessed to a priest that she had slept with her lover. The priest absolves her, but tells her that her lover is suspected of being involved in a subversive conspiracy, and that it is her duty to report upon him to the authorities. She does so and then witnesses her lover's execution after he has been tortured. This has driven her to madness and a fierce repudiation of all religious belief. Unfortunately, Keyes did not bother to go to the performance, and wrote a review of it assuming that the poem the dancers had interpreted was another of Browning's, entitled "A Last Confession". This poem is set in a Victorian English suburb. A dying man is speaking of a clandestine love affair he had many years before, and how, even now, he is unable to repent of it. Some years later, Sally Gilmour and Walter Gore included their interpretation of "The Confessional" in a programme they gave at a London theatre. They received an indignant letter from a Roman Catholic, accusing them of libelling the Catholic Church, and threatening that if they continued to include this piece in their repertory he would canvass every Catholic in England to boycott their show. What had caused his indignation was Browning's assumption that a priest might violate the seal of the confessional. But I believe that Browning was on sound ground. It has, at least sometimes, been held that the seal of the confessional is not binding when the safety of the state is endangered.

During his first year, Sidney Keyes occupied rooms on the same staircase in the back quadrangle of Queen's College that my rooms were in, though a couple of floors higher. He was once troubled by a mouse in his room and put down a trap for it baited with cheese.

The mouse ate the cheese but did not spring the trap. The college servant, when informed of this, said to Sidney: "Oh, sir, all the mice in this college have degrees." Later, Sidney was to move to rooms at Number 37, the High Street, a house lived in by a formidable lady named Mrs Taylor. The widow of a doctor who had served in Malaya, she was a strong Tory and a believer in the British Empire. Another of her lodgers, who was there during Sidney's time, was David Wright. Profoundly deaf since the age of seven, David was determined to be a poet and, when I was first introduced to him by Sidney, was learning the sound values of English words by a close study of those contemporary poets who were reputed to have the finest ear. These included Eliot, Pound and Edith Sitwell. It is difficult, now, to imagine how high Edith Sitwell's reputation stood at this time. The poems she wrote during the war years, beginning with *Street Songs*, seemed then to be very impressive. In these volumes she took a kind of prophetic stance. Today these poems appear to me to be rather empty and derivative. She survives, if she survives at all, through her early *Façade* poems, which, nonsense as they are, belong to a recognisable futuristic European movement. To some extent they have been preserved in the amber of Walton's music. Nevertheless, at this time both Sidney and I admired her work. Later on I was to meet her.

After Sidney had been called up into the army, I was also to occupy a room in Mrs Taylor's house, as later on did my friend, the poet William Bell. Number 52 became almost a traditional lodging house for poets. When, many years later, the house became an annexe of Magdalen College, who were its owners, a short article appeared in the *Oxford Mail* mentioning its poetic associations. Sidney's officer's swaggerstick, which he had left there when he visited Oxford on his last leave, still remained in the hall umbrella-stand.

Sidney Keyes is commonly thought of as a war poet and his name is mentioned along with Keith Douglas and the ill-fated Alun Lewis. This is not quite fair to Sidney, for none of his surviving poems was written after he had seen any active service. He represents a generation of very young men who lived under the shadow of war and the possibility of imminent death. The figure of death haunted him. It almost became a joke with him. Mrs Taylor had hanging in the lavatory of her house a calendar which had been printed in Malaya and had been sent to her, presumably, by one of her late husband's associates or patients. The calendar for each month was accompanied by a photograph of a British bird, with a suitable quotation from the poets. One of these pictures showed a spoonbill. The accompanying quotation, "the shovelard with his broadie beak", was attributed to a poet called Skeleton. In fact, the line comes from John Skelton's "Philip Sparrow". Sidney knew Skelton's poetry well, but found the

71

idea that there might be a poet called Skeleton irresistibly funny and was always taking visitors into the lavatory specially to read this quotation.

There were two strains in Sidney Keyes's poetry: one was pastoral – Wordsworth, Clare and Housman were among his favourite poets; the other was his interest in symbolism and mythology. A great deal of Sidney's poetry sprung from his rather anguished love affair with Milein Cosmann. He was romantically interested in women and his love for Milein was an obsessive one which she was not wholly able to reciprocate, although she liked and admired him. I do not think that she was in any way to blame for this unhappy situation. His later affair, on his last leave, with her flatmate Renée-Jane Scott might have developed into a more mature relationship. Both Milein and Renée were art students from the Slade School, which had been evacuated from London to Oxford during the war.

Sidney Keyes had, I think, some difficulty in coming to terms with women as actual human beings. It may come as a surprise to many readers today, when one considers the mores of modern teenagers, that the majority of young men and women coming up to Oxford at that time, at the age of eighteen or so, were virgins, and often remained so for several years. The fact that many of them came from single-sex schools probably added to the difficulty. No one today ought any longer to subscribe to the myth that the English single-sex boarding-school system was a breeding ground for homosexuality. It is true that many boys had minor homosexual experiences at school (this was certainly not the case with Sidney), but they usually managed to grow out of it. It was often difficult, however, for young men of my generation to come to terms with young women. The presence of female undergraduates as full members of the university did not have the kind of effect which my father and some of his friends appeared to have feared. There were four women's colleges at Oxford: Somerville, Lady Margaret Hall, St Hilda's and St Hugh's; and also the Society of Home Students, which was incorporated as St Anne's College after the war. The principals of the women's colleges kept a tight rein on their charges, and all sorts of Victorian statutes designed to protect the reputation of the women students still persisted. It was difficult for the latter to obtain permission to return late, and if they wanted to entertain male undergraduates in the college they could not do so in their own rooms – for heaven's sake they were bedsitters, unlike the men's sets – but had to hire a special guests' common room for the purpose (at least in the case of one college).

It was not easy for those of us in men's college dramatic societies to obtain permission from the women's colleges to allow girls to play the women's parts in our productions or to take part in play readings.

During the war years there were, however, a number of female civil servants, working in the various government departments which had been evacuated to or near Oxford. We were rather fortunate in Queen's that our Egglesfield Players had access to some delightful girls stationed at Cuddesden, near Oxford, who worked for Queen Anne's Bounty.

Sidney Keyes was an immensely prolific writer. He wrote with perhaps too much facility. He had had a lonely childhood, and there was a strong streak of neurosis in the family. I have never met anyone who was more certain of his poetic vocation, and the corpus of his poetry is remarkable by any standard when one remembers that he was killed in the North African campaign before his twenty-first birthday. While Sidney was still an undergraduate, two plays of his were produced in Oxford. One of these was on the biblical subject of Hosea and his faithless wife Gomer. This, given a modern setting, and accompanied by jazz choruses, was one of his best works in this field. A second was called *The Prisoners*. It was set in an imaginary Central European state, ruled by a fascist regime. In a prison cell are a young communist, played by Drummond Allison, and the Orthodox archbishop of the country, who has been commanded to pronounce an anathema against the insurgents. I took the role of the archbishop. The play was produced in the church hall of the parish of St Ebbes, along with a piece of my own, of which the least said the better. The performance of *The Prisoners* – there was only one – was marked by a somewhat sensational accident. An actor playing a fascist guard hit Drummond on the head with a pistol so effectively that the blow severed a small artery in the scalp, and a great spurt of blood shot up and fell on the stage. I was downstage, unaware of what was going on upstage, and after being shot, I fell into a pool of blood. This created sensational headlines in the *Oxford Mail* the next morning: "Stage Blood was Real". Drummond was not seriously injured, but sufficiently so to have his call-up deferred for another term. Since, when he was eventually drafted into the army, he was to be killed in the Italian campaign within a year, it gave him a few more months of life.

As for college dramatic productions, I had a small role in Dryden's *The Conquest of Granada* and also played the peasant, Costar Pearmain, in Farquhar's *The Recruiting Officer*. This play, which was written in the reign of Queen Anne, had a certain topicality for us undergraduates, as in the last scene almost all the characters are drafted into the army. Before producing a play in any college, one had to ask permission from the principal, who could exercise a certain degree of

73

censorship. Provost Hodgkin, of my college, was a bit doubtful about *The Recruiting Officer*. This was simply because the heroine, daughter of the local Justice of the Peace, having fallen in love with the recruiting officer, Captain Plume, of whom her father does not approve, disguises herself as a young man and is given by her father to Plume as an army recruit. But this episode aroused the suspicion of the college authorities who, believing they saw a homosexual implication in it, thought it would be a bad example for young men about to be drafted into the army.

In my postgraduate year I directed *The Revenger's Tragedy*, a play at that time attributed to Cyril Tourneur, but now generally held to be possibly Middleton's. I think this was the first presentation of this play since the seventeenth century. I tried to give it an expressionistic production, presenting it as a kind of dance of death. One scene was so horrifying that Mrs Hodgkin, my Provost's wife, had to leave the theatre. I regarded this as a bit of a compliment. I only got one laugh, in the wrong place. This was when, in the final scene, the Duke's son, having discovered that his father has been murdered, rises to his feet and says: "What – old Dad dead? So I am Duke." At this point his bastard brother stabs him: "Brother, you lie." It must be the shortest tenure of a dukedom in any play.

Naturally I had acted in school plays. In the junior school at Bembridge I made my début as the Chief Weasel in A. A. Milne's adaptation of Kenneth Grahame's *The Wind in the Willows*, and I followed this up with the Mad Hatter in *Alice in Wonderland*. Although I have a good memory for facts, I have always had trouble in learning words accurately by heart. For this reason, I never undertook any major acting role. I wish now I had paid more attention to directing plays. I could not, however, have competed with the most brilliant director – apart from Nevill Coghill – we had at Oxford at that time. This was the youthful Peter Brook. I have distinct memories of his productions of Oscar Wilde's *Salome* and Sheridan's *The Critic*. In these, his friend Freddie Hurdis-Jones played Herod in the one and Sir Fretful Plagiary in the other. Brook and he also made a silent film based on Sterne's *Sentimental Journey* in which Hurdis-Jones played the part of Yorick (Sterne's self-portrait). Hurdis-Jones later worked for the Parisian radio, but, although he published one novel, never really fulfilled his early promise. Brook also produced plays in London during the vacation. These included a production of Marlowe's *Dr Faustus* and one of *Hamlet* based on the First Quarto text. After he had gone down, I remember seeing a production by Brook of Cocteau's *The Infernal Machine* in a small theatre in Notting Hill Gate.

Apart from dramatic societies, there were musical societies, and concerts in the Sheldonian Theatre and in the Holywell music rooms (said to be the oldest concert hall in England) were frequent. I remember hearing in the latter one of the earliest performances of Britten's *Serenade*. There was also a gramophone library from which one could borrow records. These had to be played with a thorn needle. Previously all gramophone records were played with steel needles, which tended eventually to destroy the wax. Thorn needles did not have this effect, but could be shattered if the music was too loud. Later, expensive diamond and sapphire needles were introduced. I was told that a method of playing records with a ray of light, a forerunner of the present system, had been patented in the 1930s, but one of the larger record companies had bought up the patent since they depended for part of their revenue on records not lasting indefinitely. By present-day standards there was not a very wide selection of records available, but this library widened my own horizons. The presence of Central European refugees in Oxford, and other parts of the country, was making more widely known the modern music which was being produced on the Continent, especially in Central Europe, including what is called the Second Viennese School. I was captivated by Mahler's *Das Lied von der Erde*. The music of Mahler was new to many listeners at this time, since he had not often been performed in Britain. Now I learn he has overtaken Tchaikovsky in the classical music charts. The composer Egon Wellesz was then residing in Oxford, and at a music society lecture I heard him explain, with remarkable clarity, Schoenberg's twelve-tone system. For most of us, brought up on the BBC's pre-war music policy, contemporary music largely meant British composers such as Vaughan Williams, Holst, Constant Lambert, Bax and Ireland. Among continental composers, there was a vogue for Sibelius, who was Sidney Keyes's favourite composer. When Mr Rhys Lloyd, the Bembridge master, protested against the detestable modern music that "that man Adrian Boult" was trying to foist on the British public, he probably meant middle-period Vaughan Williams.

Among the literary clubs was the English Club (there was, then, no Poetry Society at Oxford) which invited distinguished authors to come and address it from time to time. I remember lectures and readings by Stella Gibbons, William Empson, Stephen Spender and Dylan Thomas. Stella Gibbons's lecture expounded an interesting idea that writers could be divided into once-born and twice-born. She said that nurses in maternity hospitals applied this classification to babies. The once-born babies were disturbed and continually exhibited distress at the conditions of the world in which they found themselves, while the twice-born babies, having been here before, observed the world with an ironic equanimity. Stella Gibbons went on to apply this to writers. Jane Austen, for example, was twice-born, Charlotte Brontë once-born.

William Empson chose to talk not about poetry but about the current situation in China and Japan. He had lectured in both these countries, was deeply concerned about the situation there, and believed that the Japanese might succeed in uniting the diverse ethnic components of China where other forces had failed. At the end of the meeting, Sidney Keyes was invited by the president of the English Club to join him and Empson for a drink. According to Sidney, the evening ended with Empson reciting the Buddhist Fire Sermon to the entire bar. The Fire Sermon, it will be recalled, is a key Buddhist text in which the Buddha expounds his central doctrine that desire is the cause of all suffering, and all man's senses are on fire with desire. Empson was, I believe, somewhat attracted to Buddhism. He bitterly opposed Christianity, especially in his last work, *Milton's God*. In fact, he compiled a book on Buddhist art, *Some Faces of the Buddha*, but the manuscript – text, plates and all – was lost in a taxi by the infamous Tambimuttu.

I do not quite remember what was the subject of Stephen Spender's talk. Sidney Keyes, on seeing him, remarked to me: "What a long, gaunt man he is. No wonder he's written all that dead stuff." This was unkind, of course, but it was said not so much cruelly as with the arrogance and self-confidence of youth. The hungry generations tread each other down. Sidney had no very high opinion of Auden, and this lack of enthusiasm extended to those three poets most commonly associated with him, Spender, Day Lewis and MacNeice. When, in 1942, Sidney published his first volume of poetry, *The Iron Laurel*, a reviewer in the *New Statesman* said that Keyes had evidently been strongly influenced by Spender. Sidney was annoyed and said: "This is a new line of attack." The truth of the matter is, I think, that they were both influenced by Rilke and other German models.

Dylan Thomas read his own work, including some of the poems which were to be published in 1946 as *Deaths and Entrances*, and a parody of Auden – but in the style of Kipling. It was entitled "Sisters under the Skin". He also read the parodies which he and John Davenport had written for their joint satirical novel: *The Death of the King's Canary*. This book was not published until some years after the death of both writers. Written during the war years, it imagines that the Poet Laureate has died, and in the first chapter the Prime Minister's literary adviser is receiving specimens of the work of various living poets in order that he may select one to recommend to the sovereign for the appointment of Poet Laureate. Among those parodied are Eliot, Auden, MacNeice and Day Lewis, and some whose names are little remembered now, such as Humbert Wolfe. The poet whom the

Prime Minister selects is, judging from the parody of his work in this first chapter, Cecil Day Lewis. But his character as it is later developed in the novel is not at all like that poet. Day Lewis, indeed, seems to have been tipped by the establishment for many years before he was finally appointed Laureate. *The Death of the King's Canary* makes interesting reading if one knows the background, for it is quite fun identifying the poets. But I think many readers nowadays would find difficulty in doing this. The method used by Davenport and Dylan Thomas, in most cases, was to play on variations on the names of the poets; for example, George Barker appears as Albert Ponting. (King George VI had been generally known before his accession as Albert, and Ponting's was a large store next door to Barker's in Kensington High Street.) The three Sitwells appear as the Lacey family, but this family consists of two sisters and a brother. There was another occasion when Dylan Thomas was billed to appear at the English Club, along with Louis MacNeice. However, they never turned up, sending a telegram: "Unable to come. Both killed in the black-out."

Some years ago I was invited by the Dylan Thomas Society to give a lecture. I chose to talk on *The Death of the King's Canary*, identifying the characters in this *roman-à-clef*. I could do this with about 80 per cent of the names. I still have my notes on this (inside my copy of the book) and I gave a copy of them to the Dylan Thomas Society for its archive. When the society was disbanded I suggested that its archive be handed over to the University of Wales, but I do not know if this took place.

An old boy of Worcester College for the Blind, who was in his third year at St Catherine's Society (later incorporated as St Catherine's College), was John Wilson – now Sir John, and justly honoured for the excellent work he has done for the welfare of the blind, especially in the countries of the British Commonwealth. At Oxford he thought of himself as something of a poet, and he took me on two or three occasions to a poetry group, the Apollo Society, which met at St Catherine's Society. At one of these meetings an Indian student gave an interesting interpretation of Shelley's *Prometheus Unbound* in the light of Hindu mysticism; at another, a senior member of St Catherine's Society spoke about Housman, the most popular of English poets during the war years. On a third occasion members read their own work. I was much too shy to say that I had written verse or to offer to read any of it. A year or so previously the Apollo Society had organised, among its members, a competition for an original poem. Nevill Coghill had been invited to judge this competition and to set a subject for the prize poem. He had decided that they should write a poem in honour of St Catherine of Alexandria, the patron of St Catherine's Society. I do not recall the name of the author of the prize-winning poem which was read out on this occasion, but I was impressed with it, and there are, perhaps, a few actual reminiscences of it in a poem I was to write many years later on the same subject.

Another great extra-curricular activity was university journalism. Before the war there had been two Oxford undergraduate periodicals, *Isis* and *Cherwell*. The latter had been founded in the twenties by George Eddinger. I remember this writer and journalist lecturing at Bembridge on historical mysteries. The early *Cherwell* was the organ of the bright young things of the day, but during the Second World War, when there was strict paper rationing, *Isis* was unable to appear, and *Cherwell* more or less took its place, publishing news and articles of a more serious character, as well as regular book, theatre, film and music reviews.

I myself often wrote the theatrical reviews, covering the plays which were performed at the Oxford Playhouse. This theatre supported a repertory company which played popular successes of the day, but which also had enough integrity to do, fairly frequently, plays by Shakespeare, Ibsen or Chekhov. Its star actress was Pamela Brown. James Agate, on visiting Oxford, was so impressed by her acting that he subsidised, from his own pocket, a production of *Hedda Gabler*. This led to her London début. Although her career in theatre and films was successful, she did not quite reach the heights which Agate had expected for her. I also wrote music criticisms, which because of my background and my mother's profession I felt reasonably qualified to do, but it aroused some resentment from Arthur Jacobs, later to become an eminent musicologist and a biographer of Sullivan. Jacobs felt, I think, that I had no right to review concerts, for he, after all, was actually reading music.

At one point, for some reason, the word went forth that *Cherwell* ought to be more entertaining. Michael Meyer and Sidney Keyes, who were at that time the editors, decided to do something about it. Michael Meyer, then as now a keen aficionado of cricket, commissioned a series of reminiscences of Oxford cricket. I am sure these were fascinating to those who were interested in cricket – which did not include me. However, I contributed under a pseudonym, and in disguised handwriting, what purported to be the reminiscences of a surviving, almost centenarian, Victorian on the subject of Oxford cricket in his time. Sidney's contribution on this occasion was a parody of A. L. Rowse reviewing his own poems, signed A. L. Mouse. Rowse had a high opinion of his own poetry – largely flaccid imitations of D. H. Lawrence. To his credit, he had the considerable achievement of coming from a working-class background and reaching an All Souls' Fellowship. We may suppose that he identified with Lawrence, another working-class boy who made it to a university. Sidney's review concluded with the following sentence: "The cover design, representing a turning worm, executed by my friend, Lord Passwater, is alone worth the money." Rowse was not pleased at this review, though subsequently I heard he had said that he had forgiven Sidney. He never forgave the Warden of his college, John Sparrow, for certain remarks that the latter had published about him. I only met Rowse once, at a tea party given by the Provost of my college, Dr Hodgkin. Hodgkin once described Rowse's politics to me as a mixture of communism and All Soulsism.

Cherwell, under Sidney Keyes's literary editorship, frequently published poetry. There was also a cyclostyled magazine, *Platitude*, edited by Ian Bancroft, who later, as Sir Ian Bancroft, became head of the Civil Service. There were other poets in Oxford who did not belong either to our Queen's group or to the other group of poets, at St John's (including Philip Larkin and Kingsley Amis, of whom more later). There was, for example, Alan Ross, but we were unaware of his existence (he never published anything at this time). Another poet was John Waller, whom I got to know very well later on in London, but never met in his Oxford days. He was a flamboyant character, and on his twenty-first birthday gave a wild party in which he distributed privately printed copies of a longish poem he had written for the occasion, "The Confessions of Peter Pan". Waller founded during these war years his own literary magazine, *Kingdom Come*. Later on, under the editorship of Henry Treece and Stefan Schimanski (after Waller had entered the army), it was one of the little magazines which managed to survive through the war years.

It had long been customary, since before the war, for Basil Blackwell, the Oxford bookseller and publisher, to sponsor every year a small anthology of Oxford poetry. Many of the past volumes of these, published in the 1920s and 1930s, make interesting reading. One can find poems by authors who were to gain wide reputations, though not as poets – Graham Greene, for example, and Dorothy L. Sayers – as well as by politicians such as Tom Driberg. Because of the paper shortage Blackwell's could not undertake the publication of Oxford poetry during the war. Sidney Keyes and Michael Meyer were anxious to publish a selection of the work of those Oxford contemporaries whom they admired. They naturally approached T. S. Eliot at Faber and Faber, who replied that he was unable to publish the proposed volume but that Herbert Read was starting a poetry list for Routledge and might be interested. It appears that Eliot and Read worked very closely together, discussing with each other the poetry manuscripts submitted to their respective firms. In the event, the anthology, *Eight Oxford Poets*, was published by Routledge. This firm also published, in little 2s. 6d. and later 5s. books, the first volumes of Sidney Keyes, and of myself. Other poets in this series included the Welsh poet Keidrych Rhys and the Scottish poet Norman Mac-Caig. The poems in the latter volume, which are of a wildly surrealistic nature, Norman now repudiates absolutely. The series also included two women poets who ought to be better known. One was E. J. Scovell. She is an Oxford poet and is still producing excellent work, which is not, in my opinion, widely enough appreciated. The other woman poet was Morwenna Donnelly. This very beautiful Irish girl, very much part of the Protestant establishment, interested in horses and, I was told, a friend of the Queen, suddenly appeared in Rout-ledge's office with a long poem entitled "Beauty for Ashes", de-manding to show it to Herbert Read. He published it. It is, in my opinion, a remarkable piece of work, the record apparently of a genu-ine mystical experience. It now seems to be almost completely forgot-ten. Morwenna, whom I got to know later on in London, published a few other poems, and a not wholly successful novel. She married, and I do not know what her subsequent career has been. Sidney Keyes greatly admired her work and wrote to her. It was through this correspondence that I later came to meet her myself.

As for the *Eight Oxford Poets* volume itself, it contained work by Keith Douglas, who was up at Merton College during my first year, but whom neither Sidney Keyes nor I ever met. Sidney greatly admired the work of Douglas, who was, in my estimation, the best poet of the Second World War. This, I hope, is now generally recog-nised, though the growth of his reputation was delayed. This was partly due to the total, and typical, mismanagement of his publisher Tambimuttu. After Douglas's death, Tambimuttu had the manu-script of the poems in his hands but made no attempt to publish them. Eventually John Waller and G. S. Fraser, who had known Douglas when he was serving in the Middle East, came to Tambi-muttu, wrested the manuscript from him, and undertook to edit it for publication, without asking any fee for themselves. They found the manuscript in an appalling condition. Tambimuttu had scribbled emendations on the poems. Incidentally, I know of no instance where a poet's work has passed posthumously into the hands of another poet and the latter has not emended the work. This was done by Robert Bridges to the manuscripts of Hopkins, by Charlotte Brontë to those of her sister Emily, by Rossetti when he edited the manuscripts of Blake, and there are several other cases including that of Thomas Lovell Beddoes. In the Douglas file there were also poems which turned out to be not by Douglas at all, but the work of Kathleen Raine, whose publisher was also Tambimuttu. Douglas's poems, which appeared some years after the end of the war when the public was getting a little tired of war poetry, did not immediately get the attention they deserved, though eventually their excellence came to be generally accepted.

The remaining poets in this anthology were Gordon Swaine, Alan Shaw, Roy Porter, Drummond Allison, Michael Meyer, Sidney Keyes and myself. Michael Meyer will be a name familiar to the reader for his excellent work on Strindberg and Ibsen, and his autobiography *Not Prince Hamlet*. Of the remaining names (I shall say nothing about my own work) Gordon Swaine remains a mystery. Sidney found his poems in back numbers of *Cherwell* and liked them. None of us knew Swaine personally, or anything about him. I did see one or two poems of his in a periodical some ten or so years ago. Alan Shaw became a canon of Wakefield Cathedral. I met him when I was Gregory Fellow of Poetry at the University of Leeds. At this time he was about to resign his canonry and take up a teaching post in London. He was still writing poetry, though he never became well known as a poet. Roy Porter has remained a close friend of mine. Like Alan Shaw, he was studying for the Anglican ministry, and was to become Professor of Old Testament Studies at Exeter University and a canon of Exeter Cathedral. He is now retired. He regarded his poetry as an entirely private matter, and subsidiary to his religious vocation. It was Drummond, with his enormous charm, who wheedled him into showing it to us. Sidney thought very highly of it, as did I, and insisted on including it in *Eight Oxford Poets*. I do not know whether he still writes poetry. Along with several other Oxford poets of this period, including Drummond, he later published poetry with the rather notorious Fortune Press. How this came about I will explain later.

Sidney Keyes and Michael Meyer had originally intended to include a selection of poems by Paulina Brandt, a friend of Drummond Allison, but Herbert Read did not think they came up to the standard of the others. Personally, I wish the editors had stuck to their guns. Paulina Brandt's family were of German origin, though not refugees from Nazism. They had cousins in Germany, and Paulina told a story of how, before the war, one of these cousins had come to visit the family, and they had taken her to see Oxford. Brought up with the monstrous architecture of the Third Reich, she appeared to have been totally unimpressed by the architecture of Oxford. Her only comment, after drawing her finger across the wall of the Sheldonian Theatre and gazing at it disapprovingly, was to say: *"Schmutzig!"*

A curious diversion occurred when a young man called Anthony Brown, who had been a schoolfellow of Drummond Allison at Bishop's Stortford, appeared in Oxford. He had some talent for poetry and had become a protégé of John Lehmann. The latter, having evacuated himself from his London flat, was living in Portugal Place, Cambridge.

Lehmann had a scheme for founding a literary magazine which would be jointly produced from the two universities of Oxford and Cambridge, and Tony Brown had come to Oxford for the purpose of contacting Oxford poets. This resulted in a party of Oxford poets going up to Cambridge to meet some Cambridge poets, and to discuss the proposed magazine at a meeting in Lehmann's flat. Oxford was represented by Sidney Keyes, Drummond Allison and myself, and also by Francis King, who was to become a distinguished novelist but then thought of himself primarily as a poet. Tony Brown was an undergraduate at King's College, Cambridge, and guest rooms had been booked there for our party. The meeting with Lehmann and the Cambridge poets seemed to go quite well, though there was very little common ground between the representatives of the two universities, as the ethos of Oxford and that of Cambridge are subtly different. In literary matters one can best pinpoint this difference by remembering that the most distinguished teachers of English literature at this time at Cambridge were I. A. Richards and F. R. Leavis, while at Oxford they were C. S. Lewis and those others whom I have mentioned. I cannot recall the names of the Cambridge poets, except for one, Maurice James Craig, who achieved some reputation at the time. The proposed magazine eventually appeared under the title of Z, but it only ran to one number and made very little impact.

At the end of the evening it appeared that an error had been made in booking the guest rooms at King's, and that there was one too few. John Lehmann said that if that was the case one of our party would be welcome to spend the night on the window-seat of his flat, which would make quite a comfortable bed. In view of Lehmann's reputation, none of the Oxford party was particularly anxious to avail himself of this kind offer. Eventually I volunteered to do so, was welcomed by Lehmann, and did spend the night on the window-seat – in perfect respectability. Those who were accommodated in the King's College guest rooms were warned not to be alarmed if in the middle of the night they should suddenly find an old man standing beside their beds, saying these words: "I've brought you a copy of Landor's poems to read. Such a great poet, I think, and so neglected." This would be a former Master of King's, Sir John Shepherd, a charming old man who remained resident right down to the 1960s.

Another Oxford poet whom I was to get to know well was Michael Hamburger. He introduced himself to me by explaining that he suffered from melancholia. He had already made his first translation of the poems of the German poet Hölderlin when he was still a schoolboy at Westminster, after which he went up to Christ Church. This translation was to be published a few years later by Tambimuttu. Sidney Keyes shared Hamburger's enthusiasm for Hölderlin. Some previous translations had appeared before the war by Frederick Prokosch, a poet of Central European background who was fairly well known in England in the late 1930s, and who later emigrated to America. There were also free versions by David Gascoyne. Since Hölderlin became mad, and was to remain so for most of the rest of his life, he seemed to fit into the cult of madness in which the surrealists of the late thirties indulged. In fact, the poems of his youth are neo-classical, and belong to the same European movement as those of Leopardi, Chénier, Landor and others.

When Sidney Keyes became the literary editor of *Cherwell*, his rooms in Queen's became a centre for those who were interested in the writing of poetry in the university. There was, however, another group of poets, largely unknown to us, whose centre was St John's College. I now realise that there was some ill-feeling on their part regarding Sidney and his influence. The two most prominent members of this group were Kingsley Amis and Philip Larkin. I never met Kingsley Amis at this time, although he was being talked about among undergraduates. Many years later, when I was teaching at the College of St Mark and St John, Chelsea, I was introduced to a member of the staff whom I had not met before. He said: "I've seen you in the common room but I have never approached you because I was a friend of Kingsley Amis, and I have in my possession the manuscript of his first, unpublished, novel, the opening scene of which takes place at a party in your rooms in Queen's." As I have already said, I had never met Amis at Oxford. The implication seemed to be that he imagined that any amount of decadent things might have gone on at any party that I gave. In fact, I only gave one party and nothing sensational occurred at it. I was not, in fact, to meet Amis himself till years after this. His wife, Elizabeth Jane Howard, had been invited to be guest speaker at the annual lunch of the English Association, on whose council I sat, and Amis accompanied her. I found myself sitting next to him at the table and we seemed to get on very well.

The next occasion we met was at a party given by the poet Dannie Abse at his house in Hampstead. Before Amis arrived Dannie was showing his guests, with a certain pride, a fine antique chair which he had acquired. When Amis came, Dannie being out of the room, he sat down on the chair and immediately spilt his gin all over it. We all had to cover up and mop up the gin as hastily as possible. The scene was reminiscent of something from *Lucky Jim*. I would like to assure Dannie Abse, if he sees this, that there is no reason to think that his chair was seriously damaged. It was not until 1954, with the publication of *Lucky Jim*, that Kingsley Amis became widely known. I enjoy his novels, though I have always thought that *Lucky Jim* is about a very nice professor being very patient and kind to a very tiresome young man. A professor in a provincial university who invites members of his staff to musical weekends is really doing rather a good job. Unfortunately, Amis seems to show some ignorance of Elizabethan music when he describes one of these weekends. We are told that Jim Dixon is a tenor. When asked to take part in a madrigal, and being ashamed to confess that he cannot sing, he mimes his vocal part, and gets away with it for a time. In fact, in the music of the sixteenth century and earlier, the tenor holds the main part (that is why it is called a tenor). The fact that Jim Dixon was not singing would have been apparent immediately.

With Philip Larkin, on the other hand, I was quite well acquainted at Oxford, and we were on friendly terms. Sidney Keyes admired his poetry and published some of it in *Cherwell*. But when Sidney and Michael Meyer decided to publish *Eight Oxford Poets* Larkin was, after some consideration, excluded. One should remember that the poems which were so considered were even earlier than those that were to appear in his first volume, *The North Ship*. These latter are largely a pastiche of Yeats, and very unlike Larkin's mature style. I cannot wholly subscribe to the almost universal critical acclaim given to his poetry, which seems to me limited, both technically and in its range of ideas, and to display too much negativity. Larkin never forgave Sidney for this omission, and in later years spared no opportunity of attacking his memory. After Larkin and I had gone down, I corresponded with him for a time. We were both finding difficulty in getting a job. He compared this with one of those bicycle races in which the person who wins is the first person to fall off. His real ambition was to be a novelist. *Jill*, which obviously draws on his own experience as an undergraduate at St John's, mirrors the Oxford of that time rather well. Later on, in the 1950s, when I was Gregory Fellow of Poetry at Leeds University, the students wanted to include a review of a volume of my verse in their cyclostyled magazine, *Poetry and Audience*, and were kind enough to ask me for suggestions as to who might review it. I put forward Larkin's name, since I thought he was a friend, but not such a close friend as not to be able to give an objective review. The review, when it appeared in the magazine, shook me rather. It showed that he had, in many ways, a great deal less sympathy with my own attempts at verse than I had expected. He was, of course, perfectly honest in expressing his views, though it might have been more tactful to decline the invitation to review the poems.

We were not to meet again until the sixties, when Philip Larkin had a temporary fellowship at All Souls to give him the opportunity of studying in the Bodleian to compile his edition of *The Oxford Book of Modern Verse*. I met him at John and Eirian Wain's house at Wolvercote, where I was staying for the weekend; Wain being a good friend of both of us. Larkin was very cordial and expressed great pleasure that we had met again, but for my own part I was somewhat appalled at what he had become. He seemed incapable of opening his mouth without saying something malicious, mostly about academic or librarian colleagues. He also struck me as unnecessarily foul-mouthed. After lunch we all went out for a spin in the nearby countryside, Eirian Wain and her children travelling in the Wains' own family car, Wain and myself going in Larkin's. The dashboard of Larkin's car was fitted with a kind of shelf. Wain remarked on this rather unusual feature and how convenient it must be. Larkin replied that it was: "We" (he meant himself and his female companion) "find it useful for having meals in the car. I hate eating in the open air – wasps always come." Somehow this remark seemed to typify Larkin's timid and negative attitude to life. We returned to the house for tea, and afterwards Larkin said he must go or, rather, he said to Eirian Wain: "I must piss off now."

My last meeting with Philip Larkin was in 1977 when he received the honour of Companion of Literature from the Royal Society of Literature. This is an honour which that august body hands out from time to time to distinguished authors. I have never really understood what the phrase is supposed to mean. When the sovereign makes someone a Companion of Honour, this is presumably meant to suggest that the sovereign might actually like to have that person's company, and in the mediaeval courts I suppose this was often the case, but what on earth it means to be a Companion of Literature I cannot figure out. There was a reception to mark the ceremony. The same honour was being given to the veteran poet, Ruth Pitter, and to Sir Stephen Spender. In the seventies the Royal Society of Literature gave rather lavish receptions, using a bequest they had received from the late Marie Stopes. At these receptions quails' eggs and rather good wines were served. Naturally I went to congratulate each of the recipients. It so happened that the first I encountered was Ruth Pitter, then aged eighty. When I said how glad I was that she had received this honour, her reaction was: "Good, give us a kiss." I next encountered Stephen Spender, who was characteristically vague and bashful when I congratulated him. Then I went up to Philip Larkin. "Oh," he said, "how good of you to come" – very much *de haut en bas*. I could not help replying, rather in his own manner, "I only came here for the quails' eggs." But then, perhaps wickedly, I added: "I really came here because of Ruth Pitter who is an old friend of mine."

The recent publication of Philip Larkin's letters seems rather to have confirmed my unfavourable impression of him – at any rate in his later years. Larkin was, I believe, in many ways an unhappy man with a great fear of age and "the only end of age".

85

6

The Merton Circle

At the end of three years I took my final examination in English language and literature, and secured first-class honours. My tutor, Brett-Smith, in a letter congratulating me, did say, however, that it was a close-run thing. I was persuaded, partly by my mother, to remain for a fourth, postgraduate year to take a B.Litt. degree which could be converted later on into a doctorate. This move was not altogether the right one, for my fourth year was not productive of the promised degree, and the time was in some ways wasted.

I moved out of college to Mrs Taylor's rooms in the High Street, and I had to make a new circle of friends. Sidney Keyes and Drummond Allison had both gone into the army. Sidney was to be killed in North Africa in 1943, and Drummond in the Italian campaign of the following year. Sidney made a last visit to Oxford in the year of his death, and I accompanied him on a visit to his old school, Tonbridge, where I met Tom Staveley, who had been his form master and had played an important role in encouraging his early writings. After that we went on to London, where we were to attend a poetry reading in the crypt of the Ethical Church, Bayswater. London was covered with the black-out, and taxis and other transport were difficult to get. Consequently we ended up at the Ethical Church too late, just as people were leaving. A group of them included Tambimuttu and other literary figures. Sidney said to one man: "Are you Nicholas Moore?" "No," came the reply, "I'm Charles Wrey Gardiner." Wrey Gardiner refers to this incident in one of the volumes of his published journals, *The Dark Thorn*, and regrets that he had not invited Sidney to join the rest of them as they proceeded to the pub.

On this last leave, Sidney showed me, in typescript, his longest poem, "The Wilderness". This picture of a red rock desert is a semi-allegorical poem in which the poet imagines himself crossing a wilderness. He knew that he would probably soon be drafted to North Africa, and I suppose an imagined North African landscape did, to some extent, influence the imagery of the poem, but it has sometimes, quite wrongly, been mistaken for a war poem. Sidney was interested in symbolism, and had been reading at this time Maud Bodkin's *Archetypal Patterns in Poetry*, which attempted to apply the psychology of Carl Jung to poetry. Sidney saw the wilderness as representing a spiritual state of mind which Eliot had visited in *The Waste Land*, Chaucer in the desert which he describes at the beginning of the *House of Fame*, and George Darley in his long poem "Nepenthe".

One more poem was written after "The Wilderness", and this is his last extant writing. It is a poem on the Holy Grail, in which he sees it as flung down as a challenge from heaven. This poem shows the influence of Charles Williams, who was lecturing in Oxford at this time. Sidney had begun to be aware of Williams's work when he reviewed the latter's "Witchcraft" for *Cherwell*. He was immensely impressed with *The Descent of the Dove*, which its author described as the history of the operation of the Holy Spirit in the Church, especially that part of the work which deals with the early Church. The influence of this work is seen not only in Sidney's last poem on the Grail but also in that on Simon Magus. Sidney Keyes was eventually posted to North Africa. In letters written from there to various friends he seems to indicate that he was still writing poetry. If there were any such poems, they would have been removed from his pockets with other documents when he was taken prisoner by the Germans, and, presumably, destroyed.

After I had finished my final examinations at the end of the summer term of 1942, I found myself for the time unable to read any more English literature. I went into Blackwell's shop and bought a small anthology of Italian poetry designed for students. It was a sensibly compiled anthology, the editor opining that people generally took up the study of Italian, not at school, but when they were relatively mature. It therefore contained easy Italian poems, but chosen for adult readers, including specimens of the great Italian classics: Dante, Petrarch, Ariosto, Tasso and Leopardi. Leopardi was represented in this anthology only by "The Chorus of the Dead", taken from one of his prose dialogues. I had already come across Leopardi's prose works in a not very good translation. Later on, hunting about in the back room of Blackwell's shop, I found, by climbing a ladder, a series of classics, published, I think, by Routledge, which were each priced at three shillings. Among these was James Thomson's translation of Leopardi, edited posthumously by his publisher, Bertrand Dobell. This was a unique copy, for it was signed by Dobell as a presentation gift to Edward Garnett. Blackwell's staff had evidently overlooked this interesting volume, for it was priced at the same sum as all the others in this series.

"The Chorus of the Dead" was, however, the first poem of Leopardi that I was to read in the original. Frederick Ruysch, a contemporary of Leopardi, travelled with his collection of mummies, which he exhibited as a curiosity, all over Europe. In Leopardi's dialogue,

Ruysch is awakened in the middle of the night by hearing his mummies singing. They explain to him that once in a thousand years they are permitted to do this. He questions them about death. They can tell him nothing: "I was not conscious at the moment of my death," says one of them. I was so impressed with this dialogue that I returned to Blackwell's, bought a selection of Leopardi's verse and began to teach myself Italian in order to read it. If you already know French and Latin, as I did, and have some knowledge of the way words develop and take on different forms in related languages, it is not difficult to learn Italian. At the same time I began to study French verse, of which I had been given little knowledge in my schooldays, apart from the obvious fables from La Fontaine. I bought a copy of Roger Fry's edition of Mallarmé, in which the French text is accompanied by translations and commentary, and began to explore the French symbolists. I knew that they had been important for Sidney Keyes. Enid Starkie's life of Rimbaud and Norman Cameron's translations of that poet also opened up a new world to me.

I had begun to make a new circle of friends from outside my college. One of these friends was Philip Rawson, who had come up to Queen's. It was he who had recommended Roger Fry's edition of Mallarmé to me. As a youth of nineteen, he seemed to be immensely talented in a number of fields. He wrote verse, had a fine tenor voice, and was later accepted as a pupil by Janni Strasse who acted as *répétiteur* for Glyndebourne. Philip painted, and later developed his talents as a sculptor. Eventually he was to take a particular interest in Indian art and philosophy, and published important works on Tantric art. Our friendship, which began in my fourth year, has continued ever since, though we very rarely meet nowadays. But I hope that, if he reads this, he will realise the high regard I still hold him in. He had better read it because I have named him in my will, as he knows, as one of my literary executors.

One day two young men from Merton College called on me. These were Ronald Bright and William Bell. They had become committee members of a college literary society called the Bodley Club. Discovering that its rules – if it ever had any – had been lost, they were running it in a rather idiosyncratic way, and inviting odd and eccentric characters, of whom they took me to be one, to address it. Other such characters whom they had invited included Montague Summers, the writer on witchcraft, who disappointed them by giving a very dull paper on an obscure case of witchcraft in Jamaica in the eighteenth century. When I knew them, one of their guest speakers was Count Potocki of Montalk, a well-known London eccentric who claimed to be hereditary heir to the throne of Poland. Potocki was, in fact, a New Zealander, but he may well have been of Polish descent, and his claim may have been genuine, since he had extensive knowledge of genealogy. He was also certainly a little mad and had vaguely fascist connections. A well-known figure in some of the London pubs, he dressed in a long red robe, with a silver star on his breast, and his hair was worn in a pigtail tied with a bow. Besides the throne of Poland, he claimed other titles, including Grand Duke of Lithuania, Hospidar of Moldavia and High Priest of the Sun. This last, rather mysterious title was not one which he claimed to have inherited, but pointed to his occultist interests. At the time he came to Oxford he was sharing lodgings with an eccentric character whom he referred to as Harvey. They had met when they were both placing a wreath on the statue of Charles I at Charing Cross. Harvey's mother, Potocki casually remarked, worshipped trees.

Potocki was invited to address the Bodley Club on "the Grand Duchy of Lithuania and its ancient connection with this university". This latter demand was a bit of a conundrum for him to solve, but he did so, discovering that both Oxford and Lithuania were astrologically under the sign of Capricorn. He then launched into a perfectly serious talk about the Katyn atrocities, which had recently come to light. It is now generally admitted that the massacre of Polish officers which took place in a Lithuanian forest was undertaken on the orders of Stalin, and anybody who read with care the evidence that appeared in the English papers at the time would have suspected this, but the official Allied version during the war, of course, was that it had been perpetrated by the Germans. Nobody dared say anything that might offend the Russians. Potocki, with his fascist sympathies, claimed that it had been carried out by the Russians. He was sent to prison for a short time during the war for a black-out offence – he had refused to observe the air-raid regulations in his London flat, on the grounds that he had extra-territorial rights. Later on, I was occasionally to encounter him in Soho, or to pick up from friends of his, who hawked them, curious little books which he wrote and had privately printed. One of these, entitled *Social Climbers in Bloomsbury*, is full of violent attacks on his literary contemporaries who are very thinly disguised. Dylan Thomas, for example, appears as Andyl Thomas, and Ruthven Todd, a poet of some reputation in the 1940s, as Driven Mud. These little books, full of malice and reactionary and anti-Semitic senti-ments, are the work of a sick mind, but their vituperative power is at times impressive.

My own address to the Bodley Club led to a lasting friendship with a new circle at Merton. Ronald Bright was doing postgraduate work in physics and was working at the laboratory in North Oxford which was one of those engaged in research that led to the production of the atomic bomb. Once, when I was visiting Oxford, a year or so after I had gone down, I brought with me the manuscript of a poem I had written. Ronald arranged to have it typed for me by the laboratory typist. The next evening, after the pubs closed, we went up to collect the typescript. We were accompanied by Dickie James, a fellow Queensman who was reading chemistry. Having found the poem, Ronald showed us a rather elaborate Heath-Robinson-type structure which was erected on the table. "This is rather fun," he said. James casually picked up a notebook. "Oh," said he, "you're working on uranium isotopes, are you?" "My dear Dickie," said Ronald, "what are you finding out? Never mind, the enemy know all about it anyway." Later on, I mentioned this incident to Geoffrey Midgely, a friend and schoolfellow of Drummond Allison, who had a background in physics. "Oh," said Geoffrey, "I know what that's about. It's the biggest thing that science has ever been on to."

Most of this Merton circle were committed Anglo-Catholics, while I, during the whole of my undergraduate years at Oxford, had never, I think, either attended my college chapel or any of the numerous churches in Oxford. My Merton friends began to take me to church, especially to St Paul's, Walton Street. This church, built in the Byzantine style shortly after the Oxford Movement, and intended to serve the workers of the Clarendon Press, whose buildings are opposite it, had a flourishing congregation in those days. It is very sad that it has now become redundant. For a time it was run as an arts centre, and I remember reading there in the 1960s along with Mrs Pasternak Slater, who read some of her translations of the poems of her brother, Boris Pasternak. The building is now, I believe, a restaurant or a bar. Another leading Oxford Anglo-Catholic church was St Mary Magdalen. Its priest, Father Hack, was described as one of the last of the old-fashioned High Churchmen. There is a story about a guest who, having visited him, found that he had missed his last train out of Oxford. Father Hack naturally offered to put him up. The guest asked if Hack could possibly lend him some pyjamas. "No," said Hack. The guest persisted: "Are you quite sure you can't lend me some pyjamas?" "No," replied Hack. When the guest repeated the question a third time, Hack responded: "No – nightshirt."

We also, on one or two occasions, attended the small Russian Orthodox chapel at Cowley. I was immensely impressed by the Orthodox liturgy, and have been ever since. The priest, Father Nicholas Gibb, was an Englishman. He had been a tutor to the late Tsar's children, had been converted to the Russian Orthodox Church, and had taken orders in it.

Under the influence of Ronald Bright, I began a journey back to the church of my childhood which, in a sense, I had never wholly left. This was a long and slow process, involving some experiences of a personal nature which I am not prepared to go into, and I did not become a fully committed and regular churchgoer till almost ten years later. Ronald, after a year or so, became a convert to the Roman Catholic Church, later joining the Dominican Order. I think he was profoundly shocked when the atomic bomb, to the devising of which he had contributed research, was eventually exploded over Hiroshima. I visited him when he was studying at Fribourg in Switzerland during the 1950s, but we did not meet again till many years later. He had become well known as Father Lawrence Bright OP, and during the heady days of the sixties, with its revolutionary ferment, had come forward as a leading Catholic Marxist. This was a surprise to those of us who had known him in his early days, for his views as a student at Oxford had been, I would say, somewhat to the right of official Conservatism. This altered position was partly due, I believe, to his friendship with Terry Eagleton (now a Professor in English at Oxford) who had similar views. Ronald Bright was something of an embarrassment to his own order, who eventually laicised him and put him in charge of a bookshop. My own political stance has always been very far from Marxism, which I have always seen as an imprisoning and dogmatic philosophy based on false principles and inevitably leading to tyranny, but this difference in our political views did not at all affect our friendship in Ronald's later years. After his death, I read a poem as a tribute to him at his memorial service, which was held in London at St Etheldreda's church in Ely Place.

William Bell, a firm friend of Ronald Bright, was a very talented poet who might have achieved much, but for his early death at the age of twenty-four, after the war, in a mountaineering accident on the Matterhorn. He took the literary precepts of Ezra Pound very seriously, and had made a careful study of mediaeval English lyrics and Elizabethan madrigal verse. His poems were carefully crafted in elaborate rhyme stanzas. He was an Anglo-Catholic, though his family roots were in Ulster Protestantism. He boasted, in fact, that one of his ancestors had been the last man to be hanged in that province for sheep-stealing. He was also an adept at those poetic games I have already spoken of, such as bouts-rimés. He once composed a sonnet in which the octave rhymed on the word lobster and the sestet on the word oyster. When challenged by me, he converted the Thirty-Nine Articles of the Church of England into a ballade whose refrain was "and this is all the strictest Bishops need".

Eight Oxford Poets had given an outlet for at least some undergraduate poets. At that time Blackwell had not had enough paper available to publish their traditional anthology of Oxford poetry, but two years later William Bell did succeed in persuading them to publish such a volume, which he edited himself. Blackwell's, however, were unable to publish William's second collection. Perhaps unfortunately, William approached the Fortune Press in London which was run by R. A. Caton. Caton was an odd character. He was not exactly a vanity publisher, though it is said that Dylan Thomas was the only poet who ever got a contract out of him. Caton did not pay his authors, but on the other hand they did not pay him. They had to guarantee to buy a certain number of copies of their work which they were obliged to market themselves.

The Fortune Press also published what would now be considered very inoffensive homosexual works. These included an extremely sentimental novel entitled *Bachelors' Hall*; a translation of Huysmans's *A Rebours*, billed on the blurb as the work in which Dorian Gray delighted in Oscar Wilde's novel, which is indeed the case; and a novel called *Boy* by James Hanley. Hanley was known for his books about the merchant navy, but his publishers obviously refused to handle *Boy*, which in Caton's edition was more than once the subject of police prosecution. It has now been reprinted by Penguin with an introduction by Anthony Burgess. Its story is that of a cabin boy on board a merchant ship, who, in consequence of the treatment he receives from other members of the crew, contracts venereal disease and is finally suffocated in the steam locker. Sweating was, before the discovery of effective drugs for syphilis, the traditional way of curing this disease. There are references to it in Shakespeare.

Because of his tastes, Caton had a bad reputation, and his books were not generally reviewed in the literary journals, or stocked by booksellers unless specially requested. However, he did have a stock of paper. William Bell published with Caton not only a collection of Oxford verse but also a volume of his own poems. (William's later poems were edited, posthumously, by myself, and published by Faber and Faber.) No sooner had William's Fortune Press anthology appeared than Caton wrote to all the poets included in it and offered to publish their works. Rather inadvisedly, many of them fell for his offer, including Roy Porter, Gerard Irvine, Drummond Allison (whose volume appeared after his death), Philip Larkin and Kingsley Amis. This is reflected in the episode in *Lucky Jim* in which Jim Dixon discovers that the editor who has published an article of his, on which he has staked his future hopes for academic promotion, has no reputation whatever. Caton also published a reprint of Dylan Thomas's first book, *Eighteen Poems*, which had been published by David Archer at his small Parton Press. Archer was remarkable for his insight in publishing the first volumes of Dylan Thomas, W. S. Graham and David Gascoyne. The fourth poet whom he added to his list, the Indian poet Dom Moraes, although he won the Hawthornden Prize, did not, perhaps, fulfil his early promise as much as the other three have done. When, with *Deaths and Entrances* (published in 1946), Thomas's reputation began to stand very high, Caton reissued his edition of *Eighteen Poems* with a very large print run. I am afraid that many collectors may have been deceived into buying this, thinking it was the first edition. The first edition, that of the Parton Press, is very rare indeed.

My new set of friends at Merton brought new interests into my life. To some extent, I began to fritter away my time and behave more as, traditionally, an undergraduate in his first year or the beginning of his second year should behave. I had not really done this in my early years: I had been too much damaged by my school experience, and had difficulties in relating to other people. But I now lived a much more bohemian life, drinking almost every night in the pub with my new friends, and directing *The Revenger's Tragedy* for the Egglesfield Players. My academic work suffered. I was getting very little help from dry old David Nichol Smith, my supervisor. The subject of my proposed thesis was the philosophical background of James Thomson (the eighteenth-century Scottish author of *The Seasons*). Nichol Smith simply told me to go off and read more and more eighteenth-century philosophy, and declined to allow me to write anything for him to see. As I have already indicated, Nichol Smith must be greatly respected for his scholarship, but he was an uninspiring supervisor. He was rather proud of the fact that he had given W. H. Auden a third-class honours degree and would refer to this fact whenever Auden's name was mentioned.

Among other eccentric pursuits, my friends and I made an investigation of the Spiritualist Church in Oxford. This was not the first time I had engaged in student investigations of the spiritualist cult. When a schoolboy at Worcester, I had visited a spiritualist church with some of my friends, out of curiosity. There was a kind of religious service with hymns, after which a medium retailed spirit messages to members of the congregation. There was nothing in what she said to make one think, for a moment, that she was in touch with the supernatural, but she was a very good psychologist. "I've a message for that gentleman over there," she said to a man at the back of the hall. "A message from a lady, a lady who was very close to you. Do you know who she could be?" The man answered, "No. I'm not sure that I do." "A lady who was very close to you, a lady whom you deeply loved," continued the medium. "Well, there were several," came the reply. "Is your mother still alive?" she asked. The man was over sixty and she had a pretty good chance of his answering "No". "Indeed she is not," he replied. "Did you not love your mother, then?" said the medium. She had now got him where she wanted, and relayed from his departed mother a series of suitable moral platitudes.

During my second year at Oxford, a group of undergraduates from colleges other than my own also got interested in spiritualism and the paranormal, having read some of the works of Harry Price, a psychic investigator whose experiments acquired great notice, though later examination of his career has suggested that he was not always honest in his reports. These undergraduates decided to do some experiments off their own bat. There was a staircase in University College which was said to be haunted. Whoever occupied the room at the top of the staircase would hear footsteps coming up the stairs and pausing before his door. When the occupant of the room opened the door, there would be no one there. On one occasion, the room's occupant, believing that someone was playing a trick on him, opened the door as soon as he heard the footsteps at the bottom of the stairs. There was nobody there, but he still heard the footsteps coming up. It was decided, therefore, to perform a kind of séance in this room. The ghost was rumoured to be that of Obadiah Walker, a former Master of University College. Walker, who occupied this position in the reign of James II, is said to have had undeclared Roman Catholic sympathies and to have played a disastrous part in the events leading up to the Revolution of 1688 by the advice which he gave the King. One of the precipitating factors of that revolution was James II's losing the traditional loyalty to the Crown of the University of Oxford by forcing the Fellows of Magdalen to elect a Benedictine as their president. Walker is believed to have advised the King on this matter.

These undergraduate experimenters, having read that the medium was usually someone of a neurotic and unstable temperament, picked on one of their fellows, a medical student called David, who they felt probably fitted this bill. His prime interest was in the ballet, but his parents had insisted on his taking medicine with a view to a stable career. We therefore gathered in this room. Sidney Keyes and Drummond Allison were with me. The light was turned off and only the glow from an electric fire showed. David indulged in some deep breathing and eventually went off into what was presumed to be a trance. What he then said did not make a lot of sense, but was a little disturbing just for that reason. "It's coming towards me," he said. "It's red and burning, it's red and burning. It's like a wishbone. Now it's like a heart. Domine, Domine, Domine, Domine. It's going away now. It's blue and gracious. It's blue and gracious." I had a feeling at this time, and so did Sidney (as he assured me afterwards), that we might be in the presence of something paranormal, something rather threatening, and that the other members of the party would be unable to deal with any further phenomena which might appear, and it would be incumbent upon us to do so. Drummond said, characteristically: "All that entered my mind was that David must be ill, and I felt very sorry for him." It was not a pleasant experience and I would never undertake, frivolously, such an investigation again. It was rather curious that David kept on repeating the word "Domine". Maybe it was simply that it had liturgical associations for him, but it has to be remembered that Latin was still a spoken language in Oxford at the end of the seventeenth century and that Obadiah Walker, as Master of his college, would frequently have been addressed as "Domine".

Sidney Keyes, like Yeats whom he so much admired, had a great interest in the paranormal. He claimed to have experienced a sudden feeling of cold in the little passage within Queen's College which led from the college itself to Drawda Hall, which was an annexe of the college. Other people claimed to have experienced this feeling of cold, and it may have been due to the presence of an underground stream. Drawda Hall was, however, said to be haunted by the ghost of its founder, William of Drogheda, though I never met anyone who claimed to have encountered him. The ghost was said sometimes to have been observed, but you could not see his feet because the floor had been raised since his day and was now above the level of his ankles. Drawda Hall had been one of the old independent halls, which in mediaeval Oxford preceded the foundation of most of the colleges, and which were later subsumed into them.

Oxford is full of ghosts. I was once at a party in rooms in Merton College when there was a noise in the passage: "Oh, don't take any notice," said somebody, probably Ronald Bright. "It's only Duns Scotus." The great schoolman was said to have starved himself to death in the college, or possibly the report referred to excessive fasting on his part.

The same group who had investigated Obadiah Walker's rooms in University College decided to visit the Spiritualist Church at Oxford. Drummond Allison got into conversation with a respectable couple who were members of this congregation. The husband said that his wife had mediumistic powers, and was there anyone who had passed over whom Drummond would like to contact. Drummond said he would like to contact his brother who had been killed in the RAF not long before. These good people therefore invited Drummond, Sidney and myself to their house in one of the new housing estates on the outskirts of Oxford. Their front room had been prepared as a kind of spiritualist shrine, decorated with pictures supposedly painted by mediums in trance. It was obvious that these were good and simple people who had a genuine faith in spiritualism. The wife appeared to go into some kind of a trance and delivered a message to Drummond purporting to be from his brother, the effect of which was that

95

Drummond was not to worry for "I liveth for evermore". It was not very impressive. Drummond said, afterwards, that he really did not think his brother would say "I liveth".

In my fourth year I began to indulge in some of the more frivolous social pursuits of Oxford society. On Sunday afternoons there was an open invitation to Mary Stanley Smith's house in Ship Street. Large mugs of tea, which Mary called jorums, were served, and also dough-cake from Cooper and Boffin's shop in the Cornmarket. Mary was a delightful hostess who seemed to be a kind of relic of the 1920s. Much witty conversation went on at her at-homes. Peter Brook was a regular guest. Another was an elderly actor from the Playhouse called Terence Greenidge. He had suffered some kind of mental breakdown which made it difficult for him to learn his lines and he could therefore only take very small parts. He later appeared in one of these parts, with I think a single line, in the great Laurence Olivier film of *Richard III*. He had been a friend of Evelyn Waugh at Oxford in the 1920s, and told a story of how he and Waugh had jointly made a film in their undergraduate days. The hero was the Prince of Wales (later Edward VIII, and subsequently the Duke of Windsor), who also was an undergraduate at Oxford at about the same time. In this film the Prince is in danger of becoming a Catholic, which would lead to a constitutional crisis and his having to give up his claim to the throne. But he is saved from this fate by encountering a good girl of strong evangelical Protestant views. Many years later, I received a little anonymous pamphlet of poems celebrating the stations on the old Oxford to Bletchley line (this was pre-Beeching), written as by a Master of Arts of Oxford University. I am pretty certain that Terence Greenidge was the author of these poems.

Anybody who was anybody in Oxford society in those days used to go to Mary Stanley Smith's. The parties would terminate some time after five o'clock, when Mary would declare her intention of going to evensong at the Church of the Cowley Fathers – "the Dear Dads", as she called them. I remember on one occasion a girl asking Mary if she could lend her a veil, for some purpose. "Well, dear," said Mary, "you can have my first communion veil or else the one I wore when I played Francesca da Rimini." I had the happiness of meeting Mary Stanley Smith not long ago, after many years. Some of her friends were advising her to donate her visitors' book, full as it was of names that were later to become famous, to the Bodleian Library.

It was in my fourth year that I encountered Charles Williams, both the man and his thought. I attended a series of his lectures on Wordsworth in the Oxford English School. I am not sure that I understood them at the time, but in spite of his mannerisms and his rather harsh south-east English accent (incorrectly described by some of his biographers as cockney) one passage stands out vividly in my memory. He was dealing with the passage in *The Prelude* where Wordsworth dreams he encounters an Arab, who, in that strange way in which dreams can incorporate double identities, is also, somehow, Don Quixote. The Arab is holding a stone and a shell which are also one and the same. He tells the dreamer that a great disaster is about to overwhelm the world and it is the Arab's destiny to preserve these two precious objects: the stone, which represents mathematics (Wordsworth read mathematics at Cambridge), and the shell, which represents poetry. As the Arab is speaking, the dreamer sees a long line of destructive waters mustering themselves on the horizon. "One of the meanings of this passage," Williams said, "is this: if bombs were to fall on Oxford at this moment and Wordsworth were among us, he would grab the most important volume of poems he could find and endeavour to save it from the cataclysm. Being Wordsworth, he would probably seize his own poems – and," Williams added, "he would probably be right." In the course of these lectures Williams gave a clear exposition of his own theory of what he called "the romantic experience". This was a means whereby one could obtain through the affirmation of images an experience of transcendental reality. This experience could mediate itself in different ways. One was the religious experience, of which Williams proposed to say nothing further. The next was the experience of love for another human being, typified by Dante in *The Divine Comedy*. Then there was the experience of nature, explored by Wordsworth. The next category was the experience of the city: the vision of a just society. Williams cited "those who until recently we called our younger poets, but are now, of course, hopelessly middle-aged and old-fashioned" (he meant Auden and Spender and their circle) "who gave a partial vision of the unjust city". Finally, there was the vision of great art, of which Keats's "Ode on a Grecian Urn" was a partial exploration. If he had not been lecturing to English students, it is probable that he would have cited Virgil as exemplifying the image of the city rather than Auden and the others.

I also heard Charles Williams read to an undergraduate society from his Arthurian poems, both the already published cycle, *Taliessin through Logres*, and *The Region of the Summer Stars*, which he was then working on and which was to be published by Tambimuttu a few years later. Williams's reading was remarkable, in spite of a voice which some would have found unpleasant. Like many poets, he read in a kind of chant. The *Taliessin* poems are irregularly rhymed. Using a technique derived, probably, from Gerard Manley Hopkins, whose poems he had edited, Williams sometimes put the rhymes at the end of the lines and sometimes within the lines themselves. In his reading one noticed how his voice always seemed to return to the same note on the rhyme word. This, in spite of the fact that he was, as he told me, quite unmusical. His way of reading was, in some ways, liturgical. In his Oxford days he used to attend the St Cross church, slightly to the north of the old city boundary. He would join in the responses with enormous gusto and in a loud voice, but I never witnessed this myself.

Apart from the undergraduate literary societies, there were public poetry readings organised by a Mrs Dunne, in which she and her friends took part. William Bell, Ronald Bright and their friends rather wickedly cooked up a spoof poem called "Lusby Magna", which they read in parts at one of these meetings. The poem was a collage consisting of verses from the poems of a certain Mr Lusby (a retired tobacconist who had published his poems at his own expense, and which were available in Blackwell's), some passages from Bertrand Russell's *The Pursuit of Happiness* and others from a French prose translation of Hamlet ("O mon âme prophétique, mon oncle"). These were all scrambled up together. We gave it out that this was a work by a well-known contemporary poet who did not wish his identity to be revealed. It should be remembered that T. S. Eliot's *Four Quartets* were appearing in pamphlet form at this time. After the reading, I asked an undergraduate in the audience whether he thought it possible that "Lusby Magna" might be an unpublished work by Eliot. "No," came the reply, "I don't think it can be – it's too intellectual."

Another of Mrs Dunne's readings was organised for her by a young poet, Ian Davie of St John's, who later became a master at Ampleforth. He invited me to read, and also secured Charles Williams. This was the first opportunity I had of meeting this poet. The reading was preceded by a dinner at the George restaurant. I determined to draw Williams out, and, knowing his admiration for Milton and his championship of that great poet against the disparaging criticism of F. R. Leavis, deliberately embraced Leavis's view that Milton was oversonorous and that his perception of the musical value of language was at the expense of the intellectual content of his verse. Williams rose to this magnificently. He quoted to me the lines "Satst dove-like brooding on the vast abyss, / And madst it pregnant", which refer to the action of the Holy Spirit in creation. As he did so he thrust his short-sighted face into mine and pronounced the words in his strong accent. He explained, quite rightly, that it was impossible to pronounce this line loudly. It was the clotting effect of the consonants that gave it a whispering and mysterious effect.

Apart from Milton, Wordsworth and Shakespeare, Charles Williams's supreme model of poetic excellence was Dante. I think it was under the influence of Williams's lectures that I became interested in Dante, while still in my undergraduate years. I was reading him in a rather bad translation by Redwood Anderson, and Drummond Allison had given me the little pamphlet on *Religion and Love in Dante* by Williams which had just been published. But my real perception of Dante came in my fourth year. Sidney Keyes had an aunt, Miss Phyllis Keyes, who had become a Roman Catholic. For this reason her father and the rest of his strongly Protestant family severed relations with her. She was living in Oxford, and knew that Sidney was an undergraduate there, but had made no attempt to get in touch with him lest the family should accuse her of having designs upon his religious faith. However, they met by chance in Cooper and Boffin's teashop, and immediately struck up a warm friendship. When Sidney left to go into the army he particularly requested me to visit her, because he felt she needed company. I did so on several occasions, and a very remarkable, though eccentric, lady she was. It was she who gave me a copy of Charles Williams's major work on Dante, *The Figure of Beatrice*, which opened a whole new world, both of poetry and of religious belief, to me. She also lent me *The Wisdom of God*, a work by the Russian theologian, Sergei Bulgakov, a relative of the novelist of the same name. This book had a profound influence on me. It deals with the theology of Sophia, the feminine hypostasis of God, which is also to be identified with "Shekinah", a word translated as "glory" in the Authorised Version of the Old Testament, but, especially in cabbalistic thought, regarded as a kind of feminine hypostasis of God. Bulgakov's work was condemned by the Russian Orthodox Church of his time as not quite theologically correct. Nevertheless I found it valuable, and I think it should still be studied, especially by those theologians who wish to integrate Christianity with their feminism. It also inoculated me against the extravagant claims made for a goddess figure in Robert Graves's *The White Goddess*. Phyllis Keyes was a Dominican Tertiary, but many years later I learned that she had become a Quaker.

My first little volume – or rather pamphlet – of verse, a long poem in three parts entitled *Wounded Thammuz*, was published by Routledge during my fourth year, along with Sidney Keyes's first volume, *The Iron Laurel*. I had not submitted *Wounded Thammuz* to Routledge, but Sidney, on going up to London to discuss the publication of his own volume, showed my manuscript to Herbert Read, who immediately undertook to publish it. Routledge remained my publishers for some years after this until Read was succeeded by Geoffrey Grigson, who was less sympathetic to my work or, indeed, to the kind of poetry which Read had recommended to the firm. When Read started the poetry list for Routledge he found numerous manuscripts from unknown poets submitted for his consideration. One had a covering letter which said: "It may interest you to know that I have always used your firm's rhyming dictionary." "The rhymes," said Read, "were excellent."

I met Herbert Read on one or two occasions during this period. I shall always be grateful to him. I doubt if any other editor would have recommended for publication poetry in some ways so apart from the fashionable trends of the time as mine was. I found him an extremely kind and sympathetic editor, though I had little sympathy with either his mildly anarchistic political views or his continual championing of every new trend in art and literature, whether surrealism, constructivism, existentialism or whatever. In the second edition of one of his critical works he altered the sentence "I have always been a surrealist" to "I have always been an existentialist". I admired, however, the best of the rather unequal corpus of his poetry. "End of a War", included in Michael Roberts's *Faber Book of Modern Verse*, is, in my opinion, along with David Jones's *In Parenthesis*, the best poetic writing to come out of the First World War. Unlike the war poetry of Sassoon, Owen and the rest, neither of these works was published, and presumably not written, until the war had been over for more than a decade and a half. It is precisely this which gives them their value, for – in Wordsworth's phrase – they take their origin "from emotion recollected in tranquillity".

There were a number of movements in poetry in the 1940s which reacted against what some of us saw as the intellectualism of some of the poets of the 1930s and their commitment to the ideas of Sigmund Freud and Karl Marx. Marxism had begun to be discredited in the late thirties with the publication of works such as Arthur Koestler's *Darkness at Noon*, and in the 1940s the influence of Freud was giving way to that of Jung with his theory of the collective unconscious, and his rather more complex attitude to myth and symbol. Sidney Keyes and others of his contemporaries wanted to extend the language of poetry to incorporate wider meanings, rather than be limited to mere social comment. Perhaps the most influential works of the period in this field, in English, were the last poems of W. B. Yeats (1939), T. S. Eliot's *Four Quartets* (1935–42) and James Joyce's *Finnegans Wake* (1939). There sprang up in various centres in Britain a number of groups of poets who called themselves Neo-Romantics or Personalists. The Personalists' philosophy owed something to the thought of the Russian Orthodox philosopher, Nikolay Aleksandrovich Berdyayev, one of a number of Russian thinkers living in exile in Paris. Among these groups was the so-called "New Apocalypse" which started at St Andrew's University in 1939. The work of this movement was published in three anthologies: *The New Apocalypse* (1940), *The White*

Horseman (1941) and *The Crown and the Sickle* (1945). The Apocalyptics were a kind of English offshoot of surrealism. The theory behind their writings, and the reason for the name they adopted, seems to have been that the violent imagery of the biblical Apocalypse (the Book of Revelation) would become actual, and had so become, with the outbreak of a Second World War. The poets originally associated with the Apocalypse at St Andrew's seem to have been Nicholas Moore, G. S. Fraser and Tom Scott, but the acknowledged leaders of the movement became J. F. Hendry and Henry Treece. *The White Horseman* also included poems by Dylan Thomas and Vernon Watkins, but these poets repudiated their association with this group.

Nicholas Moore was the son of the Cambridge philosopher G. E. Moore, one of the ideologues of the Bloomsbury Group. I once met someone who had been an undergraduate at Cambridge during the First World War, when the university was almost empty. My friend attended lectures by G. E. Moore and was almost the only student in the class. Because of the shortage of domestic help, G. E. Moore had brought a perambulator with him which stood on the platform. In this perambulator was the infant Nicholas. G. E. Moore, perhaps wisely, did not send his son to Cambridge but to St Andrew's. Nicholas Moore was a very precocious poet. He had more poems in *The Threshold* (the anthology of schoolboys' poems) than anybody else, including a kind of motto poem for the entire collection. His style had already reached what, I suppose, we must call its maturity. Later he became one of the assistants in the publishing venture founded by Tambimuttu – PL Publications. Tambimuttu and the rest of his associates used to go for lunch to a pub at the corner of Oxford Street and Bond Street called the Hog in Pound. Moore did not drink and remained behind in the office. Whenever the others returned they found that at least six new poems had been written on the typewriter by him. One could not open a little magazine anywhere in the English-speaking world without finding several poems by Nicholas Moore. In my judgement they were of an extreme banality. The commonest metre was a five-stressed, four-line stanza, with the second and fourth lines rhyming. This is one of the easiest metres to write in English and one of the most boring. The content was a mixture of souped-up Freudianism and watered-down Marxism. I have declared privately, and must now do so publicly, my opinion that Nicholas Moore is just about the worst poet who has ever written in the English language, beside whom Martin Tupper was an intellectual giant and William McGonagall a metrical virtuoso. I note with some alarm that in recent years there have been signs of a resurgence of interest in his work. I once put my view of Moore to an American acquaintance and suggested that the worst line in Moore's whole work was one that read:

"Darling, I still remember the warmth of your legs." My American friend capped it with a line from Peter Vierek, the American poet and conservative philosopher. It was from a poem addressed to Hart Crane, who, it will be remembered, drowned himself by leaping overboard from a ship in the Gulf of Mexico: "Hey Hart, don't jump!" As Dr Johnson said, there is no setting the precedence between a louse and a flea. In their badness, these two quoted lines perhaps represent, respectively, a characteristically English sloppiness and a characteristically American brashness. I only once met Nicholas Moore and have nothing against him personally, though I did not find him very attractive. He had a peculiarly harsh voice, a kind of coarsened version of the Bloomsbury–Cambridge voice, characteristic of the circles he had been brought up in.

J. F. Hendry perhaps expressed more typically than any of the rest the initial programme of the Apocalyptics, but the one who was generally accepted as representing the group was Henry Treece. He was published by Faber, and Eliot continued for a long time to be his editor in spite of a generally hostile reaction to Treece's work by responsible critics. It was, perhaps, because Treece so totally did not resemble Eliot, or the poets whom Eliot had championed in the thirties – Auden, MacNeice, Spender, etc. – that Eliot remained for a long time loyal to him. Treece later gave up poetry and wrote adventure stories and historical novels intended mainly for boys. They are not without merit, though marked by rather extreme violence, not to say sadism.

I have treated the New Apocalypse here in some detail, not because of its intrinsic importance, but to correct an impression which still seems to be widespread among critics of modern poetry. It seems to be used as a term to cover most of the poetry that was written in the 1940s. In fact, the Apocalypse was quite a short-lived movement and not many of us took it seriously. I myself met no member of the group until long after it had ceased to be of any importance. G. S. Fraser continued to write poetry, though hardly of an Apocalyptic cast, until his death in 1980. He was a very amiable man and an industrious writer of criticism as well as verse. If he had a fault it was that he was too apt to jump on to bandwagons as they rolled past, and was too good-natured ever really to criticise anyone strongly. Norman MacCaig also contributed some poems to *The White Horseman*. They were more formless and more unintelligible than the others. He has now become one of the best poets in Britain and I apologise for reminding him of these youthful indiscretions. Tom Scott, who contributed to *The White Horseman* some poems which seemed to be obsessed with the fear of drowning, is still with us. He became strongly influenced, at one point, by the psychology of Jung, and later turned to writing in Lallans – the literary Scottish language championed by Hugh MacDiarmid and his school. Scott's best work, in my opinion, is his translation of François Villon into Lallans. The use of Lallans works extremely well. One should remember that, when Villon was writing in France, Scottish vernacular literature was at its height. He was an exact contemporary of William Dunbar who died in 1513, and the two poets might even have met when Dunbar was part of a Scottish embassy to the French court. The later Scottish school of Burns and others, as MacDiarmid always maintained, is almost provincial compared with Dunbar and his contemporaries. MacDiarmid used to get furious if anybody said he was the greatest Scottish poet since Burns. "No," he would say, "since Dunbar."

On more than one occasion reviewers have actually described my own work as if I had belonged to the New Apocalypse. This has elicited from me violent letters of protest to editors. One reviewer, indeed, repeated this libel when reviewing my collected poems, in the introduction to which I had specifically repudiated any connection with the Apocalyptics whatever. This reviewer must have been of the same opinion as the Reverend Sydney Smith, who said he never read the books he reviewed as it tended to bias his judgement.

During my fourth year at Oxford, I had the melancholy duty of correcting the proofs of Sidney Keyes's second volume, *The Cruel Solstice*, and of Drummond Allison's *The Yellow Night*, since both poets were dead. I had been appointed Sidney's literary executor – along with Michael Meyer and Herbert Read – by the terms of Sidney's will, and the same function devolved on me as far as Drummond's poems were concerned. Meantime, my academic work on James Thomson was not going well. Before submitting my B.Litt. thesis I had to pass a necessary examination in palaeography, bibliography and the resources of the Bodleian Library. These subjects did not engage me and I wasted more and more of my time, or at least, if it was not wasted, it was spent in acquiring non-academic knowledge. Furthermore, I underwent an emotional crisis which brought me at times very close to the bounds of rationality. There were possibilities that I might have taken other than pursuing the work for my B.Litt. Nichol Smith informed me that the Swedish University of Lund – Sweden being a neutral country – required a lecturer in English, and suggested that I might like to apply for this post. I was, in fact, interviewed for it in London by the British Council. I cannot quite remember whether I was turned down or whether I decided – it now seems to me a wrong decision – that I had better go on working on my thesis. At the end of my fourth year, I failed to satisfy the examiners on bibliography, etc. In my final interview with the Provost and Fellows of Queen's, I was told that if I wanted to pursue my postgraduate studies I would have to be rusticated for a time. But I preferred to leave with these studies incomplete. "Professor Nichol Smith", said Provost Hodgkin, "does not think you are fitted to be a scholar." Nichol Smith was, I believe, entirely right. I have an enormous magpie-like appetite for acquiring knowledge of all kinds and for fitting together and relating facts in new ways – my interests range over many subjects besides literature – but the patient dedication to the pursuit of a single subject and the careful checking of research, and preparation of references, is not for me.

So it was that I now returned to New Milton, with no postgraduate degree under my belt, and endeavoured to find a job. This was a difficult and lonely period in my life. I had made many friends at Oxford and continued to correspond with Philip Larkin, Ian Davie, Philip Rawson, Ronald Bright and William Bell, who was now in the navy. In one of Larkin's letters he told me that he had given up writing poetry: "it is not my métier." His ambition at this time was to become a novelist, and he published his first novel, *Jill*, in 1946, followed by *A Girl in Winter* in 1947. Many years later, I reminded him in a letter that he had said that his true vocation was as a novelist. His reply was that the trouble was that people would publish his poems and would not publish his novels.

The only war work which I ever did was to act as a telephonist at the local fire station in New Milton. I waited, with several other men, in case an alarm call was telephoned through, reporting an air raid on Southampton. This, in fact, never happened during my time, though a bomb from a stray German plane did fall on New Milton, causing a few deaths and considerable damage. It fell at about six o'clock on a summer evening when shops were closing and many people were gathered in the High Street, greeting each other and preparing to go home. I think the bomb had probably been aimed at the impressive Gothic water-tower which stood behind the High Street, and which had been rather ineffectually camouflaged by being wrapped in green cloth. The local council wrote and complained about it to the War Office, who, according to the local paper, wrote back and promised it would not occur again.

I was totally exempt from military service, but in applying for posts I had to explain my weakness of eyesight, and this told against me. I applied for various schoolmastering jobs in different parts of England. This involved long journeys in badly heated and ill-lighted railway carriages to see various headmasters who interviewed me and always turned me down. These interviews did, however, give me some strange insights into the English public school system. I was put up in his guest room by one headmaster, who had evidently been nicknamed "The Crocodile" by the boys. His whole house seemed to be entirely furnished with bric-à-brac in the form of crocodiles: ashtrays, flower vases, and so on. They did not, however, seem to have penetrated as far as the guest room, where all I had for my solace during the night was a copy of the scriptures and a book on how to teach the facts of life to boys.

I usually managed to fix the journeys to these interviews so that I could travel back by a route that included Oxford where I could stay overnight with Ronald Bright and recontact some of my old friends. I was still continuing to make up the defects in my education, and spent many of these long train journeys trying to read Proust in the Scott Moncrieff translation. I never, in fact, got any further than halfway through the first volume, and I cannot say that it gripped my attention at all. Possibly I was too young for Proust, though I was then in my middle twenties, or perhaps it gets more interesting as it goes on. It is not the length of the novel that daunts me; one of my greatest reading experiences, undertaken fairly recently, was to plough right through Samuel Richardson's *Clarissa*. This was an absolute delight to me. I am convinced that it is not only the longest but also the greatest novel in the English language, and the only real tragedy written in the eighteenth century.

My poem, *Wounded Thammuz*, was written in a curious mixture of styles, involving echoes of eighteenth-century poetry, which many of the critics took for echoes of Milton. The subject, deriving to some extent from my reading of Frazer's *The Golden Bough*, was the seasonal death and resurrection of the Babylonian god Thammuz (identical with the Greek Adonis, supposed to have been killed by a wild boar). I incorporated into it my intuition of death and resurrection as a universal cosmic pattern, historically realised in the death and resurrection of Christ. The poem had a mixed reception, but was not unnoticed. It was broadcast by the BBC, the producer being Edward Sackville-West, for whom Tony Brown was now working as an assistant. I did not, myself, read *Wounded Thammuz*. As it was a longish poem, it was divided between three readers. Two of these were actors, and the third was Cecil Day Lewis. The latter had evidently been trained as a speaker, and, in fact, often read verse on the same platform as his actress wife Jill Balcon. In those days it was not usual for poets to be invited to read their own work on the air. The received opinion among many people, dating from the early years of this century, was that poets were never good readers of their own work and that it should always be read by actors. Many older people who had heard Yeats read said this of him, but when the BBC released recordings, which they had discovered in the archives, of Yeats reading his works, this seemed very much to alter the received opinion. I do, in fact, remember hearing Yeats reading on the radio, not long before his death. It is strange that even then, when he had written some of his finest work, he was still only expected to read "The Lake Isle of Innisfree", "The Fiddler of Dooney" and "The Song of Wandering Aengus" – all early poems. It was Dylan Thomas, I think, who really brought about the change in policy which took place during the 1950s. Thomas, too, had had some professional training in speaking. His father had arranged for him to have elocution lessons, wishing "to iron the Welshness out of his voice". Day Lewis's reading was too elocutionary for my taste, and during the rehearsal of *Wounded Thammuz* I found myself making, with some embarrassment, more criticisms of his interpretation than of that of any of the others, especially where the pointing of the ends of lines was concerned. In my opinion, and I think in that of most poets, the ends of the lines should always be marked. If the sense runs on, the voice should be slightly raised in pitch, and the word lengthened. I have to say that Day Lewis was extremely courteous and perfectly amenable to my suggestions.

A year later Routledge followed the publication of *Wounded Thammuz* by producing another little volume of my poems, entitled *Beauty and the Beast*. I sent a copy of this book to Charles Williams, expressing my admiration for him. He wrote back a kind letter of acknowledgement in which he mentioned one of the poems which he particularly looked forward to reading. This was one which I had written in my last year at Oxford entitled "An Heroic Epistle". In the form of a monologue, it deals with the ambiguous and possibly platonic relationship between William Congreve, the playwright, and Anne Bracegirdle, who acted the principal parts in his plays, including that of Millamant. In this poem I endeavoured to explore the relationship of creative genius and personal love. I am still not ashamed of this poem, written when I was only twenty-three, and which was strongly influenced by Williams's ideas, without being in any way an imitation of his style. I like to think that he had already glanced at the poem and wished to read it again more carefully. He concluded his letter by saying that if I were ever in Oxford he would be glad if I would telephone him and have tea with him at his Oxford University Press office.

On the next occasion that I had the opportunity of visiting Oxford, I gladly availed myself of this invitation. Charles Williams received me hospitably, and I spent two or three hours having a memorable conversation with him, in which we touched upon several subjects of mutual interest. Herbert Read's book on Wordsworth, which had appeared a few years earlier, came up in discussion. Williams disliked

Read's thesis, which was based on the discovery of the facts (now well known, but then only recently come to light) of Wordsworth's affair, while he was in France, with Annette Vallon, on whom he fathered an illegitimate daughter. Read's approach was semi-psychoanalytical. He identified Wordsworth's supposed desertion of Annette with his defection from the cause of the French Revolution. The guilt engendered by this was supposed to account for the later decline of Wordsworth's poetry. I now think that this argument is total nonsense: for one thing, Annette herself came from a royalist family; for another, Wordsworth made contact with her and her daughter as soon as he was able to revisit France after the Peace of Amiens. The facts of his daughter's existence were perfectly well known to his sister, Dorothy, and other members of his family. It was the Victorian biographers who suppressed the information. Williams said that we did not know enough about the facts to justify this psychoanalytical interpretation. "For all we know," he said, "when, so to speak, Wordsworth got into the coach going home, he said: 'Thank God I've got away from that woman.'" He also talked about Herbert Read's essay, "A Defence of Shelley". Read's approach here was again based on Freudian theories. He claimed that Shelley was a suppressed homosexual (that was a phrase often bandied about in those days. I have no idea what it is supposed to mean. Every homo-sexual surely, by definition, is a suppressed heterosexual) and that this somehow explained his intense sympathy and identification with humanity at large, and his espousing of the cause of the poor and the rejected. There are a whole lot of non sequiturs in this argument, and how it was supposed to defend Shelley against the strictures of his hostile critics – T. S. Eliot and F. R. Leavis in particular – on his actual use of language and imagery is not clear at all. Williams also thought that it was a very odd defence of Shelley. Of homosexuals, he said we ought to be very kind to such people. Williams illustrated his own use of psychology to interpret the work of writers by referring to some work he was at that time engaged in on St Augustine. There is an emphasis on the doctrine of predestination in St Augustine's theology. We also know, as Williams explained, that the saint had a dominant mother in St Monica. This is a fact which can clearly be demonstrated from the *Confessions*. Therefore, Williams said, having established this, we might say, in a footnote, that, although his relation to his mother was not the source of his intuition of the doctrine of predestination, it might have made it more real to him.

We discussed other points of English poetry. I said that I admired Byron's *Manfred*, although it is a very imperfect work. The point about this poem is that we never find out exactly what crime Manfred has committed, and why he is continually haunted by guilt. Some modern interpretations have held that Byron was referring cryptically to his incest with his half-sister, Augusta Leigh, though this may not be absolutely proven. For me, this theme of a source of guilt which is never named was impressive, seeming to prefigure Franz Kafka's *The Trial*, or the existentialists, who were now being widely read and publicised in England (for example, Sartre's play *Les Mouches*). Williams would have nothing of this. If only Byron would stop and tell us exactly what Manfred has done, he said. Rising from his seat at his desk he quite spontaneously acted out the end of the final scene of the play with dramatic gesture, and in his strong south-eastern accent: "Back, ye baffled fiends! – / The hand of death is on me – but not yours! / . . . Old man! it is not difficult to die" – the last words being, of course, addressed to the abbot in whose monastery Manfred has found refuge. Williams considered the final lines of the scene, spoken by the abbot, a dreadful anticlimax after that. The abbot says: "He's gone – his soul hath ta'en its earthless flight; / Whither? I dread to think – but he is gone."

Charles Williams was rather severe on Shelley. In Williams's remarkable anthology, *The New Book of English Verse*, which he edited along with Lord David Cecil, de Selincourt and some other scholars, but which very much bears his own stamp, he quotes Keats's advice to Shelley: "to load every rift with ore". The trouble about Shelley, Williams goes on, is that some people might say that he is all rift. This general depreciation of Shelley Williams seemed to share with critics very different from himself, not only Eliot and Leavis, but Aldous Huxley, who had unpleasantly described Shelley as a "little white slug staining the radiance of eternity". Williams and I spoke of Shelley's drama *The Cenci*. Williams said that Shelley seemed to be saying: "Here are a lot of cardinals and priests, and people like that, condemning a poor young girl to death because she has murdered her father. Isn't that what you'd expect of the Catholic Church?"

I asked Williams about Coventry Patmore, whose ideas somewhat resembled his own, and for whom at that time I had an enormous admiration. I wondered if Williams thought, as I then did, that Patmore was really the greatest of the Victorian poets. He would not go all the way with me, but said that if he were to name two or three of the greatest Victorian poets Coventry Patmore would certainly be included.

We spoke of women poets. I expressed a distaste for the verse of Elizabeth Barrett Browning, with its flamboyant rhetoric and imagery, adding that I preferred the poetry of Christina Rossetti. Interestingly, Williams did not agree with me. He said he would rather have Mrs Browning with all her faults than Christina on her desert island. Christina's desert island was, of course, her restrictive

Anglican faith – in essentials the same faith as that of Williams himself – which thwarted her emotionally. She turned down two suitors for marriage on grounds of the divergence of their religious beliefs. One was an agnostic, the other became a Roman Catholic and then returned to Anglicanism. Christina rejected the latter twice, first because of the diversity of their faiths, secondly because he was unstable.

I asked him about the poetry of Lascelles Abercrombie, a poet usually classed among the so-called Georgians. Abercrombie has been dismissed by the modernists as of no importance. There is even a story that Ezra Pound challenged him to a duel. In reply Abercrombie said that, as the challenged party, he had the right to choose their weapons, and that they should meet in Hyde Park and throw unsold copies of their own books at each other. Roy Porter had contributed an essay to *Cherwell* making out a claim for Abercrombie, and he had become something of a cult figure in our circle. I still think he is a neglected poet, but he cannot readily be anthologised because he wrote long verse dramas, dramatic monologues and narrative poems. Williams admired him, and when I said that I thought that Abercrombie was underrated he agreed with me but said that he and Sir Humphrey Milford had put Abercrombie's *Collected Poems* in the Press's "Oxford Standard Authors" series and the volume had not sold.

In talking about Christian beliefs Williams told me that Stephen Spender had published an article in the *New Statesman* in which he had stated that modern science made it impossible to believe in the dogmas of Christianity. Williams had written to the *New Statesman* asking what scientific discovery of the last hundred years had made it more difficult to believe in these dogmas than it had ever been. "Nobody", he said, "ever maintained that it was likely that a virgin would have a baby or that a dead man would rise from his tomb." The *New Statesman* apparently did not see the point and did not publish the letter.

At the end of our talk Williams kindly presented me with a copy of his drama, *A Myth of Shakespeare*, and said with obvious sincerity that he hoped that I would call on him again. It was some time before I had another opportunity to visit Oxford. This was in 1945, when I was working in London as a schoolmaster. I came up on a visit to Oxford and was met by Ronald Bright. I told him that I must ring up Charles Williams as soon as possible and arrange to meet him. "Oh, haven't you heard?" replied Ronald. "He died yesterday."

I tried to earn a little money, while living in New Milton in my mother's house and endeavouring to find a job, by doing some private coaching to local children. One of my pupils was a sixteen-year-old girl living in Boscombe, a suburb of Bournemouth, whose mother was Irish, and a nurse by profession. I taught the girl English literature, history and some other subjects. While doing this work, I had a curious experience, which I have never been quite able to explain. On one occasion, as the lesson was coming to an end, my pupil's mother came into the room and said that she wanted a word with me. Apparently, a young man had come to the door and told her that he had followed me, and that he worked for a private detective agency in Bournemouth. He added that his father was the head of this agency. I was a most reprehensible person, an agent of the Germans who posed as a private tutor, and I had already corrupted several of my pupils. This young man was obviously a paranoiac, and why he had fixed on me and followed me in this way I cannot tell. My pupil's mother's first reaction was an Irish one – she said to me that I ought to be given a chance to get away. But when I had convinced her that I was not guilty of any of these wicked actions, she became alarmed that an obvious madman might do me some injury on my way from her house to the station, where I was to catch the train back to New Milton. To put her mind at rest, I told her to ring the police, and ask a policeman to escort me to the station. I found that the detective agency, for which the young man declared that he worked, did, in fact, exist. So I went to call on them and told them the story. The agency seemed to be largely staffed by retired policemen who probably did such boring duties as guarding the presents at posh wedding receptions, or following men and women whose spouses wanted to find grounds for divorce. My story was received without comment, and, realising that I was being thought of as the paranoiac, I withdrew.

At least these vacant months in New Milton gave me leisure to get on with my writing. I continued to work on poems, including "The Divided Ways", an elegy on the death of Sidney Keyes, which was to be the title poem of my next collection. Mr Bradnock, the head-master of Worcester College for the Blind, who continued to take an interest in me, had written to the only friend he had in the literary world of London to see if anything could be done for me. This friend was the novelist Charles Morgan, who also wrote a column called "Menander's Mirror" in the *Times Literary Supplement*. Later on I was to meet Charles Morgan and have dinner with him. He was kind and sympathetic to me. The trouble was he was on the way out. He had had a high reputation in the thirties, for his rather pretentious pseudo-Platonic novels, and now had become almost a whipping-boy for the more progressive critics. In consequence he was not really able to do anything for me at all, though I enjoyed his conversation. He had a great reputation in France, and when that country was liberated was invited to recite an ode of his own composition, written especially for the occasion, from the stage of the Comédie Française. About this time, I met a young French writer who was visiting England for the first time. He had called on Charles Morgan, whom the French regarded as very pure, and had been rather shocked that the novelist's conversation, which the latter obviously thought suitable for a French guest, was all about sexual techniques.

However, at this juncture, while I was still living in New Milton, Charles Morgan, by way of Bradnock, gave me some good advice. This was that I should set to work to write a solid book in prose which might establish my reputation. Accordingly, I embarked on my only full-length critical book, *The Darkling Plain*. Sidney Keyes had had a particular admiration for certain minor poets who occupy a curious little trough between the end of the high Romantic movement with the death of Keats, Shelley and Byron, and the beginning of high Victorian poetry, perhaps with Tennyson's 1848 volume. These poets were Thomas Lovell Beddoes, George Darley and John Clare. Sidney also admired the serious poems of Thomas Hood, who is better known for his light and humorous verse. These might be regarded as a generation of English *poètes maudits*. Darley was prevented from mixing in literary circles by the social handicap of a bad stammer. Beddoes spent much of his time in Germany, where he was involved in the underground revolutionary movements of the period. His life ended in suicide. Hood was plagued by chronic poverty and consumption. John Clare, the Northamptonshire peasant, died mad confined to an asylum. Beddoes was obsessed with images of death, as was his almost exact contemporary Edgar Allan Poe. Poe is, whether you like it or not, a major figure in American literature, and his discovery by Baudelaire and the French symbolists made him a major influence on continental literature. Poe has this importance partly because he was an American. Beddoes, who, by any objective standards, was much his superior as a poet, is simply a minor and marginal figure in English literature, as, to some extent, are the other three of the group, though John Clare's reputation has steadily risen in recent years. Sidney Keyes had introduced me to the work of these poets and had said that somebody should write about them. When I undertook the critical work which Charles Morgan's advice had prompted, I began with two chapters on these poets. I almost felt I was fulfilling a mission delegated to me by my dead friend. An article based on the chapter in my book which dealt with Beddoes, Darley and Hood was published by John Lehmann in the Penguin "New Writing", and this was followed up by an article, which has never been reprinted, on George Crabbe. *The Darkling Plain* became an overall study of poetry down to the end of the nineteenth century. I had missed out on the Victorians at Oxford as they were not on the syllabus. In *The Darkling Plain*, which was to be published some years after the war, I tried to take an oblique look at the Victorian age, stressing those elements in it which were at odds with its dominant compromise. There are such elements in the work of its two greatest poets, Tennyson and Browning, and I wrote a chapter on these as well, but, finding that I had not, then, sufficient knowledge to deal with them adequately, I deleted the chapter.

Other chapters dealt with Victorian poetry of doubt and despair, that of Matthew Arnold, whose poem "Dover Beach" furnished the title of my book, Arthur Hugh Clough and James Thomson (BV). Another chapter treated the Roman Catholic poets, Coventry Patmore and Gerard Manley Hopkins. I also tried to deal with the Pre-Raphaelites and the Aesthetic Movement, and finished with a section on W. B. Yeats. *The Darkling Plain*, from the scholarly point of view, was an extraordinarily unprofessional book. I had not read much modern criticism. I had skimmed through the works of F. R. Leavis and I. A. Richards, but had very little idea of how to deal with a text. I was deeply influenced by a critic who was later to become well known as a television personality. This was Jacob Bronowski, a mathematician and a scientist. In his later years he strongly emphasised the essential unity of poetry and science, but the book which impressed me in my undergraduate days was his early and I think very much neglected work, *The Poet's Defence*. In this book Bronowski sees the history of English poetry since the Elizabethan age of Philip Sidney as a steady decline. The poets abandoned the Platonic sense that they were dealing with a real world of ideas, for a psychological view of poetry (in Coleridge and Shelley) which led on to the sensationalism of Swinburne, Housman and Yeats. Bronowski's next work was *The Man without a Mask*, a study of Blake for which he became much better known, but it is, in my opinion, his worst book, influenced by a Marxist interpretation of Blake, quite inappropriate to that poet. When I glance again at *The Darkling Plain*, I am surprised at how much of it I still agree with, despite all the shortcomings.

The other project I undertook during this year in New Milton was my translation of a selection of Leopardi's poems. As I have already indicated, I learnt Italian as I went along. It was rather cheeky of me under these circumstances (and I had never been to Italy) to undertake the translation of a major Italian author. The translations were eventually to be published by John Lehmann in 1946. Later, in 1966, the Oxford University Press undertook a second edition to which I added the translation of one poem (the "Bruto Minore", in English "The Younger Brutus") that had not been included in the 1946 collection. The volume also contained a selection of Leopardi's prose works, made by his biographer, Iris Origo. This distinguished interpreter of Italian culture was a member of the great Liberal intellectual family of the Lubbocks, but married to an Italian marquis. She undertook to vet my translations, and it was quite surprising that there were only one or two phrases that needed to be altered.

Charles Williams had told me he regarded Leopardi as a poet who made positive the negative. A contemporary of the Romantics, Leopardi (1798–1837) was himself a classicist. There was, in fact, a classical movement in European literature at this time which ran parallel with the Romantic movement. It was not a continuation of the Augustanism of the eighteenth century, but influenced by an improvement in Greek studies and Greek archaeology, and also by the discovery of Pompeii. Its major representatives are Leopardi, Hölderlin, Chénier and, in England, Walter Savage Landor. There are, of course, elements of this classicism in the work of other poets of the period – in Goethe and Schiller, in Wordsworth, Shelley and Keats – but the pure neo-classicism of the late eighteenth and early nineteenth centuries is more closely related to some of the art of the period, that of David or Ingres, for example.

Leopardi came from a family of poor aristocrats of the Romagna. His father was weak and impractical, and the Pope, his secular overlord, had stripped him of the control of his own estates, and handed them over to his wife. This lady, Leopardi's mother, was a formidable, pious Catholic who kept the family economy on a tight rein. She combined this with a rigidly puritanical regime, ostentatiously thanking the Almighty when any of her numerous children died. It has been said that compared with life in the Casa Leopardi, that of Haworth Parsonage was one reckless round of gaiety. This background, combined with his chronic ill health – he suffered from a number of congenital diseases, including weak eyesight – led Leopardi to a total repudiation of religious faith. One of the greatest classical scholars of his time, he found himself for most of his life trapped in the dull little provincial town of Recanati, continually longing to get to Rome or to Florence, where intellectual life existed. Eventually he did achieve this, only to be disillusioned by the frivolity and dilettantism of Italian society. To compare small things with great, I myself felt I was stuck in the dull town of New Milton in rather the same way. Leopardi's last poem, written more or less on his deathbed, "Il trammonto della luna" ("The Setting of the Moon"), is an uncompromising statement of his total despair. All positive human values – beauty, love, virtue itself – are, for Leopardi, as illusory as moonlight. In this last poem the moon sets and the world is plunged in total darkness. This desperate philosophy of Leopardi's is stated in the most cool classical terms and without any forced rhetoric in his prose dialogues – *operette morale*. It is notable that Leopardi was almost the only important writer of his generation in continental Europe not to be hoodwinked by the reputation of Byron. One of the might-have-beens of history happened when Leopardi, in the course of his wanderings around Italy, arrived in Pisa ten days after Byron and Shelley had left. I like to imagine what the conversation of these three great poets might have been had they met.

When one is closely concerned with the study of a deceased author one can feel very close to his spirit, as if it were almost present looking over one's shoulder, and occasionally nudging one. Many years later I was to meet the author E. H. Visiak. Among other things he had edited the Nonsuch edition of Milton. Milton apparently meant a lot to him. It seemed that in his youth Visiak made a rash vow of some kind, and, discovering in Milton's divorce pamphlets the doctrine that one is not bound by a vow that one has taken in youth rashly, found this had a liberating effect on him. I was told by a friend of his that there was a passage in Milton with a disputed reading. Visiak did not know which reading to adopt in the Nonsuch edition, but he had a dream in which a voice seemed to call out to him: "The correct reading is . . ." He therefore adopted this, with a note: "emendation by John Milton". If the spirit one is in touch with is a tormented spirit, as I think Leopardi's was, the effect can be a painful one. I have already spoken of my abandonment of religious belief in my teens, and of my gradual journey back to it. This journey necessitated following Leopardi through the heart of darkness. It seemed to me, in the end, that the idea of God can include the idea of this darkness. The reverse is not true. If there is nothing but darkness then the idea of God is meaningless. I have never really parted with my initial scepticism. It remains with me, snapping at my heels like a faithful mongrel, and probably will to the end, ensuring that my belief does not degenerate into escapist fairy-tale.

Eventually, the long-hoped-for opportunity of leaving New Milton and finding a job in London arrived. I had applied for a post as English master at a private preparatory school situated in Hampstead. London had gone through the Blitz, and after the Blitz had come the flying-bombs. This was, apparently, the last straw for one of the masters at the school, for he suffered a nervous breakdown, and Percival Hale Coke, the English master, was leaving for another post. I received a telegram from the headmaster asking me if I could come at once. So I packed my bags and went.

7

Teaching in Hampstead

As soon as I arrived in London I went to the school. The headmaster interviewed me and instructed me in my duties. He wished me to start work immediately. There was the question of where I was to live. I was to succeed the present English master, Percival Hale Coke, who was taking up a post in University College School the following term. Coke told me that there was a room available at his own digs in West Hampstead, and so I moved in there.

The house in which I was to live for several years was an old-fashioned lodging house in which we were served breakfast and an evening meal, cooked by the owner, Miss Schaumburger. We were provided with bedrooms and there was also a common sitting-room. Miss Schaumburger was not, like so many expatriate Germans in Hampstead and elsewhere at that period, a Jewish refugee, but came from Silesian farming stock. She was a remarkable woman with considerable intelligence and a deep Protestant rectitude. She had some admirable and strongly traditional values deriving from her background. At the very end of the war, although bread was still rationed, the government was able to increase the quantity that could be purchased. In consequence of this, many people bought more bread than they needed and there was a certain amount of stale bread lying around in dustbins, and so on. Miss Schaumburger was shocked at this waste. "My mother", she said, "always used to make the sign of the cross before she cut a loaf of bread." This attitude to bread, as being something sacred because it is the staff of life, is widespread. In Egypt I was told that a Muslim, if he finds a piece of bread lying by the roadside, picks it up, kisses it, and after uttering certain prayers places it in the cranny of a wall in case some poor person may need it. I have also, in Crete, seen a piece of bread placed under a roadside icon, doubtless for the same reason. I do not quite know why or when Miss Schaumburger had emigrated to England. Before the outbreak of the war she had been approached by the Nazi-sponsored Bund, an organisation which attempted to get in touch with expatriate Germans and instil in them a proper loyalty to the fatherland and its prevailing Nazi ideology. She would have nothing to do with them. She simply knew in her bones that they were wrong. Naturally, she took a

115

motherly interest in her lodgers, including Coke and myself, and provided us with excellent meals in the rather heavy German style.

As for Coke, I came to know him very well. He was then in his late forties and thought of himself as a minor poet. His poems, which had been published in *Chambers's Journal*, a rather old-fashioned literary periodical, did not appeal to me at all, but he was extremely interesting company. He came of an old Yorkshire family and his most famous ancestor was the great Sir Edward Coke, Lord Chief Justice in the reign of James I. Coke had been a journalist – first on the *Yorkshire Post* and then on some London paper – before becoming an English master at the preparatory school where I was now engaged. He had a good knowledge of the literature of the 1890s and the early twentieth century. I also learnt from him quite a lot of worldly wisdom, and some literary anecdotes recalled from the earlier years of the century. Among the latter is one concerning Oscar Wilde. Coke recalled that he had met a man who told him that as a young lad he had worked for a firm of furniture removers and had helped install Wilde's furniture in his house in Tite Street. As the boy was straining and sweating, trying to get a grand piano up the stairs, Wilde said: "Don't worry, dear boy, just let it happen." This remark is, perhaps, quite profound and capable of universal application. Coke had an unfortunate tendency to fall in love with small boys. The present object of his passion, a Jewish boy whose first name was Aaron, had been a pupil at this Hampstead school, and had now secured a place at University College School, which was why Coke was migrating from one institution to the other. Of course, as soon as these boys reached puberty Coke lost interest in them. He was a mass of psychological problems and an unhappy man. Once, in my youthful brashness, I tried to suggest that a solution to some of his problems might be arrived at by some knowledge of Freudian psychology. "Don't tell me", he said indignantly, "that Aaron's cousin had the secret of the universe." Aaron was, in fact, a distant relative of Freud.

After some years, Coke left University College School and set up as a private tutor and coach. I was later to recommend the poet, James Burns Singer, to him as his assistant. Coke died rather suddenly at the age of forty-eight. He had left Miss Schaumburger's house and was living in a private hotel. In the same hotel, there resided a Mrs Macbeth who claimed to have the second sight. She told Coke's fortune and said, among other things, that his circumstances would improve and that he would shortly emigrate to South America. This pleased him a great deal, since Aaron's widowed mother had plans to do exactly that, and to take her son with her. A few days after this, Coke was interviewing a parent in the office he used as a tutor when suddenly he said, "I don't feel well," and collapsed and died.

A friend of Coke from his Yorkshire days who visited Miss Schaum-burger's house was the poet, Wilfred Rowland Childe. A Professor of English at Leeds University, he was a Roman Catholic and might be considered a minor poet of the school of Chesterton and Belloc. He told me that Hutchinson were starting a poetry list, of which he had been asked to be the editor. The first poet whom Childe proposed to recommend to Hutchinson was Dannie Abse, whose name I had not heard of, and whom he praised highly. Not long afterwards, walking down Piccadilly after a visit to the London Library, I encountered Dannie Abse who recognised me and introduced himself. He was then a medical student, living not far from me in Hampstead. We became firm friends and have remained so ever since.

Another Hampstead neighbour at this time was Alfred Marnau. Fred (as he was always called) was born in Czechoslovakia, but he was German-speaking and regarded himself as a citizen of the Aus-trian Empire. Married to a Norwegian cellist, he was certainly a good European. His poems, written in German, were widely published in small magazines during the 1940s, accompanied by translations by his friend, Ernst Sigler. Some of these poems were published in book form by the Grey Walls Press with the title *The Wounds of the Apostles*. Fred is now a prominent member of the Latin Mass Society. He introduced me to the German poet, Jesse Tor. The latter's surname – the German word for gate – was a pseudonym. Tor had a working-class background, and had, apparently, been trained as a goldsmith or jeweller. He was very poor and if he received any help from patrons would repay them by presenting them with a gift of hand-made jewel-lery. He had been a communist, but was now converted to a mystical Catholicism. He seemed to me rather as Blake might have been. I have met other visionary poets, such as Charles Williams and David Jones, who also reminded me of Blake, but in different ways. Tor at this time had a scheme to approach T. S. Eliot, whom he wanted to provide him with a boat. Tor intended to cruise on this boat over the oceans of the world. There would shortly be an atomic holocaust, and when this was over there would be, as in the days of Noah, a rainbow, the seven colours of the rainbow symbolising the seven sacraments. Tor would come to land again and convert the surviving representa-tives of the human race to his own visionary Catholicism. He impressed me with his insights. At that time I had become emotionally involved with a young German who was on the fringes of the Stefan George circle. Later, I had become disillusioned with George's ideas and was trying to write a novel, modelled all too closely on those of Charles Williams, in which a figure resembling George appeared as a false religious prophet. I mentioned this to Tor, who replied, "If

George is doing his work why do you want to interfere with him?"
(Tor was, of course, aware that George had died in 1933, but he was
speaking in terms of eternity.) Tor did not, on the other hand, admire
Rilke. He was, he said, the kind of person who would talk about the
Lord at an afternoon drawing-room tea party. Michael Hamburger
has given a full account of his own meeting with Tor in his book, *A
Mug's Game*. His acquaintance with the poet ended with Tor rounding
on him for being irredeemably bourgeois. My own acquaintance with
Tor did not, perhaps, last long enough for this to happen.

My career as a schoolteacher only lasted for about a term and a
half. It was an old-fashioned prep school and the curriculum and
the teaching methods did not seem to differ much from those I had
experienced at Dorset House some twenty years before. A high proportion of the pupils drawn from the local Hampstead catchment area
was Jewish. They were intelligent and receptive, but highly excitable,
especially as there was a continual threat of flying-bombs in the day
as well as at night. I was mainly engaged to teach them English
literature, and I was careful about the texts that I chose. Deeply
influenced by the puristic conception of style that I had derived from
a study of Ezra Pound's critical works, I was unwilling for them to
study inferior poetry. "The Ancient Mariner" was one of the poems
I chose without reservation. This great work is absolutely universal
in its appeal: boys will enjoy it for its exciting story, more sophisticated
readers will find profound symbolism in it. On one occasion, reading
it to the boys in class, I came to the stanza:

> O Wedding-Guest! this soul hath been
> Alone on a wide wide sea:
> So lonely 'twas, that God himself
> Scarce seemèd there to be.

Suddenly the full impact of these lines, written out of Coleridge's own
anguish, struck me like a blow in the face. They seemed to speak to
my own condition, for I had plenty of emotional and intellectual
problems of my own. It was with difficulty that I refrained from
bursting into tears before the entire class.

I found the English ballads also infallibly good material for teaching, and I also read them some translations of Chinese poems from
Soame Jenyns's *Poems of the Tang Dynasty*. These translations give a
much wider view of classical Chinese poetry than do the better-known
ones of Waley. They had been recommended to me at Oxford by a
contemporary and friend, Roger Sharrock, whom I was later to know
as Professor of English at King's College, London. The impression
one gets of Chinese poetry from Waley is of elegant mandarins,

drinking wine under the shade of the willow, and speaking of friend-ship and tranquillity. The astonishing thing about Jenyns's collection of Tang poems is that they contain some of the greatest war poems ever written. They tell of terrible frontier wars against the outer bar-barians that drag on for generations, so that whole villages go out of cultivation, and the Chinese peasants even find it better to bear girls rather than boys, because boys would be taken for military service. One of the poems I read to my boys was "The Peach Blossom Foun-tain", which relates an old legend in which a certain man finds a pool into which a stream runs. This pool is overshadowed by peach trees whose blossoms fall into the water. Tracing the stream to its source, the man finds himself in a strange world, the world of the Han dynasty of some centuries before, which from the point of view of the Tang poets was a Golden Age. It is rather as if an Anglo-Saxon contemporary of King Alfred were to find himself back in the world of the empire of Augustus. Eventually the man returns to his own contemporary world and is never able to find the peach blossom fountain again. I explained to the boys that this was one of a universal family of stories. The best-known example is, of course, the story of Rip Van Winkle, which Washington Irving took from the folklore of the New York Dutch. I also told them a mediaeval version of the same story. A monk, walking in the woods near his monastery, and contemplating the line in the psalm, "A thousand ages in thy sight are but as an evening", pauses for a moment to listen to the song of a bird. He then returns to his monastery and finds it full of monks who are unknown to him. They tell him that there is a tradition among them that one of the brothers, many years before, had walked off into the woods and had never come back. What astonished me was that the rather sophisticated notion incorporated in these stories of the relativity of time was immediately intelligible to these boys of ten or eleven.

As well as the flying-bombs, another source of disruption during the summer term was the incursion of wasps into the classroom. These excitable boys would try to flap the wasps. This is the worst possible thing you can do to a wasp. It only infuriates it and it is much more likely to sting. I have a certain sympathy with wasps. They work very hard all through the summer catching grubs and caterpillars and other insects that do damage to our crops, and with these they feed their young. Unlike bees, they have made no provision for the winter by storing honey. So when the end of the summer comes, with the plums and the apples, they know that only their queen will survive the approaching winter in some nook or cranny, and that they are doomed. They have no more work to do in feeding their young, and so they go on a binge in orchards or invade our kitchens when good housewives are making their jam – and this is when we get stung. I therefore forbade any boy to flap a wasp and anyone who disobeyed my order had to write out a hundred times: "The wasp is a friend of man."

I began quite well as a teacher. The boys seemed to like me and found my classes interesting, but I soon found difficulties with discipline. The trouble was that with my restricted eyesight I could not be quite sure which boy was causing a disturbance, and I could not punish unjustly; that would have completely undermined my position. Gradually my classes became more and more chaotic and I saw that I could not continue at this school. After finding another job I informed the headmaster that I would be leaving at the end of my second term. He told me that had I not handed in my resignation I would not have been retained. One of the boys whom I found particularly disruptive was Derek Hart, who was later to have a distinguished career on radio and television. He was, of course, brighter than the other boys and could work at a quicker pace. Consequently he got bored and then played the fool. I remember the very last class I took. I had, for some reason, to explain the different meanings of the words "crop" and "gizzard", for which purpose I drew an anatomical drawing of a hen upon the blackboard. The boys were delighted by my sketch and insisted on my repeating it individually for each of them on a piece of paper and autographing it. This delayed my leaving the class, and when I reached the staff room I found that one of the mistresses had arranged a little farewell tea for me with cakes and so on. They were all wondering what had happened to me.

In 1944 France was liberated. Not long after, I received a phone call from the British Council asking me if I would come to William Empson's house in Hampstead where there was to be a reception for the French poet, Pierre Emmanuel. A number of English poets would read their own work in honour of him. I went along to this. It was a very informal gathering indeed. We were served beer in pint mugs – wine and spirits were hardly obtainable at this time – and most of us sat on the floor and ate lettuce sandwiches. But because of the symbolic importance of the occasion – that a representative of newly freed France was among us – a distinguished gathering had turned up. Michael Roberts, the editor of *The Faber Book of Modern Verse* (an anthology which formed the taste of a whole generation), was in the chair. Other poets included T. S. Eliot, George Barker, Dylan Thomas, Rayner Heppenstall, Ruthven Todd, Paul Potts, Kathleen Raine and Anne Ridler. A message was received from Edith Sitwell, regretting that she could not be present. I was the youngest poet there. While Roberts was reading his poems, the veteran poet, Anna Wickham, suddenly entered. She was acclaimed with great warmth and affection by everybody and a chair was brought for her. The other two women were seated, but Anna, who was unusually tall, towered over the company, making loud, though not wholly relevant, comments on the poems. She was obviously slightly drunk.

As the reading went on, after all those pints of beer I found it necessary to retire to the lavatory. I shall never forget that when I came back I heard for the first time the extraordinary flat, but intensely individual and significant, voice of Eliot reading the lines:

> . . . As we grow older
> The world becomes stranger, the pattern more complicated
> Of dead and living . . .

At the end of the reading there was a general social get-together. I had never met any of these persons before, though nearly all of them were later to become close friends. I was far too shy to address any of them. Michael Roberts, with characteristic kindness, thanked me for the one poem of my own which I had read, and praised my reading of it. Ruthven Todd, perhaps the least distinguished poet present, took it upon himself to buttonhole Eliot, demanding to know what was being done to try to get Ezra Pound released from the American mental hospital in which he was then confined. Eliot looked extremely embarrassed by this brash advance. It was his own policy, I have been told, not to support any movements for the release of Pound at that time (he was to be released some quarter of a century later). Eliot felt, probably rightly, that if Pound, with his violent and, admittedly, not quite sane temperament, were released, he would probably make some ill-advised public statement, which would simply lead to the charge of treason being urged once more against him, and because he had been released a defence of mental illness, which might save him from the electric chair, could hardly be made.

I have earlier mentioned the pioneer work which was done by Harold Monro at his Poetry Bookshop in Bloomsbury during the 1920s and 1930s to popularise the public reading by poets of their own work. Public poetry readings continued in various venues throughout the war years and down to the present time. The main centre for poetry readings in London during the 1940s and 1950s was the Ethical Church in Bayswater, where Alec Craig organised readings for the Progressive League. The Ethical Church might be called the high church of secularism, while the much more successful South Place Ethical Society in Red Lion Square was its low church. At the time that I encountered these readings, the Ethical Church occupied only the crypt of its Bayswater building. The top half had been leased to some sect of fundamentalist evangelical Christians. Both have since departed and the building is now a Roman Catholic church, Our Lady, Queen of Angels. The Progressive League was in some way affiliated to the Ethical Church. Craig was, in fact, a good Anglican Christian, though stricken with guilt because, finding it impossible to be faithful to his wife, he had a permanent relationship with another woman. As well as poetry readings, the meetings, which took place in the evening once a month, included a musical recital organised by Craig's colleague Ashton Burrell. Craig, who himself had had a volume of poems, *The Aspirin Eaters*, published (inevitably by the Fortune Press), succeeded in persuading many well-known and less well-known poets to read on these occasions and – it might be added – without fee. The idea that poets should actually receive a fee for their public readings did not come to be generally recognised until the 1960s.

I was, myself, asked to read at the Ethical Church later on. My first volume of poems had been enthusiastically reviewed by Ross Nichols in the *New English Weekly*. He had sent me a copy of his review and invited me to call on him if I were ever in London. This I did. He was a strange and rather confused character who sponsored various not very talented poets on a vague programme which had something to do with symbolism and myth. He became a member of a body known as the Ancient British Church who practised what purported to be Druidism. Nichols's group of Druids must be distinguished from the main body of Druids who still operate and who have a respectable pedigree going back to the eighteenth century.

The one poet Nichols sponsored who had real talent, though too much facility, was James Kirkup, who was a close personal friend of his. Nichols organised a group of poets, including myself, to read at one of these Bayswater Progressive League events. I read a single sonnet, but it seemed to go down quite well. I was to read at the Ethical Church on several occasions. Others whom I heard there included George Barker, Dylan Thomas and Maurice Carpenter. It was usually the practice to invite a poet to read his own poems in the first half of the evening, and poems by writers of his choice in the second half. I remember that Dylan Thomas chose to read some of Lawrence's poems about animals, and George Barker gave a striking performance of the mediaeval mystical poem "Quia amore langueo", which was of particular significance to him, and of which he had once prepared a small edition. Another poem he read was the border ballad of "Tam Lin". The best-known version of this is one edited, and a bit touched up, by Sir Walter Scott. It tells the story of a mortal carried off to the world of the fairies. He can only be redeemed from it by the steadfast love of a woman. He has to be redeemed, for:

> . . . pleasant is the fairy land,
> But, an eerie tale to tell,
> Ay at the end of seven years
> We pay a teind to hell;
> I am sae fair and fu' o flesh,
> I'm feard it be mysel'.

The word "teind" means a tribute or sacrifice, and Tam may be the chosen victim. Anyone who knew George Barker would see how close this story was to his own inner experience.

Perhaps the most notable reading at the Ethical Church, and one which has almost passed into legend, was the occasion, some years later, when Stephen Spender was on the platform. At this time Ross Nichols was in the chair, for Alec Craig, who worked in the army pay department, had been stationed for some time in Egypt which was still under British occupation. Many accounts have been given of this event, but most of them are inaccurate in one detail or another. As Spender was about to mount the podium to read, there was a noise at the back of the hall as a number of people entered. They were led by Roy Campbell, whose friends, including John Gawsworth, were trying to restrain him and drag him back. Campbell shouted out in his South African accent: "Is that Mr Spender? I have a message for him from the sergeants' mess." (Campbell had served as a sergeant during the Second World War.) Campbell then began to accuse Spender and his friends of using their influence with Faber, who were also Campbell's publishers, to get the latter's books suppressed. I have no reason to think there was any truth at all in these accusations, though there was a longstanding feud between Campbell and the left-wing poets of the Auden group – MacNeice, Spender, Auden and Day Lewis – whom Campbell collectively satirised as "MacSpaunday". Spender was completely taken aback, and Campbell aimed a blow – not a violent one – at his face. Campbell was then dragged off by his friends. As they did so, his parting shot was: "You're nothing but a horrible old lesbian governess." Most of the audience were completely mystified and had no idea what was going on. It would appear that Campbell and his cronies had been drinking in a nearby pub, and, knowing that Spender was reading, had formed a resolution to break the meeting up. One of the audience said: "Who is this Roy Campbell? Is he a poet?" "Yes," said Spender, "and a very good one."

After the Ethical Church sold its buildings, its congregation, along with the Progressive League and its poetry and music circle, moved to smaller premises – purchased from a sect of female freemasons – on the other side of the park in Prince of Wales Terrace. The Ethical

Church brought their service book with them, featuring hymns by Shelley and other free-thinking poets, and prose passages by Matthew Arnold, Emerson and others, which were, presumably, recited to Anglican chants. The Ethicals also brought their icons which consisted of portraits of John Stuart Mill and other Victorian worthies. These mingled rather uneasily, I thought, with the images of Isis, Osiris and similar Egyptian gods left behind by the original owners. The poetry and music circle continued to meet there monthly till the death of Alec Craig in the sixties. Of these events, I particularly remember a recital by the great singer, Sophie Weiss, who, though in retirement, had retained her voice. She sang to an audience who did not really appreciate her art, and had not even the courtesy to extinguish their cigarettes. Malcolm Williamson, now the Master of the Queen's Music, played, on one occasion, some of his compositions.

Among the poets, I particularly remember hearing, for the first time, Stevie Smith read there. I had been introduced to her poetry by Sidney Keyes at Oxford. It was quite a long time before she was really taken seriously as a poet. Her volumes, with their quirky verses and amusing drawings, must have seemed to many intellectuals more like light entertainment than serious poetry, but in the end people came to realise that she was "not waving but drowning". Her readings – I also heard her on several later occasions – were very carefully rehearsed performances, not only the poems which she read, but the commentary with which she introduced them. She would sometimes burst into song in her little schoolgirl voice, for she often composed her poems, as she later told me, to hymns or other well-known tunes. The poem entitled "Le singe qui swing" went to the tune of "Greensleeves". It has sometimes struck me that her sophisticated, yet extraordinarily simplistic, use of language, both in her verse and her prose, shared some affinities with Gertrude Stein's, although for my money Stevie Smith is the much more readable of the two. I asked Stevie about this once. She replied that she had read Gertrude Stein, but was not aware of any influence.

During the war years, and for some time afterwards, there were a number of small poetry magazines. The most widely read of these were Tambimuttu's *Poetry London* and Charles Wrey Gardiner's *Poetry Quarterly*. Tambimuttu – or Tambi as he was commonly called – whom one was always encountering in the pubs of Soho, was a Tamil from Sri Lanka, then known as Ceylon. His initials were M.J. These stood for Mary James, for his family were Roman Catholics, but he repudiated his Catholicism and dropped these initials, sometimes using a Hindu name. His magazine, and later his publishing house, Editions Poetry London, under the imprint of Nicholson and Watson, were very influential, though of varying quality. My own feeling is that he had very little natural taste at all, but published good stuff when he had good advisers. Eliot helped him a great deal, at least financially. Eliot had a soft spot for Indians. Later on Anne Ridler and Kathleen Raine were among Tambi's advisers. Among the pluses in his publishing programme, I would name his publication of David Gascoyne's poems (with illustrations by Graham Sutherland), W. S. Graham's *Poems*, Charles Williams's later Arthurian cycle, *The Region of the Summer Stars* (which the OUP, for whom he worked, could not undertake to publish), and the first volume of David Wright's poems. But Tambi also started a lot of very bad poets on their careers. He published only two poems of mine in his magazine: one of these I never thought worth reprinting; the other, which consisted of two four-line stanzas – the second of which ended in a comma – he succeeded in printing on two sides of a page and changed the comma into a full stop. Tambi has become a sort of legendary figure. Personally, I found it difficult to like him, but also difficult to quarrel with him, for he had a kind of soft, easy charm. His appearance was not attractive. He had lost his front teeth, his hair was usually too long and dirty, and his personal habits were often immensely squalid. Peter Russell, who once gave him the loan of his flat for a month or so, told me that he could not find words to describe the condition it was in when he returned. But Tambi was good-hearted and gentle by nature. I cannot say that I gained much from him in terms of helping the progress of my poetry, but he did teach me the proper way of eating a pomegranate.

On the occasion of T. S. Eliot's sixtieth birthday in 1948, Tambi published a large volume of personal tributes to, and reminiscences of, Eliot, written by various poets, to which I contributed. I have reason to think that it was a source of some embarrassment to Eliot, who had an intense dislike of the cult of personality in poetry, and would, I suppose, rather have welcomed a collection of academic critical essays. Most of these tributes were in the form of prose reminiscences, but some were poems. These included one by Nicholas Moore which expresses with unerring accuracy exactly what Eliot's spiritual progress was not. Tambi himself intended to contribute a poem, but it grew and grew to gigantic proportions. I encountered him in a street in Soho with the manuscript of this work in his hands. He had been showing it to all the literary colleagues he had met in the course of the evening, and asking them what he was to do with it. It was a long, mystical outpouring, with an Indian title, and vaguely modelled on the less substantial parts of Eliot's *Four Quartets*. My friend, Bob Pocock, witnessed Tambi's showing it to Dylan Thomas. "You should", said Bob, "have seen a little Welsh dumpling turn into a Gorgon." More tactfully, I suggested that Tambi should not publish it in the volume he was planning, but on its own in a pamphlet. He gratefully accepted this advice.

Charles Wrey Gardiner was a very different man. He had started his Grey Walls Press at his home in Billericay, Essex, but later moved his offices to London, where, as well as publishing his magazine, he also took to publishing poetry. He shared his offices and distribution with Peter Baker, who had founded the Falcon Press. The Grey Walls Press and the Falcon Press eventually amalgamated. Baker was a junior Conservative MP and undoubtedly unbalanced. He was eventually sent to prison for forging cheques, including one on the millionaire Sir Bernard Docker. I did not, myself, have much contact with Baker, and the reader should be referred to Muriel Spark's autobiography for a fuller account of this affair. As well as publishing original verse, Wrey Gardiner issued some quite attractively produced little pocket selections from standard English poets. I edited for him the selections of Swift, Shelley and Tennyson. Wrey Gardiner was a good-natured and well-meaning man, though immensely selfish and self-centred. He published two volumes of his journals: *The Dark Thorn* and (towards the end of his life) *The Answer to Life is No*, a sentiment which I have a cold feeling he sincerely meant. The Grey Walls Press published several volumes of his own verse, of which all that I can say is what Dryden postulated of the verse of Shadwell – that it never deviated into sense. The fashion for writing what its practitioners call "pure poetry" – that is, unending verbal drivel – was all too common in this post-surrealist, post-Apocalyptic period, but I suspect it may be coming back. A few years ago I attended a reading by the American poet John Ashbery – it was quite like old times.

After the war Peter Russell founded his magazine *Nine*. Then a student at Queen Mary College, and now living in Italy, he was an enthusiastic proponent of the poetry of Ezra Pound, and did some valuable work in rehabilitating the latter's reputation. Peter maintained that a rejection of Pound's scarcely sane political views need not mean the repudiation of his poetic and critical work. *Nine* was important in redirecting attention, as Pound had already done, to the central traditions of European literature, particularly classical Greek and Roman, and Italian literature. Peter would sometimes have gatherings of poets at his flat in Oxford Street. It was here that I first met David Gascoyne.

After the war, when relations were re-established with Italy, the Italian ambassador was Count Galleotti-Scotti. He was a liberal-minded, cultured man who during the fascist period had had a good record in the Italian Senate of opposing Mussolini's policies. He was obviously anxious to mend fences and to revive the traditional English respect for Italian culture and literature which, after all, goes back as far as Chaucer. He organised an exhibition of contemporary Italian art at which two very distinguished writers, the poet Eugenio Montale and the novelist Alberto Moravia, were invited to read from their work. I was also invited to read, from the same platform, some of my translations of Leopardi, recently published by John Lehmann. I had a brief but interesting conversation with Montale, during which the name of Ezra Pound came up. "Why", said Montale, "did he not try and get in touch with *us*?" He meant himself and those writers who were his colleagues. This remark, made without any bitterness, was, I think, the final and devastating condemnation of Pound, made by one who had every right to make it. Montale, the leader of a group of Italian poets known as *I ermetici* – so called because of their deliberate cultivation of obscurity – is, it might be said, the Italian equivalent of T. S. Eliot. The hermetics were similar to the early modernist British and American poets championed by Pound. Although these hermetics did not openly oppose fascism, or commit themselves to communism, their deliberate hermeticism was a subtle way of undermining the false values, and particularly the false rhetoric, of the regime, whose poet in its early days was the flamboyant, immoral and largely derivative d'Annunzio.

Another Italian intellectual, Orlando Ruggiero, who was resident as a refugee in England at this time, once quoted to me a line from d'Annunzio: "O perche, perche, non son io con i miei pastorie?" "Only a bad and wicked citizen", Ruggiero said, "could write a bad line like that." All the line means is, "Oh why, oh why, am I not with my shepherds?", a piece of false sentimental pastoralism. But the music of the Italian language, which d'Annunzio shamelessly exploits here, seduces one into thinking it is something greater. In fairness, I have seen it stated that d'Annunzio is really at his best when writing about his native Abruzzi, a wild and primitive part of Italy. Pound cannot be accused of falling for d'Annunzio, but he was scarcely interested in anything that had happened in Italian literature after the sixteenth century. His collected poems do include one, very bad, translation from Leopardi, but nothing else of post-Renaissance date. This blinkered refusal to look at the contemporary world of Italy was contradictory to his stated principles and led to the fatal trap of his support for Mussolini's policies, with the poet's consequent arrest as a traitor. The *Pisan Cantos*, written during Pound's captivity, contain some of his best work, but also some of his most revoltingly anti-Semitic passages. It is said that at the end of his life Pound found out what Hitler had really done to the Jews. Pound had previously dismissed it as Allied propaganda. He then became so stricken with guilt and shame that he ceased to utter anything more in print.

8

Hutchinson

The job which followed on my brief, and not very distinguished, career as a schoolmaster was with the publishers, Hutchinson. They were issuing a popular illustrated encyclopaedia, and I was engaged as an editorial assistant. Hutchinson's central London offices had, apparently, been destroyed by bombing. Consequently the encyclopaedia department, and some others, were lodged in what had been a private house in Prince's Gate, Kensington. It was pretty cramped quarters and later we moved to another such house in Pont Street, where we had a little more space. The encyclopaedia department consisted of about half a dozen men and women. We divided the whole of human knowledge between us. Our office was provided with a copy of the *Encyclopaedia Britannica*, and at Pont Street we found a very old copy of *Chambers Encyclopaedia* which had been left behind in a cupboard. We also had *Keesing's Contemporary Archives, Who's Who* and files of *The Times* for the past few years. Our main task was to write short popular articles for the encyclopaedia, copying, for the most part, from our reference books, but being careful, for copyright reasons, subtly to change the words. When the encyclopaedia eventually appeared it had Walter Hutchinson's name on the title-page as editor. In fact, he hardly ever came near the office. The real editorial work was done by an admirable man, a Mr Royston Pyke, a close relation of Magnus Pyke, the naturalist. Yet no acknowledgement was given to Royston Pyke, not even as a sub-editor. When the encyclopaedia was completed, everyone, including Pyke, was given a fortnight's notice. Royston Pyke, a serious-minded man, had written books on ethics and was a pillar of the Rationalist Society, but he was anxious to be a good popular journalist and make this into a book suitable for family reading. We were still, even at that date, only allowed to state about Oscar Wilde: "Scandals concerning his private life led to his being tried and imprisoned." At Pont Street, Pyke occupied an office next to the one I shared with two others, and, through the wall, one could hear the conversations that were going on. Pyke's secretary was a devout Anglo-Catholic and spent a great deal of her office time attempting to convert him.

The encyclopaedia staff, and especially Pyke, were treated by other departments of Hutchinson as reliable sources of information on many different areas, including the translation of French correspondence. I remember one letter from a French author who approached Hutchinson hoping that they would publish English translations of his work. This author was a romantic novelist who specialised in exotic locations. The title of one of his books, whose setting was Bali, was *The Island of Bare Bosoms*. Pyke, in translating this letter, showed considerable embarrassment in rendering the title.

Other members of the staff included a refugee from Austria, a really learned man with a doctorate whose speciality was in continental literatures. There was a lady who had been engaged by Walter Hutchinson to deal with subjects related to the Soviet Union. He felt, rightly as it happened, that the Soviet Union was going to be of great importance and interest to readers in the years following the war. The lady once came into my office with the words: "While I was doing Lake Baikal, Mr Heath-Stubbs, I found a fish in it which I thought might interest you." There was also a young man with no particular qualifications, and not much ability, who worked extremely slowly and inefficiently. He had suffered some kind of mental breakdown and Pyke tolerated his deficiencies out of the goodness of his heart. My office at Pont Street was shared with a man called Canon Hobday – Canon was his Christian name – who had a degree in history; and a young woman who was obviously working for pin-money until she married. She was a Roman Catholic and was designated the task of compiling the lives of the saints. Hobday was writing the general articles on history. He was at that time a Marxist, and this gave a slant to his history articles which would probably not have been welcome to Walter Hutchinson. Another member of our staff, who joined us later, had, I am sorry to say, a rather prurient mind. He pursued with eagerness the word "epicene", only to discover that it was defined as a grammatical term applied to words which can be of either masculine or feminine gender.

At my interview, Pyke asked me what my qualifications were. I explained that I had a first-class honours degree in English literature, but this did not seem to impress him. He enquired, however, if I happened to have any knowledge of biology. I replied that, as a matter of fact, I did have such knowledge, and had at one time hoped to make that my speciality. Consequently I found myself engaged to write articles on cookery (biology was held to include that subject), and on all the animals, plants and birds (except for the mammals, the articles on which were contributed from outside by Magnus Pyke), but I soon seemed to acquire other specialities and ended up by covering, in addition, English literature, theology and music. Once I had to write an article on the two plants which were used in the

129

Soviet Union for the manufacture of synthetic rubber. This was an achievement of which the country was extremely proud, and during the 1940s an epic on this subject, by a Soviet poet, had appeared. The two plants were called the *krim saghiz* and the *kok saghiz* and they were both species of dandelion. The milky juice, which every country child knows exudes from a dandelion's leaves or stem when they are broken, provided the latex which was converted into rubber. This was more or less the substance of my article. It was distilled from a pile of literature about four feet high which had been sent by the Soviet Embassy when Pyke had requested information from them.

Compiling this encyclopaedia was, for the whole department, a race against time, and one had always to cut articles out or reduce them in size. As I was writing articles on poets, including modern poets, Pyke very kindly suggested I should write one on myself. I did, though limiting it to a couple of lines, for I had made it a rule not to include any contemporaries younger than David Gascoyne, who was born in 1916 (two years before my birth), as I thought that younger reputations might turn out to be unstable. I was quite right, especially for this wartime period. When the encyclopaedia finally appeared – some time after I had left its staff – the cutting of articles had become so ruthless as the later letters of the alphabet were reached that, while the entry on myself still stood, there was no article on W. B. Yeats.

In the course of my work, I became rather knowledgeable about the way that the earlier encyclopaedias, which we used as our sources, were compiled, and how the minds of the contributors had worked. We wrote our copy by hand and it was then passed to a typist. It is easy not to check dates and I found that this had occurred before. Also, there were signs, in much more respectable encyclopaedias than ours, of the indiscriminate combining of sources, a practice which we ourselves were more or less forced to use. An article on a sixteenth-century composer in a very reputable encyclopaedia stated, in one paragraph, that he had studied with Jodocus Pratensis, and, in another, that apparently later on he had studied with Josquin des Prés. The writer of the article had obviously not been aware that Jodocus Pratensis was simply the Latinised form of Josquin des Prés. Other evidence of how encyclopaedias have been compiled was gleaned from articles in various encyclopaedias on the Egyptian Christian community of the Copts. The source for these entries was E. W. Lane's *Manners and Customs of the Modern Egyptians*, published in 1836. Lane is extremely interesting and reliable on the beliefs and customs of the Muslims of Egypt, but wrote only two short chapters on the Jewish and Christian communities. It would seem possible that he became a Muslim or at least passed himself off as one. Of the Copts, he says, among other things, that they are characterised by "a surly expression". I was later to make many good friends among the Copts and it never struck me that they were noticeably surly. I am inclined to think that the Copts adopted a surly expression whenever they saw Lane coming, and I do not blame them, if indeed he had apostatised to the Muslims. This piece of misinformation about the Copts is copied again and again from encyclopaedia to encyclopaedia.

I had also been entrusted with weeding out a lot of unnecessary articles which were simply dictionary definitions and not really the kind of articles one needs in encyclopaedias. Some I rejected with regret, for example, one on the bass-viol which ran as follows: "Bass-viol – an old name for the violin[*sic*]-cello, an instrument of some charm which has often been used to lure the nightingale for BBC purposes." Beatrice Harrison's famous broadcast, in which the tones of her cello were mingled with those of the nightingale in her garden, will be remembered. Another such article was the work of Mr Pyke himself, and admirable in its succinctness. It was on the word "amoral". Pyke wrote: "The word is applied to primitive savages, children, and persons of extreme artistic sensibility to whom, had they reached a higher stage of ethical evolution, the term 'immoral' would be applied."

Walter Hutchinson, the head of the firm, was the son of its founder, Sir George Hutchinson. Sir George had, apparently, not very much confidence in his son's abilities. I was told he had left all his money to his two daughters, while the son was left the firm to get on with and make the best of. Walter Hutchinson was anxious to establish a public reputation and, perhaps, to gain a knighthood like his father. For this reason he amassed a collection of British sporting art – which he hoped to give to the nation – and purchased a house just off Oxford Street which was to become a gallery for these pictures. Any British painting that had the remotest connection with sport was eligible for inclusion. There was, indeed, one painting by Constable, but it was only there because, in the background, a figure was fishing from a bridge. While the gallery was being made ready, the collection was hung in our Pont Street offices. Occasionally Walter Hutchinson would bring an influential friend to look at these pictures. In the end, the house that Walter Hutchinson had purchased for the collection was found not to conform to fire safety regulations, and so the planned exhibition did not take place. As far as I know, the collection was dispersed after Hutchinson's death.

While I was working in Pont Street, there was a notorious murderer called Neville George Heath. His first victim, Marjorie Gardiner, had been picked up by Heath in a Soho pub and murdered in an hotel room in Notting Hill. This murder was a particularly horrible and sadistic one. An old schoolfellow of mine, from Bembridge days, had a bookshop near Pont Street. I would occasionally spend my lunch hour chatting to him, but if any customer came in I would break off and start browsing among the books. On one occasion a little man came in with some publicity flyers and said: "I will have copies of the books ready for you soon, and will bring them in." When the man left, my friend said to me: "Do you know who that was?" I replied: "No." "That was Marjorie Gardiner's husband." He showed me the flyer, which was advance publicity for a posthumous collection of her poems, the profits to be used for the education of her daughter. After his execution, Heath became something of a mythical figure in the pubs of Soho and Notting Hill Gate which he had frequented. I told the story of what I had witnessed in the bookshop to an old friend of mine who was now working in the Foreign Office. "Supervacuo", as I will call him (that was the role he played in my production of *The Revenger's Tragedy*), said: "Good Heavens! That child might have been my daughter." Marjorie Gardiner had been well known for her promiscuity.

I left Hutchinson, having been with the firm for about eighteen months, at the time we had reached the letter "G". I think that the last article I wrote was on the composer Gluck. I now tried to make my way by freelance writing and reviewing. My work was beginning to become known. I was a fairly frequent contributor to John Lehmann's *New Writing*, and was invited by C. V. Wedgwood to write reviews for *Time and Tide* (then under the editorship of Lady Rhondda) – an extremely intelligent liberal paper with an early feminist slant. I also wrote for the *New English Weekly*. This little periodical, which in wartime consisted of only about eight sheets, had been founded by A. R. Orage in 1931, but was now under the editorship of Philip Mairet. It was not usually on sale at bookstalls, but I have been informed that it was quite widely read among journalists, for it was considered to be well informed on economic topics. At the time I was contributing to it, its ideology was largely that of the Christendom Group, who were mostly Anglo-Catholics. T. S. Eliot was a contributor to the *New English Weekly* and the last three of the *Four Quartets* had first appeared in its pages before being published in pamphlet form. Although it did not pay at all well, it encouraged younger writers, and many who subsequently made their names had begun by contributing to its columns. I wrote book reviews and occasional poems. One of the features of the *New English Weekly* was its editorial meetings which took place – I think at quarterly intervals – in a room of a public house in Fleet Street. Eliot was always present on these occasions. I was immensely impressed by the democratic atmosphere which prevailed at these meetings. Any contributor, however humble and unknown, as I myself was, seemed to be free to put forward his opinions and was listened to with respect. Once, the question came up of increasing the circulation of the *New English Weekly* by making it more lively. Eliot noted, as an example, the back pages (which contained the reviews and competitions) of the *New Statesman and Nation*, then under the editorship of Kingsley Martin. Eliot said: "Many people read it for its back pages. I should be sorry to think they read its front pages."

But, perhaps, my most important editor at this time was Hugh Kingsmill, who was responsible for the literary section of the fortnightly *New English Review*. Hugh Kingsmill Lunn was the son of Sir Henry Lunn, a leading Methodist who had founded Lunn's tours, originally as a means of providing Methodist ministers with well-needed holidays. Kingsmill's elder brother, Sir Arnold Lunn, the mountaineer, had become a Roman Catholic. Kingsmill did not wish to be associated with his brother's views and thus dropped the surname. He was a close friend of Malcolm Muggeridge and Clifford Bax, and the three of them had had a common guru in "Oxo" Holmes who had died young, and whose exact significance and influence on them I was never quite able to fathom. Kingsmill himself was in many ways a religious thinker, though scarcely an orthodox Christian. In an article in the *New English Review* he compared the human condition to that of prisoners confined within a high-walled jail. Every now and then leaves, blossoms and twigs blow over the wall. This proves that there is a world outside the jail, and this should be enough for us. Theologians and others attempt, on the evidence of these small fragments, to reconstruct in detail the whole world outside the jail. Kingsmill was a close friend of Denis Saurat, Professor of French at King's College, London. Saurat had written about such figures as Milton, Blake, Victor Hugo and Wagner, and had attempted to define an eternal philosophy, which they all held in common, that differed from orthodox theology. He believed that he could detect similar principles in English folk-religion from ideas he had heard propounded by speakers at Hyde Park Corner. Later he developed some highly eccentric views, such as the theory that the world was created at the birth of Christ and that since then time has flowed both forwards and backwards.

Kingsmill, however, was a thoroughly practical and down-to-earth literary editor and journalist, who had written lives of Samuel Johnson, Dickens and Frank Harris. I shall always be grateful for the help that Kingsmill gave me in those years. He would send me a book to review every fortnight, deliberately stretching me by sending me books on all kinds of subjects, which I then had to learn about in order to review the books adequately. I reviewed for the *New English Review* a

133

book by the Russian Orthodox thinker Semyon Ludwigovich Frank, a member of the same Paris School which had included Sergei Bulgakov and Berdyayev. Kingsmill also sent me an edition of a mediaeval poem, and Sir Sacheverell Sitwell's book on English baroque architecture.

Kingsmill would invite me, almost every month, to dinner at his house in Holland Park Avenue, where he nearly always arranged that a writer whom he thought I would like to meet should be present. On these occasions I was to meet Edwin Muir, Graham Greene and Kathleen Raine. The *New English Review* was published by Eyre and Spottiswoode, for whom Greene was then an editor. Later on, this firm was to publish my critical book, *The Darkling Plain*, and a volume of my poems. I remember having lunch with Greene, who was then forty, but extraordinarily youthful in appearance and in manner. Another guest was a French lady whose work Eyre and Spottiswoode were about to publish. There were some Americans lunching at a nearby table in the restaurant. Greene remarked, alluding to a well-known sonnet by Sir Philip Sidney, that he did not think anyone would ever speak of "that sweet enemy, America", as Sidney had of "that sweet enemy, France". There is plenty of other evidence for Greene's antipathy towards Americans. Since Eyre and Spottiswoode had opened a poetry list, Greene was, of course, being overwhelmed with manuscripts from unknown writers. He told me how a young girl had sent him a volume of poems, with the covering note saying: "I don't know whether you will find these poems good enough to publish; perhaps I have not suffered enough." He was obviously touched by this. It is also worth noting that he asked me if I admired Wordsworth, as he himself obviously did.

Hugh Kingsmill was, I think, equally helpful to Michael Meyer whom he trained to be his dramatic critic. It was through Kingsmill that Michael Meyer originally met Graham Greene, with whom he became close friends.

9

Soho

Before the end of the war I had already begun regularly to frequent the literary pubs and clubs of Soho, as well as others which lay to the north of Oxford Street, in Rathbone Place and Charlotte Street. This latter area was sometimes known as Fitzrovia, but this term was certainly not applied to the whole area (including Soho proper), nor were all those who frequented it known as Fitzrovians, as some recent writers seem to imagine. It was through Tony Brown, who now had a flat in Percy Street, that I first found an entry into this world. I soon ran into David Wright, who had become a regular frequenter of these pubs. He was working as an indexer on the *Sunday Times*. When I had first met David, at Oxford, I was, to my shame, too shy and nervous to make the effort of communicating with him by lip-reading, but I now learnt to do this, and he became, and continues to be, one of my closest friends, with whom I have collaborated on a number of projects. The whole area of Soho, with its Fitzrovia annexe, stretched from Fitzroy Square in the north to Shaftesbury Avenue in the south, taking in Dean Street, Frith Street and Greek Street. In the area of Soho proper, which lay within the limits of the City of Westminster, all the pubs stayed open until eleven at night. Fitzrovia (for I shall apply this term to the northern area) was where three boroughs – Westminster, St Pancras and St Marylebone – met. At the time I am speaking of, closing hours for public houses were fixed by the licensing authorities of the various boroughs, so that some of the pubs in Fitzrovia closed at half past ten and others at eleven. One planned an evening's drinking. One would normally start in the Charlotte Street area, and, as time went by towards ten o'clock, move south of Oxford Street into Soho proper. Each pub had its own character and its own clientele, though the clientele varied as landlords changed or retired, or, in some cases, if the police had warned them that they were allowing their bars to be used by undesirable elements.

Fitzrovia had been before the war a sort of colony, where rather cheaper lodgings could be found, of the then fashionable intellectual quarter of Bloomsbury. The centre of Fitzrovia had been the Fitzroy Tavern, but at the end of the war, when I first came to frequent the area, it had degenerated into nothing much more than a homosexual pick-up place. Julian Maclaren Ross's publishers wanted to feature a drawing of the Fitzroy on the dust-jacket of a collection of his short stories, but he objected strongly, saying that he would not want to be seen dead in the place. Things had been different in the Fitzroy before the war, and a few of its old clientele lingered. Among these was Sylvia Gough, one of the queens of Soho, along with Nina Hamnett. Sylvia, who must once have been beautiful, was a sad and pathetic character. She had, though I did not know this at the time, seen one of her lovers beaten to death before her eyes in the Fitzroy. Sylvia would sit in the Fitzroy of an evening waiting for some friend or other to buy her a gin. If, as might happen, one could not afford that, she would say, "Oh well, dear, I'll have to make a noise like a whore," hoping that some stranger under this misapprehension would buy her a drink. There is a story that a group of people who were more or less slumming in the area got into conversation with her and bought her drinks. She happened to mention that she had lived in Paris in the early years of the century. "Oh," said one of these people, "were you in Paris then?" "Young man," said Sylvia, "I was in Paris when the graffiti on the lavatory walls were drawn by Toulouse-Lautrec." Sylvia, like Nina Hamnett, was a relic of the old pre-war days, when the Café Royal in Piccadilly Circus had been the great meeting place for writers and artists. She once told me how she used to spend much of her time there talking to Ronald Firbank. As I was a great admirer of Firbank's work, I asked her eagerly what they had talked about. "Oh, my dear," she answered, "ourselves mostly." The Café Royal in my time had been redecorated and remodelled. The old 1890s décor had gone, and it gradually ceased to be a meeting place for artists and writers, though I do remember a saying current in Soho in the 1940s: "If you go to the back door of the Café Royal round about three o'clock, and see a little pig with a halo coming out, that will be Dylan Thomas." The halo was, in fact, his rather fluffy hair.

The landlord of the Fitzroy Tavern was Charlie Allchild (now deceased), who appears to have acquired a spurious reputation as a kindly "mine host". He attempted to give a patriotic and philanthropic image to his pub. He decorated it with recruiting posters from the First World War, twinned it with the battleship HMS *Fitzroy*, and collected money for an annual Fitzroy children's outing. It was widely believed that Charlie protected himself from prosecution for keeping a disorderly house by bribing the police. There were certainly stories of the chief police officer of the area calling on him from time to time, seeing him in his private office, and going away with several bottles of whisky. It was said that Charlie intended to keep going until he had married his daughter into the aristocracy. The Fitzroy closed at half past ten and Charlie's largely undesirable customers then flooded into the neighbouring pubs on the other side of the borough boundaries, much to the annoyance of the landlords. The ill-will thus incurred, and a change of police commissioner in the area in 1955, led to Charlie's final downfall, though he successfully defended a prosecution brought against him. One of his customers who volunteered to appear for the defence was John Waller, who rightly declared that the police could not possibly have overheard the indecent conversations and propositions which they alleged went on in the bar, because of the racket created by a monstrous musical instrument (a kind of hybrid between a piano and an electric organ) which was situated there. Waller added that he regarded the Fitzroy as an extremely respectable place, and had quite often taken his mother and sister there. His mother and sister, however, were quite sophisticated enough, and knew their son and brother well enough, to be perfectly happy to frequent the Fitzroy with him. Charlie Allchild decided to call it a day and sold the pub, which is now of an entirely respectable and different character.

The most important pub in this area, from the literary point of view, was the Wheatsheaf in Rathbone Place, which closed at ten thirty. Many writers and artists were regular frequenters of its bar until this pub also had its downfall, a little before the Fitzroy. The manager is said to have been convicted of income tax fraud. The firm which owned it, Younger's, brought in a new manager, and the clientele also changed. Julian Maclaren Ross held court every night in the Wheatsheaf, standing at a corner of the bar and playing a game called "Spoof" with his friends. I never joined this game and do not quite know what its rules were. It had something to do with holding matches between your fingers, concealing how many there were, and asking your opponent to guess the number. Later, Julian was barred from the pub because he took to playing "Spoof" for money. Gambling of any kind was, of course, illegal in English public houses. Maclaren Ross was a writer of considerable talent in the short story. His little book, *The Nine Men of Soho*, is one of the best fictional accounts of Soho in the period I am talking about. When the Wheatsheaf closed at half past ten, Julian used to retire to a café in Charlotte Street where he would order a cheap meal and make notes on the conversations, and any incidents, he had witnessed during the evening, all of which were potential material for his writings.

Next along Rathbone Place was the Black Horse, which after things changed at the Wheatsheaf tended to take its place. It served excellent sausages, totally unlike what pass for sausages nowadays. The same caterer later supplied them to the Highlander, but I have never seen them since. A little further on, up a side street, was the Bricklayer's Arms, affectionately known as the "Burglar's Rest". It served excellent fishcakes and mussels. I once found a very small pearl, about the size of a pin's head, in one of the mussels. I showed it to the barman but he dropped it and it proved impossible to retrieve. On the south side of Oxford Street there are now no licensed premises. Then, there were Mooney's Irish House, and the Old Queen's Head. Having left the ten-thirty area, one would have a quick drink at one or other of these pubs and then walk through Soho Square into Dean Street. On the right was the Highlander, so called because its original licence dated from 1745. It has now had its name changed to the vulgar and unhistorical Nelly Dean. Proceeding down Dean Street on the left, one came to a club – the Caves de France – run by a Frenchman and intended originally to simulate a French bar, serving only wine, but it soon degenerated into an English beer bar. It had a permanent exhibition of pictures on the walls. I cannot remember who the artist was. One of the paintings was quite extraordinarily Freudian in its iconography. It showed a little girl in school uniform looking into a large stone circle, in the middle of which was a large stone man, or possibly a snowman, holding in his hand – as if jutting up from between his loins – a red golfing umbrella. The barman of the Caves de France was an Italian, Secundo Carnera, younger brother of the heavyweight champion Primo Carnera. A girl I knew once witnessed Secundo pouring the contents of one half-empty bottle of white wine into another. "What are you doing?" she enquired. "Madam," he replied, "I am making a Madeira." Unfortunately, the Caves de France eventually became a striptease club. A little further down on the left-hand side was the Crown and Two Chairmen, run by a lady known as Aunty May, who had her own clientele of rather doubtful characters. Anyone who did not belong to it was not welcome, and, as soon as he had entered, was usually asked to leave in extremely violent and abusive tones. Just round the corner was the Dog and Duck. If one needed to use its lavatory, which opened not into the bar but on to the street, one had to first obtain the key, which, in order that it should not be lost, was chained to a large dried marrowbone.

Further down on the left of Dean Street was the York Minster or the French, as it came to be called. It was kept by a Frenchman, Gaston Berlemont, who had inherited the pub from his elderly father who used sometimes to be seen in the bar. Berlemont père was an almost stereotypical old-fashioned Frenchman, with large bristling moustaches. The Berlemonts, who came from Burgundy, were Protestants and formed part of the Huguenot community which had first settled in Soho, after the Greeks, in the seventeenth century. This was in the days of Bishop Compton, after whom Old Compton Street is named, who built St Anne's, the parish church of the area, on the western side of Dean Street. It was he who had allowed the Greeks and, later, the French Huguenots – fleeing from France after the Revocation of the Edict of Nantes – to establish places of worship in this area, which in those days had been newly developed on the fringe of the City of Westminster. Soho had originally been Soho Fields. The name, an old hare-coursing cry, had also been the war cry at the Battle of Sedgemoor, for the Duke of Monmouth had a house in Soho Square. The nineteenth-century French Huguenot church in the north-western corner of Soho Square is built in an interesting Protestant French style – rather similar to the Dutch – and still retains its minister and its small congregation. In the nineteenth century one of its ministers was Peter Mark Roget, the compiler of the *Thesaurus*.

To the east of Greek Street, and at the end of the short Manette Street, is an archway leading to Charing Cross Road, called the Pillars of Hercules. The nearby pub with the same name was also one we used to go to from time to time. It had been frequented by the poet Francis Thompson in his down-and-out days, after he had run away from home. He was allowed to sit in the bar, though obviously too poor to buy a drink, and slept at nights, as many down-and-outs still do, in the crypt of St Martin-in-the-Fields. His only forwarding address was the poste restante at Charing Cross, where Francis and Alice Meynell finally traced him. He had sent a contribution to their periodical *Merry England*. They rescued him, rehabilitated him from his opium addiction, and he continued to contribute to the periodical for the rest of his short life.

The artists, writers and musicians who regularly frequented this area formed a kind of coherent society, with its own hierarchy and its own codes. There were other societies there as well, but they seldom interpenetrated. There was the violent society of the razor gangs, the society of the spivs and black-marketeers, and that of the prostitutes of both sexes who frequented the streets. One of the male prostitutes of the area during the war years was said to have been known to the police as Doodle-bug Daisy because he faithfully stayed on his beat near Leicester Square throughout the worst of the bombing.

Among the painters the most prominent were Robert Colquhoun and Robert MacBryde, John Minton, Keith Vaughan, John Craxton and Lucian Freud. The last two were close friends at this time and indulged in the sort of eccentric pranks which young men often get up to, such as stuffing toffee into each other's ears. John Minton, unlike most in this society, was wealthy and generous to his friends. His lively and humorous personality must have concealed a depressive streak, for he eventually took his own life.

One of the musicians was Arthur Oldham, a pupil of Benjamin Britten. Oldham later became organist of St Mary's Roman Catholic Cathedral in Edinburgh, but never quite fulfilled his promise as a composer. Another musician was Cyril Clark, who had been a pupil of Donald Tovey. Cyril claimed to have written the first television opera, but when I knew him he had become a hopeless alcoholic. Towards the end of his life, in the 1960s, he invited me to write the libretto for another television opera. I adapted Rossetti's long ballad-like *Rose Marie*, which has a mediaeval setting and involves sorcery. As it was written almost entirely in dialogue and had only a few characters, it could be converted into an opera libretto with very few changes. I sent my script to Cyril and, a little later, called on him to discuss it, only to find that he had completely forgotten that he had received it. I do not think he did any work on it, and if any other composers would like to pick it up they are welcome. Peter Warlock (Philip Heseltine) and Constant Lambert had been regular habitués of the area, but Warlock had died tragically in 1930, and Lambert had disappeared from the scene by the time I had got there.

Cyril Clark was a regular drinking companion of Gilbert Wood, a scenic designer, Bob Pocock and John Leper. I became very much part of their circle at one time. Wood had once worked in a theatre which was showing, among other entertainments, a fire-eating act. He told us how, after the show, the lady fire-eater came into the pub and demanded a cigarette. She said she had been desperate for a smoke all evening. Bob Pocock, who was of Wiltshire farming stock, later became a BBC producer. He was a close friend of Dylan Thomas and one of the most intelligent men I have ever met. After war service in India he had joined the Metropolitan police force. His superior officer warned him to be on his guard against a terrible area called Soho, full of all kinds of undesirable types. He immediately headed for Soho, and after he had resigned from the police force became a regular habitué.

The fourth member of the group, and a particularly close friend of mine, was John Leper. He has a brief mention, for his short stories, in John Lehmann's *New Writing in Europe*, which was published at the beginning of the war and is a very useful guide to the literary scene of the thirties. Before the Second World War Leper had volunteered to fight for the Republican side in Spain, where he got to know Tony Hindmarsh, Stephen Spender's friend who had formerly been a Welsh guardsman. Spender had persuaded Hindmarsh to volunteer to fight, though Spender himself had been engaged in non-combatant propaganda work behind the lines. Leper and Hindmarsh became disenchanted with the way the Republican cause was directed, and both deserted. John Leper was an Irishman from the ancient family of the

Lepers of Leopardstown. He had an excellent singing voice and had compiled a collection of traditional soldiers' songs. These, and other similar material, he used to sing very charmingly. The oldest of his soldiers' songs was a round, dating from Elizabethan times:

> We be soldiers three
> pardonnez moy je vous en prie
> lately come from the low country
> with never a deal of money.
>
> Charge it again, boy, charge it again
> as long as there's any ink in your pen
> with never a deal of money.

These lines vividly recall Elizabethan London after the disastrous Netherlands campaign in which Sir Philip Sidney lost his life. The capital was full of discharged soldiers who had not been paid.

Leper and his three companions used to drink together in the Duke of York at the top of Upper Rathbone Place. The landlord, Major Alf Klein, was assisted by his wife Blanche. Blanche was strongly orthodox in her Jewish religious beliefs and insisted that the pub close on Yom Kippur. Her barman, Stanley, was an ex-merchant seaman. Some years later he was told that he must take another job as he was drinking too much. He did take another job, but he still died within twelve months, and he might as well have enjoyed another year's drinking.

After eleven o'clock, when all the pubs were closed, one could go to a club and continue drinking till twelve, as long as food was served. There was the expensive and flashy Gargoyle Club in Dean Street and, for most of us, the Mandrake Club, round the corner in Meard Street. Here one could buy a pint of beer and a sandwich. One did not have to eat the sandwiches, which remained in constant use. Someone once complained about this, but was told firmly: "This is a sandwich for drinking with, not a sandwich for eating." The pro-prietor of the Mandrake was Boris Watson, a Russian who had been educated at St Paul's School. His real name was Protopopoff. His elderly father, who was still alive in the 1940s, was that A. D. Protopopoff who had been the last tsarist Minister of the Interior. From the point of view of the licensing magistrates, a drinking club had to have some *raison d'être*, and the Mandrake was officially a social and chess club. Boris himself possessed the Russian national talent for chess, and several quite distinguished chess players, including Vicky, the cartoonist, did frequent the back room of the club. But its principal use was for after-hours drinking. Boris would also cash your cheques, provided that half the value of the cheque went in credit to his bar. This was convenient, but tended to lead to frightening over-drafts. As well as artists and writers, some of the underworld fre-quented this club. Once, after a trip to Paris, I went into the Mandrake to have a drink in the afternoon – for it was also open between three and six, when the pubs were closed. Before leaving, I found that my passport had been stolen from my pocket. When I told Boris he answered, "Don't say anything," and within five minutes returned it to me. He knew exactly who had stolen it. "It's all part of the service," he said.

On another occasion, my friend Noel Sircar and I went in for a drink, and Boris said: "Would you like to see our totem?" He pro-duced several large specimens of real mandrake roots. The man-drake's use as a love charm goes right back to Old Testament times. Rachel conceived Benjamin only with the aid of mandrakes which her sister, Leah, had been given by one of her own sons. When Boris showed us his totem, Noel asked: "Can you explain to us how to get it with child?" "That", he replied, "is a very technical and difficult process."

Noel Sirkar was a good friend and frequent drinking companion of mine. The son of an Indian father and an Irish mother, he worked at the Indian High Commission, and had published a charming account of his own early years, *An Indian Boyhood*. He also wrote a children's book: *News from the Lesser Burrows*. The characters were animals, and the illustrator had shown a badger smoking a cigarette in a long holder. Those who knew him would recognise this as a portrait of Julian Maclaren Ross. Noel's family were Christian, and he himself was sincere in his religion, in spite of his weakness as an alcoholic. One afternoon, while we were drinking together in the Mandrake, he spoke to me of his friendship and affection for me, and told me how sorry he was that I had such trouble with my eyes. "Give me your hand," he said. "You know I come from a Brahmin family." I saw that he was serious and gave him my hand. I cannot accurately describe what happened, but I had a sense, though not a physical one, of some kind of power passing from him to me. "I mustn't do this too often," he said. There is no miraculous sequel to this story, but I am sure that a gesture made in such good faith and with such goodwill must, somehow, have had its effects, even though it did not prevent the deterioration of my eyesight. Noel was once arrested by the police in St Anne's churchyard. His defence was that he was striking matches while trying to find Hazlitt's tomb. Hazlitt is, in fact, buried there, and his epitaph tells us that he was happy to have lived to see the end of the hated Bourbons. Sadly, Noel was later mugged by thugs in a back ally in Soho and his brain was badly affected. He had slowly to learn to speak again, for the most common words had dropped out of his memory. He had been warned by his doctors that there must be an end to his drinking, but, of course, there was not, and he finally relapsed into nothing but a vegetable state.

I have already mentioned Nina Hamnett as one of the queens of Soho. One met her in various pubs and also in the Mandrake. One bought her a gin. She gave very good value in the anecdotes she would tell and the songs she would sing. In her youth she had gone on folk-song-collecting forays with the composer E. J. Moeran – whom she once briefly introduced me to – in the pubs of Norfolk. In those days, before the radio and then the television had obliterated much of our traditional culture, it was possible to hear genuine and ancient English folk-songs performed in the bars of such places. Nina had a repertoire of some of these – especially, I think, the more risqué ones which had been rejected for publication – and others which were not folk-songs in the purist sense of the word, but fragments of old Victorian and Edwardian music-hall ballads. A particular favourite was:

Every Saturday afternoon we tries to drown our sorrers.
We always goes to the waxworks shows to see the Chamber of
  Horrors.
There's a beautiful statue of mother there, what gives us pleasure
  rather,
With the same old smile on her dear old dial as the night she
  strangled father.

Once Nina said to me, rather sadly: "Everybody used to sing when I was young, but now nobody sings any more." This was not quite true. I have already mentioned John Leper's talent in this respect. Another singer of folk-songs was Gordon ("Kit") Barker, George Barker's artist brother. He had a large repertoire of ballads – for some of which, I think, he had composed his own tunes – including such classics as "Edward, Edward" and "The Demon Lover". These ballads had been collected at the end of the eighteenth century or the beginning of the nineteenth, but the early collectors had not been interested in the music. Quite often when George Barker and Kit, myself and other friends had spent an evening drinking together, we would buy a few bottles of beer before the pub closed and find our way to somebody's flat where we would go on singing songs – some of them English, Scottish and Irish ballads, some American, and some old music-hall songs – until after midnight. This was done quite unpretentiously and spontaneously and everybody was expected to contribute. Another singer was Colin Davis, who had a good

143

repertoire of mostly nineteenth-century street ballads which he used to sing in the Mandrake. All this was long before the modern fashion for folk clubs grew up. Nowadays, any oaf who can strum a few chords on a guitar and string a few verses together, with probably a simplistic left-wing political message, can call himself a folk-singer. It has got nothing to do with the real tradition of English folk-song, which seldom, or never, used instrumental accompaniment, except for dancing.

There were many people who found their way to Soho, and occasionally one would meet writers of distinction, like John Lehmann and Louis MacNeice, though they were never regular frequenters of the area. I was once introduced in the Mandrake by Nina Hamnett to the Irish writer, Liam O'Flaherty. He asked me who I was and what I did. I replied that I was a poet. "In my day", he said, "young men did not say, 'I am a poet,' they said, 'I write verse.'" I took this admonition to heart and have never introduced myself as a poet since. Perhaps the most memorable non-event among these chance meetings is an encounter I had in the Wheatsheaf shortly after the liberation of France. I was with Lazarus Aaronson, a poet whose true worth, I feel, has not been appreciated. His work combines a sense of his deep Jewish roots with his conversion to Christianity. "That man over there", said Laz, "is Samuel Beckett. He was James Joyce's amanuensis and has written many great works which have not yet been published." At that time I had not read any of Joyce's books, and one was always meeting people who had written masterpieces which had not yet been published. Nothing of any significance by Beckett had been published at that time. Laz took me over to a table where a man in a soft felt hat and horn-rimmed glasses was seated. I was introduced and shook hands with Beckett. That was about all. Beckett was obviously a very shy man and we did not engage in any conversation.

There were some habitués of Soho who could not afford to drink. Many of these frequented a café run by Greeks, next door to the Black Horse, generally known as the Café Alix. Among these was Bernard Kops, later to be well known as a playwright. Another was the Countess Eileen de Vigne. She was an Englishwoman, but had once been married to a rich South American with an hereditary European title. She had had, I believe, a rather tragic history, including a period of drug addiction. She was cured of this, but was now rumoured to live almost entirely on benzedrine and jam puffs. At this time, amphetamines were freely prescribed, not only for those who had formerly been drug addicts, but also as anti-depressants, and even as an aid to slimming. Benzedrine inhalers, produced to relieve congestion in the sinuses, were available in chemists' shops. Some people would open the plastic cases of the inhalers, and steep the little pieces of benzedrine-impregnated cotton in cups of tea or coffee. Probably because of insomnia, which would have been exacerbated by the benzedrine, the countess wandered about the streets at night, and was, to some extent, a professional ragpicker, finding in the dustbins of fashionable areas like Park Lane and Mayfair pieces of material, or slightly cracked china ornaments, which had been thrown away and which were saleable. A young man with whom I was very friendly, whom Sylvia Gough had christened "Dear Dirty Little Les", once informed me that he had been appointed literary agent to "Iron Boot Jack". "Iron Boot Jack" was a curious character, a dealer in junk who also advertised himself as an astrologer and mystic, and wrote poetry of a sort. He wore his hair in a pigtail tied with a bow, and, presumably because of some childhood accident, one of his legs was much shorter than the other and was supported by a large iron boot.

Paddy Maguire was an elderly Irish journalist. One generally encountered him in the street: "Sure and can you lend me a lousy half-crown?" One gave him the half-crown (something one learnt in Soho was that there was no semantic distinction between the verb "to give" and the verb "to lend"). The next time it would be five shillings, and the time after that ten shillings, doubling with mathematical precision until he reached the limits of his benefactors' generosity – let us say four pounds. If refused, Paddy showed no hard feelings, but at the next encounter the request would be halved to two pounds and so on with the same precision until the original half-crown demand was reached. It was said that there were rare occasions when Paddy was in funds, and that then he would pay everybody back precisely what they had lent him. I never experienced one of these happy events, though I was told that one occurred when I was out of London. Gilbert Wood composed the following epitaph for him, in case it should be needed:

> Here beneath this trembling spire
> Lies the corpse of Pat Maguire.
> The bones that all around him lie
> Are the stiffs that he sucked dry.
> And while his body feeds the clover
> His spirit tries to touch Jehovah.

Perhaps the most notable frequenters of Soho were its poets, which included some of real talent, even genius. Dylan Thomas, when in London, was, of course, a fairly regular frequenter of Soho, though I think he did his best work when living in his boathouse at Laugharne. Dylan had a fine voice. Because of his early speech-training his Welsh accent was not as marked as one might suppose, though he retained a great deal of native Welsh eloquence. Dylan had also done some acting in the Little Theatre in his native Swansea. In London he seemed to be something of a show-off. He often gathered round him a circle of friends who were not really his intellectual equals. I remember him one evening in the Wheatsheaf reciting parts of *Under Milk Wood*, which was then in process of composition. This included some scenes which did not find a place in the final version. One of these was set in the town hall where alarming messages were coming through on the ticker tape such as "The fish have declared war!" and "Anti-Christ has reached Carnarvon!" The legendary feats of Dylan as a drinker have, to some extent, been exaggerated. Like all the rest of us he only drank beer and would get quite elated on a couple of pints. There is reason to think that he had an undiagnosed thyroid condition which would have lowered his resistance to alcohol. This appears obvious in the Augustus John portrait. John has somewhat exaggerated Dylan's features, but you can see eyes which seem to be slightly popping out of his head and a prominent swollen gland in his throat. Dylan may also have had a diabetic condition. It is notable that he was fond of Mars bars and other sweets, and was often found with a hoard of them in his bed. It is unusual for beer drinkers to want sweets, as they get enough sugar from their beer. During the war his friends used to give Dylan their sweet ration.

When he went to America the legend of his drinking had, of course, preceded him. In America, hard drinking meant hard liquor, and his hosts pressed it upon him. He did not refuse it, but it was this which in the end killed him. Some of the American academics at whose colleges he read shamelessly exploited him. I was told that members of the faculty of such a college, at which Dylan was billed to read, said before he came: "Let's get him drunk. It will be amusing." This behaviour is quite disgraceful. Dylan did not really enjoy the academic parties which he was compelled to attend. He preferred the cosy atmosphere of a British pub, which is scarcely to be found in America except, perhaps, in some old taverns in Greenwich Village, New York. American bars are uncivilised. They are either sleazy chromium-plated cocktail bars, or places designed mainly for hopeless drunks in which there are not even individual toilet stalls for men, but a large trough into which everyone makes water communally. Dylan's second and last visit to America was undertaken very unwillingly. He had to pay off the enormous debt which he had incurred through his improvidence and his persistent failure to fill up income tax returns. He hated leaving behind his wife and children, to whom he was devoted.

As with Dylan Thomas, I first heard George Barker read at the Ethical Church, and was briefly introduced to him on that occasion.

But he really became my friend when we met in the Wheatsheaf on VJ Night. The final end of the war, and our victory over Japan, had a bitter taste to it, for that victory had involved the dropping of the atom bombs on Hiroshima and Nagasaki, the terrible implications of which we had all come to realise. George's sequence of three poems, *News of the World*, should be read in this light. Their meaning was obvious at the time. The first two poems have as their subject a wife complaining of her faithless husband, and a husband who looks with pity on his doomed wife. These are followed by a brief poem which sees our earth as a star under a curse wandering in the universe. It should be realised that these poems are not only about George's own experience (he had left his first wife Jessica when in America and begun his longstanding relationship with Elizabeth Smart, the mother of four of his children). They are also allegories of the world which has been betrayed by its husband, "man", by the dropping of the atom bomb. They are, in my opinion, among the finest poems to have come out of the Second World War.

George had gone to Japan immediately before the war to take up an academic post. It was a bad time to be in that country. According to his own account, the maid whom he and his wife employed was a government spy. She could not understand much English, but ostentatiously listened at keyholes so that her superiors should know that she was doing her duty. George had some difficulty in getting the Japanese students adequately to understand English poetry. He set them for comment a poem of A. E. Housman (always one of his favourite poets) beginning "The chestnut casts its flambeaux". The students came to him in a body and said: "We find this poem extremely obscure. We have looked up the words in the dictionary, and it appears to say that the chestnut tree is throwing away torches. We cannot comprehend how a chestnut tree can have torches to throw away." The reason for this misunderstanding was that classical Japanese poetry makes no use whatsoever of metaphor or simile. Their place is taken by a subtle use of symbolism. As metaphors are the very soul of English poetry, it was the slightly unusual "flambeaux" which had brought the matter to a head. George tried to explain to them about metaphor and simile, but felt that he was not getting through to them at all, and, in fact, that he had been wasting his time all along. The entry of Japan into the war meant that George and his wife were hastily evacuated to America where they found themselves stranded without any real resources. Elizabeth Smart, who was already an admirer of George's poetry, came to their rescue, but it led to a passionate affair between the two writers and the final break with Jessica. George was a Roman Catholic and so there was no possibility of divorce. Jessica remained his legal wife for another forty years. George was to have relationships with several women during this period, and to father a large number of children. It was only after Jessica's death that he was able to marry his second wife, Elspeth. The number of George's children was, according to the usual estimates, round about sixteen. I do not think in this respect he reached the status of Augustus John, who was said always to pat small children on the head on the offchance that they might be his.

George is, in my opinion, the best poet of his generation – the generation born just before or during the First World War. His first volume of poems, *Thirty Preliminary Poems*, was published in 1933 by his friend David Archer at the Parton Press. Barker therefore came into prominence at the same time as Dylan Thomas, whose first volume, *Eighteen Poems*, appeared in the following year with the same publisher. The two poets had something in common. In the course of the thirties, the intellectual and rather didactic style established by W. H. Auden and others was giving place to a freer style which involved a highly idiosyncratic use of language and was, to some extent, influenced by continental surrealism. The International Surrealist Exhibition, mounted in London in 1936, had a great impact not only on painting but on poetry. The only important English poet definitely associated with surrealism was David Gascoyne, though his later work is much more in an English Romantic tradition. He published his first volume, *Man's Life is this Meat*, with the Parton Press at the age of sixteen, and wrote a history of surrealism. Dylan Thomas denied that he himself was a surrealist. Strict surrealistic doctrine of poetry advocated a kind of automatic writing. Everything which the subconscious threw up was to be set down, the poet himself exercising no kind of control or censorship. Thomas, however, was a very careful craftsman and could not accept this. But, for all that, he was there at the International Surrealist Exhibition, offering people cups of boiled string and asking them if they took milk and sugar in it.

George Barker's poetry, like Dylan Thomas's, employed a mannered and baroque use of language, and the two poets were often compared in their early years. Melchiori, in his critical book *The Tightrope Walkers*, subsumes Dylan Thomas, Christopher Fry and Charles Williams under the common descriptive label of "Mannerism". Thomas attended Williams's lectures at the City Literary Institute, and at least one of Thomas's poems, "The Conversation of Prayers", seems to show the influence of Williams's doctrine of substitution. The appearance of *Deaths and Entrances* in 1946, along with his successes as a broadcaster, led to Thomas's widespread popularity – he even became a kind of cult – but some responsible critics and poets, notably W. B. Yeats and T. S. Eliot, had rated the poetry of George Barker more highly. Barker once told me how, when he was sitting in a bar in New York, his friend, the American poet Dunstan Thompson, came rushing in, showing him with triumph that Yeats had included Barker in his *Oxford Book of Modern Verse*. Barker was the youngest poet to be included in that volume. Eliot, I think, favoured Barker against Thomas, for much the same reasons that he preferred Joyce to Lawrence. He saw in both Barker and Joyce an essentially Catholic sensibility, whereas the roots of Thomas were in Welsh Nonconformity as those of Lawrence were in English Nonconformity.

Barker always remained loyal to the Roman Catholicism he had been brought up in – however far from the Church's moral code he might depart – and most of his friends, including myself, came under fairly persistent pressure to be converted. I cannot remember that he was successful in accomplishing this in any instance. Edith Sitwell admired George's work, as she did that of Dylan Thomas, and George was often a guest at her London lunch parties held at the Sesame Club. After her own conversion to Roman Catholicism she seems to have thought that, apart from her immediate family, only her Catholic friends should be her guests on these occasions. Consequently George found himself invited to lunch with her, the only other member of the party being Osbert Sitwell. It was Lent or a fast day. When the menu came round, Osbert firmly ordered steak. Naturally, Edith did not follow him in this, and said to George: "I expect you would like some of this nice pasta." "I want steak," said George. "I'm not going to heaven for eating pasta. In any case I don't want to go to heaven – I want to go to hell." On one of George's visits to Italy, he was overwhelmed by the shrine of St Francis at Assisi, and became a Franciscan Tertiary, though I do not think he followed very strictly the rules of the Third Order. Among the Catholic figures he particularly revered were Gerard Manley Hopkins and Cardinal Newman. He was fond of quoting the latter's dictum that "the whole creation labours under an aboriginal catastrophe". It is this strong sense of original sin, sometimes almost to the exclusion of any concept of redemption, combined with a post-Freudian, post-Lawrentian idea of sex, which gives to Barker's poetry its particular strengths, and which makes it so repugnant to some of his readers.

I became a quite frequent visitor to George's parents' flat in South Kensington. Here his elderly Irish mother presided in the kitchen, dispensing unlimited cups of tea to her extended family of two sons, two daughters and numerous nephews and nieces. She is, of course, the subject of perhaps George's best-known poem. He told me that when he showed this poem in manuscript to T. S. Eliot the latter said: "I must congratulate you on having written an anthology piece." This, indeed, became the case, but an anthology piece is not always a poet's best work, as Eliot himself knew only too well. Such a piece can hang round a poet's neck like an albatross. At the age of about thirty I myself was guilty of an ironical epitaph written in a mood of self-depreciation. It unfortunately became an anthology piece. I had put a weapon into the hands of my enemies. When I reprinted it in my collected poems, I accompanied it by a companion piece in the same metre, falling just short of delivering a formal curse on anyone who wished further to reproduce it.

George's father had been a policeman in his younger days, but was very proud of his First World War commission in the Guards. He was a formidable old man. On the occasion of a party for George's birthday, I arrived early, finding the colonel, as he was known, in the sitting-room, most courteously receiving the guests, and happy with a box of cigars with which he had been presented. After an hour or so he retired to bed, but some time between eleven and twelve a message came down to George, saying: "Your father says that the party will now stop or else he will come down with a horsewhip." It was fairly clear that this was more or less literally true, and the party quietly dissolved. When his wife died, George's father became a recluse, saying that none of his children was ever to enter his house again.

I was to see a lot more of George when I lived for a time in a cottage near Zennor in north-west Cornwall which I shared with David Wright and George's nephew, John Fairfax. George and his companion, Betty Cashenden Cass, occupied another cottage about half a mile away. Kit Barker and his wife Ilse also had a cottage close by, and we all met together frequently. The cottage which David, John and I lived in had once been occupied by Katherine Mansfield. Peter Warlock live in a cottage on Zennor hill. One sometimes felt that there was a sinister atmosphere about this house. Whether this was due to the presence of the undoubtedly unquiet spirit of Peter Warlock, who is believed to have been involved in occultism and eventually committed suicide, I would not like to say. Cornwall, in any case, is full of such legendary presences. It is said that Aleister Crowley had lived in the parish of Zennor at one period with a party of his female disciples. Crowley and they were said later to have been run out of the county by the local magistrates. It is told that Crowley had a conflict with the vicar of Zennor who threw holy water over him in the churchyard in the presence of the congregation. Crowley's retort was: "He's not a real priest and it's not real holy water. If he were, and it were, I would sizzle."

North-west Cornwall was, for us, the sea-coast of Bohemia. In that period of the forties and early fifties one could rent a cottage there for as little as half a crown a week. The cottages were traditional

Cornish stone houses with, sometimes, no more than two rooms, no running water and no water closet. This was certainly the case in a cottage at Nancledra which I shared with two other friends on a later visit to the county. First thing in the morning one had to go down to the local stream and draw water in a bucket. This then had to be boiled on a spirit-stove before one could even wash. Covering one wall of the cottage was an enormous old-fashioned Cornish range, a formidable object which was much too daunting for us to try to use. The chimney would have needed cleaning anyway.

The nearest town to Zennor was St Ives, a fashionable artists' colony. I did not know the real grandees of the place such as Barbara Hepworth and Ben Nicholson, but there were other artists who were friends. The locals, not unnaturally, somewhat resisted these incomers. David Wright has written about their deviousness and their veiled hostility, with which he does not seem easily to have come to terms. For my own part – I do not know if it is the streak of Welsh blood in me – I felt a kind of fellow feeling with the locals, rather than resentment. Later on, at Leeds, I had much more difficulty in coming to terms with Yorkshire bluntness. Cornwall is a large county with a great variation in landscape. My friendship with the Cornish poet, Charles Causley, who lives in Launceston in east Cornwall, belongs to a later stage of my life.

Then, in Cornwall, and at other times, George Barker became in some ways my chief poetic mentor. I would submit what I wrote to his scrutiny, and he never made any difficulties about reading my verses. This is not true of all poets. I am prepared to read the work of young poets, if they show it to me, although I cannot stand being sent poems by post. One has to write a long and detailed criticism, for which one is very seldom thanked. Criticism face to face can be given with a smile, and combined with a constructive discussion of the point at issue.

Some have regarded Barker as an undisciplined and self-indulgent poet. This is very far from the truth. He was a most rigid and ruthless critic of the work of myself and of others. So strong was the influence of his personality that some poets, notably Dunstan Thompson and Maurice Carpenter, were almost prevented from reaching their full potential through being too much under his influence. Maurice Carpenter is an interesting and, I think, neglected poet who began to publish during the thirties. At that time he was a close friend of George and Kit Barker. All of them were fascinated by the English poetry of the fourteenth and fifteenth centuries. Maurice's principal work was *The Tall Interpreter*, on the theme of Orpheus. It was finally published by a minor poetry publisher not long before Maurice's death, but the text thus given seems to be abridged from the fuller and superior version which Maurice had lent to me in typescript some twenty or so years earlier.

George Barker had a complex and sometimes difficult personality. He made enemies only too easily, for he would not suffer fools gladly, and a great deal of prejudice still exists against him. One of those whom he had alienated was Kingsley Martin, the great editor of the *New Statesman*, whom Barker had described in print as a "denatured old liberal tom cat". Barker undoubtedly could behave badly, especially to women, although he was obviously very attractive to the latter. From his friends he always elicited a long and enduring loyalty. His best poem, perhaps, is the long, semi-autobiographical *The True Confession of George Barker*, which is partly modelled on Villon's *Grand Testament*. In George's poem there are certain passages on sex, combining fascination with loathing, which deeply offended his publisher Faber, particularly, I believe, T. S. Eliot. Faber refused to publish this poem until the very last edition of George's *Collected Poems*, which appeared a year before his death. It was, in fact, published in 1950 by the communist poet and translator, Jack Lindsay, in a series of pamphlets entitled "Key Poets". A further edition, to which a second part was appended, was later published by David Archer in 1955 when he refounded his old publishing venture of the Parton Press. When *The True Confession* first appeared, it was broadcast by the BBC on the Third Programme, and this led to violent protests against its alleged obscenity, and questions being asked in the House of Commons. A spokesman for the BBC apologised abjectly for their allowing the poem to be broadcast, and stated that the producer of the programme had been severely disciplined. This was, surely, a gratuitous slur on the poet himself, almost as bad as the BBC's own supineness in the matter. George completed *The True Confession* in 1948 upon his thirty-fifth birthday, or so he maintained. He regarded it as his greatest work and in adopting this strategy wished to align himself with Dante, who began *The Divine Comedy* "in mezzo del cammin" ("in the middle of the way of this our mortal life"). Mediaeval writers, following the biblical text which states threescore years and ten as the allotted span of man, regarded thirty-five as the midpoint of life. I well remember George's phoning me up and asking me round to his flat to hear him read the poem on its completion. I must have been the first person ever to hear it read aloud.

David Archer himself was a fairly regular frequenter of Soho. George Barker wrote of him with great affection and loyalty. To me he seemed a rather sad man. He came of a wealthy landowning family in Wiltshire, and had devoted most of his private fortune to the promotion of poetry, even borrowing on expectations. In the 1930s his bookshop in Parton Street, Bloomsbury, had been a well-known meeting place for poets and others, mostly political dissidents and rebels against the establishment of their time. After the original Parton Bookshop failed, Archer opened another one in Glasgow, and this also became a meeting place, bringing together many Scottish poets and painters of the time. This was, perhaps, the original link between Robert Colquhoun, Robert MacBryde and George Barker. Archer claimed to have no knowledge of poetry at all; nevertheless he seemed to have had an uncanny aptitude for picking winners. A homosexual who tended to form relationships with the most deplorable young men – brainless thugs, I would almost say – he gradually sank into deeper poverty and degradation. In 1957 he briefly reopened his book-shop, this time in Soho, but ended by selling lampshades in Selfridges. In his last years he lived in a doss-house where, sadly, he took his own life. After his cremation, a girl who was one of his friends took the urn containing his ashes back to his native village in Wiltshire to have them deposited in the family vault. In the pub she met some of the locals, and when she told them of her mission they replied: "Oh, we wanted to know what had happened to Mr David. There is a large sum of money owing to him from the War Office as compensation for use by the army of his family estates during the war."

Among the poets whom I regard as my immediate contemporaries (those whose work did not appear till the Second World War), W. S. Graham was, in the 1940s, a fairly regular frequenter of Soho. My relationship with him was always difficult, though there was a great deal of goodwill on both sides. I had the greatest admiration for his poetry, but it was hard for me to come to terms with his Scottish directness. Of working-class origin, he came from Greenock in Lanarkshire, where he had, I believe, worked in the shipbuilding yards in his early years. Indeed, his attitude to language was that of a welder or riveter, and he was strongly influenced by *Finnegans Wake*. Graham worked for a time in an advertising agency, writing slogans for commercial campaigns. The Shell Company ran a series of adver-tisements at this time, involving a rhyming couplet in which the second line was always: "The motorist he dreams of Shell." Some of Graham's contributions were too over the top for his employers, for example: "The apple dreams of William Tell, the motorist he dreams of Shell." Advertising companies were said to be the only commercial organisations who would gladly employ poets. There were several poets who did work in advertising for many years, including Norman Cameron, a member of Robert Graves's circle and a fine poet, though with a pathetically small body of work to his credit. Towards the end of his life he resigned, determined to devote himself exclusively to writing, but he did not live very much longer. In the early fifties the BBC formed a project to broadcast a selection of French poems of the Romantic period, the original texts to be read by an actor from the Comédie Française, accompanied by translations commissioned from various English poets. My own contribution was a version of Alfred de Vigny's "Le Cor". Cameron contributed a translation of de Musset's "Nuit d'été". This was of such high quality that the BBC commissioned him to follow it with a complete translation of de Musset's "Nuits" sequence. These remarkable translations have, I believe, never been printed, and they ought to be. I do not know whether they are somewhere concealed in a forgotten BBC file (the producer on this occasion was Rayner Heppenstall), or are to be found among Cameron's papers, but someone ought to look for them.

Sydney Graham (known as Jock by his Scottish friends) did not remain very long with the advertising agency, and after a spell of lecturing in America settled at Mevagissey in Cornwall with his wife Nessie Dunsmuir. Intensely devoted to poetry, he endured a life of extreme poverty for many years. Recognition came very slowly. He tried to earn a living by growing flowers commercially, but he lived largely on crabs and other crustaceans which he caught on the beach, and sometimes earned money by helping out the fishermen (his longest and best poem is "The Night Fishing"). I was told that he was reduced to eating Kit-e-Kat sandwiches, though I cannot vouch for this. Sydney had immense charm, but when drunk could be very aggressive. I was once in the Wheatsheaf with William Bell and an Oxford friend of ours, John Robinson. Sydney came up, in one of his less amiable, drunkenly aggressive and incoherent moods. I introduced him to my two Oxford friends. When he had left us, John Robinson said: "Who is that man? Surely he can't be a poet?" "John," said William Bell, "you don't know how lucky you are. Poets you happen to know, like John Heath-Stubbs and me, are, in fact, quite nice people, but the majority of poets are not." In spite of all this I had a very deep admiration for Sydney's poetry and affection for the man, which lasted until his death.

Another member of this Soho circle was Paul Potts. Canadian by birth, he was of Irish descent and had been educated at Ampleforth. I first encountered him at that gathering at Empson's house on the occasion of Pierre Emmanuel's visit to London which I have already described. Paul was, with difficulty, persuaded to read from his own work at that event. Ruthven Todd explained to the company, on Paul's behalf, that he was used to reading his poetry to "people", and not in literary salons. He had begun as a populist poet, reading aloud in Hyde Park, and peddling small pamphlets of his poems. In those days he identified strongly, among others, with Walt Whitman. Towards the end of his life he said that he had hoped to be a poet reading his work to vast crowds of people, but had ended up, like all the others, reading to a small specialised audience. Paul had a deep belief in libertarian values and in a kind of non-dogmatic Tolstoyan Christianity. In the forties, when I was still living in West Hampstead, he occupied a top back room somewhere in Hampstead proper. We would often walk home together at nights, having missed the last train and not having any money to spare for taxis. We would proceed up the Finchley Road until our ways diverged, he going up Haverstock Hill, and I going down West End Lane. I learnt a lot from the conversations we had in the evenings, at the pubs or on these walks. My own background and my political instincts were deeply traditionalist. From Paul I learnt to value the libertarian traditions of Britain and America. How he survived at all was always a bit of a mystery. He may have had a very small private income, and I believe he received a legacy from George Orwell, but his life was spent in extreme poverty and, one has to add, in his later years, squalor. Milein Cosmann, with an artist's insight, remarked of his face that it revealed the two aspects of his nature: in full face he appeared rather noble, in profile weak and shifty. Paul was notorious, not only for sponging on his friends, but also for petty-thieving from them. As George Barker said: "He just expected you to forgive him – and you did." His later years were to be increasingly sad and lonely. His person became so offensive that he was banned by the landlords from most of his usual haunts, and he also became mentally confused. He died in a fire in his flat – probably he fell asleep while smoking his pipe. Burning ash from the pipe must have ignited the mass of papers and other rubbish which cluttered the place.

I cannot speak with as much intimacy of the painters who regularly frequented Soho, or pretend to be competent to judge their work. The two most celebrated were, of course, Robert Colquhoun and Robert MacBryde. They seem to have become, since their deaths, almost legendary figures, and in 1992 were the subject of a play which received a certain amount of notice. I never saw this play. I do not care to watch actors impersonating characters whom I have known, but the general consensus among those of the Roberts' friends who did see it was that it robbed them of their essential dignity, turning them into a kind of Laurel and Hardy cross-talk act. I heard a clip from the play in a broadcast review. The first thing that struck me was that the actors had given the two artists stereotypical Aberdeen accents, when they actually came from Ayrshire. Whatever may be the final evaluation of their artistic work, and however disorderly the lives they led, it must be emphasised that they were serious artists. Colquhoun was probably the more talented of the two. He was more introverted than MacBryde, and exhibited a certain dourness. MacBryde had immense charm. He could sing Scottish ballads in a light tenor voice quite bewitchingly. Colquhoun died in 1962, collapsing from a heart attack while hanging pictures for a forthcoming exhibition of his work. MacBryde was, naturally, deeply cast down by the death of the friend he had lived with since they were both in their teens. He managed, however, to create a new life for himself, taking a teaching post in Dublin, and making a new circle of friends in that city. MacBryde died dancing, outside a pub which had just closed, when a truck swung round a corner and killed him.

During the 1940s Colquhoun and MacBryde had a studio in Notting Hill Gate, and on Sunday evenings, when the pubs in Soho were largely deserted, they and their friends used to drink in the Old Swan at the top of Kensington Church Street. This pub was pulled down in 1956 in accordance with a scheme for widening the road at Notting Hill Gate. One of the features of its décor had been two large mirrors, and inset in their reflecting glass were two images of swans, executed in white, with the beaks picked out in yellow and black glass. These were of some interest, and were illustrated in *English Popular and Traditional Art* by M. Lambert and E. Marks. The Roberts had a studio in Campden Hill, not far away. After some years they lost this, and for the rest of their lives never had a permanent address. Sunday evening drinking then generally went on in Chelsea.

In her novel, *The Girls of Slender Means*, Muriel Spark says: "Long ago in 1945 all the nice people in England were poor, allowing for exceptions." This certainly describes not only her own situation in Kensington but also that of myself and my friends in the Soho of the 1940s and 1950s. Soho was, in its way, a subculture, or a society within a society, with its own codes and its own hierarchies. There was a real sense in which, to many of those who frequented it, it was their home, the only place where, for an afternoon's or evening's drinking, they need not be alone and could relate to other people. David Wright, in one of his poems, has described Soho as his "second university". One did learn certain, not contemptible, values there: a certain generosity, a certain tolerance of other people's weaknesses and eccentricities, and, above all, not to be pretentious about one's own work.

Many will say, I know, that the artists and writers I have mentioned here were nothing but drunken layabouts. This was, in some cases, true, but many of them had real talent which they devotedly pursued. Full-time writing or painting can be a demanding occupation, and the temptations to relax and use drink as a crutch can be strong. In a production, some years ago, of Puccini's *La Bohème*, passages adapted from Murger were read before each scene. One of them went like this: "Bohemia is a country bordered on the north by poverty, on the east by hunger, and the road through it leads either to the

156

hospital or the morgue or the academy." This, *mutatis mutandis*, was also true of Soho in my day. Soho was a bohemia comparable to Montmartre in the 1840s, and it lasted for about a generation. There is nothing left of it now except, perhaps, the Coach and Horses, which has been given an artificial fame by Jeffrey Bernard. Jeffrey and his two brothers, Bruce, the painter and photographer, and Oliver, the poet and translator of Rimbaud and Apollinaire – all of them talented, and all of them remarkably handsome – were familiar figures, though Jeffrey was then very young and seemed to be unhappy and confused. His constant companion was a girl who was said to have tried to cut her throat as a result of a curse placed upon her by Anna Wickham, who was popularly reputed to be a witch. I do not think Anna was into any occultist or wicca cult – witchcraft was just one among her natural talents.

When Gaston Berlemont finally retired from the French pub in 1991, a last link with the old Soho was severed. Some years before, the brewers who were the actual landlords of the pub had sent an inspector round. He was surprised to find that there was no jukebox or pin-table in the bar, and told Gaston that he should install them. Gaston replied that if the landlords were to insist on that he would retire immediately. It is the almost universal installation of loud mechanised music in public houses which has ruined the traditional English pub. Conversation against such noise is impossible. Probably the brewers know this, since if people do not talk they will drink faster.

Before the end of the 1940s I moved from Miss Schaumburger's house in West Hampstead to Kensington. I had the offer of two unfurnished rooms in a house belonging to John Waller, whom I had met in Soho. As I have already mentioned, he had been a contemporary of mine at Oxford, but had then been known to me only by name. During the Second World War in Cairo (Waller served with some distinction in the Middle East) he had edited, along with Lawrence Durrell, G. S. Fraser, Iain Fletcher, Hugh Gordon Porteous and some others, a literary periodical entitled *Salamander*. Other writers who were in Egypt at that time included P. H. Newby, Terence Tiller and Hamish Henderson. Waller had begun what seemed to be a promising literary career. Two volumes of his poems, *The Merry Ghosts* and *The Kiss of Stars*, were published by Tambimuttu in his Editions Poetry London. They contain some poems, especially those of a more personal character, which have considerable merit. Robert Graves, indeed, gave it as his opinion that Waller was the best poet of the Second World War. This claim is too extravagant, and I believe Graves made it simply because he needed a stick with which to beat Sidney Keyes. Sidney, who greatly admired Graves's work, had written a rather tactless review of his poems in *Cherwell*. He had said that there were several Graveses: "Graves the journalist, Graves the historical novelist, and Graves the member of the Graves–Riding mutual admiration society – but the real Robert Graves is Graves the poet." I think that Graves might well have agreed with this as far as the first two statements, and the last, were concerned. Sidney was not to know that at just about this time Graves had broken with Laura Riding. After this breach, Laura Riding remained at the centre of Graves's work in the mythological guise of the White Goddess.

Waller, a collateral descendant of the seventeenth-century poet Edmund Waller, was heir to a baronetcy to which he has now succeeded. His father, when an undergraduate at Oxford, had committed the classic blunder of marrying the landlady's daughter – but sadly he took his own life before he himself could succeed to the title. John had inherited a certain amount of family property, but stood to inherit the bulk of it only when his uncle, Sir Wathen, who was in a mental home, should eventually die. After the death of John's father, two elderly aunts offered to become guardians of his two children – a boy and a girl – and to pay for their education, provided their mother gave up any claim over them. John's mother, Amy Waller, a woman of great character and toughness, refused to do this. She let rooms in Oxford, and by rigid economies and hard work managed to send both the children to good schools. Later on, John entered Worcester College, Oxford. As a consequence of this background, John lived partly in a world of expectations in which he should succeed to a title and fortune, and partly in a world of penny-pinching economies. Paul Potts said of him that he was mean in small things but generous in great. The estate which he was eventually to inherit was held in a trust. John was not allowed to touch the capital until he had produced a male heir who would survive to the age of ten. John did eventually marry. His bride was a journalist, whom he had got to know at the Press Club (Waller was a member, having been a press officer in Cairo during the war), and their wedding duly took place in St Bride's, Fleet Street. At the reception in the Press Club he became so drunk that he forgot what the occasion was and went home to his house in Isleworth. His wife was left knocking at the door of her Chelsea flat in her wedding dress, with her bridal bouquet in her hand. She subsequently joined John at Isleworth, but after the birth of her daughter the marriage ended in divorce.

The house that Waller occupied in Kensington had been bought for him by his mother. It was a large building, consisting of four flats (including the basement) which he let to some of his friends. John himself occupied the ground-floor flat. I lived in the maisonette at the top, sharing with others the use of the kitchen and the bathroom. It was here that I first began to learn to cook for myself. I have continued to do this ever since. I equipped myself with an excellent book, *Cookery for Men Only*, by a certain Mr Midgeley. The author, a Yorkshireman, had in his youth emigrated to Canada. His mother had said to him: "You're not going to live in a log cabin in the middle of nowhere without I teach you how to cook and look after yourself." It was on the basis of his mother's principles that the book had been written. It was intended, primarily, for men who had been temporarily or permanently deserted by their wives. It was assumed that they would go into the larder and make the best of what they found there. It was full of sensible instructions: for instance, take about twice as much cabbage as you think you can eat. Of soufflés, the author said: "Do not heed feminine warnings about these." He went on to point out that they are really quite easy. I have progressed beyond Mr Midgeley's standards by now, I hope, though I do not pretend to be an elaborate cook. I take pleasure in cooking, and, as someone who works mainly with his brain, find it both relaxing and creative. Now that I am quite blind, and have to rely on the help of others for reading and for typing my correspondence, it is a great pleasure to be able to offer such friends an occasional square meal.

Various characters, mostly artists or writers, but also an old drunken major, lived in Waller's house. Among them was Hugh Kingsmill's stepson, Tony Kingsmill, a painter who became a good friend of mine. But perhaps the most remarkable character was Kostik. Kostik was a Russian or, to be precise, an ethnic St Petersburg Finn. I do not know whether Kostik was his real name – it is a Polish abbreviation of Constantine – but in the course of his extraordinary wartime career my friend had somehow acquired Polish identity papers, and with the help of these had come to England. Kostik was an artist who painted with a great deal of panache. I still have his portrait of myself. It is not very flattering, for I was suffering from an attack of jaundice at the time it was painted. By degrees Kostik told me his story. As a schoolboy in St Petersburg (Leningrad, as it then was) he had apparently joined some mildly subversive under-ground organisation. It had been uncovered by the secret police, but presumably because of his youth he appears not to have been imprisoned. But there was a black mark against him. Consequently, as soon as the Germans invaded Russia he volunteered for the front line, and then, like many other Russians at that time, surrendered to the Germans. He spent some time in a prisoner-of-war camp in Lithuania, and was nearly shot by a Nazi guard for venturing too near the boundary, but he seems to have persuaded the guard that he was merely, as an artist, surveying the landscape. Later on he seems to have been used as slave labour in Germany, and was in Berlin during the worst of the bombing of that city. Somehow or other he managed to make his way to Italy, where he joined a group of Italian partisans and lived in a brothel, being fed by the prostitutes almost exclusively on eggs. At one point he found himself in Rome. He told a story of how he was observing the Colosseum at night. As he stood there a hooded figure emerged from the shadows and came up to him. It slowly pulled back its hood to reveal a face with no nose or lips. The figure was presumably a leper who was seeking to obtain alms. Kostik had a broken nose, which seems to have been the only damage that he suffered during the whole of his adventures, and it came about from his falling off a bar stool in Berlin.

When Kostik was living in Waller's house, one of his patrons gave him five pounds to buy a pair of shoes. Instead of spending the money on shoes he decided to purchase a bottle of whisky and to hold an impromptu party. Vodka was not then readily obtainable in England, nor was it as fashionable as it later became. Kostik's party was to be in the Russian style and the whisky was treated as if it were vodka. As my sitting-room was the largest one, the party took place there. In all, there were about four of us. Kostik poured each guest a glass of whisky, and then started cutting up pieces of sausage, pickled gherkins, and so on, disposing them on plates on the table. When he gave me my glass of whisky I said, "Thank you very much, Kostik," and raised it to my lips. "Oh no," he said, "you do not drink until I say drink." It appears that the Russian custom is that each guest should eat a few pickles until the host says "Drink". Everyone then drains his glass immediately, and the party resumes as before. This may be all right if one is drinking vodka, which is largely pure spirit, but hardly works with whisky. We all became quite atrociously drunk, and it was after this that Kostik confided to me his true Russian identity and some of the story of his life. His English was not very good, and he once suggested that I should write his memoirs for him. I wish I had done this.

Kensington had its own literary and artistic pubs. It was here that I met Muriel Spark, and came to know Roy Campbell. Roy was a regular frequenter of the Catherine Wheel in Kensington Church Street. He was an excellent companion and a good friend. The image of a fascist bully which seems to have been created of him is quite false. It is true that, before the war, he had written for Oswald Mosley's paper, but so had several other people who later followed very different careers – political or literary. Roy and his wife Mary had been in Spain at the outbreak of the Civil War, and as newly converted Roman Catholics had been deeply shocked by the violence that had been shown against the Church by unruly elements on the Republican side. After hostilities began in Spain the Campbells left for England. It is quite true that their sympathies were with Franco. Roy made a journalistic visit from England to Franco's front, and published a long and rather foolish poem entitled "Flowering Rifle" in support of Franco's cause, but it is quite untrue that he ever actually fought in the Civil War (as is widely believed), though he never seems to have denied this publicly. In South Africa he had been friends with William Plomer and Laurence van der Post. The three of them had edited a periodical which was far too liberal in its outlook, especially on the race question, to be acceptable to the South African government.

In many ways Roy was an immature character who never quite grew up. He had violent prejudices against communists and against homosexuals – this in spite of the fact that at Oxford he had himself gone through a homosexual phase. He would always make exceptions for those homosexuals who were his personal friends. Among these was the American poet, Hart Crane, who had been his neighbour for a time in Provence. Another of Campbell's neighbours in Provence (though not, of course, homosexual) had been Aldous Huxley. The Campbells and Huxley used to catch lobsters for the table. Roy remarked that Huxley knew everything about the lobster – except how to cook it. Roy would embarrass another of his homosexual friends by saying: "He's different, he's like Shakespeare." In this attitude of Roy's there was a parallel with that of Robert Graves. The two poets had, on one occasion, met on a Spanish boat, and had become fast friends. When they reached the end of their voyage Roy suggested that they continue their acquaintance, but Graves replied that this was, unfortunately, not possible, since Miss Riding was on board. Roy, in his satirical poem, "The Georgiad", a pastiche of Augustan verse, had included the couplet: "Inspire me, Fun, and set my fancy gliding / I'll be your Graves and you my Laura Riding."

"The Georgiad" takes its name from the so-called Georgian school of poets, but the main targets are the Bloomsbury Group. Roy had an undying hatred for these writers. The quarrel had started in Roy's early years after he left Oxford. (He never took a degree at Oxford because he could not reach the necessary standard in Greek.) Harold Nicolson and his wife, Vita Sackville-West, had offered a cottage on their estate to the Campbells, who were very poor. Roy's story was that he had found out there were strings attached. Harold Nicolson had sexual designs on Roy, who was remarkably handsome in his youth, and Vita Sackville-West had similar designs on Mary. I thought at the time that this was part of Roy's paranoia, but it would appear from Peter Alexander's biography of the poet that there was truth in the story. Vita, in fact, succeeded in her designs, and Roy, learning that his wife was having an affair with her, went up to London and got drunk. Here he rather surprisingly ran into

C. S. Lewis, whom he had known at Oxford. Lewis, on hearing Roy's story, said, with extraordinary lack of sensitivity, that it must be very humiliating to know that one had been cuckolded by a woman. Roy's hostility to the Bloomsbury Group was later extended to the left-wing poets of the thirties, though the connections between these and the Bloomsbury circle were really quite tenuous. It must be added that Mary continued to be a devoted and faithful wife to her husband after this unfortunate incident.

In the early fifties Roy constituted himself a champion of Edith Sitwell. Geoffrey Grigson had attacked her savagely, along with Dylan Thomas and George Barker, in a periodical article. It was also reported that Grigson had delivered a lecture to Oxford undergraduates in which he had read from Edith Sitwell's poem, "A Mother to her Dead Child". Grigson had commented: "These words could only be written by a woman whose womb had never felt the pangs of childbirth." This shocking remark infuriated Roy, for, as he said, "mankind has traditionally honoured virginity as a symbol of spiritual power and integrity." At this time Roy, who was then working for the BBC, encountered Grigson in Regent Street and threatened him personally. Grigson, fleeing into a shopping arcade, was so taken aback by Roy's behaviour that he lost control of his bladder. Hugh Gordon Porteous, a friend of Roy's and of mine, mentioned this incident in a newspaper article, adding: "Hey, Geoffrey, here's a use for your diaper now." (William Diaper was an eighteenth-century poet whose works Grigson had edited.) Grigson had regarded Roy as an ally, since they were both, to some degree, disciples of Percy Wyndham Lewis. Grigson told Roy that he would not bounce a ping-pong ball off his bald head. This did not pacify Roy. After this incident, Roy went on a kind of spree, attacking poets whom he disliked. Making an anonymous phone call to Stephen Spender, he pretended to be a youth whom Spender had met in Spain during the Civil War. Roy also phoned Louis MacNeice, challenging him to a duel. MacNeice, as an Irishman, said he was quite prepared to fight Roy, but shouldn't they have a drink first. They did, and became firm friends.

Roy had some ideas about Geoffrey Grigson which bordered on the paranoiac. Grigson had written an article on the subject of edible spiders. Some people, he maintained, appear to be addicted to eating spiders, which are said to have a nutty taste. Roy insisted that Grigson shared this addiction and, indeed, that spiders formed a principal item in his diet. Roy drew for me a little cartoon (he had a pretty talent for drawing). It depicted Grigson eating a spider sandwich, the legs of the creatures protruding from the slices of bread and butter. When the scandal of the defection of Guy Burgess and Donald Maclean to the Soviet Union broke, it seems that the police interviewed a number of Burgess's associates from among the intellectuals of the 1930s. Roy insisted that the police had pounced upon Grigson as he was sneaking along a hedgerow in search of his lunch.

When Roy was asked to lecture to an undergraduate literary society at Cambridge, he said that the title of his lecture would be "The Case of Dr Leavis versus English Poetry". I am not sure whether this lecture was actually delivered. On another occasion he was invited to give the annual lecture at Stratford-upon-Avon which is delivered every year on Shakespeare's birthday. According to his own account, having arrived at Stratford, he went into a pub to have a drink. The barmaid, recognising him as a stranger to the town, asked him, in a friendly way, what he was doing there. "I'm part of that show at the town hall," he answered. "Oh," she said with interest, "do you think he did it?" Roy, assuming she was referring to the Baconian controversy, replied: "Of course he did it." "What makes you so sure?" she asked. "Well," he said, "Ben Jonson wouldn't have said he did it if he hadn't." "Ben Jonson?" she said. "Surely it's Tom Johnson." It then turned out that she was referring to an inquest, then going on in Stratford, which might well lead to a murder verdict. A certain Tom Johnson was popularly suspected to be the culprit.

Roy Campbell's behaviour was often outrageous, not to say inexcusable, but there was no real malice in him. When he was killed in a motor accident in Portugal in 1957, I naturally wrote a letter of condolence to Mary Campbell. She replied, saying: "I did not know how much he was loved. I have had letters from all over the world, but you are one of the very few English poets who wrote."

During my Kensington period Muriel Spark was employed by the Poetry Society as secretary and editor of *The Poetry Review*. The difficulty she had with the old guard who then ran the Poetry Society has been described in her own autobiography. On a visit to Oxford at this time I was introduced to the distinguished theologian Austen Farrer. He had a great interest in poetry, indeed his book *The Glass of Vision*, which deals with the resemblances and differences between the concept of inspiration in biblical prophecy and in secular poetry, is one that I have frequently recommended to students of English literature. I gave Farrer a fairly sensational account (told to me by John Waller) of the disruptive events at the Poetry Society which Muriel Spark had been involved in. Farrer's comment was: "We thought academic life was ruthless, but this is nature red in tooth and claw."

Among those who made life difficult for Muriel Spark was Dr Marie Stopes. Marie Stopes had a good deal to be proud of in her early work for birth control. She also had a tragic history of early disappointed love, and an unfortunate marriage. But she had now become a ridiculous eccentric. Muriel Spark is of the opinion that Marie Stopes was actually demented by this time. She regarded herself as a poet, and formed an alliance with the old and sad Lord Alfred Douglas. Marie Stopes and he seemed to have had an equally high opinion of their own poetry. I once met a friend of Lord Alfred who told me he had reviewed a volume of the latter's verse and had included the sentence: "Lord Alfred Douglas is the greatest writer of the sonnet in our language since Shakespeare." He had sent a copy of the review to Lord Alfred who sent it back without comment, but with "since Shakespeare" scored out.

Marie Stopes also took up John Waller, and on one occasion he brought me with him to have tea with her at her house at Dorking. This was a beautiful house, on a hill overlooking the town. One reached it by walking through a wood. It had once belonged to Fanny Burney, and in the drawing-room had eighteenth-century wallpaper, not patterned as with Victorian wallpaper, but actually showing a sylvan landscape, so that one could, I suppose, sit there in the winter and imagine oneself in a pastoral scene. There was also a mantelpiece designed by Flaxman. Marie Stopes, who was immensely rich, had no idea of how to do justice to this house, and had furnished it with a few old sticks of ugly Edwardian furniture that could have been bought at any junk shop. The house had its own electric power generator, and there is a legend that when it broke down she sent a telegram to the local electricity company which so delighted them that they framed it and hung it in their boardroom. It read: "Please send a man at once. Last night I had to go to bed with candles."

When I met her, Marie Stopes, then in her seventies, had become a grotesquely vain old woman, and was heavily and obviously made up, with dyed hair. She served us generously with tea and thick slices of slab cake. She pointed out, with pride, a herd of Jersey cows on her estate which provided unpasteurised milk. She seemed to regard pasteurisation as contrary to nature.

10

St Anne's

While living in Kensington I still continued regularly to frequent the pubs of Soho. One evening in the Wheatsheaf I met Peter Avery, then a student at the London School of Oriental and African Studies. During the war Peter had been in naval intelligence in what is now Pakistan, where he had learnt Urdu, and was now studying Persian, the mother language of Urdu. Urdu, which is derived from a word meaning a military camp, was originally a lingua franca, compounded of a mixture of Persian, Sanskrit and other native Indian languages, whereby the followers of the Muslim Moguls who had conquered India in the sixteenth century could communicate with their Indian subjects. When I met Peter I had been reading Hafiz, the great Persian poet of the fourteenth century of our era, in the translations made by Gertrude Bell. These versions are in a florid post-Pre-Raphaelite, or Swinburnean, style, but something of the poetic quality of the original communicated itself to me. I mentioned this to Peter, who was an enthusiast for the poetry of Hafiz, and out of this meeting arose our project for making joint translations of a selection of the poems of Hafiz.

I did not, and do not, know more than a bare few words of Persian, but our work was not just a matter of Peter's giving me a prose translation which I was to versify. Our translating Hafiz involved a close collaboration between us. We weighed the significance of each particular word and image, and we engaged in a considerable amount of research, especially into the Sufi background of these poems. There have been other translations of Hafiz. The originals are in rhymed metres which are derived from classical Arabic poetry. The forms include the cassida and the ghazal. Persian is an Indo-European language. But when Iran was conquered by the Muslims – a generation after the Prophet Muhammad – not only was Islam adopted, but also, to a large extent, Arabic culture and a modified Arabic script. The much older Zoroastrian religion, with its culture, was not accorded the tolerance which Islam allows to the so-called "Peoples of the Book". This term, applied to the followers of monotheistic religions which can claim a revealed scripture, includes Jews, Christians and some others. Zoroastrianism was held to be a dualistic religion.

Other translators have used conventional English stanza forms, but this is to substitute one effect for another, and most of the metres which previous translators have employed might seem to a contemporary reader to be characteristic of nineteenth-century English verse. In approaching Hafiz I had in mind Ezra Pound's translations from the Chinese. Pound used free verse (whereas the Chinese poems were regularly rhymed) and concentrated on the imagery of the originals. Peter pointed out how the structure of the Persian poems was dependent on their image structure. Each image led to another, and the whole often had a circular rather than a linear design. Our joint translations were eventually published in John Murray's "Wisdom of the East" series. I found our work together on this poetry very instructive, and have sometimes attempted to plan my own poems on an image sequence, in something of the same way.

Peter Avery left England a year or so after I met him to work in the Iranian oilfields, teaching some Persian to the English workers there, and English to the Iranians. In 1951 the Iranian government, under Prime Minister Mussadeq, nationalised the oilfields, and provoked a crisis in Anglo-Iranian relations. Peter was indignant at the way in which this crisis was handled, and resigned. He later worked in Iraq, and eventually became a Fellow of King's College, Cambridge, as Reader in Persian. My close friendship with him has continued over the years.

Much later on, in the 1970s, Peter and I translated the *Rubáiyát* (or Quatrains) of Omar Khayyám, using the same method. There was no intention of challenging comparison with Edward Fitzgerald's masterpiece. Fitzgerald was a very free translator and welded a selection of the individual quatrains of Omar into a kind of unity which they did not really possess, but his general approach to Omar, and his treatment of this poetry as essentially unorthodox and sceptical, was correct. Our version was eventually published by Penguin Books. Previously they had published a version by Robert Graves. Graves was prejudiced against Fitzgerald's translations, as he was against almost all nineteenth-century poetry. He had been persuaded by a disingenuous Afghan collaborator into thinking that Oman's poems conveyed a secret Sufi doctrine. Many of the classical mediaeval Persian poets, including Hafiz, were strongly influenced by Sufi mysticism, but this was not the case with Omar, whose real importance, in fact, was as an astronomer and mathematician.

I have since engaged in other projects of joint translation, working with native speakers of languages which I do not know. These have included work in Arabic and in Russian.

I think it was my notice in the *New English Review* of the Russian theologian Semyon Frank which led to George Every's getting in touch with me. George Every, a scholar and a poet, was at that time a lay brother in the Society of the Sacred Mission, an Anglican monastic order whose headquarters was at Kelham, near Newark in Nottinghamshire. He is now a Roman Catholic and lives at Oscott College in Birmingham. After he had written to me, we met, and have continued to do so over the years. We had many interests in common, and I frequently stayed at Kelham. George lectured in Church history and had a special interest in Byzantium. It was he who introduced me to Patrick McLaughlin, then the vicar of St Anne's, Soho. The church, apart from its tower, had been destroyed by enemy action during the war. Regular Sunday services were held in St Thomas's in Tennison Court, off Regent Street. The church house adjacent to St Anne's remained standing, and many important activities went on there during the 1940s and 1950s. Patrick McLaughlin founded St Anne's Society which he described as "a centre of Christian discourse". Many distinguished speakers addressed this society, including T. S. Eliot, Charles Williams, Nikolay Berdyayev, the Russian thinker, and Dorothy L. Sayers.

Patrick McLaughlin was a remarkable man, though a somewhat unstable personality. As well as having a wide range of intellectual interests, he was a member of the Christendom group, and a pioneer of liturgical reform. He created his own liturgy at St Thomas's, and many of the liturgical forms and customs which he introduced there have been incorporated in both new Anglican and the Roman Catholic rites. Patrick became a close personal friend and a strong influence on the direction my thought was taking. I began to attend services at St Thomas's regularly. I served both on the Advisory Council of St Anne's House and on the Council of St Anne's Society. The reader may be slightly puzzled to find that I was serving on these councils at the same time as I was frequenting the bars and clubs of Soho. I was, myself, aware of this contradiction which caused me some mental anguish, but somehow or other, whatever guardian angel was looking after me, and whatever demon was turning me into a poet, seemed to be driving me along two neighbouring, and sometimes convergent, paths:

> For half a beast is the great god Pan
> Making a poet out of a man
> Down in the reeds by the river.

St Thomas's church was later demolished because of a redevelopment area off Regent Street. The congregation of St Anne's now used the chapel of St Barnabas's House in Manette Street, near the Pillars of Hercules. St Barnabas's House was a refuge for distressed women which had been founded by William Ewart Gladstone. The site of St Anne's church itself was eventually deconsecrated and turned into a car park. The tower, however, remained, and Patrick Mc-Laughlin dedicated a small chapel within it, with the title of St Charles-in-the-Tower. St Charles was, of course, Charles I, king and martyr, but he was never in the Tower. When he was brought to London, before his trial and execution, he was lodged in his palace of Whitehall.

The deconsecration service was a memorable affair. I arrived rather late and sat down hastily on a block of masonry. The service was followed by a reception in St Anne's House, and I found myself talking to T. S. Eliot, whom I had met on a previous occasion. Later on, I mentioned the conversation I had had with Eliot to David Wright, who was also present. He replied: "But you were sitting next to him all through the service. I thought you'd done that deliberately." Patrick McLaughlin finally retired as vicar of the parish and went to work in Rome with an organisation connected with the Council of Europe. He became a Roman Catholic layman, though his own theology was such that he did not see this as a definitive break. St Anne's Society continued at different venues and under different chairmanships. Its final home was at St Matthew's, Westminster, where my old friend, Gerard Irvine, who had once been McLaughlin's curate, was now vicar.

In 1990 it was decided to rebuild St Anne's church and reconsecrate the site. The foundation stone was laid by Princess Anne, the Princess Royal. The present vicar wrote to me and asked me if, as an old member of the congregation, I would write a poem to be recited on this occasion. I was happy to do this. Her Royal Highness seemed to have liked the poem as she particularly asked to have me presented to her. We had a brief conversation, but the band of the London School of Brass was playing rather loudly at the time, and neither of us heard very well what the other was saying.

Through my work with St Anne's, I got to know Dorothy Sayers, though I cannot say that I formed a close friendship with her. Hers was a formidable, though kindly, personality. Although she was witty and outspoken, one now knows from her biographers that this façade concealed a vulnerable personality who had had a great deal of stress and suffering in her early life. Dorothy Sayers was an efficient chairman of the Advisory Council of St Anne's House. Some degree of trouble developed between St Anne's parish and the London Diocese while Patrick McLaughlin was in office. In spite of his brilliant intellectual achievements, Patrick must have presented something of a problem, and there was the possibility of the parish being amalgamated with another. Dorothy Sayers compared this tactic to the mediaeval practice of first castrating a man and then declaring him incapable of holding office on account of this.

She once invited me to dine with her at a restaurant. She was at the time engaged in her memorable translation of Dante. It is invaluable for its notes, though I think she stops just short of being a poet in her own right. The diction she uses is uncertain and a little old-fashioned. For myself, I have found the old Temple Classics edition (now out of print), in which the Italian text is accompanied by an English prose translation, more helpful. Both T. S. Eliot and Charles Williams are said to have first read Dante by using this book. Laurence Binyon's translation, praised by Ezra Pound, gives a better idea of Dante's metre than any other, but somehow it is not very readable. There is a lot to be said for good old Longfellow, but Cary, whose English version became the standard one in the nineteenth century, although he has his merits, tried to interpret Dante in terms of Milton, which is to interpret the Gothic in terms of the Baroque. In a recent number of the periodical, *Temenos*, I saw some specimens of a translation by the contemporary poet, Jeremy Reed. I hope some enterprising publisher will commission him to finish the entire work because these are far and away the best poetic translations of Dante I have seen. At the dinner I do not think I had the courage to discuss Dante with her. In the restaurant she played very much the *grande dame*, treating the waiter as a particular friend, in what I can only think was a slightly patronising manner. I have never been in the habit of asking waiters which dish on the menu they recommend, being cynically inclined to think that they will recommend you the one which is selling least well.

Dorothy Sayers's Anglican orthodoxy was, of course, passionately held. She told me how she had recently attended the funeral of a friend who had belonged to the Anthroposophists and who was given a funeral according to the rites and ceremonies of that cult. It seemed to her that, if it were possible, they were pushing her friend straight into hell. She tried to save the situation by mentally repeating to herself as much as she could remember of the Prayer Book funeral service. The Anthroposophists were founded by Rudolf Steiner, who had a Catholic background but entered the Theosophist movement. When its founder, Madame Blavatsky, claimed that a Hindu youth named Krishnamurti was a new avatar of the divine – of equal status with Jesus Christ – Steiner was unable to accept this and withdrew. Madame Blavatsky and the rather suspect Bishop Leadbeater had seen the boy in an Indian village. The bishop had had an immediate revelation of Krishnamurti's divine status and the Theosophists adopted him. Leadbeater was a bishop of the Liberal Catholic Church. This is really a wing of the Theosophists, but using Christian

169

language and ceremonies. It claimed valid episcopal orders derived from the Old Catholic Church of Holland (a perfectly respectable Christian church which ultimately owed its origins to the Jansenist controversy of the seventeenth century). I would go so far as to say that the Liberal Catholic Church was neither Liberal, nor Catholic, nor a church. Madame Blavatsky claimed psychic powers, but she has certainly been accused of cheating. There is a story current in Oxford that she visited that city and asked permission from the Professor of Natural Sciences to use his laboratory for certain experiments. He gave her a key, but one day let himself in by his own key and found her levitating. This so shocked his scientific presuppositions that he vomited there and then, and said: "You wicked woman. Come down from there immediately." He took away her key and never let her in again.

During my early days in London I was still searching for some kind of religious basis to my thought. I had been influenced by the psychology of Carl Jung and his interest in religious symbolism, and by my reading in some German poets – Hölderlin, Stefan George and Rilke – who sought to reconcile Christian and Hellenic symbolism. I had also been interested in the ancient gnostic heresies. I think it was at a party given by Morwenna Donnelly that I was first introduced to Oscar Kollerstrom. A New Zealander of Swedish descent, he had an hereditary Swedish title of nobility which he did not use. His story, as partly told me by Hugh Kingsmill's wife, Dorothy, was as follows. When the Theosophists adopted Krishnamurti, it was deemed necessary that he should have twelve apostles, and Bishop Leadbeater appears to have selected twelve small boys for this purpose. One of these was Oscar, whom Leadbeater declared to be a reincarnation of St Francis of Assisi. Eventually, Krishnamurti repudiated the claims that had been made for him, though he continued to teach his own personalistic philosophy. Leadbeater was refused entry into the United States because of alleged immoral practices. Oscar had been ordained a priest in the Liberal Catholic Church, and now underwent psychoanalytical treatment, becoming a patient and pupil of Georg Groddek, one of the most eccentric of Freud's disciples. Groddek appears to have believed that the subconscious, or id, was the basis of everything which we call objective reality. The whole phenomenal world was a kind of enormous pun created by the id. Oscar told me, for example, that while living with Groddek he mentioned to him that whenever he sat in the garden he was liable to be stung by bees. "Well," said Groddek, "you are rather malicious, aren't you? You do sting people." Oscar faced up to this defect in his character, and once he had come to terms with it the bees left him alone. Oscar also told me that there was some evidence that during the war people got wounded by bullets in those parts of their bodies which they wished to punish.

When I met him, Oscar was practising as a psychologist, though continuing as a priest in the Liberal Catholic Church. I joined a series of seminars which he was conducting on religion and psychology. I remember an occasion when he was expounding the story of the Transfiguration as it occurs in St Mark's gospel. It will be remembered that when Jesus came down from the mountain, which he had ascended with Peter, James and John, who had witnessed his Transfiguration, he cured an epileptic boy. Oscar was trying to postulate some relationship between the vision of the Transfiguration and the visual hallucinations to which epileptics may be subject. In the course of telling the story he quoted the words of the epileptic boy's father: "Lord, I believe; help thou mine unbelief." They did not seem to have any particular significance for Oscar, but they did for me. I realised I was in what John Bunyan called Bypass Meadow, and that I must somehow find again the main road. I therefore discontinued my attendance at these seminars and did not see Oscar very often. Some years later Oscar's wife wished to have their second son baptised in the Church of England. Oscar approached Patrick McLaughlin at St Thomas's, Regent Street, about this. Patrick insisted that at least one of the godparents should be a communicant member of the Church of England. I therefore became godfather to the boy, who was christened Julian. Unfortunately, and I blame myself for this, I did not keep in touch with the Kollerstrom family. At this time I was in Leeds, and later I was in Egypt. I did not come into contact again with my godson until many years later.

Patrick McLaughlin, among his other schemes, was a keen promoter of Christian religious drama. Many plays, including Christopher Fry's *Sleep of Prisoners*, had their premières at St Thomas's church, and others were revived there, including Charles Williams's *Seed of Adam*, Anne Ridler's *Cain* and a shortened version of Dorothy Sayers's *Christ's Emperor*. My own play, *The Talking Ass*, on the biblical subject of Balaam, was also given there. This revival of religious drama – most of it in verse – had begun during the 1930s with the Canterbury Festival, for which T. S. Eliot's *Murder in the Cathedral*, Charles Williams's *Thomas Cranmer of Canterbury*, Dorothy Sayers's *The Zeal of Thine House* and Christopher Fry's *Thor with Angels* were written. Further work in the revival of religious verse drama was done by Martin Brown, and the Pilgrim Players. There was also an important season of verse plays at the Gate Theatre in Notting Hill in the early fifties. Eliot's *The Family Reunion* was revived, and there were performances of plays by Ronald Duncan, Norman Nicholson and others.

Murder in the Cathedral survives, perhaps, better than any other of Eliot's plays, but he himself felt that by writing a play to be performed in the cloisters of Canterbury Cathedral, sponsored by the Friends of the Cathedral, he was, in many ways, preaching to the converted. He wanted to reach a wider audience. He passed from *The Family Reunion* to *The Cocktail Party* and *The Confidential Clerk*, and finally to *The Elder Statesman* (which has never been given a London performance). In the last three of these he was attempting to adapt poetic drama, as he saw it, to the conventions of Shaftesbury Avenue drawing-room comedy, and, in both *The Family Reunion* and *The Cocktail Party*, he partly disguised his Christian message in terms of psychoanalysis. The trouble was that he moved into Shaftesbury Avenue too late, just when that kind of drawing-room comedy was about to give way to John Osborne and the kitchen-sink drama. It might have been better if Eliot had proceeded along the lines suggested by the fragmentary *Sweeney Agonistes* – I witnessed, in Oxford, a successful performance of this produced by Nevill Coghill. If Eliot had done this he might have joined hands with Samuel Beckett and Harold Pinter. It is a curious irony that the musical *Cats* has probably brought in more money to the Eliot estate than any other of his works. Eliot might not have objected to this as much as some people would suppose. I was told by George Every in the early 1950s that C. B. Cochran, the impresario, was thinking of commissioning a revue from Eliot, and that the latter was distinctly interested in the idea.

It was George Every, in fact, who introduced me to Eliot, and the latter invited us both to dinner at his club. Every informed me that he had told Eliot that I admired Charles Williams's work more than I did Eliot's. I replied that I really did not think that this was the case. George answered, rather Jesuitically, that he knew what I meant, but that he had spoken to Eliot as he had because he thought that this would recommend me to Eliot. Eliot did, in fact, greatly admire Williams's writing, and traces of Williams's influence can probably be discerned in the *Four Quartets* and *The Cocktail Party*, but it is said that he found Williams's mature poetry – his two sequences of poems on the Arthurian legend – too obscure. Eliot is reported to have said: "I have tried them with influenza and I have tried them without influenza and I still can't understand them." Eliot and Williams shared, of course, a common basis of religious belief. There is a story that the two poets both sat on a liturgical commission where revisions of the Prayer Book were being discussed. Williams moved that the phrase "from the desire of damnation, Good Lord deliver us", be inserted in the litany. The bishop who was presiding over the meeting pooh-poohed the idea, saying that he could not understand what the phrase could mean. Whereupon both Williams and Eliot are said to have risen to their feet and publicly testified that they had both frequently been tempted to desire damnation.

Before I arrived at Eliot's club, my mother and I had been spending the afternoon going through the effects of my aunt Mary, who had recently died, selecting what household objects and furniture I might wish to keep. When I mentioned this to Eliot, he said, characteristically: "I hope you took not just antique furniture and paintings, but household things like saucepans and kettles, because your aunt would have had things of that sort of good quality such as you cannot buy nowadays." I cannot remember all the topics that we discussed at dinner. Wagner's *Ring* came up. Wagner is, of course, quoted several times in *The Waste Land*. We spoke of the way in which Germanic mythology had been abused and distorted by the Nazis for their own purposes. Eliot said that it was fortunate that "our own mythology" had not been misused in the same way. By our own mythology he meant the Arthurian legend. Its influence on *The Waste Land* is more than an incidental one. Eliot had, indeed, attended a course of lectures on the subject when a student at Harvard. This also, in part, explains the high opinion he had of Charles Williams's writings, even if he did find the later poems impenetrable. While we were discussing Williams's work, I made one very foolish remark. We were discussing Williams's novel *War in Heaven*. The story deals with the discovery of the Holy Grail in contemporary Britain. An evil magician, Sir Giles Tumulty (probably based on Aleister Crowley), is trying to get possession of it, and a group of good characters is wishing to save it. In the course of their adventures, the Grail is at one point thrown out of a lavatory window. I suggested that this debased the grand symbolism of the Grail. Eliot turned to George Every and said in cool, but deadly, tones: "There is absolutely nothing you can do about persons like that." I deserved the rebuke, but it was a chilling one. Eliot impressed me, then and on later occasions when I met him, as an extremely kind and courteous man, but there were claws beneath the velvet.

I was at that time trying to write a book – never completed – on Edgar Allan Poe. Many years later, I was to use some of the material in a lecture delivered in the Cathedral of St John the Divine, New York. Eliot began to tell me, just a little ponderously, what I was already aware of, that Poe was important because of his influence on French literature, and that his reputation on the Continent was much greater than that he was accorded either in his own country or in England. I asked Eliot if there were any continental poets who were, perhaps, overvalued in England. He immediately answered: "Yes: Rilke and Lorca." This slightly shocked me, though I have come to think that he may have been right, for these were probably the two modern European poets most widely read by my generation.

Eliot mentioned two books which Faber were about to publish. One of these was Hugh Ross Williamson's *The Arrow and the Sword*. Ross Williamson had once been a curate at St Anne's, but later became a Roman Catholic. *The Arrow and the Sword* is not a good book. It puts forward the theory that the murders of William Rufus and Thomas à Becket were both ritual sacrifices, and that these two historical characters were secret adherents, not just of the witch cult, but of the Albigensian heresy. Ross Williamson had simply combined theories put forward by Margaret Murray in her *The God of the Witches* and *The Witch Cult in Western Europe*, and by Denis de Rougemont in *L'Amour et L'Occident* (its English title is *Passion and Society*), and both these sources are historically unreliable. In regard to Ross Williamson's book, Eliot said that he did not agree with its conclusions, but he felt obliged to publish it, for "otherwise I would be suppressing evidence". Possibly, Ross Williamson's idea that Thomas à Becket might have been a secret heretic and his death a secret ritual was particularly repugnant to Eliot, who probably regarded Thomas the Martyr as his patron saint.

The other book which Faber was about to publish was Robert Graves's *The White Goddess*, which had been rejected by Graves's usual publisher, Cassell. Eliot described the book as Graves's own *Golden Bough*, and said to me: "You must review it." Shortly afterwards I did so, in the *New English Weekly*. I found the book extremely interesting. Its thesis is that all poets are really worshippers of the White Goddess, the primitive mother goddess whose cult was superseded with the establishment of such patriarchal gods as the Greek Olympians or the Hebrew Jehovah. The White Goddess, whom Graves regarded as the moon, is also, he thought, the Muse. Her worship involved an annual ritual in which two divine kings, one for the summer months and the other for the winter months, ruled alternately as her son and lover. But at the end of the season one of them was sacrificed to her. Theories of this kind were not new. Many of them had been adumbrated by Frazer in *The Golden Bough*, by Jane Harrison in her *Prolegomena to Greek Religion* and by various German scholars. Graves projected on to these myths a good deal of his own personal experience, especially his relationship with Laura Riding, who had evidently been his White Goddess. There is a good deal of very slipshod scholarship in this book. In reviewing it I pointed out a number of specific errors. Knowing that Graves was a difficult man, I thought it wise to take the bull by the horns and to send him a copy of the review, with a letter in which I said that, while I disagreed with some of his theories and had pointed out a number of mistakes, I would not have reviewed the book at such length if I had not regarded it as important.

I received a very friendly reply. Graves admitted some of the errors, and said that he had written the book in England during the war and that most of his library had been at his home in Majorca, but one particular criticism of mine he declined. He had stated that the crane was sacred to the White Goddess because it had red legs. The colour red was supposed to be associated with the underworld. As an ornithologist, I pointed out that cranes do not have red legs (storks do). Graves said: "But cranes do have red legs." Accordingly, I visited the London Zoo and the Natural History Museum, and looked into *Witherby's British Birds*, the standard modern reference book on ornithology. My observations, and Witherby, all confirmed that cranes had either black or very dark grey legs. When I pointed this out to Graves he wrote back and said of course he did not mean the common crane, but the crowned crane. "This bird (its scientific name is *Balearica pavonina*)", I wrote to him, "is found in Africa and has occurred in the Balearic Islands, where you have, perhaps, met with it, but it is not found in Greece, or the Middle East, or in Celtic Britain, from which areas most of your mythological data are drawn, and anyway", I added, "it does not have red legs, either." Graves wrote back to say that he had relied upon the coloured plate of this bird in his family copy of *Morris's British Birds*. "I am familiar with this book," I told him. "It is the work of a Welsh clergyman, and is more notable for the beauty of its hand-coloured plates than for the accuracy of its text." At this point Graves gave up. Investigating the common crane further, he discovered that the front of its head is coloured black, red and white, and these colours, he decided, correspond to the three phases of the moon, and accounted for the crane's sacredness to the White Goddess. This appears in later editions, where I get an acknowledgement.

I was not to meet Robert Graves personally until some years later. I happened to have spent a night with a friend in the country, and returning in the morning I ran into the poet Martin Seymour-Smith in Charing Cross Underground Station. He had acted as tutor to Graves's children in Majorca and was later to write his biography. Seymour-Smith told me that Graves was on one of his infrequent visits to London, and asked would I like to meet him. Of course I agreed, and the next day I went to the flat Graves was occupying, where I met him and also Norman Cameron. Cameron, as I have already mentioned, was an excellent poet, but he seemed a shy man, and contributed little to the conversation. Graves I found very kind and friendly, and we had a long and interesting conversation about his ideas in *The White Goddess*. We also discussed the poetry of Pope, whom I defended, though Graves held him to be of no account at all. As I took my leave, Graves said: "I will try to like Pope, for your sake."

Some years after that, when I was teaching in an American university, I paid a visit to the University of Buffalo, where one of my former students from Leeds, Ralph Maude, an American, was now lecturing. Buffalo University has a library, the Claude Collier Abbot library, which did pioneer work in collecting the working drafts of poets. (They have the drafts of my own early sequence, *The Heart's Forest*. The much more wealthy University of Texas seems now to have overtaken them in this field.) Buffalo had just bought the entire archive of Graves, and the library was, I think, celebrating the anniversary of its foundation. Graves had been asked to come over and give a lecture, after which there was to be a reception to which I was invited. I was a little nervous about meeting him again because in the intervening period I had reviewed a volume of his poems. My review was favourable, but I had taken exception to a somewhat pretentious publisher's blurb on the dust-jacket, which I had guessed was the composition of Graves himself. It read more or less as follows: "Because Mr Graves is not connected with politics or the theatre, and is not queer, he is not widely fashionable. But, if at a cocktail party you were to take any contemporary poet aside and ask him who was the greatest living poet, he would probably reply: 'Graves, unfortunately.'" Martin Seymour-Smith told me that my assumption that Graves had written the blurb was true, and that he had been upset by my review. I therefore entered the room in which the reception was being held with some trepidation. I was taken over to Graves who was sitting down in a corner. Raising his head, he saw me and was immediately all smiles, greeting me with: "Oh John, how nice to see you. How are the birds?"

Some years after my first meeting with him, Eliot asked me to edit *The Faber Book of Twentieth Century Verse*. I went to discuss the project with him at his flat in Chelsea. Michael Roberts's *Faber Book of Modern Verse* had, as I have already said, formed the taste of a whole generation. Roberts had limited himself to British and American poets who might be classified as modernist. The book opened with Hopkins (the forerunner of modernism, and at the time generally regarded as a sort of honorary modernist) and continued to the poets of the 1930s, down to George Barker. Eliot believed that Roberts's book had done its work, and that there was room for a more comprehensive anthology which should salvage the best work of other schools, including the so-called Georgians, and should also include some neglected eccentrics and independents. I undertook this task with interest, persuading Faber to allow me to ask David Wright, with whom I had already collaborated on an anthology of verse, to edit it with me. The book is still in print, though I now feel rather ashamed of it as it was not as carefully edited or researched as it should have been, but I think we did succeed in bringing before the public some poets, very well worth reading, who were, or had been, neglected. It has gone into a number of editions, though almost all the reviewers of the first edition, with the exception of Edwin Muir, condemned it.

Eliot himself made several suggestions which throw an interesting light on his taste. One of the poets he insisted should be included was Ralph Hodgson. Hodgson was a Georgian poet and had been a friend of Eliot in his early days. He later emigrated to America and died in Eliot's own native city of St Louis, Missouri. Neither David Wright nor I could share Eliot's admiration for Hodgson's verse. One of his best-known poems, "The Song of Honour", was a kind of romantically mystical perception of nature, owing a good deal to Christopher Smart's "The Song of David". Other poems advocate kindness to animals. Almost all Hodgson's poems were well-known Georgian anthology pieces, and we included "Eve" partly because it seemed to have some metrical interest. It was obvious that Eliot had a great affection for Hodgson, and this surprised me, not only in terms of taste, but because among Eliot's poems will be found what appears to be a squib against the Georgians, beginning, in imitation of Edward Lear, "How pleasant to know Mr Hodgson", followed by another, beginning, "How unpleasant to know Mr Eliot." In a later edition we substituted for "Eve" some rather witty epigrammatic fragments belonging to Hodgson's last years.

Eliot particularly suggested A. E. Housman's "The Queen of Air and Darkness . . ." I concur in Eliot's admiration for this poem, which is not wholly typical of Housman, and has a sense of weirdness and terror about it. It was this, perhaps, which appealed to Eliot. I used to think that the Queen of Air and Darkness represents the Church seen as a reactionary and superstitious force. If the author of "The Hippopotamus" read the poem in this way too, it would not be inconsistent with his admiration of it. But Robert Percival Graves in his biography convincingly quotes Housman's own letters in which he says that the Queen of Air and Darkness is fear itself. ("You have nothing to fear but fear itself.") Eliot made one or two other suggestions, and it is noteworthy that when we followed his advice we were nearly always slated for it by the reviewers. I mentioned the name of Ruth Pitter, a Christian poet. Eliot was not all that enthusiastic. He said: "She has her following." Eliot also said that we must include Rupert Brooke – "of course". (The "of course" was spoken with obvious irony.)

Two poets who caused us a great deal of difficulty were Siegfried Sassoon and Edith Sitwell. David and I wrote to Sassoon asking for permission to include in the anthology some of his First World War poems, the work for which, of course, he is most valued. But Sassoon wished to have some of his later work included, and we had difficulty in finding any of this which really pleased us. Eventually I chose a semi-satirical poem on the demolition of Old Devonshire House. Sassoon grudgingly agreed to this, but asked a very high fee for it.

The problem with Edith Sitwell was similar. During the war years she had developed an entirely new poetic style, leaving behind the amusing, but essentially trivial, poems of her *Façade* period. She had adopted a sibylline stance in *Street Songs* and a number of subsequent volumes. They impressed me at the time, but I now find it hard to understand why I once admired them. Written in a loose free verse, the poems are full of evocative but rather vague romantic imagery. Edith's heart was in the right place. They are full of protests against the cruelty of war, and of the cruelty of man to man in general, and in *The Shadow of Cain* the dropping of the atomic bomb on Hiroshima. A Soviet critic of the time informed his readers that Edith Sitwell had written a poem in favour of the atomic bomb. These later poems prompted the brutal attacks on Edith Sitwell by Geoffrey Grigson. When she later on came to be sniped at by Hartley, the proponent of the so-called Movement School of the 1950s, she replied with lofty contempt, writing to the editor of the *Spectator*: "Please have Mr Hartley stuffed at my expense." David Wright remarked to me: "She is not the giant she thinks she is, but they are the pygmies she thinks they are." During the early fifties, Edith Sitwell had adopted a policy in regard to anthologies that she would not allow her work to be included unless she had as much space as Eliot or Yeats. When Kenneth Allot, at about this time, edited *The Penguin Anthology of Modern Verse* he apologised in the preface for not including Edith Sitwell, because he was unable to accede to her conditions. Rather sadly, in the second edition, which appeared about five years later, she was still not included, but no apology was felt needed. Considering the nature of our anthology, David Wright and I were prepared, on the whole, to give her as much, or almost as much, space as she demanded, since Eliot had suggested that the poets well represented in the Roberts anthology need be given not much more than token representation in ours. Edith Sitwell, however, insisted that we must have a generous representation of her more recent poems, written after *Street Songs*, and more and more diluted and derivative in their technique. We finally had to accede to this request and included a long anti-atom-bomb poem. Eliot said in a letter that he admired Edith Sitwell's work and certainly did not wish her to be excluded. After both Eliot and Edith Sitwell were dead, we managed to persuade Faber to allow us to drop these particular poems from a later edition, while retaining a selection from her *Façade* period.

In the 1940s I had written an enthusiastic article about Edith

Sitwell's work, which had been published in Charles Wrey Gardiner's *Poetry Quarterly*. This led to her writing a very kind letter to me and presenting me with a signed copy of *The Shadow of Cain*. She invited me to more than one of her parties at the Sesame Club. She was in the habit of coming to London once a year during the season and inviting her friends for luncheon or tea parties at this West End women's club. Essentially a warm-hearted and generous woman, she had helped several poets, including Dylan Thomas, George Barker and Maurice Carpenter, financially, although in her later years she herself was to run heavily into debt. She stood godmother to one of Maurice Carpenter's children (this was in the days before she became a Roman Catholic). One felt that she saw herself and her two brothers as embattled against a hostile world, which she identified with her childhood world of hostile grown-ups. She had suffered a great deal from her domineering and egotistical father, and her weak and foolish mother. At the time of my first meeting with Edith, she was writing her book on Elizabeth I, *Fanfare for Elizabeth*. She remarked in my presence that she had difficulty in understanding some of the characters in this Tudor drama, but "as for Henry VIII, I understand that man completely, my own father was just like him."

At her Sesame Club parties she held court, and was very much the *grande dame* of literature. One met some interesting people there. Her brothers, Osbert and Sir Sacheverell, were always present, and on one occasion I had an interesting conversation with the Chinese scholar and translator Arthur Waley. He remarked that he had never visited China, and said that he was afraid that if he did go there it would disappoint him. But many of her guests seemed to me to be somewhat sycophantic. I was embarrassed on one occasion when the conversation turned to gossip about the relationship between Coventry Patmore and Alice Meynell. Somebody asked Edith what Coventry Patmore's poetry was like. "Oh, it's very bad," she said. "Isn't it?" she added, turning to me. I had written part of a chapter in my critical book, *The Darkling Plain*, on Patmore, and had made very high claims for him. (These claims were, perhaps, exaggerated, but they were the result of youthful enthusiasm and I still rate Patmore highly.) I could not, therefore, in all honesty agree with her, and I said so, though with some diffidence. There was a distinct chill. Later on I was dropped from her guest list, though when I went up to Leeds as Gregory Fellow I had an encouraging message from her, saying she hoped I would set the town alight.

On one occasion at the Sesame Club she produced a letter which she had received from a Presbyterian minister in Glasgow who wanted her to come and lecture to a literary society run in connection with his church. She began by being rather scornful of his proposals. For example, he suggested that the title of her lecture might be "Why I hate the critics". He added that, should she come to Glasgow to lecture, his friend Sir—— would be happy to put her up. "Obviously a Glasgow shipowner," said Edith. "I couldn't possibly dream of putting up with him." Her court were dutifully giggling and smiling at her remarks. She then decided to look the minister up in *Who's Who*. There, she came upon the information that he had once lived as a down-and-out during the depression period of the thirties, wishing to share the experience of the unemployed and homeless, and to draw attention to their plight. Some of her friends still seemed to find this funny, but Edith's tone and attitude to the minister changed immediately. She admired this action of his and began reconsidering whether she should not, after all, accept his invitation to lecture.

As I have said, before David Wright and I collaborated on *The Faber Book of Twentieth Century Verse* we had worked on other joint projects. One of these, which we engaged in during the 1950s, was the compilation of an anthology of little-known Victorian verse, published by John Lehmann under the title of *The Forsaken Garden*. At this time I made one of my fairly frequent visits to my mother and stepfather in New Milton. My stepfather happened to mention that a poet called Gascoine Mackie was living a street or so away. A retired clergyman, he had been vicar of the neighbouring parish of Hordle. I went to call on him and found him a delightful old man. He had published one volume of verse in the 1890s entitled *Charmides*. He gave me a signed copy which I treasure. I was impressed with the poems; they are remarkably free from the affectations of language which infect much of the poetry of that period. These poems record a passionate friendship with another boy, when both the poet and he had been together at Magdalen College Choir School in Oxford. "Charmides" had died young, and I am certain that the relationship between these two boys had been entirely innocent. Mackie told me that he had received a visit from another verse-writing clergyman, who had published a number of volumes with titles such as *A Garland of Lad's Love*. These are regarded as collectors' pieces by those with certain tastes. They seem to me to be nauseatingly sentimental and self-indulgent. "He came to see me," said Gascoine Mackie, "for he had read my book and I think he thought I was – what is the word? Not homeopathic . . ." Mackie had also known Laurence Housman, who had lived for a time in the neighbourhood, and his brother Alfred. But he did not much care for the latter: "He had the root of bitterness in him." When I told Mackie I was compiling an anthology of Victorian verse, he was interested and showed me a poem of Swinburne which he admired. He then went on to say: "Once, many years ago, at a dinner party, I was disparaging this poem of Swinburne. The next night I had a dream in which the poet appeared to me with tears running down his face. I said to him, 'I bet it took you a long time to write that poem?' 'It took me days,' replied Swinburne." Mackie went on: "Since then I have been very careful not to speak harshly about any poet's work. I sometimes think we are being watched by angels, and what has always struck me about them is their beautiful manners."

During the 1950s George Every introduced me to Heinz Westmann, a psychiatrist who had been a pupil of Jung. Westmann organised a series of conferences which had the overall title of "The Present Question Conference", and each conference was held at some convenient place. Every morning, speakers of differing or opposing points of view were invited to speak, in pairs, to the overall subject of the conference. For example, we might have a Marxist and a Christian, or an artist and a scientist, and so on. During the afternoon, the participants were divided into small discussion groups, each of which formulated a question which would be put to the speakers at the evening session. I attended a number of these conferences and was invited by Westmann to serve on the conference council. These conferences proved to be of great value to me, and I made a number of interesting contacts there. In particular, I became friends with Rayner Heppenstall.

Rayner was a novelist and poet, and a producer for the BBC's Third Programme. His best-known novel, *Amid The Blaze of Noon*, published in 1939, had caused a degree of sensation. It dealt with a blind man whose love-making can only be expressed in tactile terms. Heppenstall came from a Yorkshire mining family, and had taken a scholarship at Leeds University. It was therefore inevitable, with the sexual frankness of this novel, that he should have been compared to D. H. Lawrence, though by temperament and talent he was, I think, really very different. He had a Methodist background, but had undergone instruction with a view to his reception into the Roman Catholic Church. But while attending a retreat at Campion Hall in Oxford he had suddenly discovered that, in conscience, he must withdraw. Neither his novels nor his poetry quite gained the attention they deserved. And he had, perhaps, always a nagging worry whether he had taken the right step in his refusal to join the Roman Catholic Church. Roy Campbell once addressed him as "You little bald-headed gnome who look as if you've swallowed an acid drop the wrong way". Rayner had an acute mind, and was, one might almost say, sceptical even of his own scepticism. He had studied in Paris as well as at Leeds. Once, at one of the seminar groups of The Present Question Conference, we were discussing whether there were any universally held human moral taboos. I put forward, as a talking point, that cannibalism might, perhaps, be considered as something which the human race had generally abhorred. Rayner then said that as the only practising cannibal present he should be allowed to comment on my thesis. When he was in Paris, he and some of his fellow students had been strongly influenced by the works of Baudelaire and other decadent writers. Finding a Lascar's ear, which had been cut off in a razor fight and was lying on the pavement, they took it home, fried it and ate it. Rayner learnt Welsh and later produced an excellent radio programme on Giraldus Cambrensis, the twelfth-century churchman and historian. He also studied astrology, though sceptical about the truth of its theory. I remember at another conference – not, this time, one organised by Westmann – Rayner and I having a very interesting conversation with the astronomer, Professor Gregory. Rayner was disturbed because he had been casting horoscopes and they seemed to come out right. He did not want this to happen. Gregory put forward the thesis that there might be, in the subconscious mind, what he called a divinatory faculty. If the conscious mind were given a complicated pattern to concentrate on, this divinatory faculty might be released. It did not really matter what the pattern was as long as one had some degree of faith in it. It could be a star chart, the arrangement of tea-leaves at the bottom of a cup, a pack of cards, the entrails of a sacrificed beast, the lines on one's palm or anything else of that kind.

Heinz Westmann was such an excellent conference organiser that Kathleen Bliss, the editor of *The Christian Newsletter*, having been asked by the BBC to prepare a report on their religious broadcasting policy, invited him to organise a conference along the same lines as The Present Question Conference for this purpose. This meeting was held at a conference house in Sussex, and a number of distinguished laymen and churchmen were present, including a Roman Catholic priest, the scientist Michael Polanyi, and the Anglican Divine and Christian Socialist, Canon Demant. There was also an American Episcopalian clergyman who had been a friend of T. S. Eliot in his early years. He told me that Eliot's first wife, Vivienne, had been involved with the Gurdjieff–Ouspensky cult. I have never had any direct contact myself with the followers of the Georgian guru, Gurdjieff, and his Russian expositor, Ouspensky. Their ideas seem to have attracted quite a number of intelligent people. According to my American informant, Laura Riding was also involved with the cult. It is well known that Katherine Mansfield died at the Gurdjieff Institute at Fontainebleau. In the evening Westmann came up to me and asked me what I thought about Dylan Thomas. I replied that I considered him a very fine poet and a good friend of mine, although there were many weaknesses and difficulties in his character. "I have had two phone calls today," said Westmann, "from patients who are in a desperate state, and Dylan Thomas is at the root of both of these crises." One of these patients I have reason to think was Margaret Taylor, the wife of the historian, A. J. P. Taylor. I once occupied the same platform as Taylor at one of The Present Question Conferences. In the course of his lecture he described himself as "an old-fashioned Marxist". It is well known that the Taylors befriended Dylan Thomas and gave him a cottage to live in on their own grounds in Oxford. He gave them a great deal of trouble, and Margaret Taylor became, unfortunately, obsessed with him.

During the 1940s and 1950s, when I visited Paris, it was not as easy to travel to the Continent as it is now. Initially one was only allowed to take £25 out of the country, but by staying at modest hotels on the Left Bank, and eating in very cheap restaurants, one could somehow make this last for a fortnight. The bars and cafés round Saint-Germain-des-Prés were a continuation of the old bohemian Paris of the nineteenth century and, to some extent, an extension of Soho. One was always running into Soho characters in this quarter. This was the time when Sartre had made famous the Café des Deux Magots, on the corner of the Boulevard Saint-Germain. I never met, or indeed saw, Sartre there, though I do remember catching a glimpse of Aldous Huxley. Another place to go was the Bar Vert in the Rue Jacob where, in a room above the bar, Edric Connor, the black folk-singer, would entertain us with negro spirituals, and American and French ballads. One would eat at a Greek restaurant called Raffi, where the cheapest dish for a few francs was stuffed tomatoes. Paris still brought back poignant memories of its occupation by, and liberation from, the Germans. One observed vases of fresh flowers placed underneath little plaques on street corners, where men had fallen during the liberation. One café had a parrot. This bird would whistle the opening bars of the "Marseillaise". I sometimes wonder if it had been deliberately taught this in order to annoy the Germans. Unfortunately it could not manage the leap of a fifth at the beginning of the third bar and always became acutely flat at this point. I usually stayed at a small hotel in the Rue de Bac, which, I am sorry to say, was infested with bed bugs.

Another conference which, on two occasions, I attended during the early fifties was held at the oecumenical centre at Bossy, near Geneva, the subject of our deliberations being Christianity and the arts. I made my first contacts here with continental Protestantism (both Lutheran and Calvinist), the atmosphere of which was very different from the Anglicanism I had known at Oxford and St Thomas's. Vladimir Weidle, the Russian theologian, and an authority on early Christian art, was also a participant. There was a rather primitive system of simultaneous translation which was undertaken by a Swiss girl.

183

Weidle addressed the conference in English, but, for the benefit of the other participants, his talk was relayed in French through headphones. In the course of his lecture, Weidle alluded to St Augustine of Hippo, but added that, although in the Eastern Church Augustine was regarded as a holy man, he had not the authority of a Father of the Church which he enjoys in the West. The roots of Lutheran and Calvinist theology are, in many ways, traceable to St Augustine. Weidle's view of St Augustine so shocked the Swiss translator that she seemed almost to stumble in restating it.

Denis de Rougemont, the Swiss Protestant literary critic, also addressed one of the conferences. His *Passion and Society* had been an influential book in my student days in Oxford. He has sometimes been described as the French-speaking equivalent of C. S. Lewis, though I think he had a less penetrating mind and certainly less learning than Lewis. In his address to the Bossy conference, de Rougemont suggested applying theological categories to literary criticism. He regarded the Provençal troubadours as expressing the ideas of the Albigensian heretics. This, according to de Rougemont, began a tradition which culminated in the death-centred passion of Wagner's *Tristan and Isolde*. In the same way, de Rougemont maintained that surrealism, for example, could be defined as a kind of Illuminism. I felt uncomfortable with this approach, and in my broken French attempted to confront him.

On my second visit to Bossy I was accompanied by Patrick McLaughlin and his elderly sister, Oonagh. After the conference concluded we had planned a little tour in Provence. One of the participants at the conference told us of a house near Tarascon which belonged to a group of religious sisters of the French Reformed Church whose leader was a Mademoiselle de Butte. These sisters would offer accommodation to guests. Accordingly, we stayed at this house for a week or two. The sisters had begun by engaging in social work among the poor of Paris, but had found that they needed a more structured organisation for their religious life. They spent their time in regular offices of prayer and in Bible study, as well as doing social and charitable work among the surrounding peasantry.

The sisters, who were of course not under vows, wore, not a conventional nun's habit, but a simple brown dress, with a light veil on their heads. Somehow or other the sun of Provence seemed to have mellowed the austere creed of Calvinism into something completely charming. Mademoiselle de Butte and her sisters had built for themselves, for use during the summer months, a little temple or grove on a hill overlooking their house. On the other side of the road was a large orphanage, or children's home, kept by a Protestant couple. One evening we were invited to dinner there, and, although my experience at Bembridge has made me thoroughly sceptical of all idealistic schemes for bringing up, or educating, children, the inmates of this place really did seem to be happy and to be treated with real love and affection. Another friend of Mademoiselle de Butte was a Protestant pastor who ministered to the sisters. He was an artist and showed us a painting of his on the subject of Abraham and Sarah. It was a delightful painting full of warmth and humanity. It showed the extremely aged Sarah in a condition of advanced pregnancy as a result of God's promise to Abraham that she would bear a son, Isaac. She was represented as an old peasant woman looking down, with a delighted smile, at her enormously swollen belly. There is a large Protestant community in Provence. These Protestants were the heirs not only of the Huguenots, but also of the earlier, though, I think, sub-Christian, Albigensian or Cathar heresy. There is a rather thin dividing-line between Calvin's rigid division between the elect (predestined to salvation) and the reprobate (predestined to damnation), and the Cathar, or Manichaean, view of humanity as divided into three classes: the *pneumatikoi* (spiritual men), the *psychikoi* (men of soul) and *hulikoi* (men of matter). In the last class no particle of the original light is present. For the Cathar, matter was not created by the supreme God, but by an inferior demiurge, and the soul is a particle of light which has been imprisoned in matter. Cathars were therefore opposed to sexuality and, particularly, marriage, since this only brought more souls into the realm of matter. It has been shown that some of the Protestant paper makers of the sixteenth century, in the South of France, used Cathar symbols in their watermarks. An underground group, of what seem to have been continuing Cathars in the strict sense of the term, emerged when all laws against non-Catholic religions were abolished by the French Revolution, though what happened to this group afterwards I do not know. One seemed to glimpse something of the Cathar philosophy as a result of the extreme sensuous beauty of the Provençal landscape. One could so easily think of this as a temptation or an illusion. The pastor said to me, rather sadly: "These people, here, they have the bullfight and the sun, and it is difficult to get them interested in the Gospel." The Provençal custom of bullfighting, which does not involve the death of the bull, is indigenous to the province. In recent years, unfortunately, the Spanish form of bullfighting has been introduced.

Mademoiselle de Butte's and her sisters' house proved a good centre for touring round the neighbouring countryside in Patrick's car. It was early summer, and I was overwhelmed by the beauty of the terrain and the brilliance of the colours. One seemed to be moving from one picture by Van Gogh into another. I was also fascinated by the history of Provence and its numerous classical ruins. The most memorable trip for me was when we crossed the desert of the Camargue and reached the shrine of Les Saintes-Maries-de-la-Mer at the mouth of the Rhône. This was my first glimpse of the Mediterranean. The legend of Les Saintes Maries is that, after the Resurrection and the beginning of the Christian Church, the Jews placed the three Marys (presumably Mary the mother of Jesus, Mary Magdalen and Mary Salome), along with St Martha and Lazarus, the brother of Martha and Mary Magdalen, in an open boat which was set adrift in the sea. By Providence it drifted to the mouth of the Rhône, where the saints landed and proceeded to Christianise the countryside. But as with the Grail legends there is a strong pre-Christian element in the story of the Saintes Maries. We may see in the three Marys a Christianisation of the triple Celtic goddesses, known as the *matres galliae* or *matres britanniae*, who presided over sacred wells and were identified by the Romans with the three Fates. This accounts for the word fairy, which is ultimately derived from the Roman *fata*. The three Marys may also, as Robert Graves suggests in *The White Goddess*, represent the three phases of the moon. They were accompanied by their black servant, Sara, who must represent the dark phase of the moon. St Sara is the patron saint of the gypsies. It is as if this submerged people had taken the dark side of the moon as their protector. There is a great annual gipsy pilgrimage to the shrine of Les Saintes-Maries-de-la-Mer. The writer Anthony Carson (Peter Brook – not to be confused with the theatrical director) told me he had once been present at this pilgrimage. A tourist, while watching the religious procession, was casually smoking a cigarette. A gypsy flicked it out of his mouth and rebuked him. This was their home, they were no longer subservient and ingratiating, as gypsies so often are. The image of St Sara is in the crypt of the church. It is nothing much to look at. It is a tawdry doll-like image and certainly not ancient, but the crypt itself has never been consecrated, and was originally an ancient Roman temple of Mithras. I am not particularly susceptible to atmosphere, but one certainly felt oneself struck by some kind of power there, if perhaps of a rather sinister kind.

Above: Myself on my first
birthday on 9 July 1919.

Above right: J. Howard
Whitehouse, founder
and warden of
Bembridge School.

Right: Outdoor
sketching at Bembridge
School, 1934.

Below: Worcester
College for the Blind in
the mid-1930s: an aerial
view.

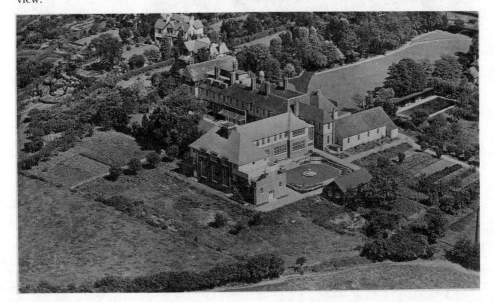

Above left: Myself, Philip Rawson and cat, in the country.

Above: Drummond Allison in uniform.

Below left: Sidney Keyes with Milein Cosmann, boating on the Cherwell.

Below: Michael Meyer.

Herbert Read.

Portrait of me at Leeds by Tom Watt.

Charles Williams in the 1930s.

Right: Portrait of Bonamy Dobrée by
Maurice de Sausmarez.

Above: Nina Hamnett by Roger Fry.

Above right: Augustus John's portrait of Roy Campbell.

Below: Tambimuttu.

Right: George Barker.

Above: Picnicking with some of my students from Alexandria; the gramophone in the foreground is playing Egyptian pop music.

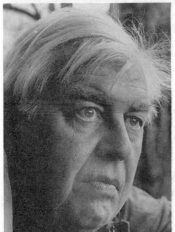

Left: David Wright

Below left: Geoffrey Hill, my colleague at Leeds and Ann Arbor.

Below: The title of the accompanying article, written in 1951, read "Are poets really necessary?" The typewriter is a pose – I never use one for composing verse.

Above: At a fancy dress party near Inverness I am in the character of Pierre Vidal, Arthur and Mary Creedy are Abelard and Eloise, and their friend is Richard the Lionheart.

Left: A recent portrait.

Below: Patrick McLaughlin, taken the year before he died.

11

Leeds

After some years, John Waller sold his house in Kensington, though retaining a flat in it for himself. I moved from one set of more or less unsatisfactory furnished rooms to another. It was difficult to find accommodation at a rent I could afford. Sometimes I lived alone and sometimes shared with a friend. One of these rooms was in a house in Tedworth Square, Chelsea. There were still parts of Chelsea which were quite shabby and run down, and had a bohemian population, although Tedworth Square had once been fashionable – it is said that Lillie Langtry had lived there in Edwardian times. One of the lodgers in this house was James Graham Murray who was known in Soho as "James the Shit". This name was given to him by Sylvia Gough, but I do not really know why. He was no more of a shit than any of the other characters on the scene, and less so than some. James was a writer, though his books were really potboilers, and I do not think any of them are remembered. One of his schemes was to write a book about secret peace feelers which had been sent out by either the Germans or the Allies during the Second World War. James was a friend of Gerald Hamilton, generally supposed to be the original of Isherwood's Mr Norris. Gerald had devised his own peace feeler which was that he should be parachuted into Germany, disguised as a nun, to make contact with Hitler. Gerald insisted that James should include this in his book, but I am not certain whether the book was ever completed. James introduced me to Gerald, who was living, as far as I could make out, entirely on credit from Fortnum and Mason's. He was not, however, forthcoming in my presence. James thought he was suspicious that I was spying on him in some way.

James told me of his own encounter with Peter Warlock in a bar the evening before the latter took his own life, under circumstances which have never been fully accounted for. James thought that if he had stayed to engage Warlock in conversation, perhaps talking over whatever problems were worrying him, he might have saved the composer. I know what this "if only" regret can be like. It is a waste of spirit.

James told me a story about Aleister Crowley which has not, I think, been included in any of the biographies of that black magician.

James was staying with a girlfriend in a hotel somewhere in the home counties. It turned out that Aleister Crowley was a guest in the same hotel, being in one of his periodical times of recession. Crowley approached James and his girlfriend in a very friendly way and offered to cast James's horoscope. However, it soon became apparent that Crowley had designs upon the girl. These manifested themselves, not so much in direct approaches, as in glances and gestures, which indicated that he was directing powerful thought waves at her. He augmented these by tapping on the wall of her room at night. James squared up to Crowley, and told him that this must stop. This was quite courageous of James, for Crowley was a very powerful man and, in his youth, had been a mountaineer in the Himalayas. Crowley took the hint and avoided the company of James and his girlfriend for the rest of their stay. When this came to an end, the couple, while waiting for a taxi to take them and their luggage to the station, were having a final drink in the bar. Suddenly Crowley appeared, all smiles: "Oh," he said, "I promised to cast your horoscope. Here it is." He took it out of his pocket. "Let me read it to you." He then read out to James, and the assembled company, a horoscope which seemed to denote for its subject every possible weakness of character and a thoroughly disastrous destiny.

I never met Aleister Crowley myself, though he had been very much part of the London and Soho scene before and during the war. Peter Brook, when he directed Marlowe's *Dr Faustus*, in London during the Oxford vacation, had asked Crowley to act as technical adviser for the magical scenes. At one point a question arose whether a certain phrase in Marlowe's text should read "Cur moreris" ("Why do you delay?"). The phrase is used by Faustus when he is evoking Mephistophilis. Crowley accepted this meaning, adding, "for quite often they do delay, you know?" He went on to say that Marlowe's invocation was a valid one and if a bucket of bull's blood had been placed in the wings a spirit would undoubtedly have appeared. On one occasion, Crowley excused himself for leaving early from rehearsals by saying that it was his custom always on that day to drink the blood of twelve virgins. This seems to have been a fairly frequent habit of his. Nina Hamnett told me that when she first met Aleister Crowley he was drinking a virgin's blood. "I didn't really go for this," she said, "but it was Sunday afternoon, and it was different from home." My friend, the poet Thomas Blackburn, also knew Crowley. He rather admired him, and wrote a series of sonnets about him. Blackburn told me how he once took a walk with Crowley through the streets of the West End after the pubs had closed. They were conversing on various subjects when they suddenly came across a group of prostitutes. Crowley then left Blackburn, and said, "Good evening, ladies," raising his hat and behaving in the most courtly manner, for in his eyes prostitutes were really priestesses.

In the 1930s Crowley brought a libel action against Nina Hamnett. In her book of reminiscences, *Laughing Torso*, she had described him as a black magician. He maintained that he was a white magician. Such an amount of revolting evidence about Crowley's practices, and the community which he had run in Italy, the Abbey of Thélème, was brought into court that the judge asked the jury if they wished to hear any more. They replied that they did not, and found for the defendant. Eventually Crowley retired to Hove. This town seems to be the place where rather sad and defeated people end up, for example those who have been at the centre of scandals. Lord Alfred Douglas and Ethel le Neve, Crippen's mistress, both died there. Crowley's last words were "I am perplexed". He was a poseur, but he was also really a wicked man who destroyed most of the people closely associated with him, though the means of their destruction were as much sex and drugs as spiritual forces of evil. Crowley's religious background was that of the Plymouth Brethren. This evangelical and fundamentalist sect seems, every now and then, to send up extraordinary sports, for example Edmund Gosse, General Wingate and Haigh, the acid bath murderer. Crowley's mother apparently told him, at an early age, that she believed she had given birth to the Great Beast of the Apocalypse. Crowley accepted this role gladly, and held that he had invented a new religion, Crowleyanity, which would supersede Christianity. Its sole principle was "Do what you will shall be the whole of the law." St Paul and St Augustine would not have disagreed, but this premise requires a major premise: love God first, and then do what you will. John Symons, the author of the first and best biography of Crowley, had, as a journalist, interviewed him in his last sad days at Hove. Crowley was so glad that someone was still taking an interest in him that he made Simons his literary executor. I was of assistance to Simons, in clearing up one or two small points, when he came to edit Crowley's journals. These are simply accounts of sexual orgies of various kinds, involving men, women and goats. Such orgies were, for Crowley, sacramental rites.

In 1916 Crowley tried to take over the Order of the Golden Dawn, a secret society of fairly harmless adepts who practised ritual magic. Their leader was MacGregor Mathers, and one of their most notable members was W. B. Yeats. Crowley wished to gain control of the society for his own sinister purposes. At one point, Yeats was forced to guard the offices of the Golden Dawn, armed with a cudgel. It is possible that the figure of the rough beast which "slouches towards Bethlehem to be born" in Yeats's poem "The Second Coming", written in 1916, may, among other things, be based upon Crowley.

Charles Williams was not a member of the original Golden Dawn, as has sometimes been stated, but belonged for a time to one of its splinter groups which included the eccentric scholar, A. E. Waite, and the mystic, Evelyn Underhill. These were orthodox Christians. This association of Williams with the Golden Dawn has been a matter of embarrassment and a puzzle to some of his admirers. But the statement made by A. N. Wilson, in his biography of C. S. Lewis, about Williams, that "Thomas Cranmer and Aleister Crowley were held in uneasy balance in his sympathies", is quite false, and indeed absurd.

It was while I was living in Tedworth Square that the magazine *Picture Post* published a feature on contemporary poetry in which there appeared a photograph of myself at the typewriter: "A scholar contemplates a line." In fact, I have never written poetry on the typewriter. I find that the mechanical rhythms of the machine conflict with the natural rhythms of verse. This feature included an article by Stephen Spender in which he remarked that poetry did not sell well, and that part of the reason might be that many readers, especially those living outside London in cities where there might not be any good bookshops, had no way of knowing what new books of verse they ought to buy and read. Spender suggested that the answer to this problem might be the foundation of a Poetry Book Society, which should select the best books of each year and recommend them to its members, who would be able to obtain them at a discount. A friend of mine, Philip Inman, who had, I believe, been in the Consular Service, but was now retired (I think through ill health), wrote to Spender saying that the idea he had put forth was a thoroughly sound one, and ought to be realised. Inman offered to do all the necessary paperwork, writing to publishers and so on, entirely without payment, if Spender would undertake to found the Poetry Book Society along the lines he had suggested in the article. Accordingly, an *ad hoc* working committee was formed, consisting of Spender, Inman and myself. We arranged a meeting at which most of the publishers of verse were represented. T. S. Eliot and Geoffrey Faber were both present, as were John Lehmann and others. At this meeting a programme for the society was worked out, and all the publishers gave it their general support. Not long after this Spender had, at rather short notice, to go to America to lecture. He handed over the whole scheme to Cecil Day Lewis without consulting Inman or myself. I have no doubt that Stephen Spender, from whom I have never received anything but kindness, was in a hurry to make arrangements for his American journey and did not fully realise that he ought to have consulted his committee. Inman was very angry and said that if Day Lewis was to have anything to do with the scheme he would resign. Although I did not have the same strong feeling against Day Lewis as Inman had, I felt that I must support him in this. The Poetry Book Society did, in fact, come into being in December 1953 and still, I am glad to say, continues. When it celebrated its twentieth anniversary in 1973, Charles Osborne, then Chairman of the Arts Council's Literary Panel, at a reception held to celebrate the event, attributed its foundation to Day Lewis. Now, I understand, the Poetry Book Society claims to have been founded by T. S. Eliot.

Inman had an extraordinarily intense animus against Day Lewis. I have already spoken about the reaction against the poetry of the 1930s, which characterised many of my generation. Day Lewis, the only one of the Auden group who had been seriously involved with the Communist Party, was now well on his way to becoming an establishment figure. He had accepted the Professorship of Poetry at Oxford, and it was widely believed that he would be the next Poet Laureate – which indeed he did become in 1968. The attitude of some of us to Day Lewis may be considered as another instance of the "lost leader syndrome". I myself was guilty of a satirical squib on his acceptance of the Oxford chair which I now regret. I only met Day Lewis on one or two occasions and found him always kind and courteous, and, although his poetry has not, perhaps, stood the test of time as much as his admirers might have hoped, he took his appointment as Laureate very seriously, acting as the official spokesman for poetry in this country.

My attempts to get by since I left Hutchinson with freelance writing and literary journalism had landed me in a great deal of financial difficulty. It was plain that I must, somehow or other, find a more secure source of income. This came about when I was offered the Gregory Fellowship of Poetry at Leeds University. Peter Gregory, a wealthy businessman, had founded Fellowships at Leeds University in 1949 for poetry, music, painting and sculpture. The committee which appointed the Gregory Fellows consisted of Herbert Read, T. S. Eliot, Henry Moore, Graham Sutherland and Bonamy Dobrée, Professor of English Literature at Leeds University. The first Gregory Fellow in Poetry was James Kirkup, whom I had known for some years. He was a prolific poet with a talent for turning the ordinary experiences of everyday life into poetry. At Leeds he put this talent to very good effect, writing about the City of Leeds and its environs. He engaged, for example, in a caving expedition. Probably his best poem is "A Correct Compassion", written when a distinguished surgeon at the Leeds Infirmary invited him to witness an open-heart operation.

I accepted the Gregory Fellowship gladly. The Fellow received a stipend, equivalent to that of a junior lecturer, but in those days had to find his own accommodation. He had no duties except to write and, in some way or other, to contact the students and encourage their reading or writing of poetry. It was not easy to find comfortable lodgings in Leeds, at least at a price I could afford, for I was heavily in debt. Most of the lodgings were heated only by coal fires. If one built a fire in the morning and then went out, when one came back in the evening it was probably going out. One then built the fire up again, and during the night was almost suffocated in a one-room lodging. It was also difficult to get a hot bath, which seemed to be regarded as rather a luxury. One landlady said to me, when I enquired about baths: "You can have a bath any time you like, as long as you make up the copper yourself." I generally went to the public baths run by the City Corporation. I seemed to have them entirely to myself. In the markets area there were so-called Russian baths. When one went inside, one was confronted by a notice which said: "It has come to the attention of the management that some customers have been acting indecently. Anyone found so doing will immediately be arrested." This, however, appeared to act as an incentive rather than a deterrent.

I was, as already explained, given no definite assignment as to how I was to occupy my time. I found this rather difficult. A painter or a sculptor, I suppose, can go every day into his studio and work. A poet does not generally work that way. No publisher is likely to issue a poet's volume of verse more than once in three years, and it may consist of anything between thirty and sixty poems. It follows from this that one good poem in a fortnight or a month is as much as any poet ought to write. It has often been said that a writer should write something every day, even if he afterwards might tear it up. T. S. Eliot was of this opinion, but his own *oeuvre*, especially in poetry, is so small that it is difficult to believe that he observed this rule, though in his early years he did write a great deal of literary and social criticism. Day Lewis, I believe, who wrote very little prose, did, in fact, write verse for several hours every day. I once met someone who had known Day Lewis and had asked him what he had done that day. "Put a full stop in", Day Lewis had replied, "and then took it out again." Frankly, a lot of Day Lewis's later work does look as if it were written under these conditions. It is competent, but is it really necessary to set it down? Shelley is wiser, I think, when he talks of the poet really working hard when he seems to be most idle: "Watching the golden bees in the ivy bloom." After a time, I adopted a kind of regime for myself. I arranged with Bonamy Dobrée to organise a small seminar on the appreciation of poetry to which a group of students could come, and I made a point of going into the students' café every morning at about eleven o'clock, during their coffee break, to talk to them. Kirkup had solved the same problem by his habit of going about the city and writing about anything interesting that took his notice, but my talent is not quite of that kind.

Regular "creative writing" classes, which are now very popular, did not, I think, exist at that time. I am not sure whether they are a good idea. You can teach people to write verse, but not to write poetry. In the 1970s I gave creative writing classes in poetry to a group of American students who, as part of their course, were spending a period in England. I only met them for a couple of weeks at a conference held at Ruskin College, Oxford, during the summer vacation. I read these students a couplet from Pope, and explained the form of the villanelle (one of the so-called artificial French forms, consisting of two recurring lines). I told the students to write a villanelle, using Pope's couplet for these two lines. This venture proved to be successful and I was asked to give them a regular course the next term in London, where they were stationed, but this course never materialised. I would like to have done something analogous to that which my old harmony master in New Milton, Mr Russe, did for me. My first lesson would consist of my reading a passage to the students in octosyllabic couplets. I would then tell them to turn this passage into decasyllabic couplets by adding two syllables to each line. For the next lesson I might, perhaps, read the students a passage in decasyllabic couplets and ask them to reduce it to octosyllabic couplets, sacrificing as little of the meaning as possible. After that I might read them a leading article from *The Times* and tell them to turn it into blank verse. And so it would go on. Once a term, for a special treat, they could write a free composition, but, I am afraid, most students would have got bored by this time and have left my class.

At Leeds I used to visit frequently the home of my colleague and friend Arthur Creedy. We often had students round and taught them how to write bouts-rimés sonnets, which they enjoyed. I also tentatively produced other bouts-rimés forms, such as a bouts-rimés ottava rima stanza in the style of Byron's *Don Juan* and, as a special *tour de force*, the bouts-rimés Pindaric ode in the style of Thomas Gray. For this, one prescribes not only the rhyme scheme of each stanza, but also the metre of each particular line, within the frame of the elaborate repeated three-stanza form of strophe, antistrophe and epode. One of my Leeds students, Ralph Maude, an American, produced a weekly cyclostyled magazine, *Poetry and Audience*, to which I contributed. Another student, Gordon Heard, who was to become a close friend of mine, was the editor of the official printed university student magazine, *Griffin*.

One of my closest friends in Leeds was Kenneth Severs. Kenneth had been a student at Leeds and was now the head of the BBC in that city. The BBC occupied a rather beautiful building which had once been a Quaker meeting house. In his last years, Severs became a lecturer in the English Department at the university. I met him within a few days of my arrival. I was walking past the door of the pub in which he generally drank, when he recognised me, I suppose from the *Picture Post* photograph, and invited me in. I came regularly to frequent this pub with Kenneth's two close friends, "David" Garrick, a lecturer in the Chemistry Department, and Edward Allan, who taught musical composition. Allan told me how once he had acquired the works of the Italian poet and librettist Metastasio in several volumes. It turned out that this particular set had once either belonged to or been lent to Coleridge. It seems that the poet had casually taken down from the shelf one of these volumes and, as was his wont, had immediately begun to annotate it. These annotations did not extend to any of the other volumes.

Kenneth Severs was a very talented man and wrote verse which was published after his death in a small volume. One of the features he produced for the BBC Northern Service was a programme in which a well-known writer or other figure addressed an audience of local artists or writers, and then took part in a broadcast discussion. I was invited to participate in two of these programmes. In one of them the speaker was Philip Toynbee, and in the other John Betjeman. I had already met Betjeman as literary editor of *Time and Tide*, to which I contributed reviews. After the programme had gone over the air, a party was held. When this was drawing to its close, Kenneth said: "Well, Mr Betjeman, I expect you would like me to call a taxi to take you to your hotel now." "Oh no," Betjeman replied, "I don't want to go to bed yet." "Well, what would you like to do?" asked Kenneth. "When I'm in a town I haven't been in before," said Betjeman, "I like to visit a music hall, if it has one. Is there one in Leeds?" "Oh yes," answered Severs, "there is a very good one: the Leeds City Varieties." "Good," said Betjeman. "Who's going to come with me?" The invited guests, who consisted largely of middlebrow Yorkshire lady novelists, were not forthcoming, so I shyly said I would like to go if he could put up with my company.

So off we went to the Leeds City Varieties. The English music hall as an institution was now very much at the end of its career. The only surviving one in London, Collins's, which I once visited with David Wright, presented a most dreary programme consisting mostly of sniggering sketches about homosexuality, and transvestite strip-tease acts. The Leeds City Varieties was only a little better than that, but Betjeman delighted in it, commenting with gusto on all the sketches we were presented with. There was, for example, a parody of the balcony scene from *Romeo and Juliet* in which an actor as Romeo, in a blond wig, impersonated Sir Laurence Olivier. This was followed by what was, by the standards of the 1950s, a rather daring act, consisting of a stripper who succeeded in preserving a measure of modesty by means of a large scarf which she draped around herself. The curtain would rise and show her in one pose, with a caption, and then fall, rising again to show her in a different attitude. Her first pose, for example, was "The Pride of the Harem", in which she reclined on a divan in the attitude of an odalisque. The curtain fell and then went up again to show "Bonny Scotland", in which a tartan scarf was draped diagonally across her body. Betjeman pointed out that there was a man sitting below us in the stalls, watching these poses through a pair of field-glasses. But the sketch which delighted us most presented a girl with marionettes. "What a nice girl," Betjeman said. "A canon's daughter, wouldn't you say?" Her first turn also had an oriental flavour. She worked a doll, dressed in exotic costume, which danced rather jerkily to "In a Persian Garden" by the Edwardian composer Ketélbey. This was followed by a dancing skeleton accompanied by Saint-Saëns's *Danse Macabre*, and, finally, what appeared to be very difficult, three teddy bears all dancing at once, manipulated by her two hands, to, of course, "The Teddy Bears' Picnic".

Another Leeds character was the artist Jacob Kramer. He had once had a considerable reputation and been a friend and contemporary of Epstein. Kramer's trouble seemed to be that he could not face leaving his elderly mother in order to return to London, where he thought he might have become better known. Every time I met him he would say: "John, I have made a decision at last. I am going to throw everything up. I am going to London." But this never happened. He once asked if he could draw me, and did a very fine sketch portrait. His idea was that, if I would give him a poem to accompany it, he would ask the Yorkshire magazine, *The Dalesman*, to publish both the poem and the drawing. He promised that if this happened he would give me the original. Unfortunately either he forgot to go to *The Dalesman*, or they rejected the project, for I never, to my regret, received the portrait.

It may seem ungrateful, since the university and Gregory's beneficence gave me security for three years, but, on the whole, I did not find the City of Leeds a congenial place. Its climate was generally cold and damp, and in the 1950s it was grimy and ugly, though it has got some fine buildings. One of the most remarkable of these is St John's Church, Briggate, said to be the last church erected in England in the real Gothic style – as distinct from the neo-Gothic – and the only church to be built under the Commonwealth. Leeds also has a fine Victorian town hall, though I do not think it is as grand as Manchester's. In City Square is an equestrian statue of the Black Prince. Apparently the Black Prince has no connection whatsoever with the City of Leeds, but some benefactor had acquired this statue and, thinking that it would look well in the square, presented it to the city. The Black Prince is surrounded by a number of half-naked ladies, holding electric globes. Facing the other way, and looking slightly embarrassed, is a statue of one of Leeds's greatest sons, the chemist Joseph Priestley, in his Unitarian minister's gown.

I also found difficulty in making friends with the local inhabitants. Yorkshire people are very fond of telling you how warm-hearted they are, but I, as a southerner, seemed to be on the wrong wavelength for them, and gave the wrong signals, for I frequently found my attempts to be friendly rebuffed. Peggy Blackburn, who came from Leeds, and was the second wife of Thomas Blackburn, told me that the university was thoroughly unpopular in that city because the workers could neither forget nor forgive that students had acted as strike breakers during the General Strike of 1926, driving buses and so on. This may have been the case. I found that if I had been working in my room at the university and wanted to take some books back to my lodgings – but planned to go into the city for a meal and a drink at a pub before going home – if I carried the books with me, they tended to elicit rather hostile comments from the locals. Consequently, I took to going back to my university rooms late at night to collect the books.

I wish I could find something more positive to say about the City of Leeds and its inhabitants, which I am sure have many sterling virtues, but to me the city seemed to breathe an air of corruption. There had been, over the years, more than one scandal involving the Leeds police. A young policeman used sometimes to drink with Kenneth Severs and the rest of us in the pub. He seemed pleasant enough. One day, while talking to him, I mentioned a paragraph that had appeared in the morning papers in which a judge had complained that, nowadays, there were far too many cases of witnesses perjuring themselves. I said, perhaps rather pompously, that it seemed obvious that the religious sanction given by the oath on the Bible did not have the force today that it formerly had, and the policeman said: "But we have to perjure ourselves – otherwise we wouldn't get convictions." It had not occurred to me that the judge might be referring to police witnesses, but to the policeman it was the immediate conclusion.

With the members of the English Department of the university, my relations were much happier. Bonamy Dobrée, the head of the department, was a most remarkable man and became one of my best friends, and one of those older men, such as Hugh Kingsmill, to whom I owe most. Bonamy liked to keep a balance in his department. He had engaged one Roman Catholic, Wilfred Childe (who had died before I arrived there), one communist, Arnold Kettle – who later became the Professor of English at the Open University – and one orthodox Jew, Harold Fisch, a specialist in the cabbala, who now teaches at the University of Jerusalem.

Another of Dobrée's appointments in the English Department was G. Wilson Knight. My Oxford friend, John Jones, who had been a pupil of Wilson Knight at Stowe School, once, in a radio talk, described him as the greatest English Shakespeare critic since Coleridge. I do not think that this is too extravagant a claim. Wilson Knight was the author of volumes covering the complete canon of Shakespeare's works. These began with an examination of *The Tempest*, stressing the structural function in this, and in others of Shakespeare's work, of the two images of music and storm. Whenever Wilson Knight moved away from Shakespeare his touch was less sure and it shaded off into the absurd, as in those philosophical books in which he attempted to reconcile Nietzsche with Christianity, or in his obsession with spiritualism. He and his brother, Jackson Knight, had both been deeply attached to their mother. After her death, neither of them married and they shared a house together near Exeter, which was named Caroline House after her. They believed that they were in touch with her spirit. Wilson Knight was an extraordinary combination of brilliant insight and sheer fudge. There was a colloquium at Leeds in which staff of the English Department discussed Eliot's *Four Quartets*. Wilson Knight was not only illuminating but full of good sense. He believed that Shakespeare's plays had to be realised in the theatre, and was an accomplished producer. I saw only one of his Shakespeare productions at Leeds. This was of *Othello*, and it was not, I have to admit, entirely successful. In his writings, Wilson Knight insists, among other things, upon the symbolic importance of nakedness in scenes of Shakespeare's plays, for instance those which present the ruined Timon of Athens, or Edgar, disguised as Poor Tom, in *King Lear*. When he had held a professorship at the University of Toronto, Wilson Knight played Timon as naked as conventions would allow. But it seems that Wilson Knight had not really got the figure for such a presentation. I was told by a Canadian friend that the production was known to the students as "Tarzan of Athens". I told this story to my American friend and former student, John Van Domelen, who used this as the title of his own interesting biographical study of Wilson Knight. Many years after I had left Leeds, I sent Wilson Knight a copy of my play *Helen in Egypt*. He very kindly sent me a detailed letter of comment. I was interested to find that these comments dealt, not with the symbolism or imagery of my play, but entirely with practicalities of stagecraft.

As a lecturer, Wilson Knight was one to whom the word "charis-matic" could well be applied. Kenneth Severs said to me once: "You listen to a lecture by Wilson Knight and you have the impression that the Holy Ghost has descended; the next day you cannot remember a word of what had been said, but it has entered your subconscious and might later come to the surface." A professor at another Yorkshire university wrote a full-length study of *King Lear*. Wilson Knight accused this critic of plagiarising his own ideas on the tragedy. I am sure that this had not deliberately been done. The author had simply absorbed Wilson Knight's ideas without realising it. I had something of the same experience myself. As an undergraduate I read Wilson Knight's book *The Starlit Dome*, a study dealing mainly with the Romantic poets. Many years later, I came to see a connection between a number of images that run through English poetry, stemming from Chaucer's *House of Fame*, through Pope's "Temple of Fame", Cole-ridge's "Kubla Khan", Shelley's "Ode to Liberty", Tennyson's "Palace of Art", to Yeats's Byzantium poems. In all of these, a build-ing, often a dome, represents the eternity of art, whereas, in most cases, shifting time is represented by a river or by melting ice. I was pleased with these ideas and thought of writing an essay upon them, but I suddenly realised that they had all emerged from my reading of *The Starlit Dome*, which I had discarded as largely unintelligible and had almost forgotten.

Bonamy Dobrée himself came from a distinguished Channel Island family, originally of Huguenot origin. His literary interests were wide, though his chief delight was in the English Augustan period, and, like many of the greatest men of that epoch, his philosophy, or religion, was a sceptical humanistic stoicism. He had served as an officer in the regular army during the First World War, but in the 1920s had become a friend of some of the leading literary figures of the day, including T. S. Eliot, Herbert Read, D. H. Lawrence and Richard Aldington. Bonamy told me that Eliot's "Dialogue on Dramatic Poetry" largely represented one of the regular dinners which Eliot and his friends used to have at that time, and at which Bonamy himself had been a guest.

Bonamy rejoined the regular army before assuming an academic career. He had evidently been a good officer and his army experience gave him a kind of worldly wisdom and a sense of order and propriety which are not always found among academics. As head of the English Department he engineered a divorce between the departments of Eng-lish Literature and English Language. He did not get on well with the head of the English Language Department, Professor Orton. Orton was a specialist in dialects, in particular those of the north of England, and, since the Literature Department and the Language

Department offices were still close together, one was always liable, when entering the former, to run into some ancient Yorkshire peasant who had come to record his dialect in the Language Department. On one occasion, at some official dinner at the university, I found myself sitting next to Orton, who reminded me that several years before he had been on a board which had interviewed me for a possible post abroad on behalf of the British Council. I could at the time have very well done with this appointment, but was turned down. "Of course we turned you down," said Orton, "because we knew you would make something of yourself." I found it a little hard to forgive this remark. Another reason why Bonamy could not work happily with the Language Department was probably that he had little feeling for the studies of Anglo-Saxon or Middle English literature. He was, as I have already suggested, essentially a man of the eighteenth-century Enlightenment, and disliked what he saw as the superstition and obscurantism of the Middle Ages.

At the end of my first year at Leeds, I was really in doubt as to whether I wished to have my appointment as Gregory Fellow renewed. Bonamy, however, begged me to stay and was kind enough to say that it was as much for his sake as for mine, as he found my company in many ways more congenial than that of most of his other colleagues. I therefore remained for the full three years. When a vacancy arose in his department, Bonamy wished to have another poet on his staff, not as Gregory Fellow, but as lecturer in English. There were two possible candidates: one was Geoffrey Hill, who was then doing a postgraduate year at Oxford, and the other, a poet of some distinction and growing prestige. The other members of the department were rather in favour of the latter, but I strongly recommended Hill, whose work I had begun to know. I told Bonamy that I was going up to Oxford the following week to give a reading to an undergraduate literary society, and hoped to meet Hill for the first time. "Tell him", said Bonamy, "that if he wishes to apply for the Leeds post it is his." I did exactly this, and Geoffrey Hill joined the Leeds staff. We became close friends and were later to be colleagues at Ann Arbor in America. I have rather lost touch with Geoffrey in recent years. He seems to have become something of a recluse. He left Leeds to become a Fellow of Emmanuel College, Cambridge, and is now, I believe, in America. I still consider him far and away the best poet of his generation.

One day, the vicar of the church in Leeds which acted as the university church asked me if I would like to compose a religious play, which could be given in the church on Easter Saturday in lieu of a sermon. I was interested in the idea and composed a play, or rather, perhaps, a spoken oratorio, on the traditional theme of the harrowing of hell. The vicar liked the play and the bishop, who acted as censor, gave it the all-clear on doctrinal grounds. A reading of the play was arranged and a provisional cast selected, but I found now that I seemed to be expected to do everything: to be casting director, producer, publicity agent and other things as well. I seemed to be getting little support, and accordingly the play was never produced in Leeds. It was eventually included, along with my two other plays, in a volume published by the OUP: *Helen in Egypt and Other Plays*. I have been told it has been performed at Kingston College, Jamaica. Presumably one of my former students at Leeds took up a post there.

My other play, *The Talking Ass*, was given in 1955 at St John's Theological College in Durham. Patrick McLaughlin had occasion to visit the Bishop of Durham, Michael Ramsey (later to be Archbishop of Canterbury), and so, accompanied by the up-and-coming theatre director, Michael Elliott, we all motored up to Durham together to see my play. This was the first time I had visited Durham Cathedral – "half house of God, half fortress 'gainst the Scot". I remember, in particular, the shrine of St Cuthbert, which had been stripped by Thomas Cromwell's commissioners of all its wealth, and now contained St Cuthbert's coffin only. Somehow or other it seemed to be a source of spiritual power. On our way back we stopped at Selby Minster. This church has been rather badly handled by the Victorian restorers and did not seem particularly impressive. However, we went in to look around and fortunately met the sacristan. He took us down to the really remarkable crypt. This proved to be the original church built by St Cuthbert. In order to enter it one has to pass through a narrow passage, wide enough to admit only one person at a time. This passage turns at a sharp right-angle before entering what was the chapel. St Cuthbert and his monks must have been always liable to attack by the surrounding pagans, and this plan of building would have served to slow up such an attack. I have never felt more directly in touch with history than at that spot.

Among the staff of the English Department, the one whose company I found most congenial was Arthur Creedy. Arthur lived in a small flat in a road with the depressing name of Cemetery Place. He seemed to subsist largely on cheese and tomato sandwiches, for he was short of funds. Much of his salary had to be paid out in alimony to his first wife. I often visited him of an evening and students would sometimes join us. We spent our time writing verses and singing songs round his piano, for he was very musical and had been a chorister of Exeter Cathedral. I found that my bass voice could go low enough to tackle Sarastro's arias in *The Magic Flute*.

In my last year as Gregory Fellow I shared a house in Armley, a working-class suburb of Leeds, with the painter, Tom Watt, who taught at Leeds College of Art. Bonamy persuaded the university to commission a portrait of me from Tom, which, hopefully, might be bought by the university for the English Department. Tom duly executed a portrait, but gave it to his girlfriend for safe keeping, since his studio was rather cluttered. However, the relationship broke up, and he was unable to secure the painting's return. He had rather hastily to paint a second portrait of me, which now does hang in the English Department at Leeds.

One remarkable work of art which the university possessed was a bas-relief by Eric Gill, which is on one side of the main Parkinson Building. Gill had been commissioned to create a war memorial for the Stock Exchange. He chose as his subject Christ driving the money-changers out of the temple. Although the figures in the sculpture are fairly formalised, one can see that the money-changers seem to be wearing something rather like the conventional frock-coats and top hats which at that time were expected at the Stock Exchange. At any rate, it was deemed unsuitable and Leeds University acquired it instead.

The Gregory Fellowships were tenable only for three years. At the end of my third year Bonamy Dobrée consulted me, unofficially, as to who should succeed me. My first suggestion was W. S. Graham who was, as I have said, living in Cornwall in a fairly dire condition of poverty. As it happened, Sydney had been invited to speak to the student literary society. He was under stress, drinking too much, and over-using amphetamines. His reading to the students was not a success, although the poems themselves were delivered brilliantly. Coming, as he did, from a working-class Scottish background, he seemed to have thought that all university students were upper class or upper middle class. Accordingly, he adopted an aggressive and patronising air towards them. This did not go down well. Many of the students, in fact, came from backgrounds not very different from his own. Later, together with Geoffrey Hill and myself, he was invited to dine with Bonamy Dobrée at his flat. Unfortunately, Sydney continued to talk in a most aggressive manner. Eventually, Bonamy, who with the best will in the world could not take much more of this, asked him what time he proposed to take the train back to London, where he would change for Cornwall. Sydney did not know the times of the trains, so we rang up the station to find out. The next train left shortly after half past ten, and there was not another till about one. Sydney declared he had no intention of leaving yet, and would catch the later train. Bonamy said that in that case he would retire to bed and leave Sydney in his sitting-room. At this point I managed to whisper to Geoffrey Hill, begging him to assist me in persuading Sydney to leave and go with us to have a drink in a public house. Fortunately, we succeeded in this, and eventually he caught the half past ten train. It was clear that this unhappy episode meant that his succeeding me as Gregory Fellow was out of the question.

My next suggestion was David Gascoyne. "But isn't he a Roman Catholic?" said Bonamy. Ancestral memories of persecution sometimes surfaced in his consciousness. He was, himself, an agnostic or, as he preferred to say, a stoic. I pointed out that Gascoyne had recently made a statement to the press that he was "a Protestant Anglican". "Then he's just a mystic," said Bonamy. "That's all right." Unfortunately, nobody seemed to know Gascoyne's address, so finally I suggested Thomas Blackburn, who did in fact succeed me. On the last day of my final term, Bonamy invited me to have breakfast with him, before I went down. While we were breakfasting, a phone call came from Biddy Crozier, the wife of Eric Crozier (the librettist of *Peter Grimes*), who was a patron and friend of David Gascoyne. She asked if the Gregory Fellowship could be available for Gascoyne. But the offer had already been made to Blackburn.

The question of what I should do next also arose. Bonamy asked me what my plans might be, and I replied that I would rather like to take some kind of academic post abroad, perhaps in the Middle East. "Why the Middle East?" he asked. "Well," I said, "many of my friends were in the Middle East – specifically in Egypt – during the war, and they seemed to have got a lot out of it." "That is the best reason for going," said Bonamy, who had himself lectured at Cairo at one period. Through a stroke of good fortune, while in London in the Athenaeum Club, Bonamy ran into a retired professor of mediaeval history who had just come back from the University of Alexandria. When Gamal Abdel Nasser came to power in 1952 all English lecturers had been dismissed from Egyptian universities and they had not been properly compensated. Consequently, the British Council was no longer recommending English teachers for Egypt, and by 1955 the Egyptians were, apparently, feeling the need for them. This retired professor had returned to England with a commission to find a visiting professor in English literature for Alexandria. Bonamy therefore suggested that I should apply for the post. Before doing so I went to see both the British Council and the Foreign Office to ask if they had any objection to my application. I was told by both bodies that they were only too delighted that I should have this post rather than a Japanese professor who was angling for it. Although the British Council could not officially sponsor me, it still had offices in Alexandria and Cairo, and would give me all the unofficial support and help that it could.

12

Egypt

Before leaving for Egypt, I was to make my first visit to the United States of America. Bill Ireland, a lecturer in the French Department at Leeds, had asked me one day if I would care to visit America as a delegate to Henry Kissinger's Harvard Summer School, which was designed to promote understanding between the United States and the Old World countries. The delegates were youngish men and women, generally under forty, who might be expected to be future leaders in their respective countries. Ireland had himself been such a delegate the year before. I had put in an application, and was accepted for the Summer School of 1955. The European delegates included representatives from Britain, Germany, Austria, France, Italy and Spain. Kissinger told me he would like to have had delegates from eastern Europe, but this had not proved possible. There were also representatives of Asian countries: India, Pakistan, Iran, Israel, Indonesia, the Philippines and Japan. The only delegate from Africa was an Egyptian. There were very few independent African countries at this time. Those of us who came from Europe crossed the Atlantic in the *Queen Mary*. Flying to America was still only for the very rich, and travelling by sea gave us, perhaps, a chance to get to know each other. We travelled tourist class, and everybody shared a cabin, generally with a representative of his own country. My own cabin mate was Jocelyn Baines who was then working on his biography of Conrad. The leader of the British delegation was the Labour MP, George Chetwynd. There were two sittings for lunch on the *Queen Mary*, one at midday and one at 1 p.m. Chetwynd took it upon himself that we should all lunch at twelve. This annoyed me. The one o'clock sitting was clearly intended for British passengers, and the twelve o'clock sitting for the Americans – the usual times of lunch in these two countries, respectively. In those days I was in the habit of getting up rather late, and I enjoyed the lavish breakfast which the Cunard Line provided. I remarked at the lunch table that this high-handed action, as it seemed to me, of Chetwynd was all too typical of the British Labour Party: "Not content with ruining my country, they have to ruin my digestion." The other three lunchers at the table, all of them serious-minded Social Democrats from Scandinavian countries, did not appear to appreciate this remark.

Another delegate to the Summer School, in fact the only woman, was the Austrian poet, Ingeborg Bachmann. She seemed to present a rather fey personality. Our tourist cabins were below the waterline, and she wanted to know why they did not have glass portholes through which we could observe deep-sea life. When we disembarked at New York she had lost her passport and for a few hours had to be escorted everywhere by two American policemen. Eventually it was found, rumour said on the *Queen Elizabeth*, but I think this was a slip of the tongue. She was to suffer a tragic death in 1973 when her bed caught fire. It was rumoured that the fire was started deliberately by a jealous girlfriend.

When we landed in New York I was immediately struck by the baking heat of that city. We were taken by long-distance bus to Harvard, where we were received by those who had been entrusted to help with our accommodation and social relations. One of these assistants was a girl who immediately recognised me. She turned out to have been a former pupil of my mother. Kissinger remarked that this was just what was to be expected of the British – wherever they went they almost immediately met compatriots, and probably founded a cricket club. Kissinger had a kindly, but shrewd, perception of the British. On one occasion he remarked to me that if one ever complained about an English hotel one would be met with the reply: "This place has been running for three hundred years and nobody has ever complained to us before."

Harvard was more or less empty of students and teachers during the long vacation, and the delegates to the Summer School were put up for a month in rooms in Harvard Yard, as the university campus is called. We were divided into three categories – politics, economics and humanities. Every morning representatives of each of the three categories met in a group seminar chaired by an American. A delegate from each country was expected to give a paper, which was then thrown open to discussion. On one afternoon a week we were taken to inspect American institutions in or around Boston; for example, Deerborn, a private boys' school (but as it was totally empty of students during the vacation this seemed to me rather pointless), the offices of the *Christian Science Monitor* and a women's reformatory. We attended a session of the State House of Representatives and were presented to the Governor. We were also given the opportunity of watching a baseball match. Since attendance at these events was voluntary, I did not go to all of them, and I did not watch the baseball match. At other afternoon sessions we were addressed by distinguished American speakers; for instance, Judge Frankfurter of the

Supreme Court, the cartoonist Al Capp, and a representative of the Pentagon. Arrangements were made for us to be given hospitality by American families. On one day we visited New York. In the evenings a group of delegates from each of the countries represented was given an opportunity to address an American audience.

Relations between the various delegates soon became very friendly. One day I came across a party of Asians sitting on the grass. Among them was an Iranian writer who was a friend of Peter Avery, and one of the group invited me to join them. "If you can make room for me," I said. "There is always room for an English poet," he replied. I think this is one of the nicest compliments that has ever been paid me.

The Harvard Summer School seemed to me to be an enlightened and liberal project, designed just as much to educate the Americans as the delegates from the Old World. Henry Kissinger impressed me as genial, intelligent and a genuine liberal. I find that many young people today, and also those who grew up during the period of the Vietnam war, find this judgement of Kissinger difficult to believe. There seems to be an impression that Kissinger has horns and a tail. If he has, then this must have come about when he commenced, shortly afterwards, his political career as adviser to the American government on defence matters, and must be an instance of Lord Acton's principle that "all power corrupts".

Altogether, I think I benefited a great deal from my stay at Harvard. I also explored downtown Boston, and made some other American friends. One of these was Jack Sweeney, who was in charge of the Harvard Poetry Library. This is a wonderful collection, not only of books, but also of records and tapes to which one can listen through headphones. Another friend I made was the American poet Donald Hall. There was at Harvard a "Poets' Theatre" which specialised in plays in verse or written by poets, and also gave poetry readings. I was invited to read at one of the latter and had the opportunity of meeting Robert Lowell. He was kind enough to tell me that he admired my Leopardi translation. Indeed, I think he made some use of it in his *Imitations*.

The Summer School humanities group was chaired by the American poet Richard Wilbur, with whom I became very friendly. Wilbur, a polished and civilised poet, was later to translate Molière, as well as writing the libretto for Leonard Bernstein's *Candide*. Wilbur and his wife had spent some time in Italy, and with them was their young son, Nathan, whom the Italians called Natanaccio di Roma (Bad Nathan of Rome). Wilbur told me that when staying in the Abruzzi they had made friends with the local village poet. The latter invited another poet from the next village to come and join them one evening, and the two Abruzzi poets engaged in an impromptu flyting; that is to say, improvising verses to a guitar accompaniment. While Wilbur and his wife were listening to this, the latter, rather inadvisedly as it turned out, told their Italian friends that her husband was a poet too. They immediately passed the guitar to him and invited him to improvise. This, of course, he was quite unable to do. I think of all the poets I know he would have been about the most unlikely to be able to do so. I believe I would have had a shot.

The Israeli delegate, Israel Zief, a journalist, was a lively and humorous character, and seemed to get on perfectly well with the Egyptian delegate, Osman Amin, a middle-aged philosopher from Cairo University who had a specialised knowledge of the philosophy of Descartes. One of Amin's achievements was to have Descartes's works placed on the syllabus of the University of Al Azhar. This is the orthodox Muslim university in Cairo, and indeed it claims to be the oldest university in the world still in existence. This university with its rector has a considerable authority in determining the interpretation of points of doctrine for the Sunni Muslim world. The studies at Al Azhar are mainly, of course, in Arabic scholastic philosophy and Koranic exegesis. However, when Amin informed the doctors of Al Azhar that Descartes's works contained a proof of the existence of God, they agreed to place the French philosopher on their syllabus. Amin explained to me that Descartes's first proposition, "I think, therefore I am", can scarcely be translated into Arabic because there is no verb "to be" in that language. The "I think" almost automatically implies the "I am". I mentioned to Zief that I was about to take up an appointment at Alexandria. "We will probably come and bomb you," said Zief, and it was agreed that I should put the meal ticket which allowed delegates to eat in the refectory of Harvard on the roof of my flat to protect me. On our return journey, I shared a cabin with Zief, Amin and a Pakistani delegate, whom Amin distrusted because of the Pakistani's commitment to a more fundamentalist view of Islam than Amin himself held. It was assumed that all racial and national prejudices and barriers would by now have been destroyed, and this was, I hope, largely true. We were all broke. Zief said: "I will look at the passenger list. There are a lot of wealthy-looking Jews on this boat and some of them are bound to be relations of mine." In further hope of improving our financial situation we regularly went in for the competition set by the P&O's newspaper, *Ocean Times*, which was provided for us every day. We hoped to win the prize of a bottle of whisky, but though by pooling our different expertise, we produced very creditable entries, we did not win the prize.

When I returned to England it was time to make preparations to go to Egypt. I had decided to take a friend with me, whom I would pay out of my salary, as secretary and general factotum. Jim, for that was his name, had been the manager of a mine in what was then the Gold Coast. Being used to life in a non-European country, he could help me in running my flat, engaging servants and so on. We travelled on a Greek boat from Liverpool. I had never visited Liverpool before and while walking from the station to the docks was suddenly accosted by somebody I knew. This was a character called "Mac the Busker", who had trained as a Shakespearean actor, but had been reduced to busking in Hyde Park and to the theatre queues. He had once been arrested in Hyde Park for indecency because he recited one of Donne's more erotic poems. His great claim to fame was that he had played Cardinal Wolsey in a production of *Henry VIII* in Ulster on 12 July and had survived all the abuse and hissing he had received from the audience as a symbol of popery. It seemed a rather fitting last glimpse of the England I had known.

As the boat steamed into the harbour of Alexandria, an Egyptian petty officer in the crew began to wax lyrical, in English, about the beauty of his beloved city which he was returning to. I suppose he was doing this partly for the benefit of the English passengers, but Alexandria really is a beautiful city. It spreads along a wide bay from west to east. At the west is the site of the Pharos, the great lighthouse of ancient Alexandria, which had been one of the Seven Wonders of the World. It was badly damaged when the British bombarded Alexandria in 1882, and only its base remains. The island of Pharos is joined to the mainland by a causeway. A broad seafront, or corniche, runs from here to the eastern end – the traditional landing place of St Mark – after which you pass from the city into the fringes of the western desert. During the summer months seabathing goes on from beach huts along the whole seafront, but if the weather is stormy, and swimming might be dangerous, black flags are hoisted by the local authorities. On one occasion, when the weather was particularly bad and there were black flags flying all along the corniche, a local newspaper columnist compared the scene to a sad poem with a melancholy recurring rhyme.

There is not much of the ancient city left. When the Arabs conquered Alexandria in AD 640 they did not seem to realise what a prize had fallen into their hands. It had been the capital of the Ptolemys, and Ptolemaic Alexandria had included the celebrated university and research institute. The city had been a centre of Hellenistic art and culture, and had an important Jewish community. Later, under the Roman and Byzantine empires it had also become a seat of Christian learning. Both the Arabs and the Christians have been accused of burning the famous library at Alexandria. There is no real evidence that either of them was responsible. Having taught in an Egyptian university, albeit one of less eminence, I can guess what happened to the library – neglected and pilfered, it finally disappeared as learning and prosperity declined. Much of this library was destroyed when Julius Caesar attacked Alexandria in the course of his struggle with Pompey, but Cleopatra endeavoured to reassemble it and to house it in the Temple of Seraphis. The ruins of this temple, and the niches in which the papyrus scrolls were placed, can still be seen.

The Arab conquerors of Alexandria, not being at that time a sea-going people, neglected the city. The port of Rosetta, on another branch of the Nile, suited their purposes for Mediterranean trade. In the nineteenth century Muhammad Ali, the Albanian ruler of Egypt, made the country virtually independent of the Ottoman Empire. He created modern Alexandria as his window on the West, encouraging Italians, Greeks and others to settle there because of their commercial skills. There had always been a continuing Greek community, but the present buildings of the Greek Patriarchate only date from the seventeenth century. To see really ancient Coptic churches you must go to Cairo. When, with the modernisation of Egypt in the nineteenth century, the Coptic community was emancipated, they pulled down most of their old churches in Alexandria, including the cathedral, and built rather ugly nineteenth-century ones. There are a few fine mediaeval mosques, but the greater part of Alexandria is modern – built by Italian architects – and consists largely of tower blocks of flats, aesthetically a great deal more pleasing than those which were erected in England in the 1960s, but less firmly built.

We landed in Alexandria and took rooms in a small hotel kept by an Armenian known as Mr Philip. He had been born in Iran and his hotel had obviously had its former glory when it was frequented by English tourists. The lounge of the hotel was decorated with photographs, both of the Shah of Persia and of our own Queen, and had various out-of-date notices, such as directions for a lady who might require the attentions of a maid during the night. The hotel was now inexpensive, and in its own way comfortable enough. We slept there for a few days until we found a flat, and always stayed in it when we arrived, and for the few days before we departed for the summer vacation, when prolonged bureaucratic negotiations for a visa were necessary. It was not difficult, however, to find a flat. Alexandria is a summer capital, and rich Egyptians from Cairo and elsewhere have flats, mostly near the seafront, which they only use during the summer months and which can be got for a very cheap rent during the rest of the year.

As soon as the boat docked, two of my colleagues, Mustapha Badawi and Mahmoud Manzalaoui, had come on board to meet me, and the next day I reported to the Faculty of Arts building which was on the corniche. Badawi and Manzalaoui were to become very good friends and loyal colleagues. They had both taken degrees at English universities. Badawi, who now teaches Arabic in the Oxford Oriental School, had been at Leicester University, and Manzalaoui, who now lives in Canada, was at Oxford, where he had been a pupil of C. S. Lewis. They came from rather different backgrounds. Badawi's roots perhaps ran deeper into the indigenous Egyptian tradition, while Manzalaoui came of an aristocratic family of Turkish origin.

Both Badawi and Manzalaoui were enthusiasts for English ideas and culture. Badawi, though his interests were wide, was mainly a Shakespearean scholar. He has recently stated in a broadcast that his generation was in love with England. Manzalaoui's speciality was in the late Middle Ages and the Renaissance. The principal interest of the head of the English Department, an Anglo-Egyptian lady named Dr Nur Sherif, was in the nineteenth-century novel. This led to my largely concentrating on the Augustan period in my teaching. This period has always delighted me and is one in which I feel at home, despite the term "neo-Romantic" which was attached to many of my generation. Among the other members of the English Department was an Irish lecturer, and an Englishwoman, Miss Elma Smith. Later on we were joined by two more Egyptian lecturers, a woman and a man. The man was, in fact, a Nubian, and he taught me how to climb a sandhill. The secret is not to try to run up it, but to run round it in a spiral until you reach the top.

The staff welcomed me because, for some bureaucratic reason, their having a professor, although he was not the head of the department, gave them the right to a certain autonomy. Before my arrival, the English Department was under the jurisdiction of the Department of European Studies, the head of which was the head of the French Department, Madame Fahmy. She had had a French education and tended to impose French traditions on the English Department. One of Madame Fahmy's ideas was that at the final examination the students should be given just one long essay to write for each paper, with no choice. With me on the staff this system could be changed and the British system of giving as wide a choice as possible, so that a student would be able to use that part of his studies in which he felt most secure, was instituted.

The Faculty of Arts, in which the English Department was situated, was a vaguely neo-Gothic building. The English Department, on the second floor, could be reached by stairs or a lift. I preferred to use the stairs. The lift could not always be relied upon to work, and, not infrequently, when one pressed the button for the second floor, the lift would proceed to the floor above, and one then had to walk down a flight of stairs. The students did not like my spurning their lift; it seemed almost a slight to the technological advance of their country. I replied gnomically: "God has given me legs." This kind of wisdom always seems to go down well with people of Arabic culture. I remember, when lecturing on *The Tempest*, a student's asking me, rather acutely, why, if Ariel had wings, or at any rate could fly, did he want to use a bat's back. I replied: "Well, you can walk, but I suppose you occasionally like to take a tram."

The students were lively and responsive, and, considering that the whole of their course was conducted in a language which was not their first, quite able. The English course which we gave them was really very ambitious. It was supposed to start with the period of Shakespeare and go down to the twentieth century, but there was also a general introductory course on the history of English literature from Anglo-Saxon times onwards, and a course on the classical background of English literature, which I was later to take over from the Irish lecturer. This general introductory course did not require any more than knowing the names of principal authors and tendencies. The examination on this paper produced the following interesting answer: "Beowulf was an Anglo-Saxon worrier. He wrote a book called 'The Wonderer' and killed a dragon called Hrothgar." It will be remembered that the King of the Danes in *Beowulf* is called Hrothgar. I remember, once, discussing with my colleagues what twentieth-century works it might be suitable to place on the syllabus. I suggested George Orwell's *Animal Farm* as a possibility. "We'd like to," I was told, "but we daren't." It seems that, when discussing the Russian Revolution, Orwell unerringly pinpointed a pattern which recurs in other revolutions. The relationship between the two pigs, Snowball and Napoleon, was meant to reflect that of Lenin and Stalin (the first a respected figure, the latter an ambitious opportunist), but in Egypt it would be taken to refer to the recent revolution which was first spearheaded by Neguib, a respected older military figure, and then taken over by the more ruthless and ambitious Colonel Gamal Abdel Nasser. The same pattern has repeated itself today in the relationship between Mikhail Gorbachev and Boris Yeltsin. I recall that when *Animal Farm* first appeared hardly any reviewers dared say that it was a satire on the Soviet Union – it was simply described as a satire on totalitarianism. Indeed, when Orwell had completed it, no publisher would touch it, for we still thought of the Soviet Union as our ally, and I am credibly informed that Orwell was about to have it published by a small anarchist press when the political climate suddenly changed.

Much of my teaching consisted of reading passages in prose or poetry and commenting upon them. The number of textbooks at our disposal was limited, though there were good bookshops in Alexandria, especially for Penguin and other paperbacks. Most of the students came from the Egyptian lower middle class. Fees at the university were not high, for they were subsidised by the state. There was widespread unemployment in the country as a whole, and by sending their sons and daughters to the university the parents hoped that their children might at least be kept out of mischief for a few years, and might, perhaps, end up with a degree which would qualify them for a post in the lower ranks of the bureaucracy. This bureaucracy, of enormous complexity, which I suppose had a tradition running back through Ottomans, Byzantines, Romans and Greeks, to the bureaucracy of the Pharaohs, was largely staffed by members of the Christian Coptic community. Under the British occupation there had been a tendency by the colonial power to favour them. Nearly half my students were Copts. There were also some Greeks, as well as a large number of Muslims. The young men and the girls sat together in the same classrooms, though this was a source of some unease. Relations with women were a problem for my male students. The boys were afraid of getting too friendly with the girls as this could lead to a compromising situation in which they would more or less be forced to marry them. This applied to any kind of relationship with a respectable girl. There was prostitution, of course, but it was expensive and rigidly controlled under a licence system such as used to pertain in France. I remember a young Egyptian saying to me, starry-eyed: "Is it true that in your country you have women serving in bars, called barmaids?" The West has fantasies about the exotic and erotic East, but these probably pale into insignificance compared with the fantasies which the East, largely prompted by the cinema, has about the West.

Dr Nur Sherif had a special fondness for the novels of Mrs Gaskell. Her teaching of the Victorians tended to stress their social message, and the students responded to this, for they were deeply socially conscious and some of them were Marxists. This approach, however, sometimes seemed to swamp their appreciation of an author. Badawi remarked to me that the students seemed to think of Charles Dickens simply as a social critic, and never as a great comic writer. Thomas Hardy, I found, was particularly congenial to the Egyptian student. The novelist describes a society which is in transition between its traditional rural structure and the impingement of new post-industrial values. This was precisely the situation in Egypt. The fatalism in Hardy also had a strong appeal. It had made it possible for a film version of *Tess* to be made in which the story was transferred to Egypt. I found this Muslim fatalism irritating. A student once said to me: "After all, sir, it is really a matter of the will of God whether we pass our exams or don't." I said: "Yes, it is a matter of the will of God, but it has also got something to do with how hard you work." A similar story was told me of an English resident in Cairo who wished to get rid of the cockroaches in his flat. Flats everywhere in Egypt are indeed infested with cockroaches, and, even more unpleasantly, with bed bugs. The bed bug, incidentally, only reached Western Europe after the Crusades. The name bug is probably of Arabic origin. This Englishman told his servant that he was determined to get rid of the cockroaches. "Impossible," said the servant. However, the Englishman went ahead with insecticides and arsenical smoke bombs and so forth. I myself once used an arsenical smoke bomb. It is a rather terrifying experience. You shut all the doors and windows, set the thing alight, then leave the house for a couple of hours. When you return you hope that the vermin have succumbed. In this case the remedies were effective, and when the Englishman and the servant returned to the flat they found it strewn with dead cockroaches. "There," said the Englishman, "it is possible to eliminate the cockroach in Cairo." "It was the will of God", replied his servant, "that the cockroaches should die."

Manzalaoui, with his interest in Renaissance literature, would have liked to teach Edmund Spenser's *The Faerie Queene* to his students, but it is unfortunate that the three Saracen brothers, Sans Loy, Sans Foy and Sans Joy, recur repeatedly in this poem as symbolic of error. Naturally, one had to be wary of offending Muslim sensibilities. I was told to use for my own lectures *The London Book of English Verse*, which had been compiled by Herbert Read and Bonamy Dobrée. When dealing with the seventeenth century, I thought that it might be amusing and instructive to teach a passage from Samuel Butler's *Hudibras*, which was included in the anthology. But glancing at the passage again I saw that it contained the following couplet, in which Butler satirises the Puritans of his day:

> The prophets of this new religion
> Like Mahomets were ass and pigeon.

This referred to the libel, current among Christians in the Middle Ages and later, that Muhammad pretended to be inspired by the Holy Ghost by training a pigeon to eat corn out of his ear. Naturally, I changed my mind about expounding this passage to the class. When lecturing upon T. S. Eliot's *Gerontion*, I tried to expound the passage about "the word within a word unable to speak a word". Eliot was echoing the phrase "verbum infans" of the seventeenth-century Lancelot Andrewes – the paradox that the Word of God should become an infant. The Latin word *infans* literally means "unspeaking". I had forgotten that according to Muslim tradition the Prophet Jesus spoke as soon as he was born.

There were in general, however, quite good relations between my Muslim students and their Coptic contemporaries. The Nasser regime was a relatively liberal and tolerant one, in spite of the way it was thought of in the West. Nasser always sent representatives of his government to the indigenous Christian churches on the occasion of the great festivals. The Muslim fundamentalists, the so-called Muslim Brotherhood, were severely repressed by Nasser, even more so than the communists. In any case, Alexandria seems to me to be a more tolerant place than Cairo.

Although the Egyptian temperament is perhaps naturally romantic, there were certain aspects of the Augustans to which my students responded; for example, to the gnomic verses of Samuel Johnson in *The Vanity of Human Wishes*. *Rasselas*, partly because it is largely set in Egypt, was also a book they found congenial. It had been one of the first books to be translated into Arabic in a recent government project, but its pessimistic, quasi-fatalistic philosophy, as well as its strong gnomic moral character, also recommended it.

The Egyptians are, and always have been since the earliest times, a lively, pleasure-loving people. On many of them the sterner precepts of Islam seem to sit fairly lightly. Because our knowledge of the ancient Egyptians is mainly derived from their funerary monuments, we tend to think of them as gloomy and death-obsessed. This is surely wrong. The whole nature of the ancient Egyptians' funerary customs arose from an intense love of physical life and the hope that it might somehow be perpetuated after death. They provided the dead man in his tomb with everything he might need in the next world, including light reading. Their tomb paintings depict scenes of ordinary life – picnics, hunting for wild fowl in the marshes (with trained cats as well as trained dogs), and parties with harp players and dancing buffoons.

The Egyptians also have a strong dramatic sense, and I had considerable pleasure, with the aid of my colleagues, in directing English plays for my students. One of these was a production, admittedly shortened to some extent, of Thomas Heywood's *A Woman Killed with Kindness*. This Elizabethan tragedy is an exercise in bourgeois realism set in the author's time and country. Mr Frankford, an English gentleman, discovers his wife, Nan, in the act of adultery. Instead of killing her, as the conventional code of honour demanded, he exiles her to a second country mansion which he owns, treating her honourably, so that she has adequate provision and servants to attend on her. He finally comes to see her on her deathbed when she is dying of a broken heart. He forgives her and they are reconciled. This play meant a lot

213

to my Egyptian students, for their own traditional code of morality was in many ways comparable. I was told, in fact, that an incident very similar to that which Heywood describes had happened in Egypt within living memory. The girl who played Nan Frankford would not allow her name to be printed on the programme. She said that if her uncles were to find out that she was acting the part of a fallen woman they would kill her.

As I have already said, a large number of my students belonged to the Christian Coptic community. The Copts belong to the indigenous Christian Church of Egypt which claims to have been founded by St Mark. The Coptic Church divided from the rest of Christendom at the time of the Council of Chalcedon (AD 451), over the so-called Monophysite heresy. According to official figures the Copts form about 10 per cent of the population of Egypt – though under pressure from resurgent Muslim fundamentalism many of them are now emigrating. There are said to be areas in Upper Egypt where Muslim guides refuse to take their European clients because the guides are afraid to enter Coptic areas. The Coptic language is a late form of ancient Egyptian written in a modified Greek script, but it is only used liturgically.

I found that many of the Copts whom I got to know had a great natural dignity, and were gentle and generally more responsible than the lively and volatile Arab Muslims. Shortly after I arrived in Alexandria, I was taken by a party of Copts to visit the monasteries of Wadi Natroum which lie in the desert in an oasis between Alexandria and Cairo. This is a little community comprising several ancient monasteries dating back to the days of the Desert Fathers. Wadi Natroum had to be reached by crossing the desert and for this purpose a jeep was hired. As the jeep drove over the sand, what I at first thought were reddish birds sprang up out of its way, but the creatures were, in fact, locusts in their non-plague stage. My Coptic hosts seemed to grow taller as they reached Wadi Natroum, for this was one of the centres of their community. In ordinary converse one sometimes found the Copts rather too subservient, and liable to suffer from minority psychology. They tended to believe that they were being discriminated against. This is quite understandable – there is a long record of persecution and discrimination against them.

A remarkable feature in the chapel of one of these monasteries was a large ostrich egg suspended from the ceiling. Our guide explained that this was placed there as a reminder to the worshippers not to let their thoughts run astray during the service. (The Coptic liturgy, by the way, is the longest in Christendom and lasts for four hours.) The ostrich, he said, abandons her eggs, and therefore they do not hatch. One should not let one's thoughts behave like her. But the cosmic egg is an ancient symbol of the universe, and I wonder if that has not something to do with the use of the ostrich egg.

One of my students was a Coptic deacon and asked me, one day, if I had ever attended a Coptic Church service. I replied that I had not, but would very much like to do so. The student said he would collect me next Sunday at eight o'clock and we would leave the service early. I said I thought it would be better, if we were not going to attend the whole service, to arrive later and stay to the end. As far as I remember, I attended the entire service. I got quite lost and committed a terrible blunder. Everybody suddenly turned round, and I thought we were turning east for the Creed. In fact, it was the Pax, and I was supposed to shake hands with my neighbour. The service, as I have said, is conducted in the Coptic language, though there was a sermon in Arabic. The most impressive moment comes when there is a great procession, accompanied by the sound of the sistrum. This is a kind of rattle, shaped like a circle with a handle. Across this circle wires are strung through beads which make a jingling sound when shaken. As we were leaving the service, we paused on the steps to buy a piece of blessed bread from an old man who had a concession from the Church to sell it. This is not consecrated bread, but the custom of eating a piece of bread after the service is a rudiment of the ancient Christian custom of the Agape, or love feast. As we were eating this bread another Coptic student appeared and was extremely jealous that his comrade had had the privilege of taking me to church, and, in order to go one better, invited me to dinner with his family the following Sunday. I was happy to accept this invitation.

My student's family was a substantial middle-class one. The men sat at one end of the table and the women at the other. I was generously served with a meal of cold meat and salad, but every time I got halfway through a plateful it was piled up again. There was a conflict between conventions here. My code of etiquette said it would be rude not to eat everything that was offered one, theirs that a guest's plate should never be empty. Finally, I realised that this was the case and pushed a full plate of food away, saying that I had had enough. The plate was accordingly taken away, but was immediately followed by others, containing, first, a large piece of cake and, then, an enormous slice of water melon. I was sitting next to the father of the family who was keeping my glass steadily filled with whisky. This helped me get everything down. I do not think that my hosts were at all offended, or thought that I was being greedy, but were rather complimented by the justice I paid to their food. I was unable to eat anything at all during the whole of the next day.

The Coptic calendar, which is a late ancient Egyptian one, consisting of twelve lunar months of twenty-eight days plus an intercalated five days, is dated, not from the birth of Christ, but from the cessation of the last great persecution of the Church in the time of Diocletian, in the third century. This persecution had been particularly severe in Egypt, and the period is remembered as an almost legendary age from which sprang the great myths of St Catherine and St George. The minority Coptic Catholic Church, which entered into communion with Rome after the Council of Trent, has its cathedral in Alexandria in St Catherine's Square. This is alleged to be the site of that saint's martyrdom. But the real centre of the cult of St Catherine is the monastery of Mount Sinai where, according to legend, her body was carried by angels after her death. She does not seem to have been known in Alexandria till the Crusaders came there. St Catherine of Alexandria is supposed to have converted several hundred pagan philosophers when she was imprisoned for her faith by the tyrant Maximin. She is, therefore, the patron saint of scholars and philosophers, and of colleges, both in Oxford and in Cambridge. Eventually, she was put to death by being tormented on a wheel.

One of the main troubles in teaching the undergraduate students was their tendency to present as their own work passages which they had either copied out or memorised from critical authors they had read. It seemed difficult to persuade them that this was an unacceptable practice. I think their approach to learning was, to some extent, influenced by traditional Arabic teaching, where learning large passages of the Koran by heart forms the main basis of religious instruction. Finally, I had to issue an ultimatum, telling them that when we, the examiners, found such a passage, we simply put a blue pencil straight through it, and gave no marks. After all, I told them, we have read the books you have copied from and will recognise the extracts. This frightened them and the practice abated. I was bluffing, of course, as one could not possibly read all the books, and there was always the danger of mistaking a really brilliant piece of writing for something copied, or vice versa.

As well as teaching the undergraduate students, I had to take classes of postgraduates who were working on various theses which they had not been able to complete without the supervision of a professor. My presence enabled some of them to carry on with work they had been engaged on for years, and with these more mature students I was able to discuss a number of literary topics. One of them was preparing a thesis on Byron, whose life and work he interpreted in terms of Freudian psychoanalysis. A few years before he had got himself involved with Marxism and had spent some time in an internment camp. In D. J. Enright's novel, *Academic Year*, which is a fictionalised account of his own period at Alexandria University some years before, there is a scene in which the members of the department go to visit such a camp in order to examine a student for his finals. The student portrayed in that scene was the original of the one I now had working on Byron. When he was released from the camp his family had tried to cure him of Marxism by sending him to a Freudian psychoanalyst. The student had not discarded his Marxism, but had simply superimposed another set of dogmas upon it.

Among the graduate students were Fuad Megally and his younger brother, Shafik. The former was writing a thesis (which he completed at Trinity College, Dublin) on some letters of George Moore, and the latter on Thomas Hardy. Shafik later went on to write a doctoral thesis on Landor. This was at my suggestion. These postgraduate students, until, and unless, they got a place in a British or American university, were hampered by the lack of books in the library at Alexandria, but I found that among the books in the Faculty of Arts Library, in the English section, which we sorted out, there were, in fact, the complete works of Landor in several volumes. These two Coptic brothers have remained close friends of mine. Fuad is now living in England and teaching Arabic, Shafik is living in Belgium where he has married a Belgian wife.

Some years ago the Coptic community in London had become sufficiently numerous to need its own church building. Previously, the Copts had used the chapel of the Ethiopian Embassy, but when Ethiopia became an atheist Marxist state this was no longer possible. The Copts acquired a building, behind Barker's in Kensington, that had originally been a Congregationalist church, but had become redundant through the union of the Congregationalists and the Presbyterians in England. The church was to be formally consecrated by the Patriarch, who visited England for this purpose. As there was now a second generation of Copts growing up in an English-speaking country, it was hoped to get a new translation of the liturgy into English, to be used at least part of the time. The Copts were using a version of their liturgy which had been prepared in Australia, but the translation was not altogether satisfactory. There is also a Victorian version by the Marquess of Bute. To make a completely new English translation would, of course, have been a very large undertaking, but it was hoped to provide at least a version of the vespers for the Patriarch's visit. A small panel was thus formed, presided over by Fuad Megally, who, himself, understood Coptic, but even so we did not manage to complete our labours in time. I was, however, invited to the consecration of the church and presented to the Patriarch. The consecration was an impressive service which included a number of lessons from the Old and New Testaments. Almost anything that could be relevant to the consecration of a church seemed to have been brought in. These lessons were read, not only by a Coptic priest, but by representatives of the Armenian, Syrian Orthodox, Greek Orthodox, Roman Catholic and Anglican churches, and by a minister of the Church of Scotland.

Examinations came at the end of the summer term, in June, just when the weather was starting to become unbearably hot. They took place in a large tent. The exam papers had to be prepared in great secrecy in a small room in the faculty building. They were cyclostyled, and the wax matrix was solemnly burnt in a brazier of coals by a servant who could neither speak nor read a word of English. In the tent the students seemed to be hoping for any aid that heaven might afford them. Although textbooks were not allowed in the tent, sacred books were. Consequently, the students' desks displayed copies of the Koran and the Gospels, as well as rosaries and crucifixes.

During the examination period we used to receive external students for a viva voce examination, the main purpose of which was to test their proficiency in spoken English. Many of these students came a long way; from Upper Egypt, for example. They were rather shy, and one had to encourage them to talk. I asked one young man to describe an average day in his village. He explained how in the morning the women went out to work in the fields, whereas the men sat in the café talking. "What do they talk about?" I asked. He replied that they talked about politics (this meant local politics) and the ginn. (The word usually transliterated "djinn" has a hard initial "g" in Egyptian Arabic. Incidentally, the word genie, commonly used in English, is due to a false etymology.) "The ginn?" I said. He went on to explain. Apparently the most popular form of evening entertainment in this Upper Egyptian village was to invite to one's house a local who claimed to be in touch with the ginn. After suitable preparations had been made, and money had passed, this man would go into a trance, and the voice of the ginn would speak through him. It was, I would surmise, a form of ventriloquism. "What does the ginn say?" I asked. "They talk local gossip and about local characters." "Do they ever reveal the whereabouts of hidden treasure?" I enquired. I knew this was often a reason for invoking spirits. "No," he said. "If you asked them any question of that sort they would reply, 'God has not revealed it to us.'"

My relations with both my university colleagues and my students were friendly. Far too many English lecturers appointed by the British Council in foreign universities, I suspect, have treated their posts as paid holidays abroad, identifying themselves with the English-speaking community wherever they happened to be. Having seen some of the English community of Egypt on the boat I travelled out in, I was determined to have as little as possible to do with them. I tried to interest myself in the problems of the country at large, and especially of my students, and to work closely with my Egyptian colleagues.

Any writer with a sense of the past cannot fail to have his imagination stimulated by Alexandria. There is, as I have said, very little left of the ancient city, but in its centre the narrow roads are still only wide enough to accommodate a Roman chariot. These roads were trodden by Theocritus, Callinachus and Apollonius of Rhodes. There is a great tradition of Arabic poetry, also, though I cannot recall that any of the classical Arabic poets were from Alexandria. It is difficult to translate Arabic poetry into English. The only translations from classical Arabic poetry which I am acquainted with, and which seem to stand up in their own right, are those made by Wilfred Scawen Blunt and his wife Lady Anne Blunt (Byron's granddaughter, and a better Arabist than her husband) of the so-called "Suspended Odes". These poems are believed to be pre-Muslim. The great poet of modern Alexandria was the Greek, Constantine P. Cavafy (1863–1933). Cavafy worked all his life as an official in the Post Office under the British administration, and published his poems in small limited editions. He had had an English education, and, as a boy, lived not very far from where I live now, in Bayswater. His use of the dramatic monologue, or short dramatic narrative, taken from ancient history, derives largely from the practice of Browning and Tennyson. Cavafy translates remarkably well into English, though I believe that the versions we have partly ignore the fact that he used rhyme in his poems. It was E. M. Forster who first made Cavafy's name known in the English-speaking world. Alexandria seems to have had a liberating effect on Forster. Before I left England for Egypt, Alec Craig, who had himself worked in that country, gave me as a parting present a copy of Forster's *Guide to Alexandria*. Although it was more than thirty years out of date, I still found it very useful, and some of the information included here is derived from it. I met Forster after my return to England. Peter Avery introduced me to him at King's College, Cambridge, where the great novelist spent his last years as an Honorary Fellow. He seemed old and tired, but when I mentioned Alexandria and Cavafy he suddenly came to life. Cavafy's house is in an inner suburb of Alexandria. The Greek community pressed, though I think without success, to have a plaque placed on it. Cavafy occupied a flat on the first floor. Underneath there was, in his time, a brothel. He is supposed to have said, "La bas le chair; ici, en haut, l'esprit." On the landing outside his flat was a stone garden seat which was chained to the floor – of course. It had apparently come from a villa, which his family had owned, somewhere in the Greek islands, and was of immense sentimental value.

I think it was in my second term that a writer and lecturer, who had taught in Alexandria before 1952, wrote to the university, saying he had heard that English lecturers were once more being engaged, and that he would like to be considered in this capacity. He would really like, he said, to have the professorship, but he had heard that I held that post. However, friends in Alexandria had informed him, he added, that I was likely to resign soon because of ill health. Although he had met me personally (this was, in fact, untrue), he did not like to write to me on so delicate a subject. This letter exhibited either unscrupulous cunning or extreme stupidity. The writer must have known that Alexandria is a hotbed of gossip, and that his statement that I was about to resign might well become a self-fulfilling prophecy. In any case, whether he had met me before or not, he surely should have had the courtesy to contact me first before writing to the university. The authorities of the Faculty of Arts were prepared to consider his application, but the trouble was, they said, he had published a novel in which he had satirised the university and some of his colleagues there. Nevertheless, they said, perhaps they should appoint him to show how liberal and tolerant they really were, but the novel was banned in Egypt. I said that I had not been aware that it was banned, and had, in fact, brought a copy with me which I would be glad to lend to the Dean of the Faculty of Arts. He accepted my offer and read the novel (it was not returned to me) and it put paid to the ambition of this particular writer to return to the university. It so happened that in the next summer vacation I was introduced to him by "Supervacuo", who was a friend of both of us, in a Soho club. I must admit that I told him exactly what I thought of him. He seems to have been taken aback, and in his own autobiography gives an account of this in which he accuses me of having actually used physical violence against him. This is not true. Many years later, when he had included a poem of mine in an anthology which he had edited, I thought it was time to write to him to clear the matter up and try to bury the hatchet. He accepted my overtures and we subsequently met on friendly terms, but, as the account of my alleged attack on him stands in his autobiography, I feel it necessary to give my own account of the affair here. He did not name me in his autobiography, nor do I name him here.

As for his comments about the state of my health, I had, in fact, only suffered a few days' illness in Egypt at that time. This was due to a poisoned foot. I went to an Egyptian doctor who cured me in an efficient and modern way by prescribing penicillin, though some of his methods appeared to be less modern and orthodox. He told me how every day he got from the slaughterhouse a supply of fresh blood, to which he attributed some therapeutic virtue. He was a pious

Muslim and perhaps something of a saint. His waiting-room was full of poor people whom he treated for nothing.

There were, in the 1940s and 1950s, and later, a spate of English novels written about Egypt. Most of the writers had been lecturers at the universities of Cairo or Alexandria. The most notable of these novels is, of course, Lawrence Durrell's *Alexandria Quartet*. Although this was a great success with the reading public, and in many ways deservedly so, I still regard Durrell's poetry, which he abandoned for prose, as his best work. *The Alexandria Quartet* is a poet's dream of Alexandria rather than the reality. One would not suppose from these novels, for example, that the city is mainly inhabited by Arab Muslims. They occur in the books only occasionally, as servants and the like. Most of the characters in these novels are what are generally called Levantines. This term covers Greeks, Syrian Christians, Armenians and some others. Durrell makes his Levantine Alexandrians far more complex and cultivated than they generally are, and although the Copts play an important role in his narrative he seems to have had no understanding of their religion. There is, for example, a description of a Coptic funeral in which passages from the Koran are read. This is obviously absurd. One of the themes which emerges in this long narration is a supposed conspiracy in which the Copts and other Egyptian Christians are represented as joining forces with the Israelis. There is no truth in this theory and if the authorities were to believe Durrell it would go hard with the Copts.

Other writers have given a more satirical picture of Alexandria, especially from the point of view of the university teacher. I have already mentioned Enright's *Academic Year*. The Caesarea of Robert Liddell's *Unreal City* combines features of Alexandria with those of Salonika, giving it the ethnic mixture of the former and the rather unpleasant climate of the latter. This book gives the portrait of an elderly Greek intellectual who is clearly based on Cavafy. Cavafy died in 1933, and Liddell could not have known him. It seems to me that P. H. Newby, especially in his *Picnic at Sakkara*, understands the Egyptian character far better than any of these other writers. This novel is a relatively slight work concerned only with university life at Cairo. No English writer has penetrated the real world of Egypt, the world of the fellahin in the fields, or the poor inhabitants of the overcrowded bustling great cities of Alexandria, Cairo or Asyût.

I got to know a little of the real Alexandria, at least its cafés and its bars, the latter mostly run by Greeks. It was pleasant to sit at a café table and watch life go by, or to spend the evening in a bar, where if you were a regular customer you were brought little snacks with each drink you took. These snacks, in themselves, formed a complete meal, beginning with shellfish or squid, followed by meat balls and beans, with something sweet at the end. In the streets one was continually pestered by beggars and touts of all kinds. In Egypt there is a great deal of desperate poverty and widespread unemployment. People try to get a living as best they can. This may be by selling something or by stealing. Anything that can be stolen is stolen. I got into a habit, which I still retain, that if I am in a public place, say on a railway station platform, and wish to put down my suitcase for a moment, I place it firmly between my legs. I heard of an Egyptian middle-class family who, having been out for the day, went back to their flat, several storeys up in a tower block, and, as they came in, saw their washing, which had been hanging out on the balcony to dry, disappearing over the edge. Somebody had climbed up the sheer vertical concrete wall of the block, with bare feet, in order to steal the laundry. One simply could not give to every beggar that one met. Jim and I formed an arbitrary plan of adopting certain beggars and giving to them, whenever we saw them, and ignoring the others. A great many of these beggars were children. These looked well cared for. I think they were probably exploited by somebody, a sort of Egyptian Fagin, who took their takings, but did feed and clothe them. There was one little boy, I presume afflicted with polio, who crawled about on all fours with great agility in his quest for alms.

Among the more interesting street traders was an old man who trundled around a small tea-trolley. On this trolley there lived a cat, a rabbit and a rat. At one point these were joined by a small pig, but the trader gave up exhibiting this creature as it was probably not popular with his Muslim customers. The proprietor of the trolley was some kind of Christian, and a fortune-teller. If you gave the man a few piastres, his rabbit would nudge the cat, which would pick up the rat and deposit it in a box, from which it would select a slip of paper on which your fortune was printed in French. The message was always reassuring, the usual formula being something like: "Your luck is about to take a turn for the better and with the aid of the Blessed Virgin all your desires will be accomplished."

Jim and I had not been in Alexandria more than a week or so when a young man attached himself to us. His name was Abdul, but he was generally known as Qassab, a word which can be translated as Butcher or Cut Throat. He was an extraordinary character who became quite a friend, and was useful for fixing all sorts of things for us, in a city where a certain amount of corruption and sailing close to the law was necessary. He came from Lake Mariout, the ancient Mareotis, where his family were fisherfolk. Like many other Egyptian boys, he had run away from the restrictions of traditional village life and gone on to the streets of Alexandria. He had taught himself to read from the headlines of newspapers and the Arabic subtitles of

American and French films. He was now working as some kind of clerk or general factotum to a Sudanese lawyer, and also for the police. It was apparent to me from the first that in his getting to know us he was partly acting as a police spy, and this turned out, indeed, to be the case. His sobriquet, Qassab, suggests to me that he may possibly have been involved in a violent crime, and had been let off the full penalty of his deeds by the police on condition of his working for them. Abdul had developed an extraordinary kind of English, in the same way that he had taught himself to read; again, largely, from the cinema. If he wanted to convey that something we were doing should not be made too obvious he would say, "No cinemascope this." The verb "to go", in his language, was always, "let's go", and "today" was always "tonight", since most of his activities took place at night. "You're looking very cheerful today" came out as "You very Charlie Chaplin tonight".

I regularly attended Sunday-morning services at the Anglican church in Alexandria, where a very old chaplain preached to a rather middle-aged, expatriate congregation. I particularly remember a sermon which he preached on the text "And Abraham planted terebinth trees in Mamre". The sermon seemed to drone on in the heat of a hot Sunday morning. "What does this text teach us? It tells us how Abraham, that great man, the Friend of God – as our Muslim neighbours call him – had planted terebinth trees in Mamre, and", he went on, "we all should plant terebinth trees. We should leave something behind us like that great man, Abraham, the Friend of God, whereby our posterity should remember us, for example, by planting terebinth trees . . ."

I had several opportunities of visiting the Egyptian countryside, and I was invited in my first year to give a lecture in Cairo, where, of course, I visited the museum which contains the treasure of Tutankhamun. Naturally, I also visited the pyramids and the Sphinx. Of the pyramids I can only say, with one of the characters in my play, *Helen in Egypt*, that "they are principally remarkable for their size, antiquity, and strictly pyramidical form". Joan Evans, in her excellent but neglected book, *Taste and Temperament* (in which she tries to correlate different styles in art with different psychological temperaments), calls the pyramids "paranoiac art". They are simply there to emphasise the power of the monarch who erected them – Khufu, whom the Greeks called Cheops. Much the same goes for the Sphinx, which symbolises the royal power of Egypt, having a lion's body and a man's head. The Greek Sphinx which Oedipus encountered was a monster with a woman's face and a lion's body. Her name means "The Strangler", and her challenging Oedipus with riddles before he assumed his sovereignty is, perhaps, the earliest version of a widespread folk-tale, the story of the Riddling Bride. The ability to solve riddles was in prehistoric times a quasi-magical gift, the mark of a king. Perhaps the Sphinx and Jocasta were originally one and the same, for Jocasta is a strangler – she strangled herself. When the Greeks came to Egypt they naturally identified this human-headed lion form with their own Sphinx, just as they called the ostrich a great big sparrow (the Greek for ostrich is *struthion*, and *struthos* is a sparrow). Similarly, the name the Romans gave to the locust originally meant lobster. This is typical soldiers' humour. On another visit to the Egyptian countryside I saw the Buff-Backed Heron, or Cattle Egret – a beautiful bird which seems like a living winged lily. I am told it is in decline owing to the indiscriminate use of pesticides in the cotton fields. The sacred ibis of the ancient Egyptians, the symbol of Thoth – the god of wisdom and learning – has now disappeared from Egypt, as have the ostrich, the crocodile and the hippopotamus.

My most enjoyable stay in the Egyptian countryside was at the villa of Dr Magdi Wahba, a wealthy Copt who lectured in English literature at Cairo University. He was at that time the squire of a village on the Delta. I spent a weekend there with some of my colleagues from Alexandria. It was almost like returning to the Edwardian age. We were served by numerous servants, played charades, and took part in an impromptu croquet match between representatives of Cairo and Alexandria universities. I finished last, partnering ex-Queen Dina of Jordan, who was now also a lecturer at Cairo University.

On Sunday a whole sheep was roasted for us on a spit over a charcoal fire in a pit in the garden. While we were having our lunch, I heard an extraordinary turkey-like gobbling sound in a neighbouring field. I asked my Egyptian friends what this bird was. They told me that in Arabic its name meant field-chicken. I was quite at a loss to identify it, but by chance, some years later, I heard, unmistakably, the same sound on a recording in a BBC natural history programme. It was the Little Bustard. I have spoken earlier of my passion for birds, but in all my observations in England I have never encountered any bird that was rare, or even scarce. When abroad, however, it is fun to meet with birds which are common there but not found in England. One experience of this kind happened a couple of years ago when I was on holiday near Arezzo in Tuscany, with friends. Before leaving England, I had listened to a series of programmes on the radio about Japanese poetry. Each programme had been planned round an image which was of significance to the Japanese; for example, rain or moonlight. One of these images was a little bird with a short song. It appears that this bird is as important for the Japanese in their poetry as the nightingale is for us. The Japanese believe that it is repeating a Buddhist sutra. It was a species of bush-warbler of the genus *Cettia*. While sitting in the garden of the Italian villa in which we had an apartment, I heard a little bird singing in the trees, and it struck me that it was not unlike that of the Japanese bird. I mentioned it to one of my friends. Looking in the direction I pointed at, he saw the bird in the upper branches of a tree. "It is smaller than a sparrow", he said, "and has a fan-shaped tail." That was what I wanted to know. The bird was indeed Cetti's Warbler, the European representative of the genus *Cettia*, a rare visitor to England – but recently a small breeding colony has established itself in the neighbourhood of Nottingham.

Magdi Wahba took us for a walk round the village of which he was the landlord. We were greeted politely by all his tenants as we passed them. The village seemed fairly squalid, and a hoopoe was feeding in the mud on the road. Magdi was building a church for his Coptic tenants. Manzalaoui asked about the iconostasis. "There won't be an iconostasis," said Magdi. "They would only hang bad modern Greek icons on it."

One evening in Magdi's villa we played a card-guessing game to determine whether any of us possessed extrasensory perception, but none of us scored more than the number of correct guesses that the law of chance would have predicted.

Magdi was an active member of his church, and concerned with oecumenical affairs. He had met the Russian theologian, Nikolay Zernob, whom I had myself once encountered in Oxford and was, later on, to get to know at St Basil's House in Bayswater, the headquarters of the Society of St Alban and St Sergius. "The trouble is", said Magdi, "that Zernob comes along, saying that Monophysitism doesn't mean a thing and we should all get together, but next thing, we shall all be shaking hands with Anglicans."

On a later occasion one of my students invited me to stay with his family at Kafr el Dauwâr, where his father worked in some managerial or executive capacity at a cotton mill. The occasion was the great festival which follows the end of Ramadan. One would see a sheep, being fattened up for the end of the fast, tethered in the courtyard of almost every home, even in the town. The species favoured seemed to be the fat-tailed sheep of central Asia. I readily agreed to the invitation and travelled by train, with my student and one of his friends, to Kafr el Dauwâr. The fast of Ramadan, of course, lasts for a whole month, during which Muslims are not permitted to eat, or even drink a drop of water, during the hours of daylight.

I arrived at Kafr el Dauwâr on the evening before the day that precedes the end of Ramadan, and was quite prepared to share my hosts' fast. When I arrived, my student presented me to his mother.

225

This was, I think, a concession to Western custom, for I never saw her again or any other female members of the family. The men ate together separately. I awoke next morning, expecting to begin a fast for the next twelve hours, but I heard an extraordinary noise going on from the bedroom which my student and his friend shared. Making my way there, I found that, the other members of the family having gone out to work, the students had quite wickedly raided the larder, and had prepared a large Egyptian-style breakfast of cold meat, bread, cheese and other things for themselves and for me. The noise I had heard was their reciting, even more wickedly, passages from their geography textbook to Koranic chants.

After the end of Ramadan all the male members of the family sat down to consume the sheep, accompanied by bread and, as far as I can remember, nothing else. I was presented with part of the jawbone (with its teeth still *in situ*) which has little gelatinous pockets, considered delicacies. My hosts explained that they were presenting it to me as an honoured guest. "If we were real Arabs living in the desert we would give you the eyeballs, but we know you don't really like those." The next day my student wished to take me on a bus journey to visit some other relatives of his who had a house by the seaside. I was a little alarmed at the prospect of even more extravagant Arab hospitality, and explained that, after eating as much of the sheep as had been pressed upon me, I did not feel very hungry. He quite understood and explained to his relatives, who presented me with little cakes. In case we should feel hungry on the journey, however, his mother had wrapped up large parts of the remains of the sheep in newspaper to take with us. This Arab hospitality is genuine and quite overwhelming. For the Westerner it often seems impossible to make any adequate return for it.

13

The Suez Crisis

One could not live in Egypt without being aware of the continual international tension brought about by the Arab–Israeli conflict. The Jewish population, who since the earliest days of the city had played an important part in its life, had now dwindled. There were a few Jewish students in Alexandria University, though they kept a low profile. One of them was a girl who was in my postgraduate class. Her first language was Latino (the mediaeval Spanish dialect with a Hebrew admixture), which the Sephardic Jews of North Africa and the Middle East, the descendants of the Spanish Jews expelled by Ferdinand and Isabella, still speak. One charming old man, whom Abdul introduced to us, was Pepe. He was an Italian Jew, and by profession a photographer. He lived alone with his cat, "Pussi". Pussi was fond of olives, and her favourite parlour trick was to take one out of Pepe's ear. Pepe would say, "Pussi, je veux que tu me dises un secret." Whereupon the cat would leap on to Pepe's lap and then on to his shoulder, appearing to whisper in his ear as she found the olive. There was also a Jewish lady who was a lecturer in German at the university. The authorities were quite aware of her origin. Born in Croatia before the end of the First World War, she would put down her nationality on official documents as either Austrian or Yugoslav, according to which way the political wind was blowing. The authorities obviously trusted her, for she was allowed to lecture in the German language to naval personnel in the dockyards. It was she who gave me, before I finally left, a little ancient statue of the god Bes. In taking it out of the country, I was, strictly speaking, breaking the law which forbids the export of antiquities, but this little figure is only an inch high and has lost his feet. I had a little stand made for him. There is no harm in the god Bes. He was represented as a pot-bellied Ethiopian dwarf, wearing the reed crown of Upper Egypt. He was the god of parties and good fellowship, sometimes shown playing a harp, and his image was stamped on ladies' make-up boxes.

I had been in Egypt for some weeks when I came home from the university to find a little pencilled note in Arabic pushed under my door. I asked my Egyptian servant what it signified and he told me that a policeman had brought it. I felt rather nervous and took it across the other side of the road to a tobacconist's kiosk which was in the charge of a Syrian Christian boy who could speak some English. He explained that I was to go the following day to the town hall to a certain office where I was to be interviewed by "one big Pasha". I duly kept this appointment, and was shown through various passages to the anteroom of the office, where a frightened-looking Greek woman was also waiting to be interviewed. I was eventually called in and found, behind the desk, a large man wearing horn-rimmed spectacles. Looking like something straight out of *1984*, he was, in fact, a member of the secret police. He began to take down my particulars – my nationality, my age, my position in Egypt and my religion. "Have you ever been to Israel?" "No." "Have you any relatives in that country?" "No. As far as I know, I have only ever met one citizen of that country, and that was when I attended a seminar in America last summer." "Oh," said the secret policeman, "was his name Zief?" "Yes," I replied, "it was." The reader will remember that Israel Zief had promised to write. "Well," he said, "he has sent you a letter and that is against the law." In fact, of course, it had been smuggled into Egypt. The Israelis delighted in showing how they could circumvent Arab security arrangements in this way. The police chief, or whoever he was, began to glance through the letter. It was obviously of a perfectly harmless and jocular character. The policeman read out the sentence, "How is old Amin?", and asked me: "Who is Amin?" "That must be Dr Osman Amin. He was one of the delegates at this conference." I pronounced the name Osman incorrectly, not stressing the second syllable. "Oswald?" he said. "Is he a Copt?" From the time of the British occupation, the Copts have tended to adopt English Christian names. I assured him that Amin was not a Copt, and explained that this letter was quite innocuous, that relationships between all the delegates at the conference had been friendly and open, and that I could only be astonished at the foolishness of this man in writing to me. This seemed to satisfy him. I was dismissed and I never heard any more of the matter. I wish I could meet Israel Zief again and tell him that he had very nearly got me into serious trouble.

My first year in Alexandria, 1955–6, turned out to be the last year of relatively peaceful relations between Egypt and Britain before the Suez crisis. During my summer vacation in London in 1956, "Supervacuo", who worked in the Foreign Office, gave me a hint that something might be brewing. I did not heed this warning and returned in the autumn to Alexandria. Shortly before the Suez conflict began I learned that Francis King, the novelist, whom I had known at Oxford, was to be appointed to a British Council post in Alexandria. I was delighted at this, for it meant that I would have a fellow Englishman with a common background to myself to talk to. I had not known Francis very well, and am inclined to think that he is the sort of person that one never gets to know very well. He duly arrived in Alexandria, but almost immediately the conflict began and he only lasted about ten days. He tells me that the Egyptians simply could not believe that his role in the British Council, since he had been appointed so shortly before the Suez crisis reached its head, could be anything but that of a spy. He was sharply cross-questioned, and followed about everywhere he went, until he was finally expelled.

The university term began as normal, but it was not to continue so. At the end of October, Israel and, at the same time, Britain and France, attacked Egypt. I was lecturing to one of my classes on Milton's *Lycidas* and, reading the poem to them, had reached the lines:

> Where the great vision of the guarded mount
> Looks towards Namancos and Bayona's hold:
> Look homeward, Angel, now, and melt with ruth . . .

I was explaining to the students that the "vision of the guarded mount" was the Archangel Michael, protector of Christians, looking out to sea from St Michael's Mount in Cornwall towards the ports in the north of Spain, to guard England against a second Spanish Armada. I was almost in tears at the thought of the greatness of vision which my country had once possessed, and what seemed to me to be a shameful threat against Egypt. It was at this point that somebody came in and said that we were at war, and that the university was, for the time being, closing down. My students said goodbye to me and it was clear that most of them thought they would never see me again, and that I would probably be shot. Among these students was Joseph (he preferred this form of his name to the Arabic Yusuf). He was the son of an old Coptic priest, and I suspect that, as a child of his father's old age, he had been rather spoilt. His academic work was poor, but he was convinced that he was a poet. On an earlier occasion I had expounded to the class Dryden's "Ode on the Death of Mrs Anne Killigrew" and had come to the lines:

> When in the Valley of Jehosaphat,
> The Judging God shall close the Book of Fate . . .
> The Sacred Poets first shall hear the Sound,
>   And formost from the Tomb shall bound:
> For they are cover'd with the lightest Ground
> And streight, with in-born Vigour, on the Wing,
> Like mounting Larkes, to the New Morning sing.

I was explaining the daring humanistic claim for poets that Dryden was making – that they should be the first to rise at the general resurrection. Joseph was pleased. "So we shall meet again, sir," he said. Now, at this moving moment of farewell at the outbreak of hostilities, he suddenly said to me that he wanted to show me his poetry. I said I would be delighted to look at it, but this was hardly the moment.

After a day or so, it was announced that all British and French subjects were to report at the town hall. Jim and I duly went there, and found the square in front of the building packed with a rather hysterical crowd. It seemed to have been forgotten that the Cypriot Greeks and the Maltese, of both of whom there was a large population in Alexandria, were at that time also British subjects. Consequently they were dealt with first and our reporting was put off for another couple of days. The Cypriots were treated as honorary Greek citizens as a gesture of sympathy for the nationalist rebellion under the leadership of Archbishop Makarios, then in progress. I felt sorry for the Maltese, many of whom were expelled. Their own island is over-crowded, and they were mostly skilled workers, for example, engineers, and would have found some difficulty in securing new employment there.

When we eventually joined the queue of British and French sub-jects, each of us was given a printed form advising, but not actually ordering, the recipient to leave Egypt within ten days. One English-man is said to have asked: "What will happen if I don't take this advice?" It was made quite clear that he would be immediately interned. Jim was ahead of me in the queue, and, of course, we both had the same address stamped on our documents. He was duly handed the form, but when it came to my turn I was asked for my particulars and what I was doing in Egypt. I explained that I was a professor at the university. "Are you still employed by the university?" the official asked. I replied: "As you know, the university is now closed, but I've had no intimation from them that my appointment has been terminated." Accordingly, he rang up the university authori-ties, who replied that they wished me to stay. Having ascertained this, the official withdrew my form and then asked me: "Who is Mr James P—?" I explained that he was my personal secretary and assistant. "Then you need him for your work, don't you?" "Yes," I replied, "I do." Jim's form was then immediately withdrawn, and we were both given temporary authorisation to stay, while our security position was investigated. Of course, the Egyptian authorities had nothing against us, especially as I had not been appointed by the British Council. I saw no reason why I should leave, abandoning my property and my job. Sooner or later it was clear the university would

230

reopen. In fact, it did so in the spring of 1957 and I resumed my teaching there.

Life went on very much as usual. Although my telephone was soon cut off, I retained my radio, which might well have been confiscated, and was able to listen continually to the BBC World Service broadcasts. There was a real threat of attack on Alexandria and a black-out was imposed. It was not difficult to observe this, since, in any case, all flats were fitted with shutters. There were anti-aircraft emplacements on the roofs of some of the blocks of flats, including, I think, the one in which I lived, but there were no serious attacks upon the city. The French plan, I believe, was to occupy Alexandria, which has never withstood a siege. Its water supply (an artificial canal connecting with an arm of the Nile) can easily be cut off. From this base the French and British could have struck directly at Cairo. This scheme perhaps made a lot of sense, and would probably have been more successful than the plan (which in fact prevailed) to seize Port Said. I am glad the French plan was not put into operation as I would probably not have survived. There were one or two air-raids on Alexandria. The Post Office Savings Bank was destroyed, as was the Scottish School (which was, of course, British property). Our intelligence seems to have been poor, for the Post Office Savings Bank building, which, some years before, had been the main post office, was no longer used for that purpose. According to Abdul, the people of his native village on Lake Mariout were provided with arms against British raids. They promptly went wild-fowling.

The financial and moral support which the Soviet Union gave to Egypt during the time of the Suez crisis resulted in a large number of Russian sailors and technical workers coming to Alexandria. For a time, the touts, who were always trying to sell something on the street by shouting "Hey Jack" to any European, started shouting "Hey Ivan", but Ivan did not have any money to spare, and was obviously quite nonplussed at finding shops relatively full of consumer goods which he had no idea how to bargain for. I was told that the Egyptian workers in the shipyards would often needle the Russian technicians who had taken the place of British ones. Whenever the Russians failed, the Egyptians would say: "Britain very good before. Russia no good today."

Shortly after the university reopened, I had occasion to go to the Dean's office on some departmental business. I found him receiving a delegation of about half a dozen Czech students. The Dean introduced me. They were obviously quite surprised to see an Englishman there. The conversation was necessarily conducted in English, since the Dean did not know any Czech. The students explained they were a fraternal delegation. I think I detected just a trace of irony which the

Czechs have always employed under various oppressive governments.

Before I left Alexandria in the summer of 1957 for my usual return to England for the vacation, I stayed, as I generally did, in Mr Philip's hotel. I found it much fuller than it usually was. There were a number of Russians staying there who kept themselves very much to themselves, but to my surprise there was also a party of Englishmen. I got into conversation with a member of this party and he explained that they were technicians sent over to service the cotton mill at Kafr el Dauwâr which I had already visited. It had originally been constructed by the British, and the Russians had proved incompetent at servicing it. These Englishmen were therefore working in Egypt on a generous expense account only.

I was never asked to make any kind of statement condemning the British aggression against Egypt, and, although I thought that the policy of the British government at this time was wrong, I would not have consented to make such a statement. Some other residents of British origin were more anxious to make their position clear. The Scottish-born wife of Osman Amin contributed some violently anti-British articles to the *Egyptian Mail*. She was probably anxious for the safety of her liberal and internationally-minded husband.

The Alexandria branch of Barclays Bank, where I had my account, was sequestrated at the beginning of the Suez conflict and put under Egyptian management. As an enemy alien, I was only allowed to draw a hundred pounds a month. When I first came to Egypt, the Egyptian pound had stood slightly higher than the pound sterling, but it now dropped to about three-quarters or less of its original value. Consequently we had some difficulty in making ends meet. We managed to buy the cheaper kinds of Egyptian food, buffalo meat, for example, which was tough, and buffalo milk. All milk has to be boiled in Egypt, but when buffalo milk is subjected to this treatment, instead of forming a skin, like boiled cow's milk, it produces, for some reason, nasty thick clots. Fortunately, the Mediterranean, though it has been exploited and polluted, still produces very good fish, and these could be bought at a reasonable price. Grey mullet and red mullet were excellent, as were shark steaks. One could also buy prawns and other shellfish. I once found an interloper among my helping of prawns. It was a crustacean called the Opossum Shrimp which had somehow perished while swimming among the prawns. It looks quite alarming, and you could not eat it because it is all shell and legs and nothing else. I only once tried oysters in Alexandria. They were obviously not fresh, or had come from polluted waters, and made me ill. The one indulgence we allowed ourselves was a fancy pastry with our afternoon tea. One could buy very good pastries at a Greek pâtisserie not far from our flat.

Cooking was all done by our Egyptian servant, a lad of about seventeen, on a spirit-stove in the kitchen, though sometimes he would borrow the baker's oven for a small fee and make a good dish of mixed fish and meat, baked with pimentos and chilli peppers. Traditionally, cooking in Egypt used to be done on charcoal-burning stoves, but the spirit-stove has become universal. Very few flats were supplied with gas. An elderly Egyptian servant, whom we employed in my first year, was unfamiliar with gas. Consequently, instead of turning off the gas taps when he had finished cooking, he would blow the burners out – as he would have done with the burners on a spirit-stove. This habit of cooking on spirit-stoves has a terrible side-effect in Egyptian urban society. Women frequently commit suicide by drenching themselves with fuel oil and then setting themselves alight. This happened in the case of the mother of one of my students. In traditional Muslim society suicide is rare. The phenomenon I have just spoken of must arise from the terrible tensions experienced by women trying to adapt to the pace of an urban and industrial society.

Social life in Alexandria ground to a standstill during the crisis and there seemed little point in my leaving the flat. I was, in fact, under surveillance from two policemen who were occupying a casino on a little pier just opposite the block of flats in which I resided. The police also, of course, had their own spy, Abdul, more or less regularly inside my flat. The corniche of Alexandria has these little piers with casinos every few hundred yards along the front. The casinos are for foreign tourists, as gambling is forbidden to Egyptian citizens, and the two policemen spent their time drinking coffee. This particular casino was always empty. It was said that this was because it was haunted by an afrit. There are three principal supernatural beings in Arabic folk-lore – djinns, afrits and ghouls. Afrits are spectres, but not, apparently, the spirits of departed human beings. Abdul claimed to have seen one once. It stood astride his village street. He admitted that he had been smoking hashish at the time. Ghouls haunt graveyards and feed on the bodies of the dead. They are not wholly distinct, I suspect, from hyenas, which, because of their human-like voices, have long been regarded as partly supernatural beings.

The hundred pounds a month I was allowed to draw from the bank was never quite enough for my needs, but my Egyptian colleagues at the university very generously helped me by granting a loan till the end of the month, and a grocer, who had his shop just round the corner from the entrance of my block of flats, always gave me credit for the same period. This was good of him. He had been a police colonel under the British administration, and this, apparently, made him trust the British. But policy could have been changed at any time. I might have been interned, or expelled, and then he would have been left with my outstanding debts unpaid. On one trip to the bank, I broke my journey to pay a call on Manzalaoui. "What are you doing here?" he said. "You're supposed to be under house arrest." "Well, they never told me," I replied. There was very little hostility from the local population or from the students. The general opinion seemed to be that if this man has been allowed to stay by our authorities he must be all right. Personal loyalties and friendships count a great deal in Egypt. Some of the students actually said that if things were to get difficult for me they would be willing to hide me in their family houses. Nor was there any hostility from the ordinary people in the street. Badawi's wife, who was Dutch and had a very northern blonde beauty, did feel it expedient to carry a little notice pinned to her dress, saying: "I am Dutch" – just in case. I think things might have been tougher in Cairo. Alexandria, with its many communities of different races and religions, has a tradition of tolerance. In Cairo, as somebody once said to me: "People are still under the delusion that life has a serious purpose." Nobody could call Cairo "an unreal city".

There were, however, some worrying moments. One was when the Rector of Al Azhar University threatened to declare a state of *jihad* or holy war. This would have made my own position, and, indeed, that of all non-Muslims in Egypt, untenable, for when *jihad* pertains the toleration of the "People of the Book" is suspended. But the next day President Nasser paid a formal visit to Al Azhar and we never heard any more about *jihad*.

One day I heard a tremendous row going on in my kitchen. Somebody had come in through the back door and was delivering a tirade, which I gathered was directed against the British, the French and the Israelis. I did not know what might happen so I thought it best discreetly to remain in my bedroom and lock the door – not that this would have been any protection from an attack from a hostile mob. After the noise had died down, I asked my Egyptian servant what it had all been about. It turned out that it was only the dustman who was complaining because he had not been tipped. Nevertheless, there was always the feeling that I might suffer mob violence, or that I would be interned. For this reason, I slept with the Gospels and Homer's *Iliad* and *Odyssey* (in Rieu's Penguin translation) beside my bed. This was partly so that if I were obliged to pack a suitcase and go into internment I could take these with me, but it was also a symbolic gesture defining my own European identity. I found that in a crisis literature as basic as this was the only kind that really seemed to make any sense. Besides Homer, another author who I found gave me continual pleasure and instruction was Herodotus. I managed to obtain the two volumes of the Everyman edition of Rawlinson's

234

translation. I had already discovered Rawlinson's Herodotus in the school library at Bembridge. Herodotus has ever since been one of my favourite authors. His account of Egypt is surprisingly accurate. He is our prime authority for the exact method used by the embalmers in preparing a mummy, for he gives a detailed and technically accurate account of this. He must have got his information mostly from tourist guides, for Egypt was already a civilisation which aroused the curiosity of the Greeks.

Herodotus is often accused of telling tall traveller's tales, but I think this is unjust. He says, for example, that the neighbourhood of Lake Mariout is famous for its vines and its excellent wine. While I was in Egypt, some police officers stationed near Lake Mariout, finding themselves with not much to do, had made a hobby of vine growing and wine production. Under the relative tolerance which the Nasser regime afforded to deviation from Muslim law and custom, this was possible. The policemen produced two vintages, Clos Matamir and Clos Mariout, and they were not bad at all.

There was nothing much to do during these months when the university was closed and I was officially under house arrest, but the bookshops of Alexandria were full of paperbacks, and we made a large collection of American science fiction. It furnished a kind of fantasy escape. These science fiction stories ranged from work of quite a high degree of literary craftsmanship to pulp-fiction nonsense. I became fed up with it after a while. Almost all the stories seemed to express a kind of paranoia, presenting a world in which your best friend may turn out really to be a malignant vegetable from outer space. I do not believe that science fiction can ever be the major literary form that some have claimed. The ingenuity of the fantastic set-up prevents the development of human character in any kind of depth. This is also true of the detective story. The title of Kingsley Amis's study of science fiction, *New Maps of Hell*, is all too accurate a description of what many works of science fiction are.

In my third academic year (1957–8), although full diplomatic relations between Egypt and Britain had not been restored, things began to be easier, now that hostilities had ceased. During this period President Nasser called a general election. Shortly before that event, on a summer evening, I felt bored with staying in my flat and ventured out to a nearby café. As I sat drinking coffee some men at a nearby table invited me, in English, to join them. Out of courtesy, I accepted their invitation. They then began to quiz me thoroughly. Who was I? What was my nationality? What was I doing in Egypt, and what was that bulge in my pocket? It was, in fact, a metal cigarette case, but they evidently suspected it might be a bomb or an offensive weapon. I replied that I was a professor at the university. Turning to his companions, my questioner said, in Arabic: "He is a student at the university." "I am not a student," I replied, "I am a professor." This made them think that I understood more Arabic than I actually did, and after that they left me alone. They were clearly members of the secret police.

Abdul, since he was working for the police, was in a position to inform us how they regarded us. In consequence of this, he was getting a double rake-off, being paid by the police, and being given small sums of money whenever he asked for them from us. This increase in his income led to a corresponding increase in his consumption of hashish. By 1958, as the political climate became easier, we were not quite so ready to accede to Abdul's every demand. He became indignant, and said he would denounce us to the police, and proposed to go to the post office, where you could obtain, across the counter, a special form for that purpose. Refusing to be intimidated, we told him that if that was the game he wanted to play there were a few things we could denounce him for, too. I accompanied him to the post office, where he duly obtained the form, but having done so his bluff suddenly collapsed. He tore up the form. "You are my friends," he said, "and I will not betray you."

During my period of house arrest I began to write a play, *Helen in Egypt*, based on the strange story, current in antiquity, that Helen never went to Troy at all, but only a phantom in her likeness. This story first occurs in Herodotus, who says that Paris and Helen fled to Egypt, but the Pharaoh detained Helen, and let Paris, accompanied by a phantom Helen, go on to Troy. But the story is earlier than Herodotus's time. The poet Stesichorus (*c*.640–*c*.555 BC) wrote a poem in which he blamed Helen for having caused the Trojan War. After this he was smitten with blindness, for Helen was now receiving divine honours. She appeared to him in a dream, and told him to write a poem retracting his strictures upon her. This he did and recovered his sight. Only one line of the poem survives: "It is not true you never went to Troy . . ." The poem was called a palinode and was the first of its kind. The word "palinode" now means a poem in which the poet retracts statements made in a previous work. The Egyptian Helen story is the subject of a play by Euripides, and, in modern times, has been used by Paul Claudel. It also furnished Hugo von Hofmannsthal's libretto for Richard Strauss's opera *Ägyptische Helena*. When I was about fifteen I had read a curious romance, written by Rider Haggard and Andrew Lang, which uses the same story, and in which Odysseus, on his last voyage, meets Helen. But I already knew the story from Herodotus.

It was fun to retell this story when I could actually look out of my windows and see the island of Pharos on which the action of my play took place. I used it as a peg on which to hang some ideas about the nature of history and the relationship between European and Asiatic civilisation, which were obviously pressing on me at this time. An Egyptian family who were friends of Manzalaoui, and whose culture had been very much influenced by an admiration for British culture, were in the habit of doing acted readings of plays in their flat. So my play was given its first presentation there. I played the Pharaoh, with a large plastic fruit bowl on my head. A beautiful Armenian girl took the part of Helen. The play has only been given one other performance. This was in 1988 by the Roman Court Theatre Company at the Westminster Community Theatre. In my treatment of the story, the same actress has to play both the real Helen, who has aged, and the phantom, which is eternally beautiful. Menelaus, shipwrecked on the island of Pharos on his return voyage after the fall of Troy, has to choose between an eternally beautiful illusion and a mortal reality. He chooses the latter, and thus history, in which freedom will be possible, can begin.

After some time, I discovered that there was a law which stated that enemy aliens who were servants of the Egyptian government were not to be regarded as enemy aliens for some purposes, including the freezing of their bank accounts. I informed the Egyptian sequestrator who was in charge of Barclays Bank, but he refused to believe me. I then obtained a copy of the law, in Arabic, from the town hall, and revisited the bank, thrusting the document under the sequestrator's nose. He was then compelled to unfreeze my bank account. A certain amount had accumulated to my credit in the intervening weeks, and I hastily spent as much of it as possible in case the authorities should change their minds. I bought myself a new suit and a nice Italian edition of Ariosto's *Orlando Furioso*. I also gave a party for my Egyptian colleagues as a way of expressing my gratitude to them for their support.

The university had reopened for the spring semester and I resumed my lectures. The first class that I took were studying Shakespeare's *Much Ado About Nothing*. During this I noticed a certain amount of disturbance at the back. Remarks were being passed which were probably hostile to me. I ignored them, for they did not seem to be a real threat, but one of my students stood up indignantly, saying that he could not stand this disrespect to a teacher, and went off to the Dean's office. In a few minutes the Dean appeared, breathing fire and fury. I explained what had happened and he told me that there were stiff penalties for serious indiscipline. I said that I could not really name the culprits, and did not think that their behaviour warranted severe punishment. Having settled down, the class were obviously grateful that I had not used any possible sanctions against them. It was now necessary to assign the parts for the scene we were about to read. "Now, who are to read the parts of the two villains, Conrad and Borachio?" I asked. "What about you two at the back?" Quite by accident I pointed at the instigators of the disturbance. Everybody laughed and I had no more trouble.

As things eased it became possible to order books from England. I recall that the first book I obtained was Rose Macaulay's *The Towers of Trebizond*. This novel, partly serious, partly comic and satirical, describes the adventures of the heroine (or hero – the sex of the narrator and protagonist is, possibly, deliberately left ambiguous) who is brought by her Anglo-Catholic aunt and an extreme High Anglican priest, Father Chantry-Pigg, to Turkey in a pilot mission for the conversion of that country. The book shows a good knowledge of Turkey, which Rose Macaulay had clearly recently visited. The Englishness of this book, and the comic effect it achieves from presenting a clash between Western and Middle Eastern values, made a lot of sense to me at this time. I had always admired Rose Macaulay's work since I had been recommended, by Miss Hunkin, to read *Orphan Island*, an extravaganza and satire on Victorian values, written during the 1930s. I had met Rose Macaulay on several occasions at St Anne's House, and she suffered the accident which led to her death on those premises. Most of the meetings took place in a large first-floor room. There was a narrow staircase leading from this room down to the ground floor, almost directly to the street door. Rose Macaulay was leaving and going down these stairs accompanied by a young man. He wished to open the front door for her, but, as he pressed forward to do so, she mistook his courtesy for rudeness, and, mustering all the dignity of the Cambridge intellectual aristocracy to which she belonged, said: "I thought ladies always went first." But in doing so she lost her balance and fell down the stairs, breaking her thigh. She was taken to hospital, but, sadly, never recovered.

After I had weathered the Suez crisis, my annual contract was renewed, and I was determined to stay in Alexandria for at least another year. First, however, I travelled, as I always did, to England for the long summer vacation. It was necessary to give up the flat I occupied, since its owner needed it for the summer months. So I went, as usual, to Mr Philip's hotel. On the evening I got there, I found the place oddly quiet. I waited a long time for dinner to be served, and eventually an Egyptian servant, who did not speak English, brought me some roast chicken which had gone cold. It transpired that Mr Philip had been arrested and interned on suspicion that he was an agent working for the British, French or Israelis. When I came back to Alexandria in the autumn and booked rooms in the same hotel, I found that Mr Philip had been released. I do not know how he had been treated during his internment, but his mind was broken. He wandered aimlessly around his hotel, sometimes into the rooms of guests, if their doors were unlocked and he saw a light on. The hotel was being managed by a brisk young Turk who treated Mr Philip with contempt: "He would like to fill the hotel with Armenians as crazy as himself."

I have not much to say about my final year in Egypt, which went off successfully. Some of my visits to the Egyptian countryside, and the production of *A Woman Killed with Kindness*, which I have already spoken of, belong to this period, but, as I cannot exactly remember the chronology, it seemed appropriate to deal with them all in their own place. I was obviously popular with the students and with the university authorities, and I could doubtless have had my appointment renewed indefinitely or until the next crisis blew up. But I decided that three years in Egypt was enough; 1958 would see my fortieth birthday, and I thought I should do something more to further my career than becoming an academic expatriate. The status of an expatriate is a dangerous one for a writer. He to some extent occupies a privileged position in the country of his choice, and is shielded from the problems which may beset its citizens, especially if they live under an oppressive government. At the same time he may be cut off from the roots of his culture. It was partly this expatriate status, I am certain, that led to the tragedy of Ezra Pound's support for Mussolini. Egypt under Nasser was a police state, if a relatively mild one. I believe that Nasser had genuine liberal intentions, but his position was insecure. In particular he had to keep in power by favouring the clique of military officers who had originally supported him.

Although I had returned to England during the previous two summers, in 1958 I found it in many ways a country very much changed from the one I had left three years before. The Suez adventure had been the last throw of Britain as an imperial power. Anthony Eden had been one of the heroes of my youth. My first overt political action was to refuse to join the Young Conservative League because I could not subscribe to a vote of confidence in Neville Chamberlain. But Eden had now shown himself to have acted in an extremely irresponsible and injudicious way. This was the age of the "Angry Young Man", and I did not feel myself wholly comfortable in it. In the theatre the honest craftsmanship of writers like Noël Coward and Terence Rattigan was disparaged in favour of the self-indulgent rant of John Osborne and his kitchen-sink followers. One influential critic actually opined that Osborne was the greatest English playwright since Shakespeare. Osborne did, however, have one failure. This was his venture into the realm of the musical – *Paul Slicky*. Round about this time I came across a young man, not personally known to me, in a side street in Soho, who seemed to be almost in tears. I asked him what was the matter. "It's terrible," he replied. "They're even attacking John Osborne now."

I found myself a basement room near Lancaster Gate. It was below street level and damp, but spacious enough for me. It was now that I renewed my friendship with John Wain. I had scarcely known him at Oxford, though I remembered his face, but I had visited Reading University, at his invitation, when he had been a lecturer there. I gave a talk to the students' literary society on the poetry of Alexander Pope. Wain was now living in London, and made it known that he would always be in the saloon bar of The Salisbury in St Martin's Lane at lunchtime on Saturdays. I often joined him there. Among other friends of his who were present at these gatherings was Harold Pinter. On one occasion the conversation turned to the young people of today and their mores. "Don't talk to me about the young," said Harold, "I was at one of Elvis Presley's films, at the height of which a young girl suddenly rushed up to the screen, crying out: 'Piss on me, Elvis.' She was then carried off by nursing staff."

There was still the problem of what employment I was to find. Eventually, I wrote to Donald Hall, a Harvard friend and poet, and asked him if there was any chance of my getting a university lectureship in America. He replied advising me to obtain a list of American universities from the United States Embassy and to write round to all of them offering my services. This seemed a rather daunting prospect, but shortly afterwards he wrote again, to inform me that he had suggested my name to the English Department of his university, Ann Arbor, Michigan. I was offered a visiting professorship for one semester. Therefore, at the beginning of 1960, I set off once again for America – this time travelling by plane.

14

Ann Arbor

I arrived at Ann Arbor in the middle of the American winter, suffering severely from jet lag. For about the first twenty-four hours all I wanted to do was to run away and take the first plane home. I heard a story of a Chinese student, from Hong Kong or Singapore, who had suffered in just the same way on his arrival in Ann Arbor. He hid in the rafters of a church for some weeks, coming down at night and pilfering coffee and biscuits from the church canteen, before he was eventually discovered. However, I soon began to settle in. I was received kindly by the head of the department, Professor Rice, and his colleagues, and given two assignments. At the beginning of the semester I was to lecture to a freshman class, using as my texts a collection of short stories and an anthology of verse. This was to be followed at the end of the course by more detailed study of a poet of my own choice. I chose Wordsworth.

The students at Ann Arbor, as is usual in American universities, took a four-year course. The work in this freshman year was more like what one might have expected in England for a sixth-form course than a university class. However, I seemed to be able to communicate readily with these young men and women. X. J. Kennedy, the poet, who had been assigned as my assistant, told me that within a few weeks of my arrival my name was being mentioned in the women's dormitories, and that the girls opined that I was "dead cool". There are Anglo-American linguistic problems which many must have encountered. The first short story in the collection I was assigned to study with them was a translation of Gogol's "The Overcoat". After my first meeting with the class I told them to go away and read this story, which we would discuss the following week. The first question I asked of one of the young male students was: "What sort of a man is the protagonist of this story? How does he fit into the Russian society of the early nineteenth century?" It will be remembered that the protagonist of "The Overcoat" is a poor clerk in the enormous Russian civil service. "He is a peasant," replied the student. I was angry. But I soon realised that the word "peasant" has a quite different meaning in American English from that which it has in British English. In American English it simply means an uncultivated person.

I suspect that this arose among immigrants from Central and Eastern Europe. When one of these families had prospered and found a niche in American society, if the wife found her husband eating peas with his knife, or something like that, she would say: "You are behaving like a peasant." In Britain I had always been taught of the peasantry as embodying sterling values of independence. The peasants represented the old rural order before the rise of capitalist farming, when the Enclosure Acts had reduced most of them to mere hands. Another problem arose out of our reading Cowper's "Epitaph on a Hare". In their essays, the students all referred to the animal as a rabbit. To me this seemed extremely odd. There is nothing surprising about a tame rabbit, whereas the whole point of Cowper's poem is that a very strange and wild creature should have been tamed. In America this point is lost, for the animals of the family *Leporidae* which inhabit the northern hemisphere of the New World are intermediate between rabbits and hares.

My other assignment was with fourth-year students. I was to lecture on three twentieth-century major English authors. I chose T. S. Eliot, James Joyce and Robert Graves. I dealt largely with these authors' use of symbolism and mythology, paying little attention to the earlier work of Joyce – *Dubliners* and *A Portrait of the Artist as a Young Man* – but spending most of my time on *Ulysses*, and not neglecting *Finnegans Wake*. The same treatment was applied in the case of Graves. I concentrated on his poems and the theories he expounded in *The White Goddess*, largely leaving out of account his historical and other novels, and his autobiographical *Goodbye to All That*. This may not have been a very balanced approach, but it made a stimulating course. The students seemed to be pleased with it, and at the end of the semester very generously subscribed to make me a presentation. The book which I chose was T. H. White's *The Once and Future King*.

X. J. Kennedy (the X stood for nothing – he had simply added it because there were a lot of Kennedys in the telephone directory, and a very high proportion of those were called Joe) was a postgraduate research student at Ann Arbor and proved to be an invaluable assistant. Together with his friend, Keith Waldrop, he had formed a lively group who met regularly to read and discuss their poetry, and who enjoyed putting on unusual dramatic productions. One of the latter was Alfred Jarry's *Ubu Roi*. Somewhat ill-advisedly an attempt was made to reproduce the conditions of the original Paris production. On that occasion the audience had been so outraged by the play's challenge to bourgeois conventions that the actors were pelted with rotten vegetables. Kennedy and Waldrop suborned members of the Ann Arbor audience to stand at strategic places and throw cauliflowers and other vegetables. This did not please the authorities who looked after the hall, for the mess had to be cleared up the next morning. Later, this same group of Kennedy's and Waldrop's friends mounted a production of my own play, *The Talking Ass*, which I myself directed. The title of my play was slightly embarrassing to present to an American audience, for American English makes no distinction, either in pronunciation or in spelling, between the word "arse", meaning fundament, and "ass", meaning donkey.

Professor Rice struck me as perhaps a sad and disappointed man. A New Englander, he seemed to be a Calvinistic Puritan who felt himself not predestined to grace. His expertise was in Milton. At the end of my stay in America he told me that he was intending shortly to retire, and recounted to me what appears to have been the only joke which he was ever recorded to relate. This concerned a professional fox-catcher, who, on deciding to retire, sold to his successor a secret which he employed in his chosen trade of fox-catching. Some time later he met this successor and asked him if he had caught many foxes. "No," he replied. "Didn't you use the trick I taught you?" asked the retired fox-catcher. "No. I thought of a better one of my own." On one occasion Professor Rice said to me: "I understand that a member of the Mathematics Department has been attending your lectures. There must be some hope for the humanities, after all." The mathematician was Kenneth Leisenring, who had been attracted by my lectures on *Finnegans Wake* which dealt with Joyce's references to Einsteinian theories of the space–time continuum. Leisenring, a man older than myself, became one of my closest friends in Ann Arbor. He was a bachelor, and his flat, which was close to the university campus, was always open to me. A mathematician with a scientific training, he also had a genuine interest in the arts of poetry, painting and music. He came from a father of German stock, whereas his mother had been of Scottish descent. His father had been a fundamentalist Methodist preacher. Leisenring had reacted against this, under the influence of the writings of Albert Schweitzer, one of his heroes. Apart from Leisenring and the Kennedy–Waldrop circle, my other constant companion was Geoffrey Hill, who was now spending a year as a visiting professor at Ann Arbor. I received a great deal of kindness and hospitality from other members of the university. There was also Dorothy Donnelly, whose husband worked for the University Press. Dorothy Donnelly is a poet whose work is published by Wesleyan University Press. She is also the author of some books in which she re-examines Darwinian theories of evolution in the light of her own Catholic beliefs. I was frequently entertained at the Donnellys' house, and have remained in correspondence with Dorothy ever since – her husband died some years ago. I regard her poetry very highly indeed and I am surprised it is not better known.

Ann Arbor is purely a university town. The nearest big city is Detroit, which was spoken of in accents of horror as a nightmare modern industrial conurbation. The centre of Ann Arbor is occupied by the university campus. Just outside that is a small shopping centre and a belt of churches of different denominations. There is a local law which forbids the sale of liquor within a quarter of a mile of a church or a school. Consequently, one has to go some distance to get a drink. This law seemed to me to show a pessimism uncharacteristically American. Whoever framed it assumed that the churchgoers were more likely to be corrupted by the drinkers than that the latter should be converted by the churchgoers.

One day I received a telephone call from – as far as I can remember – the head of the German Department, informing me that Arthur Koestler was visiting the university, and would be giving a lecture the following afternoon. Would I like to come and meet him afterwards at a private party in his honour? After I had found out whom we were talking about (the difficulty is that the German "oe" diphthong is ungrateful to the Anglo-Saxon vocal chords, and, while Americans solve this problem by making it sound like the "e" in "best", we British sound it like the "o" in "worst"), I naturally agreed. I attended the lecture, which was held in one of the larger university auditoria on a very hot American summer's afternoon. The subject of Koestler's discourse, which he later made the basis of a book, was a general theory of creativity which should apply to literature, science and humour. This theory, which did not seem to me to be particularly original, was that the creative moment in each of these fields is when the mind makes an unexpected leap which transcends the logical. For humour, Koestler illustrated this with one of the least funny stories I have ever heard, which he said was his favourite joke. It went as follows. A French nobleman of the *ancien régime*, returning home unexpectedly, found his wife in bed with the bishop. The husband's reaction was to go out on the balcony and start blessing the crowds beneath. When asked why he did this, he replied, "Monseigneur is performing my function, so I am performing his." After a while I found my attention flagging, and fell asleep. As I left the auditorium, I met Donald Hall and he asked me what I thought of the lecture. I replied that unfortunately I had fallen asleep halfway through it. He replied that so had he. As I proceeded further, and met other friends and acquaintances, I found that they all had had the same experience. I was forced to draw the conclusion that Koestler had performed the remarkable feat of sending an entire audience to sleep. After this I did not really feel very eager to go to the party, at which I had been invited to meet him. Leisenring had offered me the opportunity of what proved to be a much more interesting encounter. This was to meet Prince Ostrovsky, who lectured on Russian history in the university. Ostrovsky's lectures were so interesting that students used to go to the ones preceding them in order to be sure of getting a seat. What made his lectures so compelling was that as a young guards officer Ostrovsky had been an eyewitness of most of the key events of the Russian Revolution. He was now an old man, but very lively, and full of anecdotes about the old days in St Petersburg. One of these concerned a Prince Bogratov, a scion of the Bogratid dynasty which had once ruled Georgia. The Bogratids claimed descent from King David. This particular Prince Bogratov was regarded in St Petersburg society as a bit of an ass. One day somebody met him in the street and said: "I am surprised I didn't see you in church yesterday." (It had been Good Friday.) "Oh, you may go to church on Good Friday," replied the prince. "For us it is always a family occasion."

Prince Ostrovsky, like many Russians of his generation, had a semi-mystical interest in the occult. This was the generation which had been influenced by Merezhkovsky, Scriabin and, of course, Madame Blavatsky. On one occasion Leisenring related to Ostrovsky the saying, which is widely current among people with scientific interests, that of all the scientists that have ever lived 90 per cent are alive today. The point, of course, is to illustrate how recent the growth of science has been, but Ostrovsky misunderstood it and supposed that Leisenring meant that all the great scientists of the past were still alive on some astral plane. Ostrovsky had once been present at a house party in Detroit. Some people in another room were experimenting with the planchette, and momentarily supposed that the unintelligible jumble of letters which the spirits appeared to be dictating might possibly be Russian. Accordingly, they asked Ostrovsky to come and read these. Yes, it appeared, the message was in Russian. It was addressed to him personally in the most correct bureaucratic language. "Nikolay Alexeitch, I have the honour to request you kindly to be so good as to contact my brother" (here Ostrovsky read out a name) "in Ann Arbor and tell him that he is overworking and has a weak heart and is in danger of damaging his health."

On a later occasion, Leisenring had secured a new set of records comprising the whole of Mussorgsky's *Boris Godunov*, and had invited the prince and myself round to his house to listen to them. The words are, of course, in Russian (the opera is based on a play by Pushkin), and Ostrovsky's interpretation of the text to us was extraordinarily illuminating. I realised, for example, that the Polish scenes which have often been dismissed as inferior to the Russian scenes are not so, they are deliberately written in another idiom, for Poland as presented in this opera is a decadent Western country seen from the point of view of a nineteenth-century Russian Slavophile.

Besides Arthur Koestler several distinguished writers made visits to Ann Arbor during the time I was there. The poet E. E. Cummings gave a reading of his work. Before he started he announced that if any press photographs were taken the reading would stop immediately. Cummings is notorious for the odd typographical devices which he uses in his work. These are meant to be aids to the oral reading of the verse. He is, in fact, a rather simple lyrical poet, sometimes verging on sentimentality. During the Hungarian uprising of 1956, Cummings had written a poem in which he bitterly blamed America for not intervening on the side of the Hungarians against the Russians. If such a course had in fact been followed it might well have led to a Third World War. One is thankful in cases like these that poets remain unacknowledged legislators. But Cummings thought so highly of his poem that he chose to read it in Ann Arbor, although this was some years after the events which had prompted it.

I had been engaged for one semester only (the second semester, which started at the end of February and went on until the beginning of May) but my lectures were apparently so successful that I was invited to stay for a second semester. This began in October and continued until January. "What are you going to do during the summer?" asked Leisenring. I replied that I had really no idea. "Why don't you go to Mexico?" he said. It turned out that there was a direct flight from the local airport to Mexico City. I determined to make this journey and spend my summer vacation in Mexico. Leisenring had to take a summer school at another university, but promised to join me in Mexico later. I obtained a visa from the Mexican Consulate in Detroit.

When eventually I arrived in Mexico City, the first shock was that my suitcase, containing most of my belongings, could not be found. I booked into the Hotel Majestic, overlooking the central town square, or Zoccalo as it is called, with a fine view of the presidential palace and the cathedral, both impressive buildings of the Spanish colonial period. I had my hand-luggage, but my suitcase had contained my traveller's cheques and also my razor. I was therefore reduced to living on credit in the hotel, and spent most of my time lying on my bed waiting for phone calls from a Mr Valencia at the airport, who was trying to find my luggage. At the same time, I had nothing to read but *The Once and Future King*, which I had taken to read on the plane, and was growing more and more unshaven. I realised that I must be turning into a character out of a novel by Graham Greene. This only went on for a couple of days, though it seemed much longer. I had my meals in the restaurant of the hotel. One day I found myself sitting at the same table as two English ladies who seemed to have just taken a turn out of Kensington High Street, but I was too ashamed of

246

my unshaven appearance to try to get into conversation with them. I established something of a personal relationship with Mr Valencia, who eventually rang me up, saying delightedly: "We have found your luggage. It is in Winnipeg. It was just about to be put on a plane going to Japan."

After my luggage had duly arrived I felt free to explore Mexico City. I was furnished with an introduction to two students from Ann Arbor, Bob Loscher and his friend, who knew Mexico well and were very helpful. I liked the old city in which I was staying, and I liked the Mexicans. For me, they compared favourably with the Egyptians – although I had a considerable affection for Egyptians. I had equipped myself with a *Teach Yourself Spanish* book and a small dictionary, and soon became sufficiently proficient in the language to be able to read a newspaper, to engage in simple conversations, and even to translate a short poem by the twentieth-century Spanish poet, Ximenes. I was persuaded, I forget by whom, to move to a cheaper hotel at the other end of the city. This area bordered on what had been a forest, and was where the President's summer palace was situated. The old city had been laid out on the sensible Spanish gridiron plan, and it was difficult to get lost in it, whereas this new part of the town had a number of misleadingly forking avenues. It was only possible to find one's way around by using the names of the streets as clues. These streets had been laid out in the time of Porfirio Diaz under the influence of the positivism of Comte. There would be a block of streets named after philosophers, another block named after poets, and so on. Consequently, if one was looking for the Calle Edgar Poe and found oneself in the Calle Victor Hugo one knew that one was fairly warm, but if, on the other hand, one found oneself in the Calle Immanuel Kant one was definitely off course.

After a bit, I decided I would be happier in the old city again, and asked a taxi-driver, in Spanish, to take me back to the Hotel Majestic. He did not want me to go. He took me to several other hotels, all in the new city, which I rejected. Eventually, with a bad grace, he deposited me at the entrance of the Majestic. At this time there was a certain amount of anti-American feeling in Mexico and considerable sympathy among the people at large with Castro's Cuba. The night after my return to the Majestic, it was besieged by a hostile mob of demonstrators. I could only adopt the tactic I had followed in Alexandria when I thought for a moment I might be in a similar situation, that is, locking myself in my bedroom and hoping for the best. But there was no violence on this occasion. It had been clear from some things he had let drop in his conversation that the taxi-driver was a communist. Knowing that this demonstration was about to take place, and realising that I was British and not American, he had tried to save me from any possible dire consequences. Eventually, I moved to a smaller hotel, not far away, which I hoped would not be such an obvious target for demonstrations. I had a small room with bathroom en suite. One morning I woke up and, going to put on my clothes, found that my passport, my wallet (which contained only a few dollars, as it happened) and my metal cigarette case were missing. It was clear that a thief had slipped in through the bathroom window while I was asleep and had stolen anything that he thought might be valuable. I am a light sleeper, and what would have happened if I had woken up while he was in the room, I tremble to think. I might well have been knifed. I reported the theft to the manager of the hotel. It turned out that my passport, along with several others, had been abandoned in an empty room of the hotel. I had only lost a valueless cigarette case and a small amount of money. Before I could reclaim my passport, I had to accompany the manager to the police station and affirm that it was my property. He had not dared to pick it up from the room it had been abandoned in and hand it to me because, in that case, his fingerprints would have been upon it, and he himself would have been under suspicion.

After the demonstration at the Majestic, which was clearly spontaneous, the government arranged a pro-American demonstration in order not to scare away American tourists who were clearly important to the economy of the country. It was obvious that these demonstrators were Indians from outside Mexico City who had been offered a free trip to the capital on condition of their demonstrating. The Mexicans have a great deal of pride, and particularly resent the way America annexed Texas, which would have been, with its oil reserves, Mexico's richest province.

Next to the great cathedral in the central square of Mexico City is the pawnshop, one of the first buildings instituted by the Spanish. Tourists are recommended to visit this Mexican shop, full of jewellery pawned by poor peasant women – their jewels are their dowries. I myself did not have the heart to shop there. Also in the town square is the Museum of Ancient Art, full of Aztec and other pre-Columbian sculpture. One of the masterpieces of Mexican art is the statue of the earth goddess, Coatlicue. The name means Serpent Skirt. At first you seem to be looking at a megalithic block with carvings on it – a purely abstract art – but then you discover that what you are seeing represents a human figure. She has a necklace of skulls and of severed hands. Her head is made up of two arching serpent heads facing each other. Her hands are the claws of a vulture, or eagle, and she has a skirt of live serpents. One realises the truth of this sculpture – nature is like that. Whoever made it had a lot of fun creating it. The statue of Coatlicue in the museum in Mexico City is, in fact, a cast. The original is *in situ* on a temple site in another part of the country. I have also seen a photograph of an extraordinary piece of sculpture – a colossal figure of a goddess carved out of the living rock of a mountain. This is not like the statue of Coatlicue, formal to the point of abstraction, but intensely realistic. It shows a goddess in the very act of giving birth to her daughter.

The Once and Future King was not my only reading matter. Of much more relevance was *The Conquest of Mexico* by Bernal Diaz. He had been one of Cortés's officers and his account is extraordinarily vivid. One realised what an unmitigated disaster the discovery of the New World had been for its indigenous inhabitants, but the Aztec civilisation of Mexico would, I think, have destroyed itself anyway, sooner or later. The Aztecs were Stone Age cannibals, yet they had an immensely sophisticated art and literature, although this literature was entirely oral. The Dominican and Franciscan friars had the good sense to realise that if they were to convert these conquered people to Christianity they must try to understand their culture. The friars, therefore, got all the old men they could find to recite to them as much of their literature and historical traditions as they could remember. This literature was a great one, consisting of epic poems about the gods, ritual poems (which, strangely, have a genuine religious feeling), secular songs and two tantalising fragments of drama, just on the point of emancipating itself from ritual.

I relied for this information about pre-Columbian Mexican poetry on Irene Nicholson's book *Fireflies in the Night*. The ancient Mexicans believed that only the gods live in a world of light. We are in darkness – but poems are fireflies in that night. I had the pleasure of meeting Irene Nicholson, *The Times* correspondent in Mexico. The daughter of a wealthy Lancashire industrialist, she had arrived in Mexico, fallen in love with the country and had never gone back to England. She lived with her boyfriend, Armando, a Uruguayan right-wing political refugee, in what seemed more or less a slum. They entertained me to supper and seemed to live exclusively on spaghetti and cheese. Both of them were influenced by the philosophy of Gurdjieff and Ouspensky. Apparently, a number of Ouspenskyites had come down from North America at some period in the thirties and had settled in Mexico. I found the Ouspenskyan mode of discourse rather tiresome. I was genuinely interested in the problem as to whether the ancient civilisations of the New World were entirely of indigenous growth – as is the orthodox view of anthropologists – or whether there had been influences from the Old World, particularly from South-East Asia. When I put forward this question, Armando simply said: "Why use Aristotelian logic?" I think there is something to be said for Aristotelian logic.

Bob Loscher and his friend took me to a bullfight – a must for tourists. I enjoyed the atmosphere of fiesta which surrounds the bull-ring. People dress up for the occasion and there are mariachi bands. Mariachi is one type of Mexican folk-music, deriving I think from the folk-music of northern Spain, which is much more closely related to the main European tradition than the gypsy and Moorish-influenced Andalusian music which most people think of as Spanish. As for the bullfight itself, it has a certain glamour. The bull is, per-haps, not much more under stress than one that is slaughtered along with others in an abattoir, and the meat from the bull is distributed among the poor. On the other hand, cruelty is undoubtedly involved, and it is said that nowadays the bulls are weakened before they go into the ring. I find the glamorisation of bullfighting as a macho activity by such authors as Hemingway and, indeed, my friend Roy Campbell a rather pathetic phenomenon. Once, when the London School of Economics decided to get rid of its "dismal" image by organising an arts festival – rather an enterprising one with a new work commissioned from Benjamin Britten – Roy Campbell, David Gascoyne and I were invited to read our poetry. Roy was about to return to Spain and had secured a job as a picador. As the picador operates on horseback, Roy's lame leg – caused by treading on a land-mine during the Second World War when he served in the King's African Rifles – would not hamper him. He explained all this to the Principal of the LSE who entertained us for lunch. It was a new world to the Principal. "I hope you are insured," he said. But the English indignation about the bullfight seems to me to be as equally out of place as the Hemingwayish idealisation of it. My own feeling about bullfighting is that it is slightly more revolting than hunting, slightly less boring than cricket.

Mexico City has an excellent opera house built on the model of the Paris Opéra. It was the creation of one of the nineteenth-century presidents, and apparently the revolution that overthrew him began when he was attending the opening gala performance. The building also houses the national art gallery which possesses a number of paintings by Diego Rivera, whose murals are also displayed on various public buildings throughout the country. He was a Marxist and a revolutionary and his paintings are poster-like propaganda. They seem to me to hector the spectator into accepting the message. The other major Mexican painter of the same generation was Orozco, who was Catholic. His paintings are almost equally overpowering, frequently depicting the more gruesome scenes of martyrdom.

As he had promised, Leisenring joined me in Mexico after a few weeks. We made some excursions in the neighbourhood of Mexico City to examine ancient sites. The most impressive of these was

Teotihuacan. This had been the central holy site of the Toltecs, a race who preceded the Aztecs. It consisted of two great pyramids, one dedicated to the sun and the other to the moon, and a large sanctuary dedicated to Quetzalcoatl. This comprised a sacred enclosure, with a holy of holies at the back (not visible, presumably, to the mass of worshippers), in which were two colossal carved serpent heads with jaws agape. Into these jaws offerings were placed. Quetzalcoatl is a mysterious figure in Mexican mythology. Unlike the other gods, he was not offered human sacrifices. It was said that he wore a mask and that he was bearded. Since the indigenous inhabitants of America are of the Mongolian race, they have scanty beards or none at all. This has led to all manner of conjectures; for example, that Quetzalcoatl was a Greek, or an Irish missionary, or even the Apostle St Thomas. The two pyramids at Teotihuacan had been the site of human sacrifices. They had steps which one could climb to the top. The victim was dragged up these steps by the priest, and at the summit his heart was cut out. As this place has been developed as a tourist site, metal rings have been set into the sides of the pyramids to make it easier to ascend them. It must have been quite tough for the priest and the victim without these aids. It has been suggested, recently, that the victims went willingly to their deaths, having been drugged liberally with the cactus-derived hallucinatory substance, mescal. These pyramids, though not so ancient, impressed me rather more than the Egyptian pyramids at Giza. They were not so mathematically perfect, but had a kind of rough-hewn strength.

One day Leisenring and I ran into an Englishman and a party of English girls. They had motored down from New York, where the girls had been employed as secretaries. The girls were about to return to England by boat, but their male companion intended to drive further, first to Oaxaca, some hundred miles south of Mexico City. He said he would like to have passengers who would share the petrol expenses. This Englishman never seemed quite to realise that he was not motoring in the English home counties. He would drive out of the city and then start asking the way from Indians working in the fields who could speak little Spanish, let alone English. Usually they had never heard of the place that we wanted to go to. The result of these tactics was that we ran out of petrol in the middle of the Mexican desert. The desert at this time of the year, the rainy season, was a kind of lunar landscape punctuated by tree-high cactus plants, and the ground was covered with exquisite little flowers that had sprung up under the rain. Our driver hailed a passing truck to hitch a lift to the nearest large town, some distance away, where he could get petrol, and then hitch back with it. Leisenring and I, therefore, were left alone for hours in the middle of the desert. I was secretly a little alarmed at this situation because we might well have been murdered by bandits for the sake of the spare parts of the car. In a typically English way I suggested we should play twenty questions. We did so for several hours while night slowly fell, and wolves, or at any rate coyotes, howled in the distance.

When we eventually arrived at Oaxaca, I realised that I was in a quite different world from that of Mexico City. In Oaxaca one was in the centre of the Zapotec civilisation. The Zapotecs had been a subject people of the Aztecs, who commanded them to fast on their behalf to appease the gods. In consequence, the Zapotecs, to calm their hunger pangs, chewed a gum derived from a local shrub. This is the origin of chewing-gum. I found the Zapotecs a friendly and open people, and exceedingly clean. During the rainy season, at least, they washed themselves and their clothes as often as possible.

One of the sites which Leisenring and I visited was Miclan, which had been the capital of another pre-Aztec civilisation, that of the Mixtecs. Miclan was built on a hill, and the archaeological remains were at the top of this, near the site of the church. The church was closed. The regime, which is still in power in Mexico, is the PRI or Institutional Revolutionary Party. The name is singularly apt, for the party is institutional, though it continually uses revolutionary language. Officially, the PRI is still strongly opposed to the Catholic Church, though there is not the kind of persecution one finds described in Graham Greene's *The Power and the Glory*. The churches in Mexico City were open, and on Sundays I usually went to hear mass at the fashionable church of San Francisco near my hotel, but priests and religious were not allowed to wear their distinctive habits in the street.

At Miclan, most of what had been excavated was housed in a museum in the village. I visited this with Leisenring and we met an American archaeologist who had been working on the site for a number of years. She seemed to have got to know the local inhabitants very well and to be popular with them. The gods of the Mixtecs were different from those of the Aztecs. One of them was a bat god with large ears and a grinning mouth. Leisenring found the grin friendly and said to the archaeologist: "Those were the days when the gods had smiling faces." "It's difficult to know", she replied, "whether they are smiling or just showing their teeth." While Leisenring and I were looking at the archaeological site, there was a sudden violent downpour. The summer months are the rainy season in Mexico and it rains very heavily every afternoon. An ancient Mexican creation myth describes how the gods had various unsuccessful attempts at creating the sun. One of these attempts was the water sun. It shone down upon the primeval waters and sucked them up until it burst, thus causing the deluge. It then became the water god, Tlaloc. Next, the gods created our sun, which fed upon the blood of human beings. Men were then created, and commanded to make war against each other in order to provide the sun with sustenance. The sudden bursting of Tlaloc seems reproduced in what happens in the rainy season in Mexico every afternoon. On this occasion, the village street of Miclan suddenly became a raging torrent. We were floundering about in it up to our ankles. Some children saw us and began to laugh. I found nothing unfriendly in their laughter. I suddenly began to see myself and my companion as they would have seen us – two enormous white men, floundering helplessly in the mud. Amid the laughter and shouts of the children, I caught the word "mosquito". This was slightly alarming. I had been told by some English friends I had made in Mexico City that this "mosquito" was an aquatic insect (perhaps related to our water-boatman and water-scorpion) which lives in the fast-running mountain streams of this part of the world. It is a secondary host of a parasitic worm which can cause blindness in human beings. In consequence, there are said to be whole communities where the entire adult population is blind. These people rely on their children to do tasks for them and to lead them about. H. G. Wells must have heard of this "mosquito" when he wrote his story "The Country of the Blind".

The Zapotecs are a small people, not more than five feet six high on average. As we were coping with the flooded road, a little man at the door of his stone hut beckoned us in to take shelter. He only had a few words of Spanish, but we had a halting conversation. He asked for a pencil and a piece of paper and wrote down his name. I think that was all that he could write. It was to prove that he had at least that accomplishment. His children, he explained, did go to school. There was an extraordinary openness and friendliness about this man which I shall never forget.

Another archaeological site which we visited in the neighbourhood of Oaxaca was Monte Alban, a ruined city which had once been the capital of an even earlier civilisation, that of the mysterious Olmecs. Leisenring and the Englishman who had driven us down were hunting around in the ruined streets for some bas-reliefs of dancers, which they knew to be there. They had just, I think, located the dancers when the god Tlaloc burst up in the sky and a downpour ensued. We rushed down the hill on which Monte Alban was built and got into our car as quickly as possible. As we did so the whole silence of the hills became alive with an extraordinary sound. It was the croaking of frogs, aroused by the coming of the rain. It was a strange and eerie noise, almost as if the ghosts of the ancient Olmecs were calling out to us.

During our previous stay in Mexico City, Leisenring was able to take a plane down to Yucatan to see the remains of the second Maya Empire there. I was sorry not to be able to join him, but I had social invitations which I wished to honour. I had been furnished by the writer and psychic researcher, Renee Haines, with an introduction to her son Crispin Tickell, who at that time had a junior post in the British Embassy in Mexico City. He received me hospitably and gave me some interesting introductions. Many of the British residents in Mexico City whom I met, including Irene Nicholson, seemed originally to have come to the country with the intention of staying a short while, and had remained there ever since. In discussing poetry with one Englishman, the name of Horace came up. My host went to his bookcase to verify a quotation, and found that he had left his Horace at home in England. This must have been ten or twenty years before. The local English and American amateur dramatic society was rehearsing a performance of *Brief Encounter* – of all the incongruous plays to see in Mexico.

I am glad that I saw Mexico when I did. One hears that smoke pollution has made Mexico City intolerable, and that all the local cultures have been subsumed by the universal popularity of television. Apparently a television soap opera, in which all the actors have to be of white European type, plays a dominant role. Mexico is only superficially a Spanish country; just below the surface are the Indian cultures, each totally different from its neighbour and using a different language. There are said to be certain forest areas in remote parts of the country where Indian tribes, who have never been subdued by the Spanish, still lurk.

I had been asked to teach for a second semester at Ann Arbor. As I have already said, during my first semester there I had taught a course on major twentieth-century British authors. I have always rather resented the fact that a writer who is invited to teach in a university is supposed to be interested in, and only capable of teaching, twentieth-century works. I have considerable doubts whether the teaching of contemporary literature in universities is a good idea at all. There was no such teaching in my day at Oxford. Nowadays, the teaching of twentieth-century literature seems to me to have led to a kind of mandarinisation in this field. Poems and novels are exalted because they conform to academic standards and are easy to teach. These are not necessarily the most vital works of contemporary literature, which as often as not are written by mavericks who are breaking new ground. If twentieth-century literature had been in the syllabus during my years in Oxford I am certain that we would have had to spend a lot of time studying Robert Bridges. All the older dons regarded him as a major poet, and his now almost unreadable work,

The Testament of Beauty, as a major poem. It is true that contemporary literature is often taught by younger members of the academic staff. These will be young men and women perhaps not much more than ten years older than their students. This is precisely the generation from whom the students should not be getting their ideas about modern literature. It is this slightly older generation which the students ought to be in revolt against. Two years ago, at the time of George Barker's death, there was an extraordinary instance of academic stupidity in relation to contemporary literature. An Oxford professor, whom I will not name because I have been on friendly terms with him, reviewed, in one of the Sunday papers, a biography of Elizabeth Smart. She had been George Barker's constant companion at a crucial period of his life and was the mother of four of his children. This professor stated that in the 1930s Elizabeth Smart had formed a relationship with a minor poet of the period, George Barker, whom he seemed to assume his readers might not have heard of. It was unfortunate for this man that on the day his review appeared George Barker died. It is to be supposed that when the professor opened his *Guardian* or his *Independent* the next day – I assume that all dons read at least one of these papers – he was confronted with two long obituaries, making very high claims for George Barker's status as a poet, one written by myself, the other by Anthony Thwaite. It looked as if George Barker, like Keats, had been "snuffed out by an article" (in Byron's phrase), but, in fact, Barker had been dying for many months of emphysema.

I was, accordingly, now rather pleased to be called upon to teach a course on the Augustans. The authors whom I chose to concentrate on were Dryden, Swift and Pope. These lectures seemed to go down well with my students. Many of them had been taught at school, or pre-university colleges, the old-fashioned late-Victorian view of Dryden and Pope that they were, to quote Matthew Arnold, "not classics of our poetry, but classics of our prose". My enthusiasm for them, and my exposition of the basic philosophy of eighteenth-century Toryism, was probably something new to my students. My own political views, in so far as I have any, probably derive, as did my father's before me, from this old tradition of Toryism. This has little in common with the Conservatism of Lady Thatcher and her friends. These people are Whigs, not Tories. If I were pressed, I suppose I would define my ideological position in terms similar to that of T. S. Eliot when he stated that he was "classicist in literature, royalist in politics and an Anglo-Catholic in religion". However, I would, possibly, give rather different interpretations of all three of these terms to the ones Eliot would have given. In particular, I am not very happy with the term Anglo-Catholic. I prefer to call myself a High

Churchman, loyal to Cranmer and his Book of Common Prayer, but in my case with a strong mixture of that scepticism which I think has always been part of my character. I am sceptical with regard not only to religion but to scientific scepticism itself. As for politics, most of the intelligent people I have known have been more or less sympathetic to socialism, but the most intelligent, and these have included Eliot, Hugh Kingsmill and Bonamy Dobrée, were not.

I had the pleasure of being invited to give readings of my verse at two pre-university colleges, one of which was Calvin College in Grand Rapids. One of my students, John Van Domelen, had studied there and secured an invitation for me to give a reading to the students. The college had originally been founded to train candidates for the ministry of one of the numerous sub-sects into which the Dutch Reformed Church had split. I was motored there through a blizzard, and when I arrived I was hospitably received by the head of the English Department, who took me for a meal in a restaurant and offered me a drink. After my long and rather arduous journey, I was only too glad of a drink, and my satisfaction that I had been offered one evidently showed on my face. "We may be Calvinist here," he said, "but there's nothing of the Methodist about us."

My second semester at Ann Arbor was punctuated by a short Christmas break in New York. I had been invited there by Michael Romney who occupied a large studio in the Bowery, above the offices of a Chinese newspaper. It was fortunate that there was a stove in the studio, for the weather was bleakly bitter, but, I am afraid, the place was infested with bed bugs. I was warned that if, by any chance, I should need to go down in the morning into the lobby of this build-ing, I should always put my shoes on, for the local drunks and winos used this lobby as a shelter, and urinated on the floor. Michael shared this studio with an artist friend, who lived in the suburbs of outer New York, but liked to come and work in the centre. He had bought, as a Christmas present for his small son, a model space rocket that flew when one ignited some chemical in its rear. It sounded rather alarming, and in order to test it safely he brought his son with him to Central Park where the four of us witnessed the launching of the rocket. It turned out that it only jumped a few feet and our precautions were quite unnecessary. The Bowery seemed a rather frightening place, full of Chinese, Italian-Americans and more than its fair share of drunks and layabouts, who must suffer terribly in the bitter winter weather of New York.

During my stay I made a visit to suburban New York in order to spend a couple of days with John Guenther, then a journalist. He had been in Oxford during the war, though we had never met. His knowledge of Oxford in wartime had led him to write an excellent biography of Sidney Keyes, published by Alan Ross. Guenther had corresponded with me about the book and I had given him as much help as I could. He lived on Long Island Sound in what can only be described as Great Gatsby country. After I had arrived, he suggested that we should take a walk down to the Sound where we might see some wild geese and feed them. It seemed to me typical of the whole place that the wild geese were tame. I took a stroll around the village, and remarked afterwards that, comparing it with similar suburban areas in England, I had been struck by the absence of dogs. Guenther explained that you were not allowed to keep a dog in this community unless it had been psychoanalysed. This was said without irony, as far as I could tell, but the psychoanalysis in question really meant Pavlovian conditioning to inhibit the dogs from biting strangers. There is a real danger of rabies in North America, as the virus is carried by squirrels and other wildlife.

I felt that I should take the opportunity to attend a theatre. I decided to go to a performance of Jean Genet's *The Balcony*, showing in an off-Broadway theatre. I hailed a taxi, gave the address of the theatre and asked the driver to take me there. I am convinced that London taxi-drivers are the best in the world. Those of other cities that I have lived in simply do not compare with them in their efficiency and knowledge of the terrain. This driver had no idea whatever how to find the theatre. Having driven round for about half an hour, he eventually said, triumphantly, "Here it is," and deposited me at the entrance of a theatre. I paid off the taxi, and as it was just a few minutes before the curtain was due to rise I rushed in, bought a ticket and entered the auditorium. I found myself watching, not *The Balcony*, but a musical comedy by P. G. Wodehouse. This was a charming work about the rivalry between two American college football teams. I probably enjoyed this musical a lot more than I would the Genet.

I also attended a party in Greenwich Village. A woman sitting next to me remarked that she was writing a novel, and that she had also just given birth to her first baby. I said: "It must be very difficult to find time to write a novel when you're looking after a baby." "On the contrary," she replied, "it is very difficult to find time to look after the baby when one is writing a novel." She also told me: "We met an English poet once. He lives in a wood near London." I was a bit puzzled by this, but then a flash of inspiration entered my mind. "Do you mean Stephen Spender?" I asked. "He lives in St John's Wood." I was right, and tried to explain that St John's Wood is hardly more of a wood than Greenwich Village is a village, but she assured me that Stephen had told her that it was a rich sylvan place.

15

The Sixties

I returned from America in 1961 to my basement room near Lancaster Gate. I had kept up the rent during my absence. While in America I had read about a scholarly article on Charles Williams, published in the Jesuit magazine *The Month*. I had made a note of the article's author and title, and the number in which it had appeared, but this note had gone missing when I packed for my departure. Accordingly, I went up to the London Library soon after my return, took out the files of *The Month*, and went through the index of each volume, looking for the article. To my horror, I found that after about half an hour of this the print was fading in front of my eyes. I have spoken about the eye trouble which had dogged me since the age of three, but never before had I had any difficulty in reading even the smallest print. The operation which I had had at the age of eighteen had saved the sight of my left eye, although my vision from side to side was restricted. At that time my right eye could only just discern light. When I was in Egypt this eye had begun to degenerate and there had been a danger of its becoming infected. I had it removed by an operation in 1956 while on vacation in England and it was replaced by an artificial eye. This sudden deterioration in the sight of my remaining good eye, the left one, I now think was possibly caused by my exposure to ultraviolet light at the very high altitude of Mexico City during the previous summer. I ought, perhaps, to have worn sunglasses, but I had always despised them as an affectation. For a time I was able to read for short periods, but this soon became impossible. From now on I had to rely on the help of readers, and was very lucky in finding many people who volunteered to do this for me quite freely.

In 1962 John Wain organised a large-scale poetry festival at the Mermaid Theatre which lasted for a whole week. Among those who read was Ted Hughes, whom I briefly met at this period. A pop group, the Shadows, were also called in. They accompanied the verses of Royston Ellis, a twenty-year-old poet. He had published a small pamphlet of poems which had been advertised as the work of a beatnik genius. Taken up for a time by John Waller and others, he eventually obtained a post as secretary-companion to the owner of the small

Channel Island of Jettou. Unlike Jersey, Guernsey, Alderney and Sark, Jettou is not a Crown dependency – its owner is simply a tenant of the Crown. Royston Ellis wrote a small pamphlet of about three pages telling the entire history of the island. This work I found rather more interesting than his verse. One night, when he was in Jettou, Royston Ellis discovered that he had forgotten his latchkey. He knocked at the door of his employer's house but was unable to get an answer. Eventually, he was reduced to ringing the tocsin in the town belfry. I do not know what happened to him in the end. I think he found another position, in the Caribbean.

John Wain's poetry festival culminated in a gala night on the Saturday. Sir Ralph Richardson and Dame Flora Robson were billed to read, and I was also invited to take part, since John Wain paid me the compliment of admiring my verse-reading style. William Empson, whom John Wain had always regarded as his master, was also invited to read, and Nevill Coghill was to give one of his inimitable interpretations of Chaucer, using the reconstructed English pronunciation of the fourteenth century. When I arrived at the theatre I found chaos. The tickets had been sold out and all manner of important people were ringing up and asking for seats. John Wain should have had the foresight to reserve a few places for possible VIPs. Empson arrived, accompanied by his wife Hetta and a young man who shared their house in Hampstead. There were no seats for the last two so they had to be brought into the green room. I have come to know Hetta Empson much better in later years, and have a great deal of admiration and affection for her. But on this occasion I could cheerfully have strangled her. In the green room she continually asked people if they felt nervous. This is something one should never do, either to actors or to musicians, before a performance. I had been taught this at an early age by my mother. A further diversion was caused by a female admirer of Flora Robson. This admirer had rung up demanding that she be given a seat. She said that she was a fan of Flora Robson and had never missed any performance of hers. But when Dame Flora was consulted on the matter she said: "Oh, that woman. She's always following me around – and if it's not me it's the Archbishop of Canterbury." Until the performance began I found a certain degree of peace and calm in the room occupied by Nevill Coghill. Sir Ralph Richardson read Blake's "The Mental Traveller", and was kind enough to compliment me on my own reading. I read some poems of my own, as well as Tennyson's "Edward Grey" – a ballad which at first reading might seem naïve and sentimental, but which is really much more subtle – and Pope's little poem "A Hymn Written in Windsor Forest":

All hail! once pleasing, once inspiring Shade,
    Scene of my youthful Loves, and happier hours!
Where the kind Muses met me as I stray'd,
    And gently press'd my hand, and said, Be Ours! –
Take all thou e'er shalt have, a constant Muse:
    At Court thou may'st be lik'd, but nothing gain;
Stocks thou may'st buy and sell, but always lose;
    And love the brightest eyes, but love in vain!

During the sixties I still frequented the pubs and clubs of Soho but the area was now in its decline. It finally deteriorated when the Westminster City authorities, in their wisdom, decided to allow the opening of sex shops and striptease clubs in this area, a policy which I believe they now regret. However, there were new faces to be encountered. There were the Irish poet Patrick Kavanagh, and the playwright Brendan Behan. A new meeting place was the Colony Room, a small club over a shop in Dean Street. It was owned by the formidable Muriel Belcher who had previously run a coffee stall on a bomb-site on the other side of the road. I did not feel particularly at home in this place. It was made much too obvious by Muriel and her barman that one was not welcome if one was not prepared to spend a large amount of money behind the bar. However, I went there from time to time. One could count on meeting Francis Bacon there, if one wanted to, and the piano was played by Malcolm Williamson, who some years later was to become Master of the Queen's Music and to be given a knighthood. Malcolm suggested our collaborating on an opera libretto, but nothing came of this. I think our temperaments were too dissimilar. I did write a short solo cantata for him in the form used in the baroque period, but I do not know whether he completed his setting of it. My poem was not a very good one, anyway.

Another friend and companion of these days was Frank Norman. He had shot to fame and fortune with his prison memoirs, *Bang to Rights*, his musical, *Fings Aint Wot They Used T' Be*, and his short stories, *Stand on Me*. The last two works both deal with the seamier side of Soho life. It seems that I had been kind to Frank some years before, and he remembered this with gratitude. On one occasion, I ran into him in Soho and he insisted on taking me to a restaurant and standing me a meal. He was very drunk and went on to say that he was going to drive home in his new car and take me with him. He wanted to show me a flat he had recently acquired in Hampstead. The waiters and the proprietor of the restaurant, who knew him well, tried desperately to dissuade him, begging him to allow them to call a taxi for him, but he was adamant that he was going to drive, and was going to take me with him. I suppose I was a bit drunk myself, but a quixotic resolution formed itself in my mind. I said to myself: "If I allow Frank to drive home on his own he will almost certainly crash and perhaps be killed. If I go with him, however, there is a chance that this will make him responsible enough to get home in one piece." Accordingly I let him drive me to Hampstead, sitting beside him on the front seat and praying hard all the way. He showed me round his flat and I spent the night there. The next morning, as soon as he woke up, he rushed to the window to see if his car was still there. He had vague memories of the night before, and had apparently smashed up two or three cars on previous occasions.

It was also during the early sixties that I first met Eddie Linden, in the Highlander in Dean Street. Eddie came from a mining family in Lanarkshire, and the story of his early years is an appalling one of illegitimacy, rejection by members of his own family, and a fragmented education, which has led to his having severe reading difficulties. All this is to be found in *Who is Eddie Linden?*, his autobiography as told to Sebastian Barker. In spite of Eddie's reading and spelling difficulties he had literary ambitions and some talent, and was given money to found a poetry magazine. This was the beginning of *Aquarius*, which still continues to publish, if a little irregularly. The way it got its name is of some interest, I think. Eddie asked me what title he might use for the magazine. I suggested "Python", an image which I hoped suggested both the possibly aggressive and scaring qualities that poetry ought to have, and the Pythoness, or oracular priestess, who served the shrine of Apollo at Delphi. Stevie Smith, however, who had promised Eddie some poems, disliked the name. Her sympathy for all living creatures did not, apparently, extend to pythons. Another name, "Aquarius", was suggested by a friend of Eddie.

"Aquarius" was a buzz word of the sixties. Its origin is astrological. Those with a knowledge of astrology will know that although the sign of Aries (the Ram) governs the spring equinox (21 March) the sun does not rise in the constellation of Aries at that date but in that of Pisces (the Fishes). This is due to the phenomenon known as the procession of the equinoxes, whereby the position of the sun in relation to the signs of the zodiac shifts approximately every two thousand years. Two thousand years ago was roughly the beginning of the Christian era, and the Fish was an early Christian symbol. According to traditional chronology, the sun began to rise in the sign of the Ram at about the time of Abraham, when the substitution of a ram, caught by its horns in a thicket, for Isaac, about to be sacrificed on the altar, signalised a new covenant. Virgil was aware that the year had once begun in the sign of Taurus (the Bull). Traditional chronology would suggest that this would bring us back to the time of Adam, and, indeed, there is a rabbinical tradition that Adam's first sacrifice, after his expulsion from Eden, was a bull. It follows that round about the year AD 2000 the sun will rise at the spring equinox in the sign of Aquarius (the Water Carrier). This was taken up in the sixties by the various New Age prophets of the time, who were perhaps influenced by the ideas of Robert Graves. The sign of Aquarius was of a human being which they said would signal a new age of humanism and the end of the Christian dispensation. What will happen in the year AD 4000 when the sun rises at the spring equinox in the sign of the Goat (Capricorn), I do not like to contemplate. I felt that Eddie Linden, a Roman Catholic, should not have adopted this un-Christian iconography for the title of his magazine. However, as few people understand these things, it probably does not matter very much.

Brian Higgins was also to be found in the Soho pubs in the late fifties and sixties. He came from Hull, though he was of Irish descent. His poems were, I believe, first published by David Wright and Patrick Swift in their short-lived but excellent magazine, *X*. These poems have a kind of gritty honesty about them, together with a rejection of pretension and false values. Higgins's longest poem, "The North", is a conspectus of that part of the country which he came from. In one passage he spoke of Hull as:

> . . . the worst university in England,
> with its famous librarian,
> a sad poet, a beat-up Beverley Nichols,
> all Kodaks and missed chances.

This librarian was, of course, Philip Larkin. The passage caused offence and was rejected by the Poetry Book Society for fear of libel. Although Higgins had a degree in mathematics, and had once held a teaching post in Turkey, he seemed, by the time I knew him, to have become almost a professional layabout. He would stand around, hoping someone would buy him a drink, and, if nobody would, might end up by finishing the half-empty glasses on the bar. His career was brought to an end when a doctor warned him against any further drinking, but the warning was perhaps not necessary. Higgins turned out to be suffering from a condition known as "senile heart", and died a year or so later at the age of thirty-five.

George Barker had now settled in a National Trust farmhouse in Norfolk, where I went to stay with him on several occasions. Elspeth Langland was now living with him and was the mother of several of his children. He had met her first when visiting Greece, where she was engaged on an academic thesis, which she never completed, on traditional kleptic (literally, robber or outlaw) ballads. George was always very good company until late in the evening when a certain hysteria usually took over. He would insist on Elspeth's reading poetry aloud to him, but there were no poets whom he wanted to listen to except for the Tennyson of *In Memoriam*, and A. E. Housman. George worked regularly every morning at his writing. A few years before his death, in 1991, his wife, Jessica, died in America and George married Elspeth. The wedding was a happy occasion, attended by a vast clan of his extended family. It took place in the Roman Catholic church of a nearby town, though Elspeth remained a staunch Presbyterian. George made his confession to a priest prior to the ceremony. I asked George if this had not taken some time. He replied that he had simply said: "Father, I have committed every sin, with the possible exception of murder." Whereupon the priest had absolved him of all of them on the spot. George always remained loyal to the Roman Catholic traditions of his family, but one of his last and finest poems, "Thurgarton Church", written after the death of his father, is very bleak and seems to deny both the existence of God and any possible immortality. Oliver Bernard tells me that at this time George said to him: "I only believe in the saints."

One day, by good luck, I ran into Charles Wrey Gardiner, who told me that I could rent two unfurnished rooms in the house he owned near Westbourne Grove. He had a large front room on the first floor which he shared with his American mistress. I was offered accommodation here on the understanding that when Gardiner raised a second mortgage on his house I could have the front room as well. I eagerly accepted this offer, as unfurnished rooms, in which the tenant had security of tenure, were extremely difficult to find. Eventually, Gardiner did get his second mortgage and I moved into the larger room as well. I was able to get my furniture, pictures and books, which had been in store for years, into place. Gardiner rejoined his wife in the country but, unfortunately, abandoned the American mistress. For some time she was left derelict in the front room, where, of all Gardiner's furniture, only one armchair remained. She sat in this chair entirely surrounded by empty whisky bottles. I was now faced with the problem of how to get rid of her, courteously, so that I could occupy the room. Fortunately, however, one of her American friends arrived, rescued her and took her back to America.

Gardiner eventually returned to the house, but moved to the attic room. There were various other tenants. The most interesting of these was the poet John Gawsworth, whose real name was Terence Fytton Armstrong. On his mother's side he was descended from the Fytton family whose seat was in Gawsworth in Cheshire. The most famous member of this family was Mary Fytton, who according to one theory is the Dark Lady of the Sonnets. Her effigy in the parish church at Gawsworth shows her as fair, but it may have been repainted.

Apart from this possibly distinguished ancestry, Gawsworth was also the King of Ridonda. Ridonda is a little island, not much more than a rock, in the Leeward Islands. The story goes that, when these islands were formally annexed by the British Crown, Ridonda was overlooked. An Irishman named Shiel, cruising in his yacht in the Caribbean, landed at Ridonda and claimed it in the name of his small son. Shiel had the boy crowned by the Bishop of Antigua. It is alleged that Queen Victoria sent a gunboat to haul down Shiel's flag, and wrote a rather firm note to the Bishop of Antigua. Shiel's son grew up to be the writer, M. P. Shiel. He wrote sensational romances, some of them dealing with what used to be called the Yellow Peril – the idea that the West would be overwhelmed by the Chinese and other Asiatic peoples. M. P. Shiel, who died unmarried, made Gawsworth his literary executor and also his heir to the Kingdom of Ridonda. Among Gawsworth's most treasured possessions were the ashes of Shiel, which accompanied him to whatever lodgings he took and were kept in a little urn on the mantelpiece. Gawsworth somehow succeeded in being literary executor to a number of other writers. It was said that there was a superstition in Fleet Street that if you met Gawsworth twice in one morning you would die within the year and he would be your literary executor. Gawsworth took his position as King of Ridonda very seriously and created a number of peers. Originally these were formally named in state papers which he had privately printed. In his later years, when he was very much in decline, he was apt to make anybody a peer who lent him money or stood him a drink. Most of the aristocracy of Ridonda were dukes, though Roy Campbell was, appropriately enough, Master of the Horse. For my part, I was made a duke in about 1949. Gawsworth had asked me to contribute a poem in honour of Shiel for a volume of tributes to that author which he was planning, but which never got published. This was when I was living in John Waller's house in Kensington. I was at one of Waller's parties when Gawsworth rang up and asked to speak to me. He reminded me that I had promised him this poem and he wanted it as soon as possible as he was getting the manuscript ready for the press. Begging to be excused from the party for a moment, I retired to the lavatory and in about a quarter of an hour wrote a short ode, which I then delivered to Gawsworth over the telephone. He said he knew that I would not let him down and that the state paper nominating me a duke had already been printed. Many years afterwards, on the occasion of Shiel's centenary in the 1960s, Gawsworth was good enough to appoint me Poet Laureate of Ridonda in return for a poem in celebration of the centenary.

Gawsworth had been born in 1912, and was therefore a few years younger than Louis MacNeice and W. H. Auden. His own verse, however, was in a traditional mode, regularly rhymed and written in a conventional poetic diction. For this reason, and also, one must add, for his charm and, at that time, his youthful good looks, he was, in the 1930s, adopted by the establishment as an alternative to the modernist poets whose work that same establishment looked upon with suspicion. Early in life he had received all sorts of honours. He had been made a Fellow of the Royal Society of Literature and a Freeman of the City of London. Apparently there was a charter given to the Vintners' Company by Edward IV (in return for a loan) which allowed a public house owned by the company to remain open, whatever the local regulations might be, so long as a Freeman of the City of London was in it. It is said that Gawsworth used to exercise this privilege, carrying with him the charter which made him a freeman. He never did so in my presence, however.

When I knew him, Gawsworth had become a fairly hopeless alcoholic, and was living largely by selling off the collection of manuscripts and memorabilia he had amassed. He did me a very good service in arranging for the sale of a number of my own books and papers. At his best, Gawsworth was a good conversationalist, with many anecdotes about literary figures of the twenties. He had known T. E. Lawrence, for example. There had been two Queens of Ridonda. The first, Estelle, was a Belgian lady. I met her once. She was tough enough to handle Gawsworth successfully. His second wife was Anna. She was a rather pathetic character and got a bad deal from Gawsworth, who bullied her unmercifully. Anna eventually had the courage to leave him, and Gawsworth acquired a third consort, Eleanor, but did not marry her. He referred to Eleanor as Queen SJ (the initials standing for *sub judice*.) One day, while Anna was still living with Gawsworth, a young man came to see me. He had written an excellent pamphlet on the Swedish poet, Carl Michael Bellman (1740–95), with translations. This young man had an idea that I might be able to collaborate with him in making a freer translation of Bellman's poems, but it seemed to me that since Bellman wrote in very strict forms, setting his poems to popular operatic arias of the day, nothing much more could be done with them. He wrote lyric poems about the bohemian tavern life of the Stockholm of his day, with a cast of ongoing characters. He seems to have penetrated a world like one I knew very well. While we were talking, there was a roar from upstairs. It was Gawsworth having a row with his poor wife, Anna. This was not unusual. On occasions he would take down a family heirloom, an old cavalry sword, from its place, and brandish it at her. On other occasions he would break eggs into her hair, saying he was giving her

265

a shampoo. The young man was alarmed by the noise. "What is that?" he cried. "It is only John Gawsworth," I said. "He is a poet and he is probably drunk." "I am afraid I haven't much experience of that sort of thing," replied Bellman's translator.

Gawsworth's real name, as I have stated, was Armstrong. The Armstrongs were Irish Protestants, and Gawsworth's minute private income still included rents from a few cottages in Cork. He seems to be the Mallow of Dylan Thomas's *Death of the King's Canary*. I was puzzled to identify this character, but it turned out that Mallow is the county town of Cork. Gawsworth sometimes described himself as a black Protestant, but, according to John Waller, who had known Gawsworth in Cairo, the latter, when stationed in India during the war years, had become a convert to the Hindu religion. He had a commission at this time, and having declared his intended conversion he went to his commanding officer and demanded leave to go to the holy city of Benares to receive religious instruction. The commanding officer replied that this was unnecessary, as Gawsworth could perfectly well receive religious instruction from the local Brahmin priest. Gawsworth was forced to agree to this, but insisted that the Brahmin, by all accounts a rather squalid character, must be treated as a chaplain and entertained in the officers' mess. This was too much for the racially conscious officers of that period, and they were forced to accede to Gawsworth's request to go to Benares. Little seemed to remain of his conversion to Hinduism, but I was told that he would sometimes exclaim "Ram, Ram", this being an invocation to the demi-god Rama, the hero of the Indian epic *The Ramayana*, who is regarded as an avatar of Vishnu. However, I never witnessed this. In moments of depression Gawsworth would go into the nearby Roman Catholic church of St Mary of the Angels to kiss the foot of the statue of St Joan of Arc. Both he and Joan, he explained, had been victims of English persecution.

Perhaps the best thing that Gawsworth ever did came about when he was serving in the Italian campaign. Learning that the philosopher, Benedetto Croce, was living near where his regiment was stationed, Gawsworth went to call on Croce, and found the old man and his wife. They were obviously starving, and Gawsworth immediately went to the store and scrounged tins of bully beef and baked beans for them.

Gawsworth had no children and so the question of who should succeed to the Kingdom of Ridonda raised its head. Some time in the past a journalist who worked for the magazine *Lilliput* had apparently taken Gawsworth to his house in the country, got him drunk and persuaded him to sign a deed of succession, naming his host as his heir to the kingdom. This was regrettable, but Gawsworth was a man of his word and refused to name any other successor while this journalist was still alive. However, he predeceased Gawsworth and the latter began to think of offering his kingdom for sale to raise money. Accordingly he advertised it in the press. There were several replies. A rather sinister consortium thought that Ridonda could, perhaps, be used as an offshore gambling centre. Another company planned, rather more realistically, to exploit its guano resources. A prince of the royal house of Sweden also evinced interest, but was warned by the British Foreign Office not to pursue the matter, for the story of Shiel's annexation of Ridonda, if true, had a slight element of possible legitimacy in it which might have precipitated an awkward international situation. After Gawsworth's death I received a visit from an American, a Mr Lehmann, who presented himself as the secretary of the Micropatriological Society. This society apparently concerns itself with small realms dotted up and down the world which have some kind of claim to a real independent existence, of which Ridonda is one. Other rulers of such realms included King Lenny of Reach, who claimed that King John had given a charter of independence to that East Anglian town because it had repelled a French invasion. There was also the King of Sealand who claimed independence for a rock in the Thames estuary, and someone who purported to be the real King of Ireland. In the various documents which he issued from time to time he referred contemptuously to the Republic of Ireland as Bogland. I do not think that Gawsworth recognised any of these rulers but there is a story of his meeting the King of Poland, whom I have already mentioned, in the street. The two monarchs greeted each other with royal courtesy: "Good morning, Poland." "Good morning, Ridonda."

Eventually Gawsworth abdicated in favour of a publican whom none of his friends had ever met. This man had befriended him in some way, I presume financially. But this new King of Ridonda did not turn up for the formal abdication ceremony, so his succession may be questionable. In fact, he left London for the north of England where he was rumoured to be actively creating fresh dukedoms. Since Gawsworth's death there have been several conflicting claims to the realm of Ridonda. The publisher, John Wynne Tyson, nominated in Gawsworth's will as his literary executor, styles himself King of Ridonda. Wynne Tyson actually visited Ridonda and found that one of the American universities had already made a biological survey of it. It is mostly inhabited by sea birds and rats, though I am told that at the time that Shiel landed there there were actually a few people living on it. It is said that a group in New York formally acclaimed Ridonda a republic. The Reverend Baron de Fortis, who, oddly, combined a French hereditary title with Holy Orders in the Church of England, also interested himself in the succession, nominating a young black man. I had a communication from the baron asking me to attend a meeting of Ridonda dukes which he was holding in the Fitzroy Tavern. I replied that I thought this game had gone on long enough and that the memory of Ridonda should lie in the Fytton family vault, along with the ashes of Gawsworth and Shiel – might they rest in peace.

In the early 1960s I was still desperately trying to find some kind of employment, and applied for adult education lecturing. All I could get was a job in Battersea, teaching speech training to a class of local people. I had no expertise in speech training, though I had had a few lessons as a boy in Bournemouth in what was then called elocution, but the Director of Adult Education for Battersea seemed to think that I would be a suitable person. He assumed that my being partially sighted would somehow make me an expert in using tapes as a means of instruction in class. I never, in fact, used these tapes. Tape recorders at that time were still large and clumsy machines which had to be plugged into the mains, and which were nearly always going wrong. I simply could not face carrying one of these on the bus every evening as far as Battersea and back. The students had been told that I was going to use tapes and rather liked the idea. I had to keep fobbing them off and told them I would use the tapes in a week or so, but I never did.

These students were a motley crew who wanted to improve their accents for a variety of reasons. They mostly spoke with the local intonation, not cockney, but the gentler speech of South London. I told them that I was willing to do my best for them, but there was no reason why they should be ashamed of their own speech habits. Some of them were immigrants from the Caribbean whose native language appeared to be Creole French. Others, I suppose, wanted to improve their speech for social reasons, and one highly intelligent man had a tongue which was rather too large for his mouth. He played the clarinet and said that part of his trouble was that he was unable to pronounce the name of that instrument properly. I tried to do my best for them. I would start each class with deep breathing exercises, which seemed to be the right thing to do, and I gave them little lines of verse to recite and memorise to improve their speech habits. Among my favourite exercises to remedy the London speech were Tennyson's "In the spring a young man's fancy lightly turns to thoughts of love", and Lewis Carroll's "Will you won't you, will you won't you, won't you join the dance?" I added to these a little poem by Swinburne, which he actually wrote in his sleep, beginning, "I hid my heart in a nest of roses, under the roses I hid my heart." Each of the students (the class included both men and women) really had a different problem, and I would spend a few minutes with each of them in turn, trying to help them. I asked any new member of the class to give a short speech about himself and his background. The information thus provided was helpful and it gave me a chance to listen to the student's speech and estimate what his or her problems were.

Leisenring took the opportunity of the long vacation at Ann Arbor to visit England, and looked me up. The two of us went up to Leeds together to see Geoffrey Hill, who had returned to teach at that university. I stayed with Arthur Creedy, who had now married for the second time. His new wife was rich. They had a splendid house with all sorts of modern conveniences and contraptions, and a beautiful music-room with his piano in it. Arthur, Geoffrey and I spent an evening in our old pastime of writing bouts-rimés sonnets. We wanted Leisenring to join in, but he was too diffident about his capacity to write verse. He should not have been – anybody can write a line of verse. So we allowed him to call out the rhymes, taken from the rhyme scheme of sonnets chosen at random from the *Oxford Book of English Verse*. Arthur's life in this new house did not last very long. His wife went to see the film *On the Beach* which envisaged the aftermath of a nuclear war in which the Antipodes was the last place to be affected by radioactive fallout. She was terrified by the film and decided they would be safer in New Zealand, insisting that Arthur apply for a teaching post there. He did find one, but the marriage seems to have come to an end, for the next time I met him in London he had acquired a third wife, from New Zealand. She was a beautiful, passionate woman, from whom I was later to receive a good deal of kindness, but obviously wrong for the gentle, scholarly Arthur, for that marriage eventually broke up too. Arthur's next teaching post was at the University of Northern Nigeria, and, while on leave in England, he arranged that I should visit this university, which had two colleges – one at Zaria and the other at Kano – as an external examiner.

My Battersea job had come to an end. The turning-point in my career occurred quite by chance. Strolling one evening in Notting Hill Gate, I ran into James Smith, who taught drama at the College of St Mark and St John, Chelsea. The college had a new Principal, Alex Evans, whom I had known in Leeds, where he had been a lecturer in the Education Department. James told me that the college had taken on a new English lecturer who was supposed to start in the autumn term, but for some reason he would be unable to take up the post until the spring. Would I be prepared to fill in for one term? Naturally, I agreed, and my teaching was so successful that I remained there until 1972, when the college moved out of London to Plymouth.

Before starting teaching at St Mark and St John I went to northern Nigeria for about a fortnight. I spent about one week at Zaria and another at Kano. Two of the lecturers in the English Department at Kano (of which Arthur was the head, holding the post of professor) were the poet Tony Harrison, who had been one of Arthur's students at Leeds, and Tony's friend, the Ulster poet James Simmons. The students were extremely lively and intelligent, though having considerable difficulty in understanding the culture represented in the English books they had to study – *Middlemarch*, for example. The dominant race of northern Nigeria are the Muslim Hausa, but the cities are largely occupied by the Ibo, who tend to be traders or hold professional positions. The Ibo are largely Christian, either Roman Catholic or Anglican. There is also a sect of African Christians known as the Cherubim and Seraphim. They practise daily baptism and for this reason find it convenient to live on the beach, digging holes in the sand for shelter, if necessary.

Before I left for Africa I received a message from the Nigerian High Commission asking me if I would take a sample of solder, needed for research purposes, to the Chemistry Department at Kano. I agreed and was told that an official from the Embassy, a Miss U. Bosman, would deliver it to me at the airport. No sooner had I acceded to this than I began to panic. Nigeria was, after all, not a very stable country, and if somebody wanted to blow up the plane it seemed a fairly obvious plan to plant a bomb disguised as a packet of solder on an unsuspecting passenger. I rang up the airport at London and the officials took my theory quite seriously. However, when I reached Heathrow, Miss Bosman, a large, formidable-looking African lady, duly arrived with the packet of solder. While sending my baggage on to the plane, I showed the packet to the official in charge and told him I had already rung the airport about it. He picked it up, sniffed it and then sent it through. I felt that this was not quite good enough, but when I complained he told me that my luggage had now been placed in the hold of the aircraft and if they were to unload it again and investigate the solder the flight would be held up by at least two hours. At this point I gave up and, taking my courage into my hands, entered the plane. Nothing happened. Well, if it had I would not be telling this story. We arrived in Nigeria shortly after sunrise, just as it was beginning to get hot. I heard the cries of strange birds flying overhead. Later I was told that they were grey hornbills. Arthur introduced me to the ornithologist Hilary Fry who worked at Zaria. He was engaged on a study of the bee-eaters of Africa, and he took me for a little country stroll around Zaria, identifying for me the various birds that we encountered.

I made my second visit the following year, but in the meantime dangerous political unrest had broken out in northern Nigeria. The Muslim Hausa had begun massacring the Ibo. The English expatriate community were not threatened but were appalled at what was going on around them. These massacres had not been widely reported in the British press, and I had known nothing about them. The expatriates seemed surprised that I should have come at all. They had some appalling stories to tell; for example, how a priest had been murdered by Hausas at the altar. Some British people had hidden Ibos in their gardens. Their kindly Hausa servants, who were so good with the children, would come in the morning and explain how they had been out killing Ibos the night before. When I arrived in Kano on this occasion, an Englishman who worked for the university showed me the city. This was a remarkable experience. He first drove me to a hill overlooking the city. It had been, anciently, a sacred hill, he explained, when the majority of the population was still animist. Down below, one could see the lights of Kano, and a faint sound of drumming reached our ears. My companion then took me into the old city, the Muslim quarter. It was a Thursday evening, the eve of the Muslim holy day. Muslim leaders were holding religious prayer sessions, chanting texts from the Koran in praise of God and his gifts to small groups of young men and boys. This was accompanied by African drumming and went on all night. We then drove through a part of the city which had been burnt during the rioting. Among the ruins, there were still bodies which had not been recovered. From there we passed outside the old mediaeval walls into the new city. This was all neon lights, dance halls and bars. A young man, an acquaintance of my guide, came up to us. He was called Laurence the Applikant because, it was said, he had once applied for a job in a bank. He wanted to know if he could introduce us to any nice girls, and so on. He was, of course, an Ibo. The Ibo are a volatile people, sometimes called the Irish of Africa. It was extraordinary to see these two totally different worlds side by side, and it was inevitable that there should have been an explosion.

During my stay at Kano I was aware at nights of a Tuareg watchman, playing his flute outside the building. The Tuaregs, a notably fierce tribe of desert Berber people, provide watchmen for city dwellers. The head of the tribe contacts householders and arranges suitable watchmen, armed with daggers and whips. This watchman's flute was made out of an old piece of piping and all through the night he repeated over and over again the same melodic phrase. I bought for my mother a specimen of Tuareg jewellery, a silver chain which, interestingly, had suspended from it a little cross. It was the Coptic cross and must somehow have made its way from further east and north to become a conventional motif in the decorative art of this Muslim people.

After my first visit to Nigeria, I began to lecture at the College of St Mark and St John. This teachers' training college had originally been founded in the nineteenth century to provide teachers for the Church schools. Its founder was Berkeley Coleridge, the second son of Samuel Taylor Coleridge. The name Berkeley represented Coleridge's conversion to that Irish bishop's idealistic Christianity. St Mark and St John's prepared students for external degrees at London University, so the teaching was of quite a high order. I was given a fairly free hand as to which authors I should lecture on. I think the students particularly appreciated my exposition of T. S. Eliot's *Four Quartets*, but I also lectured upon my other favourite English poets, including Spenser, Milton, Pope, Gray, Wordsworth and Coleridge. This was the sixties, the time of the hippy culture and the fashion for drugs. We had a certain amount of student unrest at St Mark and St John. But I think the students fomented it because they would have been hopelessly out of fashion if they had not, rather than from any real discontents. I sometimes noticed in their essays passages which seemed to be totally incoherent. I suspect that these may have been written under the influence of drugs. When I announced that I was going to give a course of lectures on Coleridge, an unusually large number of students turned up. They had been told that Coleridge was a junkie. Realising that this topic would get in the way of any serious consideration of Coleridge as a poet and a thinker, I devoted the first of my lectures, and that only, to a discussion of opium. After that we could get on with properly studying Coleridge's poetry and prose.

The head of the English Department at St Mark and St John was Thomas Blackburn, whom I had known fairly well for a number of years. He was a fine and imaginative, if uneven, poet, but in some ways a tormented personality. In his autobiographical work, *The Clip of Steel*, he has gone into the sources of his childhood difficulties. His grandfather, a clergyman, had done missionary work in Mauritius and had married a Creole lady from that country. Tom's father, also a clergyman, was apparently obsessed with the idea that what he called "the taint of colour" had been inherited by his two sons. As boys, they were scrubbed every day all over with lemon juice to lighten their skins and had to do "cheek drill" – tapping their cheeks with their hands – for the elder Blackburn had an idea that healthy English boys had nice rosy cheeks. From his appearance I would judge that Tom did, indeed, have some non-European blood, probably both

Indian and African. But this mixture of genes should be a matter for pride and gratitude, not for shame and guilt. The clip of steel of the title was a device that his father made Tom wear in bed in his adolescence to inhibit nocturnal erections. As a result of all this, Tom had a nervous breakdown in his student days and it is remarkable that he recovered from this sufficiently to have a very considerable career, as both a poet and a teacher. His younger brother, John Blackburn, became a successful writer of detective stories. Before writing *The Clip of Steel* Tom used some of the material for a proposed radio talk which was advertised in advance in the *Radio Times*. It was stated that the poet would talk about his relationship with his father. To Tom's horror, the producer of the programme received a letter from one of Tom's father's old parishioners. "The late Canon Blackburn", this parishioner wrote, "was a most helpful and charming man, and we are so glad that his son is paying him this tribute." Tom had no alternative but to cancel the talk.

Tom's poetry was in many ways intensely religious, though not quite orthodox from a Christian point of view. When he succeeded me as Gregory Fellow of Poetry in Leeds, he had become friendly with Wilson Knight, who had interested him in spiritualism. After my own experiences of those amateur séances at Oxford which I have described, I would not cross the road to attend a spiritualist meeting. There is, moreover, a real danger that those who become addicted to spiritualism may fall into the hands of sharks. There have been cases of spiritualist mediums employing private detectives to spy upon their clients so that the mediums may produce accounts of personal matters in their clients' lives which the latter would suppose could not have been acquired by any but supernatural means. Tom himself was no sucker for the spiritualist movement. He told me an amusing story concerning a woman medium whom he knew and whose work he admired. Tom had been at a meeting in which she addressed a young woman in the audience, saying that she had a message for the girl from her deceased mother. The message was the usual compilation of vague spiritual uplift and encouragement. Afterwards Tom said to the medium: "Surely her mother didn't say that." "Of course she didn't," replied the medium. "What she actually said was 'Why don't you snap out of it, you silly little bitch, and start being a woman for a change?' But I couldn't tell her that, could I?"

Tom's other passion was for rock-climbing and mountaineering, a passion which had also been possessed by William Bell and which had led to his death. For both these poets mountaineering seemed to be somehow a symbol of spiritual ascent. In the end, the pressures under which Tom had lived since childhood became too much for him. In spite of the support of his second wife, Peggy, he drank too much and also misused tranquilliser drugs, which a foolish doctor had prescribed for him much too freely. He died suddenly of a heart attack in his Welsh cottage. The day before, he had written his last poem, which dealt with the imminent prospect of death, and rebirth into another life.

Because of these pressures Tom had resigned his position at St Mark and St John. Ronald Banks now became the new head of the department. He was an excellent man and an Anglo-Saxon scholar. The London external degree course in English, fortunately, still demanded Anglo-Saxon. The Music Department boasted the composer Peter Dickinson. He had set, as a kind of oratorio, a semi-dramatic poem by Blackburn, *The Judas Tree*, which had a successful performance in Liverpool Cathedral. Peter was anxious that I too should collaborate with him, and he set a short poem of mine which, many years before, had been commissioned from me for Christmas by the BBC. Later on he asked me to write a libretto for an opera, originally planned as a children's opera. I knew the kind of composers that had influenced Peter and whom he admired. These included Eric Satie, Lord Berners and Francis Poulenc. This made me think that Peter might be happier with something a little more in the nature of fantasy and irony than *The Judas Tree*.

The libretto I wrote was entitled *The Unicorns*. At this time the London Zoo had been desperately trying to induce its giant panda to mate, and had introduced it to a possible spouse from China. In my libretto two countries, one a Western capitalist democracy and the other an Eastern totalitarian state, both send expeditions to Africa to capture a unicorn. The Western country employs the well-known device of entrapping a unicorn with a virgin. The Eastern country uses the more violent method whereby you play the unicorn and dodge behind a tree. The unicorn charges and his horn gets stuck in the trunk. A clown from the state circus is employed for this purpose. The two unicorns are brought together in the hope that they will mate, but the clown and virgin discover that there are plots against the unicorns. The Western capitalist who sponsored the expedition plans to exploit the unicorn's magical properties commercially, whereas the dictator who rules the Eastern country wishes to obtain from the unicorn a drug which will make him immortal. (There is some evidence that Stalin did so experiment, hoping to find a drug which would prolong his life indefinitely.) The Western virgin and the Eastern clown, of course, fall in love but the political systems of their two countries prevent their union. The story ends with their escaping on the backs of the unicorns to the mythical island of St Brendan in the western ocean. There the unicorns can find sanctuary, whereas the human couple are sent back to our world to try to persuade people to behave more sensibly. Peter expressed himself delighted with this libretto, but owing to pressure of work he only wrote the music for a couple of songs. Later, Elisabeth Söderström recorded these. He now appears to have left his Satie–Poulenc phase behind him, and perhaps *The Unicorns* would no longer be a suitable libretto for him. He told me recently that *The Unicorns* was the best opera never written. There is, of course, an opera house in heaven and *The Unicorns* must be in its repertory. Other works which are regularly given there include Verdi's *King Lear*, Mussorgsky's *Salammbô*, Debussy's *The Fall of the House of Usher*, Elgar's *The Spanish Lady* (based on a play by Ben Jonson), and also that sequel to *The Magic Flute* for which Goethe sketched a libretto but could never find a composer to set it.

In 1970 Alex Evans retired from the post of Principal of St Mark and St John. At that time a plan was mooted to construct a ring road round London which would have cut right through the grounds of the college. The new Principal, who hated London, immediately drew up plans to move the college to a provincial location. In fact, he did not remain Principal for very long, but had to retire owing to ill health. But his successor continued with this plan. He exhibited many of the trendy qualities of the period. In discussing the English syllabus, he said to Tom Blackburn: "You must admit that, compared to Karl Marx and Max Weber, Charles Dickens and George Eliot are very small beer." Eventually, it was decided to move the college to Plymouth, where it would be associated with Exeter University. The degree courses were to be dropped. This plan pleased neither the members of the English Department nor those of the French Department, and most of them resigned *en masse*. Furthermore the new Principal decided that there should not be a chapel in the new college, merely a dedicated room. St Mark and St John had a fine chapel and a good tradition of choral services. As these would now come to an end, the Music Department also resigned. However, this department went down with flying colours, putting on a production of an opera by Michael William Balfe (the composer of *The Bohemian Girl*) entitled *A Daughter of St Mark*. The heroine, I might state, was a daughter of the Serene Republic of Venice, not of the Evangelist. I had no wish to go to Plymouth. In spite of my years spent in America and Egypt I had become a deeply addicted Londoner. My experience of provincial life in Leeds did not tempt me to experiment with it again.

During my last year at St Mark and St John a student introduced himself as Nicholas Kollerstrom. He was the elder half-brother of my godson, Julian, who was now, it turned out, a junior lecturer in mathematics at the University of Kent at Canterbury. This gave me the opportunity of getting in touch with Julian, which I ought to have done long before. He was, I was glad to discover, being prepared for confirmation by the chaplain of his university, but he was a rather sad and lonely young man. In spite of his good looks he seemed to find it difficult to make friends, or to enter into relationships with women. He played the viola, though not very well, and sang in an amateur choir, but this did not seem to have gained him many friends. I was shocked to find what a lot of daft and superstitious ideas he seemed to have got from his father, Oscar Kollerstrom. One day when Julian came to visit me, a friend of mine, who happened to be there, had with him a copy of *Old Moore's Almanac* which he had bought for fun. Julian took it seriously and became immediately engrossed in its predictions, and its advertisements for quack and magical remedies.

I invited Julian to lunch with me once in each term. I tried to wean him away from the false ideas by which he was hag-ridden, but I had to do this delicately because I did not wish to intrude on his real affection and loyalty to his father. Oscar Kollerstrom had now left Julian's mother and was living with another woman to whom Julian seemed to relate more strongly than he did to his natural mother. Oscar died some years after I had re-established relations with Julian. I attended the funeral, which was presided over by a bishop of the Liberal Catholic Church, and felt very much the same emotions as Dorothy Sayers had described to me in her account of an Anthroposophist funeral. After the ceremony Julian and Oscar's companion went straight to her house where they engaged in a séance with some of their friends. They contacted the spirit of Oscar who informed them that he had already reached the Seventh Heaven. Even they thought he had got there pretty quickly. It was less than a year after this that Oscar's companion took her own life, wishing to be with her lover. This left poor Julian even more isolated.

After a few years, I was shocked to receive a phone call from Nicholas to say that his brother had committed suicide. Julian had taken an overdose of sleeping pills, but, as these apparently did not work quickly enough, had stabbed himself repeatedly with a sharp carving knife. There must have been a great deal of suppressed aggression in him which he never showed openly. It has been alleged that Julian's suicide resulted from a curse delivered against Oscar by Aleister Crowley. I find this a shocking and horrible idea and would reject it absolutely. There were many people who were to blame, not least of all myself, for not having continued to keep in touch with the Kollerstrom family after Julian's baptism.

The years in which I was teaching at St Mark and St John roughly coincided with the decade of the sixties, when I was in my forties. It was a difficult decade in which to enter middle age. There was a real alienation between the young and their elders. Student unrest, the Vietnam war and the threat of nuclear war led to the formation of a number of protest groups, and the revival of Marxist ideology, though the dissident groups of the time usually adopted the banners of Maoism or Trotskyism or anarchism. Stalinism was dismissed as merely a disguised form of capitalism (which it was not). Although communism had been on its way out when I had been at Oxford, I had sometimes found myself under pressure from Marxists. I made some study of Marxist philosophy, no doubt very superficially, but enough to detest it. The oldest trap of all – "John, it's intelligent, independent people like yourself whom we need in the Party" – was, of course, offered to me. I was deeply unhappy at seeing these Marxist ideologies resurfacing in the sixties. Those who were involved in them had much goodness of heart and were full of goodwill, but I felt that in the end these protest movements could only be to the aid and comfort of the Soviet Union which posed a continual threat. If a Third World War had broken out the odds are that Western Europe would have been overrun by the Soviet Union, and that Britain would have become an advance base for missiles aimed at the United States. We would then, doubtless, have been bombed flat with missiles from America. I never supposed that I would live to see, some twenty-five or so years later, the total collapse of the Soviet system. Mikhail Gorbachev simply opened a window, and the whole structure, worm-eaten from top to bottom with corruption and founded on a false philosophy, collapsed almost overnight, leaving God knows what mess and muddle to be cleared up.

Besides this political ferment the sixties was the age of an emerging pop culture and the cult of drugs. The hideous music of the Beatles permeated the atmosphere, and their icons were everywhere. John Lennon, it will be recalled, issued an album, on the sleeve of which was a full frontal nude photograph of himself. He made a tactical error in this – a god should always withhold some element of mystery from his devotees. Passing by my local pub one evening I heard two young men, standing outside, discussing this album. "He makes beautiful music," said one of them, "but his cock is no bigger than yours or mine." Some years ago, on a visit to New York, I was shown the garden which Yoko Ono had created in memory of John Lennon, not far from the place where he had been shot. Yoko had bought up a piece of waste ground and laid it out in the Japanese manner with ginkgo trees and a small pond in which lived a beaver. This garden had an atmosphere of charm and peace, and made me feel more kindly towards two people whom I had previously regarded as representing the worst aspects of our contemporary culture. But I was sorry for the beaver, a social animal, all on its own in a little green patch in the middle of an urban desert from which no escape was possible.

I had the pleasure of meeting the Beat poet Allen Ginsberg in 1967 when he was visiting this country. A mutual friend introduced us and we spent an evening in the garden of a pub, together with other friends. I found him intelligent and, rather to my surprise, a great admirer of Wordsworth's poetry (Wordsworth is always a touchstone). At the end of the evening Ginsberg suddenly broke into a Buddhist chant, accompanying himself on some small musical instrument. I am not sure whether it was a miniature accordion or a portative organ. I found this chanting embarrassing, but perhaps it was his religious duty to engage in it at that hour of the evening. I was not feeling my best. I was grieving for the recent tragic death of a close and much loved friend.

The Beat poets had their apogee in a great poetry reading organised at the Albert Hall by Ginsberg and others. One of the poets who took part in that event, and one whom Ginsberg regarded as the best British poet of his generation, was Harry Fainlight, the brother of the poet Ruth Fainlight. I did not meet Harry until the late 1980s, and a very sad figure he had become. He had experimented with drugs, as was the fashion of the decade of his youth, and they had turned him into a hopeless schizophrenic. He would come to see me and tell me of some vast, undefined conspiracy which was directed at the human race in general, and himself in particular. He was not the first person so afflicted to come and visit me in this way. There seems to be little point in reasoning with such unhappy people. One can only hope that by listening patiently, and not showing that one believes that what they are saying is nonsense, some of their terrible tension may be slightly eased. But I let Harry Fainlight down. He had come to see me two or three times. On the last occasion, as I was letting him out of the front door of the house in which I lived, my friend Guthrie MacKie, who lived nearby, came along the other side of the road and called out a greeting to me. This immediately aroused Harry's suspicions. "Who was that?" he said. I replied, "That is my close friend, Guthrie MacKie." But I let a little note of irritation into my voice. Harry Fainlight never came to see me again. It was clear that he thought I had joined the conspiracy. His death was tragic and mysterious. His body was found in a cottage in which he was living alone in Wales. It was discovered so long after his death that there was no way of telling how he had died, whether by disease or, possibly, by his own hand.

The psychodelic, or hallucinatory, drugs such as LSD were also in fashion in the sixties. Some serious investigators at first thought that they might have a real function in showing how the mind works, but the dangers to which they might lead soon came to be realised. There were cases of people leaping out of windows thinking they could fly.

278

Rosalind Heywood was interested in conducting experiments with LSD from the point of view of her researches. She told me that she would never press it upon anyone but would be happy if anybody volunteered. She had given the drug to a young poet from Cambridge, but he had been a great disappointment to her. All he could see, or seem to see, under the influence of the drug was "an infinitude of fishes". I suspect that whatever visionary imagination he might, as a poet, have possessed had been eroded by the Cambridge criticism in which he had been instructed. For my part I did not feel disposed to volunteer for the experiment, though I dare say Rosalind would have liked me to have done so.

On the whole it seemed to me that the sixties was a disastrous decade, but the general breaking down of traditional taboos in this period did at least result in the abolition of capital punishment for murder and the decriminalisation of homosexual acts between consenting adults.

A year before my teaching at St Mark and St John had to come to an end, fortune came to my aid. John Jones, one of the circle of friends I had made at Merton during my fourth year at Oxford, suggested that I might do some teaching in Merton where he was now Reader in English. It is a custom in Oxford for lecturers and readers to be able to assign some of their pupils for part of the time to suitably qualified people (I had, after all, got a first) to enable the dons to give more time to research. Accordingly, I began teaching in Merton. I normally did one day a week, but every three years John Jones would take a term off in order to engage in research. He is the author of excellent books on Wordsworth, Keats, Aeschylus and Dostoevsky, and is at present working on one on Shakespeare. On these occasions I would come up for two days, spending the night in college, where I dined, and was made a temporary member of the Senior Common Room. I was told that the guest room I occupied on these visits had been once occupied by Andrew Lang. The founder of the Folklore Society and the author who had influenced some of my youthful ideas seemed to be a kindly presence. I had therefore found my way back to Oxford, after some thirty-five years, by a circuitous route.

I discovered things had changed less than I might have expected. There was more pressure on the students to work hard than there had been in my day. The students themselves were more mature in many respects, but had read less. The syllabus remained much as it had been except that the study of twentieth-century literature was now included. I have already said that I am not at all happy about the inclusion of twentieth-century literature in the syllabus, but if it is going to be taught I might as well teach it as anybody else. Not long ago I found myself sitting at a dinner party opposite a young man who reminded me that he had been one of my pupils. "The last time we met," he said, "you were talking about the women writers of the Restoration period. It had nothing whatever to do with the syllabus." This tendency to believe that the only learning worth acquiring is what can be directly related to a syllabus is understandable in modern students, but nevertheless one should be on one's guard against it. In any case if he had followed up my suggestions and read a little in this field and been able to introduce his knowledge of it at his viva voce examination it would probably have stood him in good stead, especially if there had been a feminist on the examining board.

I continued this Oxford teaching for nearly twenty years. In 1991, however, John Jones retired. Unfortunately, I was unable to finish that last term and say a formal goodbye to my students. I travelled up to Oxford by train from Paddington station, and as I was quite blind, I relied on the help of British Rail officials to get me on and off the train. One day, as we were approaching Oxford station, the lady ticket collector suggested to a young man sitting opposite me, who was also getting off at Oxford, that he might help me out of the station. Oxford station is in process of reconstruction and one had to go down a flight of roughly improvised steps to the main road where one can pick up a taxi. It turned out that the young man, in fact a sixteen-year-old boy, was going up to Merton for an open day, and hoping to enter the college to read English in two years' time. This naturally interested me and we got into lively conversation, so much so that he forgot to warn me when we approached the steps. Consequently, I fell right down them, breaking my hip, and was taken to the Radcliffe Infirmary where I remained for about a couple of weeks. I had messages of sympathy from my students, and visits from my Oxford friends. John Jones and his wife came to see me, as did John Wain. He now lives at Wolvercote and I had often stayed with him. I received visits from the poet Sally Purcell and her friend William Leaf, and also from Mustafa Badawi and his wife. Mustafa was my old colleague from Egypt who now teaches Arabic at Oxford. In the common room at Merton I had made friends with Tom Braun, the Reader in Ancient History, and he also was kind enough to come and see me.

I was now no longer living in the house that had belonged to Wrey Gardiner. Some years previously he had sold it and, having got a pension from the Royal Literary Fund, had retired with his new mistress and their Alsatian dog to a council estate on the outskirts of London. I did not visit him there, but I gather that they lived in some squalor. Some years after that he died. As an unfurnished tenant, I had security of tenure. The new landlord, a retired army officer and a gentleman, made it quite clear that he would be only too pleased if I would move. Gawsworth had no such security, but, as he could have made difficulties, the landlord offered him a thousand pounds if he would vacate his room. And this he was happy to take. Unfortunately, however, Gawsworth never found another place to live. He had to stay with various friends for as long as they would put up with him. Eventually he died in hospital still writing poetry, though one of his last poems began: "Poetry, I hate you." His was a real talent which had been ruined by too early success and over-adulation, and over-investment in that talent, as well as by over-indulgence in alcohol. I continued my unfurnished tenancy under the new landlord for several years. Eventually, I was made an offer which really seemed reasonable under the circumstances, enough to put down as a deposit on a mortgage on a flat only a few yards away. That is where I now live. I did not want to move out of the Westbourne Grove district. My eyesight was now gone but I could find my way around. The local shopkeepers and others knew me and were helpful.

Some years before, I had once more been in touch with Arthur Creedy. He had left the University of Northern Nigeria and eventually returned to New Zealand, where his third marriage broke up. In his fourth wife, Mary, he found at last the partner he needed and deserved. She combined gentleness and strength. She was a sculptor, specialising in religious work, and an Anglican. The Creedys came to England, and I had the pleasure of staying with them in Cornwall, where they rented a house. Arthur had now retired from his career. For a time they lived in Italy, in Anticoli Corrado, a village in the Alban Hills. They invited me to stay with them there for a fortnight. I had never been to Italy except for one overnight stay, but it had always exercised my imagination ever since I started reading Dante and Leopardi at Oxford.

Anticoli had once been an artists' village. The beauty of the landscape and the quality of the light had attracted artists when landscape painting was fashionable. Many English painters of some note had resided in the village and had presented some of their work to the church. This possibly made the inhabitants more used to foreigners and more disposed to be friendly than might otherwise have been the case. The Creedys had resided there for some time, and Mary, especially, had become an active supporter of the local church. Most of the other members of its congregation were elderly widows, *le vedove*. The men of the village, who were all communists, were convinced that the priest, Don Vittorio, who was over eighty years old, had secret passages from his presbytery to the houses of all the widows.

281

These men never went to church themselves but were pleased that their wives and mothers should go, and that their children should serve mass. This the children did in a lively way, being soundly cuffed by Dom Vittorio whenever they got out of line. There was an American expatriate residing at Anticoli who earned his living by teaching English to the Italians. He introduced me to the men of the village at an evening in the local tavern. They were extraordinarily friendly and the oldest of them wanted to kiss me. I was told that some years later I was still talked about in Anticoli and referred to as "Il gigante", for I am unusually tall. The Creedys occupied a flat in a block. The woman who owned these flats also ran a restaurant on the ground floor and sent cooked meals up to us. It was Eastertime, though in those high hills still very cold. Indeed, it actually snowed on Good Friday. Mary, explaining that we were Anglicans, asked Dom Vittorio if he would allow us to take communion in his church. He waved his arms about and said, "God is everywhere," which we took as an affirmative reply. As we left the church after the Good Friday devotions, all the little boys of the village were lined up outside, hitting with cudgels the stone wall which surrounded the churchyard. It was obviously great fun and I asked what they were doing. They were beating Judas Iscariot.

We made some interesting excursions in the neighbourhood. The one which most impressed itself on my memory was a visit to what is supposed to be the site of Horace's villa in the Sabine Hills. You can just see the ground-plan of the villa, which long after Horace's time became a monastery. I noticed one small ceramic tile with a simple geometrical design. This, I thought, with its classic good taste, must have been chosen by Horace. Just above the villa was a fountain, springing from the top of a hill and overshadowed by holm-oaks. This is the Bandusian spring on which Horace wrote one of his most beautiful poems. Before I came, Arthur had sent me a leaf from one of these holm-oaks. I had attached the leaf with adhesive tape inside my copy of Horace's poems. We also visited the Benedictine monastery of Subiarco, founded by St Benedict before the greater and better-known one of Monte Cassino.

Eventually the Creedys returned to Britain and settled in an old farmhouse (National Trust property, I think) beside a loch in Dumfriesshire. This farmhouse had a beautiful situation, and a statue of St John the Baptist by Henry Moore had been placed by the local landlord on an island in the loch. The Creedys invited me for a visit. The occasion was an impromptu fancy dress party, the only participants consisting of Arthur and Mary, together with an English neighbour of theirs and his wife. The theme was to be the troubadours. Arthur and Mary dressed as Héloïse and Abelard, while their friends came as Richard Coeur-de-Lion and his mother, Eleanor of Aquitaine, the great patroness of the troubadours. Richard himself was also something of a troubadour. I decided to go as Pierre Vidal. Readers of Ezra Pound will remember that this troubadour poet fell in love with a lady called Loba (wolf). Dressing up in a wolf skin, he had himself hunted by her dogs. I had made myself look as mediaeval as possible with the aid of a coloured shirt and a Japanese kimono, and by rolling up the bottoms of my trousers and tucking them inside my socks. Arthur and Mary had made a little lute for me. As a final touch, I had hired a wolf's mask from a theatrical costumiers. I ought not really to have done this. The Creedys had intended that we should not buy anything for our costumes, but I had not been aware of this prohibition.

Arthur was to live only a few years longer. Cancer was diagnosed, though after an operation he had a period of remission. I hope his end was not too painful or too prolonged. He spent his last years listening to his beloved collection of gramophone records and learning to play his newly acquired treasure, a harpsichord.

I have already stated that I had become dependent on readers. I had learnt Braille at Worcester College for the Blind but I had not reached a high proficiency in it. In my present circumstances I found I was not pressured to relearn it. Braille is rather a clumsy system and with modern electronic devices, such as recorded books and tapes, there is not much necessity for it. I had also learnt touch-typing, but in the intervening years had got into the bad habit of looking at the keyboard, and when I really needed touch-typing found myself unable to relearn it. Sometime in the 1960s I had run into an old acquaintance, Alan Whiteside, and his wife Carol. Their marriage subsequently broke up. At this time, Carol had just had her first baby and Alan was working as a stagehand at the Mermaid Theatre. Carol was to have two daughters, Sarah and Rebecca, for both of whom I stood godfather. They were baptised in the Roman Catholic Church, but the priest, who was oecumenically minded and liberal in his views, made no difficulties about my standing godfather as long as it was not too widely known. Carol offered to type for me. I would call on her most evenings and she would type at my dictation. It was under these circumstances that I undertook my poem *Artorius*. This is a poem of considerable length, but which I hesitated to call an epic, on the Arthurian legend. This, the Matter of Britain, has haunted English poets as a subject for an epic. Spenser's *The Faerie Queene* is partly an Arthurian epic, and Milton and Dryden both thought of handling this material, but abandoned it or never got around to it. Pope's projected epic was not to be an Arthurian one, but was to be on the older legend of the settlement of Britain by Brutus the Trojan.

Pope's opening lines, written rather surprisingly in blank verse, and quite good blank verse at that, survive. Later, Tennyson took up the subject, though using it for a series of idylls rather than an epic proper. Even T. S. Eliot's *The Waste Land* might be regarded as an Arthurian poem.

When I was eighteen I read Robert Graves's novel, *Count Belisarius*. This deals with the Byzantine general Belisarius, who in the reign of Justinian reconquered Italy for the Roman Empire. The main source of Graves's novel was Belisarius' contemporary, Procopius. In his preface, Graves remarked that if we had learnt about King Arthur (who would have been roughly contemporary with Belisarius) from an historian like Procopius, instead of from the writers of romances, we might have a very different picture of the British leader – as a general trying to preserve what was left of Roman civilisation in western Britain against the barbarian incursion of the Anglo-Saxons. This remark captured my imagination. It was something of a commonplace in the late 1930s that our own situation might not be altogether dissimilar to that of the Romans of the late empire, facing the barbarian threat. I began to read up the history of the sixth century in Gibbon and others, and I also investigated the sources and development of the Arthurian legend. I had read Geoffrey of Monmouth's *History of the Kings of Britain* at the age of about fourteen, when I was at Bembridge. Later, I came across the Welsh sources in Lady Charlotte Guest's translation of the *Mabinogion*. Now that Carol offered to type for me regularly every evening, it seemed the moment to embark on my Arthuriad.

The problem, as I saw it, of writing a long poem with a narrative content in the twentieth century is that one must avoid at all costs producing a novel in verse. From the beginning of the nineteenth century, narrative poetry has gradually given place to the novel and the short story. The poems of George Crabbe written in the early nineteenth century can seriously compete with anything in the way of short stories composed at that period. The same might be said of such narratives as Wordsworth's "Michael". But Scott abandoned his early verse romances for the historical novel, and Byron, had he lived, might have followed a similar course. Browning's *The Ring and the Book*, considered as a verse novel, is far in advance of any prose narrative of the nineteenth century – indeed, possibly of anything written up to the time of Virginia Woolf. But today one lives in an age when the novel and the short story have achieved enormous technical sophistication. Straightforward narrative verse, that written by John Masefield, for example, cannot possibly compete with the modern short story. For this reason I constructed my poem on an elaborate plan, partly derived from James Joyce. The work must be cyclical in structure, not a linear narrative. Furthermore, it should employ different verse or prose forms for different sections, and have a symbolic superstructure – such as Joyce used in *Ulysses* and in *Finnegans Wake* – to which each section of the poem should refer. This would control the material and prevent it from getting out of hand. The cyclical structure of my *Artorius* was based on the twelve signs of the zodiac. Other structures which I employed included the nine Muses, the twelve Olympian deities, and the twelve labours of Hercules. By this means I hoped to achieve something that could not be mistaken for yet another unsuccessful verse novel. It took me rather more than six months to complete my scheme. The Oxford University Press, who had been my publishers for a number of years, turned the poem down when I sent it to them, but, with the support of Kathleen Raine, I arranged for its publication in a limited edition by The Enitharmon Press, then owned by Alan Clodd (a grandson of the great Victorian rationalist, David Clodd, who, among other things, founded the Omar Khayyám Society).

Artorius was well received and I think it was mainly on its merits that I was nominated for the Queen's Gold Medal for Poetry. This medal, which was instituted on the advice of the then Poet Laureate, John Masefield, in the 1930s, is a rather special award. Its first recipient was Laurence Whistler and its second W. H. Auden. This was an enlightened choice for the period. During the war years the presentation of the medal lapsed, but was resumed after hostilities ceased and was awarded to Andrew Young, an older poet whom both traditionalists and modernists could respect.

My receiving the medal involved a private audience with the Queen, to whom I was presented by the then Poet Laureate, John Betjeman. Betjeman and I were ushered into Her Majesty's presence in a small drawing-room in Buckingham Palace, and had about half an hour's conversation with her. The Queen began by asking me how I set about writing my poems. It was fairly obvious to me that, with the best intentions in the world, poetry was not really her kind of thing. But we managed to switch the conversation to more general topics. The Queen had recently returned from a Commonwealth tour and she spoke of the difficulties of adjusting herself after such wide travelling to the British time zone. "But if one did not," she said, "one would have to receive the ministers in the small hours of the morning. If it were Winston that wouldn't have mattered." This led to a general conversation about foreign travel. Betjeman had plenty of experience of visiting Commonwealth countries, while I could only refer to my Egyptian experience. I made it clear that I had remained in Egypt during the Suez crisis because I thought that staying at my post was the best way of serving my country. "I am sure that was so," said the Queen. I also ventured to suggest that there was still much goodwill for the British among the common people of Egypt. They had much more difficulty in getting on with the Russians. But, not wishing to say anything controversial, I added that I was sure that the Russians were a great people when one got to know them. "The trouble is", said the Queen, "that you never do get to know them." I had been told that the Queen was a good conversationalist. She certainly had a most friendly and relaxed manner, very different from the persona which is all too often projected in her public speeches when she uses scripts that have obviously been very carefully written for her.

The medal itself is an object of some value. It is a gold disc, about two and a half inches in diameter. You cannot wear it because there is no ribbon, or anything to which a ribbon could be attached. It has a portrait of the Queen on one side, and on the other a design of a woman holding a flame (I suppose she is the Muse) by Edmond Dulac. I am proud to have received this medal. Other recent recipients have included Philip Larkin, Stevie Smith, Ted Hughes and Kathleen Raine. Stevie Smith said that her interview with the Queen was rather like going to see the headmistress. After my audience with the Queen, Betjeman took me, and a friend who had accompanied me, back to his flat in Chelsea. Betjeman amused himself by pulling books of poetry at random from his shelves, choosing a quotation and asking me if I could identify the author. The first volume which he picked out was by the Irish poet William Allingham and I think I acquitted myself fairly well by identifying this not too widely known poet.

Some years later I was to be nominated for the OBE. To receive this one goes up with a batch of other worthy recipients and has a brief moment of converse with the Queen while she pins the order on to one. She asked me if I was still writing poetry. "It becomes an ingrained habit, Ma'am," I replied. She was observed to smile.

16

Blindness

It was in 1978 that I eventually became totally blind. This was shortly before my sixtieth birthday. I have already told how I had suffered from congenital glaucoma from a very early age, had virtually lost the sight of my right eye when I was eighteen, and had had to have that eye removed in 1956. The oculists who had treated me when I was a boy had wished to discourage me from reading, which is one of the reasons why I was sent to Bembridge School with its emphasis on arts and crafts. But, although I had a certain liking for painting and drawing, I was quite hopeless at carpentry and other crafts, and the very fact of my bad eyesight actually encouraged me to read. It made cricket and football and other outdoor games a perfect torture. Because I more or less had the sight of only one eye, it was difficult for me to judge distances, and any kind of achievement in these fields was out of the question. I detested games and avoided them on all occasions. Whenever I listen to the morning news on the radio, I rush to turn off the sports news when it comes on, muttering dark things about "the opium of the people". Participation in sports was compulsory at Bembridge and one was subject to punishments, usually impositions, if one did not turn up for games. At one point I succeeded in persuading the oculist to give me a note, saying I was excused from playing cricket as a hard cricket ball might smash my glasses. He had forgotten that he had prescribed me a very thick, very unbecoming, unbreakable pair of glasses specifically for this purpose. On the basis of this exemption, I refused to turn up for football games as well. I was punished, but I found the punishment less tedious than the game itself. After a bit I won. The authorities either relinquished the struggle or believed that the prohibition which I had told them applied to cricket also extended to football.

But the deterioration of my eyesight in 1961 came as a shock to me. For the next twenty years I was putting up a struggle for independence, and was often, I know, rude and ungracious in refusing proffered help from others; for example, in assisting me across roads. But this was not just pride. I found the experience of being taken across a road by somebody else quite alarming. It is my own custom to wait at the side of the road, listening carefully until I am absolutely certain that no traffic is within earshot, and then I cross at a brisk pace. When people help they grab one by the arm and rush across the road when one is perfectly aware that a bus is approaching. One of these occasions had an unfortunate and, I fear, tragic consequence. An elderly lady, who lived in the next house to mine and whom I had greeted on several occasions, offered to take me across the road. I could not refuse her, but we rushed across the road and both fell over the kerb on the other side. She was unable to get up and I had to recross the road to get to a shop which had a telephone in order to ring for an ambulance. I very much feared that she had broken her thigh. At any rate she never returned from the hospital. As I did not know her name I was unable to make enquiries or visit her.

In the summer of 1978 my eye became infected and irritable. I consulted my doctor who prescribed an antibiotic, but as it did not clear up the trouble I was sent for a further examination at a Marylebone hospital specialising in eye diseases. It turned out that there was, in fact, no sight remaining in my left eye. I was quite unaware of this deterioration because the imagination creates what it thinks it should see. If I were standing on the kerb waiting to cross and I heard a bus coming I would "see" that bus. This effect is not generally understood. My mother once told me of her godmother to whom, in her girlhood, she had been much attached. This lady went blind in her later years, but fell into the hands of a Christian Scientist practitioner who persuaded her that he was curing her of blindness. This is all too easy. One tells somebody they can see something; they will believe you and think they are seeing it, if only in a faint and shadowy way. This probably accounts for many alleged miracles at public faith-healing sessions. A boy who was a contemporary of mine at Worcester College for the Blind told me how he was taken to a public demonstration of faith-healing. The minister who was conducting the meeting laid his hands on my friend and said: "Now you can see, can't you?" The blind boy was so embarrassed by the situation that he replied, "Yes, of course I can," in order to get away as quickly as possible.

Before the operation to remove my left eye was performed, I had already made plans to revisit America. I had received an award and had decided to go there for a holiday, with my friend Guthrie MacKie as companion. We spent a week in New York where our friends Robin Prising and Willy Coakly had booked a room for us in a hotel in Washington Square. It was one of the very few moderately priced hotels still available in New York. Most of the other smaller hotels had been taken over by the city authority to give temporary housing for the homeless. Washington Square seemed to have come down a lot in the world since it gave its name to one of Henry James's best-known novels. In fact if one visits New York one notices how the world of Henry James's early novels and Edith Wharton's *House of Mirth* has totally vanished. The hotel in which we stayed was infested with cockroaches which seemed to have learnt how to use the lift, for they were always travelling up and down in it. On arrival, we were met at the airport by Robin and Willy and took a taxi to the hotel. Unfortunately, there had been some muddle about the booking and we had to wait for almost an hour before the manager could be found to straighten this out. We were tired by our journey and wanted to sit down, but there were no seats or chairs in the lobby. We were informed that, if there had been, drunks and down-and-outs would have colonised the lobby and sat on them.

After a week in New York, I made a return visit to Ann Arbor where I met Leisenring again. It was the last time I was to meet him, for he was to die a few years later. Arrangements had been made for me to give a lecture to the students. I did not want to give a conventional academic lecture, but one which would have a wide-ranging scope. I chose as my title "Four Poets, Four Cities". The poets and cities were James Joyce and Dublin, T. S. Eliot and London, Cavafy and Alexandria, and Apollinaire and Paris. I selected these because not only were the poets four of my favourite authors, but the cities they celebrated were all places I knew and had stayed in, if not lived in, for some while. Unfortunately, at the time scheduled for my lecture my infected eye was giving me a great deal of pain. However, I think I got through the lecture with some credit. Afterwards the members of the English Department took me to a restaurant for dinner, but I was violently sick afterwards and could not eat any solid food for the rest of the two days remaining to me in America. I was given temporary relief at the university hospital. Fortunately, as a former member of the university and a visiting lecturer, I was not charged anything for this.

It is still quite easy for me to forget that I have not seen things which have been described to me; for instance, if I go to the theatre, someone has only to mention the sets or the costumes for me to have a most vivid impression of them. There also appears to be what is known as "blind sight", that is to say that the visual cortex of the brain is somehow aware at least of light and darkness, even though the eyes themselves cannot see. It is possible that the pineal gland, which is considered to be the relic of a third eye, may play a part in this. I am not certain whether I have experienced this phenomenon, but I certainly have had a very strong impression that this has been the case. If I wake up in the middle of the night the room seems to be dark, but, of course, I know whether it ought to be light or dark, anyway, if I am aware of the time. After the diagnosis of the loss of sight in my left eye, it too was removed by an operation. I had already been provided with one artificial eye for my right socket and was now given another for my left. I remember, on returning to my flat, switching the electric light on and off. I had the distinct impression that I could see whether it was on or not, but this could not, in fact, have been the case. I have been very fortunate in that, over the years, I have slowly been able to adapt to blindness. I experience it, as David Wright said in a review of my *Collected Poems*, "more as an inconvenience than as a tragedy". It must be terrible for those who in mature life lose their eyesight suddenly, for example in an accident, and who therefore have to learn, with difficulty, to adapt. But this has not been my fate. I have also been very lucky in the help I have received from various friends. Some read to me regularly and others deal with my correspondence. If I have not mentioned their names in these pages they will understand that it is not through any lack of gratitude.

I do not live in a world of total blackness. I have already spoken of the part the imagination plays in re-creating the world it knows to be there, but there is something other than this, of which I have not been able to find an explanation. In front of my left eye I have a continual display of regular, rectangular patterns within a roughly triangular frame, somewhat resembling an heraldic shield. These shapes vary in colour from pale yellow, through golden-orange to red, or from green to blue, and at their brightest have a beauty and purity scarcely to be found in nature. They are always there, but are affected by my physiology. If I am tired or hungry they are much more vivid than if I am rested. They are not in any sense dream images, and have no symbolic content. Something is going on in the visual cortex of the right side of my brain. I have been told by my friend John Newell, who is a science editor on the BBC World Service, that something of the same kind was recorded when electrodes were experimentally planted in the brain of a woman who had lost her sight. In the 1950s experiments were conducted with LSD, before the potentially dangerous effects of this drug were fully realised. It was supposed that one could bypass the long-drawn-out and tedious method of understanding the psyche through analysis. I was informed at that time that, after hallucinatory images had been produced in the brain, there was a final reduction to a stage when only geometrical forms remained and we were left with the simplest constituents of perception. I do not know whether this has anything to do with the phenomenon which I experience or not, but I must repeat that this is quite definitely a physiological, not a psychological, phenomenon. In front of the rectangular coloured forms there are a number of little moving dots, known as *mouches volantes*. They appear to be moving in a circle, and this movement seems to be either clockwise or anticlockwise. I experienced these "little flies" before I lost my sight, even in early childhood. They worried me and I asked doctors about them, but none seemed to be able to give any satisfactory explanation. I have heard it suggested that what I was seeing were the blood corpuscles circulating in the retina of the eye itself. This, however, cannot be the case since both my eyes have been removed, and I still experience the moving dots. During my childhood, they were often associated with tiredness. The specks often came on when I was in church, as a result of standing for periods of time or rising from a kneeling to a standing position. In my last year at Oxford when I was, as it happened, under considerable emotional strain, I attended a performance of Beethoven's *Missa Solemnis* in the Sheldonian Theatre. As I was listening to the music I suddenly became aware of what I at first thought were drops of rain, and supposed that the dome of the Sheldonian might have sprung a leak, but it was a severe attack of these little moving specks.

With the aid of a stick I can find my way happily around the streets where I live, within a radius of half a mile or so. I have lived in the same address, or near it, for thirty years now. I am glad of someone to guide me, but I like to be as free as possible, and a slight touch on my elbow is all I need. Steps are a problem. I like to be told when I am approaching them, and it is very important to know whether the steps are going up or down. It is quite unnecessary and, to me, very irritating for someone who is guiding a blind person to count the steps. I really do not know what this is supposed to do for the blind person. All that he wants to know is where the steps begin and end.

I have left this discussion of blindness to a final chapter. I suspect that the reader will be more interested in hearing about it from me than I have myself in giving the information. Blindness carries a high psychological charge. It was, after all, the punishment of Oedipus, and, in both biblical and classical mythology, to be struck blind is nearly always a sign of the wrath of God or the gods. In the Bible the sodomites were struck with blindness, as was the sorcerer, Elymas. In Greek tradition so was Tiresias. Furthermore the Victorian myth that blindness, like madness, is somehow the result of masturbation still lurks not very far below the surface of the folk-consciousness. It is easy to see how this came about. Blind people and mad people were kept in asylums with very little to occupy their time. They were observed to masturbate because there was nothing much else for them to do. It was therefore assumed that an early addiction to this habit was a cause of their disability. Another widely believed piece of folklore on the subject of blindness is the idea that blind people are providentially compensated by having their other senses made more acute. I do not believe there is any evidence for this at all. It is simply that a blind person learns to pay more attention to signals provided by the other senses. Most of us live primarily in a visual world and this is probably even more the case since the invention of television. When I walk down my street on a fine spring morning I can identify the songs of at least half a dozen species of birds. I doubt if many of my neighbours even hear the birds. I have a reasonably good sense of hearing, and, after all, I had a musical training, but I have not got a strong sense of smell. I am rather glad of this for most people seem to smell more unpleasant smells than pleasant ones. But if on a warm day I pass by a greengrocer's I recognise it by the aroma of oranges and other fruit.

A character in one of Iris Murdoch's novels says: "All people despise cripples, they can't help it." I believe this to be true and it is a matter of instinct brought about by natural selection. It is for the benefit of the species that physically defective individuals should be kept out of the genetic pool. We see that animals and birds will often mob injured members of their species. But man is "placed on the isthmus of a middle state". Subject, like animals, to instincts, the result of Darwinian evolution, man is nevertheless capable of imagination, altruism and compassion. Blind people, and I suspect other cripples, do not wish to have a sentimental image of themselves. The images of the blind in literature are unfortunate. I have already mentioned those ancient depictions of the blind man as the victim of the wrath of God. Others, which we remember from our early reading, are "Blind Pew", a figure of sinister menace, in Stevenson's *Treasure Island*, and the saintly figure of Nydia, the blind flower-girl, in Bulwer Lytton's *The Last Days of Pompeii*. Nydia, it will be remembered, is in love with the hero, Glaucus, who is himself in love with the Christian heroine of the novel. When, in the final chapter, Mount Vesuvius does its stuff, and Pompeii is destroyed, Nydia leads the hero and heroine through the streets of the darkened city. They all three get away in a boat, and Nydia, tactfully, drowns herself in the Bay of Naples while the attention of the other two is distracted. Bulwer Lytton gives a false picture here. Nydia would have been completely at a loss as Pompeii was destroyed. People were rushing about in panic, familiar landmarks would have been obliterated, and the shower of ashes which the volcano emitted, and which darkened the streets, would have made echo location utterly impossible for her. Blind people themselves are not prone to this kind of sentimentality.

I will relate a (doubtless fictitious) anecdote which was told me as a boy at Worcester College for the Blind. I find it funny, but it is also quite brutal. It shows the kind of stories which disadvantaged people tell about themselves. There was a young girl who was, unfortunately, very short-sighted. She refused to wear glasses, doubtless subscribing to Dorothy Parker's dictum "men seldom make passes at girls who wear glasses". This girl was walking out with a young man and was worried that he might discover her defective sight, and that this would put him off her. So, one day, she proceeded to the field where she often used to take walks with her boyfriend, and stuck a pin in the bark of an oak tree. On their next country walk, she casually remarked to him: "I have an idea that you think I don't see very well." "Well," said the young man, "I suppose I did rather think that." "In fact, I have unusually good sight. For example, you see that oak tree at the other end of the field? I can see that someone has stuck a pin in the bark." "I don't believe you," said the young man, "you couldn't possibly see a pin at that distance." "I'll prove that I'm right," she said, and, striding out briskly across the field, walked straight into a cow.

Deafness, it seems to me, must be a far worse handicap than blindness, but my friend David Wright has dealt with it with extraordinary courage and skill. He refuses to use the deaf and dumb alphabet and converses with people through lip-reading. One of the advantages he finds in using this is that in order to converse with someone in that way you have to look them straight in the eyes. Shifty people, therefore, cannot get into conversation with him. The lip-reader watches not only the mouth of the person conversing with him but the muscles of the throat as well, so the head has to be held high. David does have difficulty with proper names and foreign words, and it is therefore best to write these down for him, but one can also write in the air. He has dealt with the question most interestingly and thoroughly in his own book, *Deafness*.

As a poet, I have found that blindness actually tends to stimulate the visual imagination. T. S. Eliot's essay on Milton is in many ways misleading. Eliot was obviously influenced by his own acquaintance with James Joyce, who was almost blind for a large part of his life. Joyce was exceptionally aurally orientated, but, even so, visual imagery is very important to him, as in the famous image of the "snot green sea" in *Ulysses*. Milton was, of course, a talented musician, and he was, in many ways, aurally orientated but the visual imagery in him is powerful. In *Paradise Lost*, however, it depends upon memory rather than upon the thing actually seen. An example is the passage at the very end of the poem when the angels expel Adam and Eve from paradise:

. . . for now too nigh
Th' Archangel stood, and from the other Hill
To their fixt Station, all in bright array
The Cherubim descended; on the ground
Gliding meteorous, as Ev'ning Mist
Ris'n from a River o'er the marish glides,
And gathers ground fast at the Labourers heel
Homeward returning.

This is an extraordinarily vivid visual image. It is something that
Milton could have seen in the marshes around Rome during his
Italian visit some twenty years earlier, or in his undergraduate days
in the fenland of Cambridgeshire. The imagery of Milton's earlier
poems, such as "L'Allegro" and "Il Penseroso", is painterly. The landscape is composed with figures in foreground, middle-distance and
distance. The effect is rather like that of a painting by Milton's contemporary, Claude Lorrain, though whether Milton ever saw any of
this painter's work there is, I think, no way of telling. To Milton and
Joyce, as poets who were certainly visually handicapped in their later
years, one should probably add Wordsworth. He suffered from a great
deal of eye trouble. This is partly the cause of the falling off of his
later poetry after about 1800, though, as Edith Bathoe has shown
in her excellent *The Later Wordsworth*, this falling off has been much
exaggerated. I suspect that Wordsworth's sense of sight was never
very acute. As he admitted, he relied on his sister Dorothy as both
his eyes and his ears. Apart from "Blind Harry", the fifteenth-century
author of a Scottish epic poem, *The Wallace* (who perhaps belongs
more to folklore and the tradition of the blind minstrel than to historical fact), there have been, as far as I know, two English poets who
were blind either from birth or from a very early age. These are
Thomas Blacklock (1721–91) and Philip Bourke Marston (1850–87),
a minor member of the Pre-Raphaelite circle. Neither of them is a
very satisfactory poet. Blacklock, writing in a straightforward eighteenth-century style and diction, probably does rather better than
Marston, for Blacklock is supported by the conventions of his time.
Marston's poetry really does seem to me deficient in concrete imagery.
Incidentally, James Thomson (BV) finally succumbed to drink and
died in Marston's flat. It must have been difficult for Marston to cope
with this.

The prototype of the blind bard is, of course, Homer. It is hard to
know whether Homer was a real person or not. If he was he may
simply have been a blind bard who recited traditional material that
had come down from earlier sources. Homer's poetry is, of course,
full of visual imagery. Music and poetry were, in earlier societies,

among the callings which a blind person might take up. H. G. Wells in *The Outline of History* mentions an anthropologist who saw that the musician of a troupe of dancers in what is now Zimbabwe had actually been blinded by the chief, as we, I suppose, used to blind singing birds. The figure of the blind poet, or musician, goes along with that of the lamed smith – Hephaestus, and the Norse Volundr (Weyland Smith). This suggests that smiths were hamstrung or deliberately lamed to prevent their straying away from the tribe and revealing their secrets to enemies. With the beginning of the Iron Age the art of making iron weapons was as potent a secret as the art of making atomic bombs has become in our century. With the development in modern Western culture of a complicated system of musical notation it has not been as easy for blind musical performers to attain a proficiency in their arts as one might think, but from the eighteenth century we recall the blind organist John Stanley, who became blind at the age of two, and Madame Paradies, the blind pianist and composer, for whom Mozart wrote a concerto.

During the 1980s I was invited to serve on an Arts Council committee concerned with arts and the handicapped. This was presided over by Sir Brian Rix (now Lord Rix). The other members of the panel, mostly young, were handicapped in various ways, some being wheelchair cases. I remained on this committee for a year. It was suggested that one should serve for at least that length of time. I did not feel that I had much to contribute. The other members of the panel seemed to belong to handicapped subcultures which I, like David Wright, had carefully avoided doing. Apart from David, I had only one handicapped friend, a lady who suffered from a mild form of epilepsy. I am sure that the work the panel was doing was excellent, but it was concerned with subjects on which I had no expertise, such as the necessity of persuading theatres to install ramps for wheelchairs and so on. Somehow or other I failed to establish a good rapport with the secretary of the group, who was a permanent employee of the Arts Council. She asked me what organisation I represented. I replied: "I do not represent anybody but myself." I do not accuse her of deliberately being prejudiced against me, but it was, perhaps, psychologically significant that she invariably got my address wrong. When I wrote to correct this, the next letter informing me of a coming meeting would have another incorrect variant of my address.

At the penultimate meeting at the end of the year, when the date of the next meeting was to be fixed, I informed the panel that I intended to resign. The secretary seemed to take this as signifying that I was resigning there and then, for I was never informed of the date of the final meeting. This annoyed me as I wished to make a statement concerning my feelings of inadequacy and dissatisfaction with the panel. At one point I had been asked whether I thought I had ever been passed over on account of my eyesight. I replied that I did not think that this was the case. "If one begins to imagine things like that," I said, "it is a road to paranoia." I added that Hitler believed that he had not been given an exhibition in Vienna because the art galleries were all controlled by Jews, whereas the real reason was that he was a third-rate artist. This remark did not seem to go down very well either. On another occasion Sir Brian remarked to me that he had been talking to the head of the Arts Council Literary Panel and had mentioned that I was on his panel. "Oh," said the head of the Literary Panel, "we were thinking of inviting him on to ours." Over a number of years I have sometimes wondered why I had never been invited to serve on the Literary Panel, and it seemed to me significant that its head only expressed these views when I was safely settled on another panel. This was one of the points I wished to broach in a final statement, and I would have asked Sir Brian to inform the head of the Literary Panel that I was now free if he wanted me.

A more amusing case of my involvement with the arts and the handicapped happened, I think, a year or so later. An Irish friend of mine, Kevin Byrne, invited me to go and stay with him in Dublin, remarking vaguely that he wanted me to take part in a project he was organising. It was not clear what this project was, but the morning after I arrived he called for me at the house of a friend of his, where I was being put up, and took me to a meeting place where a large number of people seemed to be milling around in a purposeful way. I asked what this was all about and it turned out to be a festival which Kevin was organising for the arts and the handicapped. "And you", he explained, "are to take a creative writing class." At this point he was called away and somebody else came up to me and said I was also to take a journalism class as the journalist who had been selected for this purpose had not turned up. I protested that I knew nothing about journalism and despised and hated journalists, but the organisers would not take no for an answer. Fortunately, the journalist arrived just in time. My creative writing class consisted of two mentally handicapped girls – one of whom could only communicate through her friend – but they were bright and I soon had them writing bouts-rimés. While we were engaged in this, the patron of the festival, Mrs Kennedy Smith, a sister of the late President John F. Kennedy, came to see how we were getting on. I soon had her sitting down and writing bouts-rimés sonnets too. At the end of the festival there was a kind of concert-cum-exhibition. I am happy to say that one of my two girls read a sonnet she had composed in the class, and also one by her friend.

As I write this I realise that I am approaching my seventy-fifth birthday and have outlived the allotted biblical span of threescore years and ten. This is becoming more and more usual nowadays. Indeed, I am always finding in the newspapers the obituaries of people who have passed their hundredth birthday, and there must be many less distinguished people who pass their hundredth birthday but do not get their names in the papers. A few years ago, one of the first to reach her hundredth birthday was Margaret Murray, the writer on witchcraft. She published her own autobiography on that day – *My First Hundred Years*. She lived, in fact, only another year, but she gave a radio talk on the occasion of her hundredth birthday and showed she was in complete control of all her faculties.

The last quarter of a century of my life has been far happier than my early years, especially since I lost my sight and no longer had to put up a vain struggle. Philip Larkin spoke with fear of age and "the only end of age". The only end of age is, of course, death, but death in itself would appear to be merciful and nothing to fear. It is the twin horrors of pain and imbecility that guard its gates which one should fear. If anything lies beyond death it is impossible to tell. Charles Williams once said that he accepted the doctrine of the immortality of the soul on the authority of the Church, but it never would have occurred to him personally to have postulated such an idea. On another occasion he said that the acceptance of immortality might be the final act of obedience. I would like to finish with the words of that great Christian agnostic, Ralph Vaughan Williams: "It is permitted to hope."

Index

Grey Walls Press 117, 126
Griffon 193
Grigson, Geoffrey 99, 162–3, 178
Groddek, Georg 170
Guenther, John 257–8
Guest, Lady Charlotte 284
Gugnuncs 30–1
Gunter family 15

Hack, Father 90
Hafiz 165–6
Haigh, John George 189
Haines, Renee 254
Hall, Donald 205, 240, 244
Hamburger, Michael 91, 118
Hamilton, Gerald 187
Hamnett, Nina 136, 143, 144, 188–9
Hanson, Miss (teacher) 45
Hardy, Thomas 24, 50, 211, 217
Harrison, Beatrice 47, 131
Harrison, Jane 174
Harvard Poetry Library 205
Harvard Summer School 203, 204–6
Harvey (friend of Potocki) 89
Heard, Gordon 193
Heath, Neville George 131–2
Heath-Stubbs, Beatrice (JHS's aunt) 1, 3, 4
Heath-Stubbs, Edith (née Marr, later Begg,
    JHS's mother) 4–5, 8–9, 13–14, 19,
    22–3, 32, 37, 45–6, 86, 173, 180, 204,
    259, 271
Heath-Stubbs, Florence (JHS's aunt) 1, 4
Heath-Stubbs, Francis (JHS's father) 4, 5–6,
    8, 11–12, 14–15, 17, 21–2, 24, 32,
    44–5, 51, 55
Heath-Stubbs, George (JHS's brother) 21–2,
    37, 45
Heath-Stubbs, George (JHS's uncle) 4, 5
Heath-Stubbs, John
  LIFE AND CAREER
    eyesight 10, 35, 52–3, 65, 69, 104, 120,
      142, 159, 258, 280, 281, 283, 287–97
    education 16–17, 27–42, 49–51, 53–7
    confirmation 44
    religious beliefs 44, 54, 90–1, 99, 114,
      255–6, 297
      see also religion
    and alcohol 55, 58
    political views 66, 91, 239, 255–6,
      277
    at Oxford *see* Oxford
    and dramatic productions 72–4, 274–5
    graduation 86
    and languages 88
    Blitt thesis 93, 103
    as private tutor 111–2
    translation of Leopardi 112–14, 205
    as schoolmaster 115–20
    at Hutchinson 128–32

as reviewer 132–4
joint translation projects 165–6
as Gregory Fellow at Leeds University
    191–202
in United States 203–6, 240, 241–57,
    288–9
in Egypt 207–39
as teacher of speech training 268–9
at College of St Mark and St John
    269–70
in Nigeria 270–2
as teacher at Oxford 280
broken hip 280
awarded Queen's Gold Medal for Poetry
    285–6
awarded OBE 286
and Arts Council committee 295–6
  WORKS
    Artorius 12, 283–5
    Beauty and the Beast 106
    Collected Poems 290
    The Darkling Plain 111–12, 134, 179
    "The Divided Ways" 110
    The Faber Book of Twentieth Century Verse
      (ed. with David Wright) 176–80
    The Forsaken Garden (ed. with David
      Wright) 180
    The Heart's Forest 176
    Helen in Egypt and Other Plays 197,
      199–200, 223, 236–7
    The Talking Ass 171, 200, 243
    The Unicorns 274–5
    Wounded Thammuz 99, 105–6
Heath-Stubbs, John (JHS's grandfather) 1,
    4, 5–6, 18
Heath-Stubbs, Lily (JHS's aunt) 1, 4, 5
Heath-Stubbs, Mary (JHS's aunt) 1, 4, 6, 8,
    52, 173
Hemans, Felicia Dorothea 29
Henderson, Hamish 157
Hendry, J. F. 101, 102
Heppenstall, Rayner 120, 154, 181–2
Herodotus 234–5, 236
Heywood, Rosalind 279
Higgins, Brian 262
Highlander pub, Soho 137, 138, 261
Hill, Geoffrey 199, 201–2, 243, 269
Hindmarsh, Tony 140
Hobday, Canon 129
Hodgkin, Mrs D. F. 74
Hodgkin, Dr R. H. 56, 79, 104
Hodgson, Ralph 177
Hofmannsthal, Hugo von 236
Hog in Pound pub, London 101
Hölderlin, Friedrich 82–3, 113, 170
Holmes, "Oxo" 133
Homer 62, 234, 294
homosexuality 92, 107, 116, 161
Hood, Thomas 111

Hopkins, Gerard Manley 80, 97, 112, 149, 176
Housman, A. E. 57, 72, 77, 112, 147, 177, 180, 263
Housman, Laurence 180
Hughes, Mr (teacher at Bembridge) 33–4, 37
Hughes, Ted 258, 286
Hunkin, Miss 51, 52, 238
Hurdis-Jones, Freddie 74
Hutchinson (publishers) 117
  encyclopaedia 128–32
Hutchinson, Canon 54
Hutchinson, Sir George 131
Hutchinson, Mr (rector) 24
Hutchinson, Walter 128, 129, 131
Huxley, Aldous 56, 108, 161, 183
Huxley, Thomas 38, 40

Inman, Philip 190–1
International Surrealist Exhibition 148
Ireland, Bill 203
Ireland, John 75
Ireland, "King" of 267
"Iron Boot Jack" 145
Irvine, Rev. Gerard 68, 92, 168
Italy 281–2

Jacobs, Arthur 78
James, Dickie 90
Jenyns, Soame, *Poems of the Tang Dynasty* 118–19
Jettou 259
Jim (friend and secretary) 207, 222, 230
John, Augustus 146, 148
Johns, Rev. C. A. 20
Johnson, Lionel 39
Johnson, Samuel 62, 102, 133, 213
Johnson, Tom 163
Jones, David 100, 117
Jones, John 197, 279, 280
Jonson, Ben 56, 60, 163, 275
Joseph (student in Alexandria) 229–30
Joyce, James 144, 149, 242, 284–5, 289, 293, 294
  Finnegans Wake 100, 153, 243
Jung, C. G. 67, 87, 100, 102, 170, 181

Kafr el Dauwâr 225–6, 232
Kalevala 16
Kano 269, 270, 271
Keats, John 40, 64, 70, 97, 108, 111, 113, 255, 279
Kelsall, Mr (rector) 20
Kennedy Smith, Mrs 296
Kennedy, X. J. 241, 242–3
Kershaw, Miss 17
Kershaw, Roland 17
Kershaw, Warren 17

Ketélbey, A. W. 195
Keyes, Phyllis 99
Keyes, Sidney 63, 67, 69, 70–83 *passim*, 86–7, 94, 95, 99, 100, 103, 110, 111, 124, 157–9, 257
  The Prisoners 73
  The Wilderness 86–7
Khufu (Cheops) 223
King, Francis (novelist) 82, 228–9
King, Francis (writer on magical subjects) 26, 41
Kingdom Come (magazine) 79
Kingsmill, Dorothy 170
Kingsmill, Hugh 132–4, 196, 256
Kingsmill, Tony 159
Kingsnorth, Miss 33, 34
Kirke White, Col. 64
Kirke White, Henry 64
Kirkup, James 122, 191, 193
Kissinger, Henry 203, 204, 205
Klein, Major Alf 141
Klein, Blanche 141
Knight, G. Wilson 197–8, 273
Knight, Jackson 197
Koestler, Arthur 100, 244
Kollerstrom, Julian 171, 275–6
Kollerstrom, Nicholas 275, 276
Kollerstrom, Oscar 170–276
Kops, Bernard 144
Kostick 159–60
Kramer, Jacob 195
Kreisler, Fritz 47
Krishnamurti, Jiddu 169, 170

Lambert, Constant 75, 140
Lancaster, Ray 38, 40
Lane, E. W. 130–1
Lang, Andrew 29, 38, 39, 62, 236, 279
Langland, Elspeth 148, 262–3
Larkin, Philip 79, 83, 84–5, 92, 104, 262, 286, 297
Laurence "the Applikant" 271
Lawrence, D. H. 78–9, 122, 149, 150, 181, 198
le Neve, Ethel 189
Leadbeater, Bishop 169–70
Leaf, William 280
Leavis, F. R. 82, 98, 107, 108, 112, 163
Leeds 151, 179, 192, 269, 273, 275
  City Varieties music hall 194–5
  College of Art 201
  Infirmary 191
  St John's church, Briggate 195
  town hall 195–6
  University of 84, 117, 191–202, 203
Lehmann, George 66
Lehmann, John 81–2, 111, 112, 127, 132, 140, 144, 180, 190
Leigh, Augusta 108

Leisenring, Kenneth 243, 244–5, 246, 250–4, 269, 289
Leishman, J. B. 69
Leopardi, Giacomo 83, 87–8, 112–14, 127, 205, 281
Leper, John 140–1, 143
Leschetizky, Theodor 45
Lewis, Alun 71
Lewis, C. S. 61, 62–3, 64, 82, 162, 184, 190, 209
    The Lion, The Witch and the Wardrobe 63
    "A Prolegomena to Mediaeval Literature" 62
Liberal Catholic Church 169–70, 171, 276
Liddell, Robert, *Unreal City* 221
Linden, Eddie 261–2
Lindsay, Jack 152
Little Theatre, Swansea 146
Litvin, Natasha 69
Lloyd, Rhys (later Lord Lloyd of Kilgareth) 34–5, 37, 75
London *passim*
    see also Kensington; Soho
London Library 258
Loscher, Bob 247, 250
Lubbock, Mark 46–7
Lubbock, Mr 46–7
Lubbock family 113
Ludwig, Miss 50–1
Lusby, Mr 98
"Lusby Magna" 98

Mabinogion, The 284
MacBryde, Robert 139, 153, 155–6
MacCaig, Norman 80, 102
MacDonald, George 63
Mackie, Gascoine 180–1
MacKie, Guthrie 278, 288
Maclaren Ross, Julian 136, 137, 142
MacLaughlin, Oonagh 184
McLaughlin, Patrick 167, 168, 171, 184, 185, 200
McNair, Peter 32, 37, 40, 44
MacNeice, Louis 76, 77, 102, 123, 144, 162, 265
Madge, Charles 62
Maguire, Paddy 145
Mairet, Philip 132
Mandrake Club, Soho 141–4
Manzalaoui, Mahmoud 208–9, 212, 225, 234, 237
Mariout, Lake 231, 235
Marnau, Alfred 117
Marr, Fred (JHS's uncle) 22
Marr, Mrs (JHS's grandmother) 13, 22
Marr, Philip (JHS's uncle) 13
Marsh, Edward 39
Marshall, Mrs 23
Marston, Philip Bourke 294

Martin, Kingsley 133, 152
Marx, Karl, and Marxism 67, 91, 100, 216–17, 275, 277
Masefield, John 29, 284, 285
Mathers, McGregor 189
Matthay, Tobias 4–5, 45
Maude, Ralph 176, 193
"May, Aunty" (pub landlady) 138
Megally, Fuad 217
Megally, Shafik 217
Merezhkovsky, D. S. 245
Metastasio, Pietro 194
Mexico 246–54
Mexico City
    Hotel Majestic 246–8
    Museum of Ancient Art 248
Meyer, Michael 78, 79, 81, 84, 103, 134
Meynell, Alice 139, 179
Meynell, Francis 139
Miclan 252–3
Micropatriological Society 267
Midgeley, Mr (cookery writer) 159
Midgely, Geoffrey 90
Milford, Sir Humphrey 109
Milne, A. A. 74
Milton, John 29, 98, 105, 114, 133, 169, 243, 272, 283, 293–4
    Lycidas 229
    Paradise Lost 293–4
Minton, John 139
Mixtecs 252
Moeran, E. J. 143
Monahan, Father W. B. 54
Monro, Harold 51–2, 121
Monroe, Mr and Mrs 27, 29
Monte Alban 253
Mooney's Irish House, Soho 138
Moore, George (novelist) 217
Moore, Nicholas 40, 101–2, 125
Moraes, Dom 92–3
Morgan, Charles 110–11
Muhammad Ali, ruler of Egypt 208
Muirhead, Mr 36, 37
Müller, Max 38–9
Murray, James Graham 187–8
Murray, John (publishers) 166
Murray, Margaret 25, 174, 297
music 37, 45–9, 57, 74–5, 140, 274–5, 291, 294–5
music halls 194–5
Mussadeq, Mohammed 166
Mussolini, Benito 44, 126, 127, 239
Mustard Club 30, 31

Nasser, Gamal Abdel 202, 210, 213, 234, 235, 239
Neguib, Mohammed 210
New Apocalypse 100–3
New English Review 133–4, 166

304